CW00661874

Cross-Channel France

Nord-Pas de Calais: the Land Beyond the Ports

the Bradt Travel Guide

John Ruler

Contributor
Laurence Phillips

edition
I

www.bradtguides.com

Bradt Travel Guides Ltd, UK
The Globe Pequot Press Inc, USA

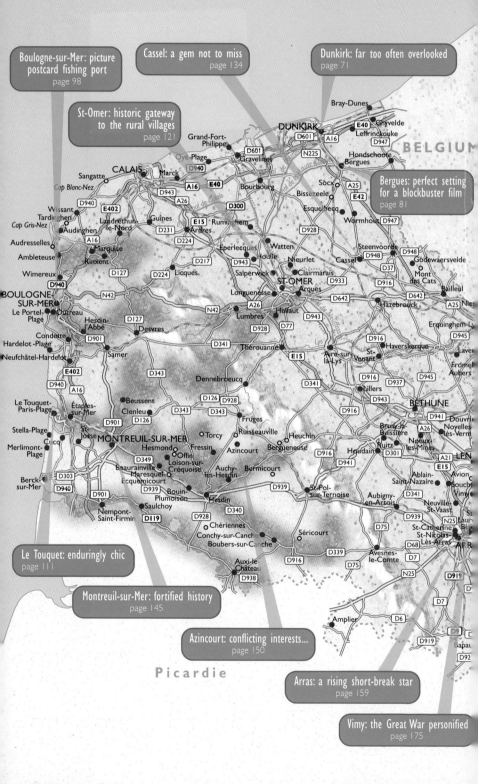

Boulogne-sur-Mer: picture postcard fishing port
page 98

Cassel: a gem not to miss
page 134

Dunkirk: far too often overlooked
page 71

St-Omer: historic gateway to the rural villages
page 121

Bergues: perfect setting for a blockbuster film
page 81

Le Touquet: enduringly chic
page 111

Montreuil-sur-Mer: fortified history
page 145

Azincourt: conflicting interests...
page 150

Arras: a rising short-break star
page 159

Vimy: the Great War personified
page 175

BELGIUM

DUNKIRK
Bray-Dunes
Ghyvelde
Leffrinckouke
E40
D947
Grand-Fort-Philippe
D601
A16
D601
Hondschoote
Oye-Plage
Gravelines
N225
Bergues
Socx
A25
Bissezeele
E42
Esquelbecq
Wormhout
D947
CALAIS
Sangatte
Marck
A16
E40
Bourbourg
Cap Blanc-Nez
D943
A26
D300
D940
E402
Ruminghem
D928
Wissant
Landrethun-le-Nord
Guînes
E15
Steenvoorde
D948
Tardinghen
D231
Ardres
Eperlecques
Watten
Cassel
D948
Godewaersvelde
Cap Gris-Nez
Audinghen
A16
D224
Houlle
Nieurlet
Mont des Cats
Audresselles
Marquise
D217
D943
Clairmarais
D37
Ambleteuse
Kinxent
D224
Licques
Salperwick
ST-OMER
D916
Bailleul
Wimereux
D127
Longuenesse
Arques
D933
Hazebrouck
A25
Nie
BOULOGNE-SUR-MER
N42
N42
A26
Helfaut
D642
Haverskerque
Erquingham-L
Le Portel-Plage
Outreau
Lumbres
D943
Aire-sur-la-Lys
D916
D945
Condette
Hesdin-l'Abbé
D127
Desvres
D928
D77
St-Venant
Lave
Hardelot-Plage
D901
Thérouanne
E15
D916
D937
Fromel
Neufchâtel-Hardelot
Samer
D341
Lillers
D945
Aubers
E402
D343
Dennebroeucq
D341
D943
BÉTHUNE
D940
A16
Beussent
D126
D928
D916
D941
Douvrin
Le Touquet-Paris-Plage
Étaples-sur-Mer
Clenleu
D343
D343
Fruges
Bruay-la-Buissière
A26
Noyelles-les-Verm
Stella-Plage
St-Josse
D901
D126
Torcy
Ruisseauville
Heuchin
Ruitz
Noeux-les-Mines
Cucq
MONTREUIL-SUR-MER
Hesmond
Fressin
Azincourt
Bergueneuse
D916
Houdain
D301
A21
LEN
Merlimont-Plage
D349
Offin
Auchy-les-Hesdin
Bermicourt
D941
E15
Berck-sur-Mer
D303
Esaurainville
Loison-sur-Créquoise
Ablain-Saint-Nazaire
Avion
D940
Maresquel
Bouin-Plumoison
St-Pol-sur-Ternoise
D341
ouch
D901
Ecquemicourt
D939
D939
Aubigny-en-Artois
Neuville-St-Vaast
Vimy
Nempont-Saint-Firmin
Saulchoy
Hesdin
D340
D939
N25
Laur
D119
D928
Chériennes
D75
St-Catherine
Bl
Conchy-sur-Canche
Séricourt
St-Nicolas-Lès-Arras
A
Boubers-sur-Canche
D68
D339
Avesnes-le-Comte
D7
D919
Auxi-le-Château
D916
D75
N25
D938
Amplier
D6
D7
Picardie
D919
Bapat
D92

KEY

Town	●
Village	○
Main road	
Other road	
Airport	✈
International boundary	
Regional boundary	
Departmental boundary	

N

Bradt

0 ——— 10km
0 ——— 10 miles

BELGIUM

Halluin
Comines
Deûlemont
Quesnoy-sur-Deûle
Tourcoing
Wattrelos
uplines
Bondues
Croix
Wasquehal
945
St-André
La Madeleine
Villeneuve-d'Ascq
E42
aubourdin
LILLE
Loos
Wattignies
Lesquin
N41
Seclin
E17
A23
Meurchin
A1
917
Orchies
Vieux-Condé
Condé-sur-l'Escaut
Courrières
D938
St-Amand-les-Eaux
E19
Courcelles-les-Lens
D938
Marchiennes
A23
Raismes
D935
St-Saulve
Hénin-umont
E17
Rieulay
Anzin
VALENCIENNES
D621
DOUAI
A21
Lewarde
Denain
Saultain
Gussignies
Brebières
Corbehem
D630
Trith-Saint-Léger
Jenlain
D649
Bavay
N2
D649
Jeumont
Gouy-sous-Bellone
Mastaing
A21
Artres
D934
Boussois
A26
Arleux
D643
Wavrechain-sous-Faulx
Bouchain
Villers-Pol
Preux-au-Sart
Maubeuge
D649
Assevent
Aubigny-au-Bac
Hordain
Le Quesnoy
Boussières-sur-Sambre
Louvroi
D936
D939
E17
A2
D630
St-Martin-sur-Écaillon
Beaudignies
Pont-sur-Sambre
N2
Naves
Cagnoncles
Neuville-en-Avesnois
Englefontaine
Sars-Poteries
Soire-le-Château
Fontaine-Notre-Dame
CAMBRAI
Solesmes
D934
St-Hilaire-sur-Helpe
Felleries
Eppe-Sauvage
D643
D962
Liessies
D930
Flesquières
Caudry
Le Cateau-Cambrésis
D959
D959
Le Favril
AVESNES-SUR-HELPE
Sains-du-Nord
E19
D644
Ors
D934
Trélon
Wallers-Trélon
Ribécourt-la-Tour
Les-Rues-des-Vignes
A26
D643
Ohain
D7
A2
Déhéries
Élincourt
N2
Fourmies
E17

Lille: the region's beating heart
page 221

Douai: big-hearted town, with even bigger giants
page 195

Le Quesnoy: quaintly different and loved by Kiwis
page 210

Le Cateau-Cambrésis: a touch of Matisse magic
page 192

Cross-Channel France Don't miss...

Douai
Meet the Gayants,
the doughty dignitaries
whose origins date back
to the 13th century
(JR) page 201

Marshlands of St-Omer
Reclaimed by 7th-century
monks, the Audomarois has a
magic of its very own
(SS) page 130

Vimy Ridge
The white, twin-columned monolith of the Canadian National Vimy Memorial seemingly soars to the clouds
(SS) page 175

Arras
A city of culture and entertainment, Arras is one of the most attractive short-break cities close to Calais
(SS) page 159

Maroilles's magical garden
Sylvie Fontaine's organic garden is just one of many providing dazzling summertime displays
(SF) page 216

left   Boulogne is beloved by the Brits for its Gallic charms, and was dubbed by Dickens as 'My French watering hole' (SS) page 98

below   Reduced to rubble in World War II, Dunkirk is now a thriving centre with a crowd-pulling marina (JR) page 71

bottom   Lille's Grand'Place is the very heartbeat of the city (SS) page 230

above   Bergues fortress — the town of
Bergues was the setting for
Bienvenue Chez les Ch'tis, the
blockbuster comedy which has
boosted interest in the region
(SS) page 81

right   Calais's lace museum — Calais
became world famous for its lace
in the 18th century (JR) page 69

below   St-Bertin's Abbey in St-Omer was
built between 1325 and 1520
(SS) page 129

The Flemish countryside is a rural haven
(SS) page 138

AUTHOR

Travel writer and photographer **John Ruler** spends considerable time in Nord-Pas de Calais, 'just down the road' from his family home in Hayes, Bromley, Kent. His initial interest in the region stemmed from idle curiosity and traditional shopping sorties to Britain's cross-Channel neighbours a mere 21 miles over from Dover. His

A keen horse rider and the author of two books on equestrian holidays, John is a Life Member of the British Guild of Travel Writers. He has travelled worldwide but is now at his happiest closer to home.

CONTRIBUTOR **Laurence Phillips** has written many and varied guides to France. He is author of *Lille: the Bradt City Guide*, which won the Guide Book of the Year award from the British Guild of Travel Writers.

AUTHOR'S STORY

Am I the only travel writer to recognise that Calais is not Nord-Pas de Calais any more than Dover is representative of the whole of Kent? It was a question I regularly asked myself. I was frustrated by the apparent obstinacy of even the most hardened Francophile to recognise that real France is real close – a phrase adopted by the hard-working regional tourist boards. And therefore I jumped at the chance to put pen to paper. Let's be honest. The French, too, know little of Kent, all adding to the pressure to put the record straight.

But conceptions are slowly changing. Not only has the recession and the need to cut our carbon footprint brought a surge of Dutch and Belgian visitors across the border into coastal France and beyond, but a growing band of short-break Brits are heading there too. Arras, for instance, has joined Boulogne, Dunkirk and Le Touquet in being at least recognisable names offering a weekend in La Belle France.

Even the French, themselves pretty sniffy about The North, which they traditionally see as a grey, rainy region riddled with old industrial towns, have had their preconceptions shattered by a blockbuster of a film which has taken France and its neighbours by storm. Written and produced by French superstar Dany Boon, *Bienvenue Chez les Ch'tis* has not simply outsold *Titanic* but shed a refreshing new light on the Nord-Pas de Calais region.

Cinderella, it seems, has at long last come in from the cold. But unlike the fairytale, this Cinders is a feisty, even wayward, fighter all too often overshadowed by squeaky-clean sisters Normandy and Brittany. Now they have a new kid on the block.

She certainly has plenty to offer, from the dazzling Giants of Douai to tiny villages tucked away in the tranquillity of the Seven Valleys, close to the coast, or the Avesnois in Le Nord. Small seaside resorts offer the best in sporting activities; flower-filled parks and gardens grace many a town or village and fortified towns add a flamboyancy rarely seen outside of tourist hotspots. Wartime history was created here. So was the industrial power of 19th-century France. If anywhere deserves exploring then it's Nord-Pas de Calais. Its lively traditions, medieval magic and rich country fare come as an added bonus.

Thanks to Bradt, for publishing the first-ever guide devoted solely to this region (rather than giving it scanter coverage within a guide to northern France). Let's hope the current crop of tour companies, of which those to France are generally more adventurous, will quickly cotton on …

PUBLISHER'S FOREWORD   *Adrian Phillips, Publishing Director*

It's rather strange that few people in Britain have even heard of the region of Nord-Pas de Calais; to us Brits, Calais usually means ferries, cheap booze and a portal to other parts of France. And yet there's no region closer to us – either geographically or in terms of shared history. So close are we that some teams will base themselves in Nord-Pas de Calais during the London Olympics in 2012 because the journey time is shorter than from towns in the UK… John Ruler has long been frustrated by our failure to recognise the merits of a region right on our doorstep. In this book he shows what we've been missing – from colourful festivals to moving reminders of the Great War. John's a passionate champion for a beautiful region; let's hope his book succeeds in putting Nord-Pas de Calais on the map!

First edition published November 2010

Bradt Travel Guides Ltd, 23 High Street, Chalfont St Peter, Bucks SL9 9QE, England
www.bradtguides.com
Published in the USA by The Globe Pequot Press Inc, PO Box 480, Guilford,
Connecticut 06437-0480

Text copyright © 2010 John Ruler
Lille chapter © Laurence Phillips
Maps copyright © 2010 Bradt Travel Guides Ltd
Photographs © 2010 Individual photographers (see below)
Project Manager: Elspeth Beidas

ISBN: 978 1 84162 327 6

British Library Cataloguing in Publication Data
A catalogue record for this book is available from the British Library

Photographs Wilmar Dik (WD), Sylvie Fontaine (SF), David R Frazier Photolibrary Inc/Alamy (DRFPI/A), David Noble Photography/Alamy (DNP/A), John Ruler (JR), SuperStock (SS), TTL Images/Alamy (TTLI/A)
Front cover Background: Cap Blanc Nez (DNP/A), left inset: colourful building, Bergues (TTLI/A), right inset: Calais Hôtel de Ville (DRFPI/A)
Back cover Canadian National Vimy Memorial (SS), Douai giant (SS)
Title page Golden Lion Square, Lille (SS), Cambrésis countryside (SS), Mont des Cats cheese (JR)

Maps Dave Priestley (based on source material from Le Nord and Pas de Calais tourist boards)

Typeset from the author's disk by D & N Publishing, Baydon, Wiltshire
Production managed by Jellyfish Print Solutions; printed in India

Acknowledgements

This guide would not have been possible without the support, enthusiasm and unstinting help and patience provided by Delphine Bartier of Nord Tourisme in Lille and Benoît Dieval in Pas de Calais. *Merci mes amis* ... Thanks, too, to Barry Warner, a long time friend, for acting as co-driver during numerous sorties across the Channel. Oh yes, and being the perfect *passe-partout* when it came to camera-carrying, picking up 'mislaid' notebooks, etc. A big hug, too, for fellow Bradt writer and editor Polly Evans for proving the perfect partner with her judicious pruning and checking of my sometimes over excitable prose!

A massive thank you must go to P&O Ferries, and in particular Brian Rees and Michelle Ulyatt, as well as Doug Goodman and Cathryn Hicks for their help in bringing fresh aspects of the area to my notice.

I am likewise indebted to Ellie Philpott of SeaFrance and Nick Stevens now of LD Lines for first introducing me to the joys of cross-Channel France, and continuing to do so over many years.

The same can be said of many others who, both before and during the writing of the guide, proved an inspiration, as well as answering a welter of queries and questions with such good grace. These include Marion Harmel at Arras, the wizard of the prompt reply, and her colleague Isabelle Pilarowski, for her incredible Great War knowledge; Stéphanie Thieffry, Audrey Avinee and Franck Hargot at Douai; Lydie Rault in Wimille for her help with Calais; Delphine Diotti in Cambrai; Laurence Baillieul in Dunkirk; Martine Leuillier in Le Touquet and Luc Tassart at Berck; likewise Jacques Martel and his staff at Bergues; Claire Lemaire and Laurence Boulogne in Bailleul; Stéphanie Berrier, Béthune; Marlene Lafere, Lens; Virginie Théret and Anne-Sophie Taufour, St-Omer; Nathalie Rocar, Cassel; Séverine Bastien, Guînes; Céline Gardier and Laurence Matoon in the Avesnois; Gérard Brigoo and Olivia Debomy, St-Amand-les-Eaux; and Guy Huart in Valenciennes.

Others, too, pulled out all the stops, come rain or shine, to ensure that I explored the hidden nooks and crannies. Too numerous to name individually, they have helped bring out that *je ne sais quoi* quality with which the region is richly endowed.

Some have already discovered this. My thanks, therefore, go to Jenny Miah and co, along with Penny Visman, for their restaurant reviews, to Noel Wills for describing his coastal walk, Brian McEwan for extolling the delight of cycling and to Alan Cheeseman for his hints on golfing.

I would also like to thank the team at Bradt: from Adrian Phillips for taking up my dream project, to Elspeth Beidas, Anna Moores and others who helped it come to fruition. Oh yes, and to my long-suffering wife, Janet, for putting up with the many hours I spent stuck upstairs in my office.

Finally, though I have never even met him, to Dany Boon, whose box office hit punctured the prejudices surrounding his native region. In doing so, he made my task that much easier. And yes, it was a good film.

Contents

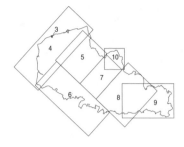

NOTE ABOUT MAPS

The Lille map uses grid lines to allow easy location of sites. Map grid references are listed in square brackets after listings in the text, with page number followed by grid number, eg: [156 C3].

LIST OF MAPS

Introduction

Explain to someone you're writing a guide to Nord-Pas de Calais and the average reaction is either to ask exactly where you mean or, worse still, automatically to assume you mean Calais. And to many – not only motorists streaming onto the southbound motorways, but even those who've never visited – that conjures images of an ugly industrial port. OK, the town is no beauty, but it does provide a handy gateway to the coast and, more importantly, the rural hinterland, which so many miss out on.

Basically Nord-Pas de Calais, though one region, is split into two *départements*, each recognisable by a number. Pas de Calais is 62 and Le Nord is 59. Both, of course, have their loyalties, but for a region fought over for centuries by warring European powers, not least the English, French and Spanish, it presents a remarkably peaceful and rewarding chequerboard of cultural differences. Just how much so is reflected in the eight areas described in the guide.

If tourism is a key to a brighter future, so, too, is the region's unique location. Already a partner with Kent in an EU Interreg (cross-border co-operation) programme, it is well placed for helping to create an economic corridor to link Paris with Germany, the Netherlands and northern Italy. This is roughly the old 12th-century route between England, Flanders (including France, Belgium and the Netherlands) and northern Italy described on page 7. This, and the role already played by ports such as Calais and Dunkirk, the Channel Tunnel, the Eurostar to Lille and the changing face of its once industrial cities, is already helping tackle the transition of this remarkable, yet often misunderstood, region to one very much in tune with the times.

FEEDBACK REQUEST

Every effort has been made to ensure that the details contained within this book are as accurate and up to date as possible. Inevitably, however, things move on. Any information regarding such changes, or relating to your experiences in Nord-Pas de Calais – good or bad – would be very gratefully received. Such feedback is invaluable when compiling further editions. Send your comments to Bradt Travel Guides, 23 High Street, Chalfont St Peter, Bucks SL9 9QE, UK; e info@bradtguides.com.

Part One

GENERAL INFORMATION

Country name France

Location North of France, 140km of shoreline. The region shares a common border with Belgium and, at the nearest point between Cap Gris-Nez and Dover, is only 34km from the English coast.

Size/area 12,414km² of which 5,743km² comprises Le Nord and 6,671km² the Pas de Calais

Population Around 4 million inhabitants of which there are 2,555,020 in Le Nord and 1,441,568 in Pas de Calais

Regional capital Lille

Languages French. National statistics show less than 4% in Le Nord, and less than 2% in Pas de Calais, say they, or their parents, can talk or at least understand Flemish. Far more people probably speak Ch'ti (see page 12) than Flemish.

Currency Euro

Exchange rate £1 = €1.20, US$ = €0.76 (August 2010)

International telephone code 0033 (0)3 or if calling a mobile phone 0033 (0)6

Time GMT+1

Electrical voltage 220–230 volt socket

Tourist Board websites www.tourisme-nord.fr and www.pas-de-calais.com

Public holidays 1 January (New Year's Day), Easter Monday, 1 May (Labour Day), 8 May (1945 Victory Day), May Ascension Day (always on a Thursday, 39 days after Easter), May Whit Monday (Lundi de Pentecôte, always a Monday, 50 days after Easter), 14 July (Bastille Day), 15 August (Assumption), 1 November (All Saints' Day), 11 November (Remembrance Day), 25 December (Christmas Day)

School holidays Usually from beginning of July until beginning of September; 10 days for All Saints (around 1 November); two weeks around Christmas and New Year; two weeks in February and two weeks for Easter

Background Information

GEOGRAPHY

Nord-Pas de Calais is the northernmost pimple of the 22 regions marked on the map of France. It is also, for its size, one of the most densely populated. Originally a part of the historic provinces of Artois, French Flanders (or Flandre), and Picardy, it lies directly south of England, whose southern pre-Ice Age chalklands were linked with those of northern France. Even now the cross-Channel neighbours remain only 34km apart across the Straits of Dover.

Bounded by the North Sea to the north and northwest, the region shares a common border with Belgium to the northeast and with Picardy, which includes the Somme, to the south.

Bar the chalk cliffs along the Channel coast, whose vast sandy beaches butt onto a hilly hinterland, the region is flattish; this is what has led south-bound motorway drivers to all too often blithely dismiss it as boring. But don't be fooled. Nord-Pas de Calais is far more fragmented than that.

To the east, the windy sand dunes of Coastal Flanders have been reclaimed by engineers, mostly from the Low Countries, since the Middle Ages. This is now a thriving agricultural region rich in vegetables, as well as pig, sheep and dairy farms. Windmills, belfries and bell towers dominate the landscape. Inland, French Flanders gives way to the lusher lowlands and a series of summits, the Monts des Flandres. The area includes the fertile marshland marketing gardens of the Marais Audomarois surrounding St-Omer (see *Chapter 5*, page 131). Between Lille, Douai, Béthune and Valenciennes lies the former industrial region; once dominated by coalfields this area has been transformed by urban regeneration.

The Avesnois, the region's toe tucked away to the west, is crossed by the River Helpe Majeure and the River Helpe Mineure, tributaries of the River Sambre. It, too, has its summits, rising to 250m in places. This is rural France famous for its dairy cows and cheeses, especially the ubiquitous Maroilles (see *Chapter 9*, page 216).

The Boulonnais coastal region boasts both a chalky plateau and a lower-level countryside of woods and meadows, home to the award-winning Boulonnais working horses. The Artois, or what remains of the former province, lies on an extension of the Picardy plateaux running northwest to southeast. This ends in an escarpment, including Vimy Ridge (see *Chapter 7*, page 175), from whose foot the plain of Flanders spreads out before you. Equally, the well-watered Artois hills to the northwest have produced a lush countryside which includes the Hesdin area, a highlight in the delightful Seven Valleys (see *Chapter 6*, page 151).

While the Hainaut and Cambrésis regions are extensions of the Artois plateaux, the wide valleys of the rivers Escaut, Sambre and Scarpes help create farm land, whose produce shapes the regional fare (see *Eating and drinking*, page 36). They are just three of many other rivers which, interconnected by networks of canals and waterways, have boosted the region's economy, both in terms of trade and tourism.

Indeed water has witnessed the birth of towns, has supplied scores of mills and provides yet another green way to explore the countryside.

CLIMATE

Lined on the north and west respectively, by the North Sea and the English Channel, Nord-Pas de Calais has a climate similar to that of southern England. Roughly speaking, this means year-long cool temperatures, especially during winter months, but with generally sunny weather in summer. This is usually at its most pleasant from late May to late September, with the peak holiday period between mid-July and mid-August. The region benefits from 1,600 sunshine hours a year and it actually rains less in the north of France than it does in the south.

The average summer temperature is around 18° C climbing to 25°C; the average in winter is 3.2°C. The highest level of rainfall statistically is in November, the lowest in April. The wettest areas are Artois, Haut Boulonnais and Avesnois, while certain areas to the north are as dry as the Côte d'Azur.

Mild spring and autumn months make the region ideal for off-season breaks, especially for outdoors types keen on walking, horseriding or sampling the string of beach activities along the Côte d'Opale (see *Chapter 4*). Buffeting wind is fine for kite-fliers, the chill waters less so for swimmers.

GREEN NORD-PAS DE CALAIS

Nord-Pas de Calais is blessed with a large number of the *forêts domaniale*, or 'state forests' (see *www.sceren.fr/svt/foret/CompDiv_Nord-Pas-De-Calais-Imp.htm*), with which the whole of northern France is well endowed. Of these, nine are in Le Nord, of which **Mormal Forest** (see page 213) – at 9,163ha – is the largest in northern France. Oak, beech, hornbeam and ash trees predominate. There are a further eight state forests in Pas de Calais, with the **Forest of Boulogne** sporting 2,000ha. Between them they provide 90,750ha, featuring walking, cycling, horseriding and nature trails, as highlighted in *Part Two* of the guide. Nord-Pas de Calais is also a great bird-watching area. Canals, locks, churches, chapels and mining cottages add to the green mosaic and so, too, do local markets and traditional games. Timber-built accommodation using environmentally friendly paints and varnishes has also been introduced.

Nord-Pas de Calais also has three regional nature parks, one of which, the **Parc Naturel Régional Scarpe-Escaut**, was once hideously pockmarked by coal mining. Situated between the Scarpe and Escaut rivers, it is now geared to the growing demands of a more sustainable kind of tourism. Located only 20 minutes from Lille, between Valenciennes, Douai and the Franco-Belgian border, the park stretches over nearly 43,000ha and covers up to 48 towns. Restoration began as far back as 1968, creating the first such park of its kind in France. Uniquely different are the 'hills', or rather the now grass-and-shrub-covered slag heaps (see *chapters 7 and 8*); a trail traces the mining heritage and the extraordinary ecosystem which has grown up around the slopes, some of them 100m high.

The seriousness with which both Le Nord and Pas de Calais treat green tourism is borne out as follows:

- New initiatives have been put into practice by technical teams working from a Parks Charter
- The three parks have gained EU certificates for sustainable tourism
- Between them, the regional parks contain 80% of the flora and fauna of Nord-Pas de Calais
- Around 30,000 schoolchildren a year take part in environmental projects
- A total of 29 fragile sites (*espaces naturels sensible*) are now protected under the Eden 62 project set up by Pas de Calais. These include not just the cliffs, limestone fields and forests, but also the old industrial slag heaps around Lens and Béthune.

Also in Le Nord, situated to the east, is the **Avesnois National Park** (see *Chapter 9*, page 209). This stretches nearly 125,000ha and covers 129 towns and villages. The landscape is mainly farmland, whose fields are lined with hawthorn hedges and dotted with apple trees. The forests of Mormal, Bois-L'Evêque and Fourmies, covering 20,000-plus hectares, provide signposted paths for walkers, horseriders and cyclists.

Val Joly, an 180ha lake (see *Chapter 9*, page 218), is the largest reservoir north of Paris. Perhaps better known, due to its proximity to Calais, is the **Parc Naturel des Caps et Marais d'Opale**. This includes the Cap Gris-Nez (Grey Nose) and the Cap Blanc-Nez (White Nose), both of which will be familiar to coastal visitors (see *Chapter 4*, page 89). Covering some 130,000ha and 152 towns and villages, the park covers the coastal dunes, estuaries and beaches, as well as the forests, farmland and rural villages lying behind Boulogne. It also encompasses the Audomarois – the canal-riddled home of the marshland market gardeners with some 160km of navigable waterways around St-Omer (see *Chapter 5*, page 131). This includes the 100ha **Nature Reserve of Romelaëre** home to 200 animals and 150 plants (see *Chapter 5*, page 131).

Useful websites are: www.parc-naturel-avesnois.fr, www.parc-opale.fr and www.pnr-scarpe-escaut.fr. See also *Sports and activities* on page 47 and *Parks and gardens* on page 49.

A BRIEF HISTORY OF NORD-PAS DE CALAIS

On the morning of 25 January 1658, the citizens of Dunkirk were Spanish. By noon they were French, and by the evening English. This small, but far from insignificant, fact starkly illustrates the fluctuating fortunes of Nord-Pas de Calais, for centuries ravaged by war between rival nations and even regions.

The fact that it has managed to assimilate the characteristics of each occupying force is astonishing. Even more so is the way in which these have been turned to mutual advantage. But then these sturdy northern folk are nothing if not adaptable, honed by history into fighting for a corner of France which, located between Germany, England and the Benelux countries, has long been one of the most contested regions in Europe. Charles de Gaulle was later to dub it a 'fatal avenue' through which invading armies repeatedly passed.

Originally part of the historic provinces of Artois, French Flanders (Flandre) and Picardie to the south, present-day Nord-Pas de Calais is split into two *départements*. Basically the medieval principality of French Flanders, in what used to be the southwestern part of the Low Countries, now largely forms the *département* of Le Nord, which takes up the northeastern section of the region. However, it continues to have much in common with the neighbouring Low Countries in terms of terrain and Flemish culture. Similarly the old French province of Artois is designated as Pas de Calais. This does not, as is sometimes quoted, include Picardy. The historical flip-flopping which led to this is outlined over the following pages.

ROMAN TIMES Two millennia ago, the Romans ruled this part of what was then northern Gaul for two centuries. Their governance led to huge road-building projects and a burgeoning economy. By the 1st century Nord-Pas de Calais, then part of Belgium, was one of four administrative areas. Within it, Arras (Nemecatum in Roman), and Thérouanne (or Tarvanna), became forerunners of France's regional capitals, or *préfectures*, built under Augustus. Bagacum (present-day Bavay – see *Chapter 9*, page 214), whose Roman forum covering nearly 2.5ha remains the largest of its kind north of Rome, was another. Bavay was also the centre of seven roads initiated by Augustus. Castellum Menaporum, now Cassel (see *Chapter 8*, page 134), was the centre of six. Traces of the roads remain in both towns.

Earlier Roman defences likewise provided the foundations for Boulogne's old town fortifications. Julius Caesar's botched attempt to seize Britain in 55BC began here at what was then the old fishing village of Gesoriacum, the port's original name. Other towns such as Ardres (see *Chapter 4,* page 94) and Cambrai (see *Chapter 8*, page 181) developed as 1st-century textile centres; production included Roman linen togas. This helped open up the trade route between northern Europe and Italy.

INTO THE MIDDLE AGES The eventual break-up of the Roman Empire saw the gradual evangelising of Europe. Nowhere was this felt more strongly than in Nord-Pas de Calais. The region now lay in the hands of the Franks, one of a succession of barbarian tribes that invaded from the 3rd century onwards.

However, following the example of Clovis, successive Merovingian kings relied on the Church to encourage intermarriage between the earlier Gallo-Roman population and the Frankish (or indeed any other) invaders. This gave birth to the Flemish and the Picards, both of whom were to play a pivotal part throughout the following centuries.

This was also the time of superstar saints. Amand, who founded a Benedictine monastery that he named after himself, gave the name to present-day Saint-Amand-les-Eaux (see *Chapter 8*, page 206). And it was a chapel, built by Omer, Bishop of Thérouanne, that led to the rapid growth of St-Omer which, though a small town, was well served by a network of roads in the Middle Ages – as it is today (see *Chapter 5*, page 121). By 1127 St-Omer was a prominent city, thanks largely to its commercial centre, which sprang up around the streets linking the monastery and the chapel. Cambrai (see *Chapter 8*, page 181) similarly developed around the abbey founded by Bishop Géry. Calais, too, (see *Chapter 3*, page 57) was a great monastic centre in the 7th century. Heavily influenced by the powerful Celtic connection, the port developed a handy religious and cultural route between Britain, Nord-Pas de Calais and Italy. Trade links rapidly followed.

But by the end of the 9th century trouble was brewing. The fall of Carolingians, of which Charlemagne was the greatest monarch, saw the region split into counties. This eventually led to the administrative set-up we have today.

FLANDERS FLOURISHES One county emerged triumphant from the conflict between Charlemagne's grandchildren – Flanders. Militarily independent from the outset, it rapidly founded new 12th-century coastal towns, Gravelines and Dunkirk among them (see *Chapter 4*, page 71). Trade centres sprung up in the North Sea and Mediterranean as Flanders became renowned for high-class drapery. Gold, spices and precious objects were sold by Italian merchants at Flemish fairs. Flemish goods were traded as far afield as Russia.

But the flourishing economy, though well administered by a growing dynasty of Flemish counts, led to in-fighting. There were clashes between the counts of Flanders and local lords; there were also, and in a foretaste of things to come, accusations of meddling by the early 12th-century King of France, Louis VI (nicknamed Louis The Fat, and son of Philip I of France and Bertha of Holland).

More royal entanglements were to follow. In 1180 King Philip Augustus of France married Isabelle de Hainaut, thus gaining control of Artois and sovereignty over St-Omer, Hesdin, Lens, Boulogne and Guînes. But by 1214, having been abandoned by old allies, he was fighting a combined force of Flemish and English at the battle of Bouvines. It is said that every Flemish farm provided a soldier to oppose him; still, he won.

THE ENGLISH CAPTURE CALAIS After further skirmishes, the argument over who had the rights to Flanders and Artois escalated into the biggest clash of all: the Hundred Years War (1337–1453) between France and England. This began with conflicting claims to the French throne between the Burgundian House of Valois and the English Plantagenets, known as the House of Anjou (in western France), the latter contending they were heirs to both the English and French thrones.

In 1347, several months after defeating the French at Créchy, the English laid siege to Calais. After resisting for 11 months, the city was forced to surrender. What happened to the six burghers is now the stuff of legend, captured by the famous Rodin statue in the town hall square (see page 57).

REMEMBER AGINCOURT Neither the French, nor certainly the victorious English, will forget the famous Battle of Agincourt (or 'Azincourt' in French). It was here, on 25 October 1415, that French forces superior in number, and sporting their finest knights, were roundly defeated thanks to the dominant role played by the longbow archers, a large proportion of whom were Welsh. The episode is now recalled in all its gory glory in the high-tech museum at the surprisingly small site at Azincourt (see *Chapter 6*, page 150).

One beneficiary of the Hundred Years War was Philip the Good, Duke of Burgundy, whose grandfather, Philip the Bold, had already acquired the province and that of Artois through his marriage to Margaret, heiress to Flanders. To these he added Hainaut, again through marriage. Power struggles and shifting alliances, including playing off England against France and vice-versa, helped bolster his position. In 1430 it was Philip the Good's troops that captured Joan of Arc and handed her over to the English. He was known as a great patron of the arts – as well as for having 24 mistresses and around 18 illegitimate children.

It was his son and heir, Charles the Bold, who helped change the course of European history. Shortly after his death in January 1477 – he was killed while waging a vicious war against Louis XI – his unmarried daughter, 19-year-old Mary of Burgundy, married Maximilian of Hapsburg, Archduke of Austria. Their son, Philip the Handsome, in turn married Joanna of Castile, thus shrewdly creating an alliance against the growing power of the French.

But it was their second son, Charles, born in 1500, who became the major force throughout Europe and beyond. As Charles V (or Charles Quint in French) he united three dynasties by inheriting not only the earlier gains of Artois and Flanders, Spain and the Spanish Netherlands, but the old Hapsburg Empire, including Austria and Germany. The continent was virtually in his clutches.

It was against this background that in June 1520 François I of France called for a summit at the famous Field of the Cloth of Gold, located roughly mid-way between the towns of Guînes and Ardres (see *Chapter 4*, page 43). His aim: to seek support from England's Henry VIII against what he considered a common threat, particularly at a time when Guînes and Calais still remained English-held territory. But Henry had other things on his mind, not least Anne Boleyn. The summit proved a flop.

Two other major events in Anglo-French cross-Channel history followed. In 1558 Calais, England's last remaining foothold in France, was taken over by the French – much to the chagrin of England's Mary I (see *Chapter 3*, page 57). And it was her husband Philip II of Spain who launched the famous Armada which, following a quarrel with the Protestant Queen Elizabeth I, set out to conquer England in 1588 only to be defeated off the French coast close to Gravelines (see *Chapter 4*, page 84).

In the meantime, an exasperated Charles Quint, eager to absorb France, waged war on François during which Thérouanne and its cathedral were razed to the ground (see *Chapter 5*, page 133). This quickly dissolved into the 30 Years War (1618–48), one of the most savage in Europe. It was not until 1659 that the Treaty of the Pyrenees restored Artois province to the French crown. Flanders was handed over under treaties in 1668 and 1678.

Other major cities of the region were also drawn in around the late 17th and early 18th centuries. Some were destroyed and rebuilt; others were occupied by whichever forces were winning at the time. Even local celebrations, like the early giants festival at Douai, reflected whoever was victorious at that point – in effect booing either the Spanish Flemish or the French.

France's Louis XIV, the Sun King (see box below), who engaged in fighting throughout his reign, including the War of the Spanish Succession, played one of the biggest roles by laying down strict rules concerning his preferred style of architecture. In many instances this meant toning down the more flamboyant Spanish nuances. This is still obvious today, especially with the distinctive shapes of what we loosely describe as Flemish style (see page 9). He was also influenced

SUN KING'S ROLE STILL SHINES

You can't avoid the role played by Louis XIV in establishing Nord-Pas de Calais as part of France. Scores of Sun King symbols appear commemorating the 17th-century monarch, who saw himself as second only to God from the age of five. Born in September 1638 and named Louis Dieudonne ('God given'), he not only reigned for 72 years, the longest reign in French history, but for 54 of them personally controlled the French government.

His fine living, evident from his palace in Versailles, is said to have set the seal on the perceived superiority of French culture on the world stage. He also personally led the French army to besiege border towns in the Spanish Netherlands, often taking much of the court with him. This enabled him to spend his evenings with the ladies and playing cards. He also insisted that both the Queen and his mistress came too, even if they were pregnant. What he fortunately failed to do was to squash a Flemish legacy, which lingers on in French Flanders, bringing a unique and rich diversity to this relatively small corner of France.

In the same way as art, Flemish architecture takes many forms, and therefore should not be seen as a singular style, but rather as coming in many shapes and sizes. Initially strongly influenced by the likes of traders from northern Italy, encouraging artistic exchanges, it inevitably fell foul of religious and royal preferences. What one ruler liked another didn't, and what was fine for one set of Catholics was frowned upon by another for being over the top. The Protestant influence also helped tone down what remains a flamboyant style, despite individual quirks. Belfries, town halls and other city buildings would look far less romantic without their richly embellished façades, niches, statues, gables and pinnacles. Towns such as Arras and Douai were among those wise enough to realise this and rebuild war-shattered buildings in this most refreshing and all-embracing of styles. So don't be confused when told some landmarks are built in Spanish Flemish, others in French Flemish or perhaps even Dutch Flemish style – they all look great.

by Vauban (see page 12), whose military defences helped protect towns already conquered but still under threat.

REVOLUTIONARY TIMES In 1789, the French Revolution did more damage to the highly industrial and cultural cities in Nord-Pas de Calais than perhaps anywhere else. Not only were there the inevitable beheadings, but lands were confiscated and castles and abbeys destroyed. One more strand was thus added to the region's already chequered past. Robespierre, who played a major role, was initially well respected in his native town of Arras, but later became increasingly unpopular as the autocratic head of the Revolution's Reign of Terror (see *Chapter 7*, page 161).

Unfortunately for Arras, the town suffered a triple whammy during the Revolution; not only did the townsfolk become disillusioned with Robespierre, but Joseph Lebon (see *Chapter 7*, page 161), his revolutionary replacement – also Arras born – proved particularly vicious towards his fellow residents. The town's cathedral, one of the most beautiful Gothic structures in northern France, was also destroyed.

So, too, were other cathedrals, including those at Boulogne and Cambrai. The bishops and the Church were regarded in the same negative light as the aristocracy for the huge amount of land and buildings that they owned, especially in the north. Other casualties included St-Bertin's Abbey, St-Omer (though not the impressive cathedral – see *Chapter 5*, page 128) and the abbey church whose vast grounds remain a feature at St Amand-les-Eaux (see *Chapter 8*, page 208).

It should be remembered that our apparent fascination with the French Revolution is not always shared by our Gallic neighbours. While recognised as a major event, it is overshadowed by other destructive historic episodes, not least the appalling hammering Nord-Pas de Calais took in World War I (see *20th-century alliances*, page 10).

THE NAPOLEONIC ERA A new figure was to take centre-stage following the Revolution: the Corsican-born Napoleon Bonaparte, whose military achievements saw him rapidly rise to prominence under the First French Republic. In 1799 he staged a *coup d'état* and installed himself as First Consul. He soon fixed his eyes on England, amassing a Grande Armée of 80,000 men at his base at Boulogne in 1798 (see *Chapter 4*, page 98). However, the planned invasion was sidelined by more pressing campaigns in Egypt and Austria. Instead Napoleon was forced to head east, where he triumphed at the famous battle of Austerlitz. However, still angry with his old enemy he imposed a total blockade on imports from Britain from 1806

THE COAL-MINING LEGACY LINGERS ON

It was not until 1682 that the first coal mine was opened in Nord-Pas de Calais, at Hardinghem near Boulogne-sur-Mer. Though only a small and uneconomic deposit was discovered, it sparked a flurry of interest in the potential offered by the coal seams, which had formed a deep running crust on both sides of the Channel over millions of year (the 19th-century Kent coalfields were likewise founded on it).

By 1716 prospecting for the 'black gold' had begun in earnest around Valenciennes; the first hints of mineable amounts were discovered in 1720 at Fresnes-sur-Escaut in the same area. In 1734 François-Joseph Desandrouin, the owner of the original Boulonnais mine, discovered a seam some 500m deep at Anzin, again in the vicinity of Valenciennes.

Life as a miner was tough: knotted climbing ropes, or *cuffats*, were used to descend into the darkness and the only light came from candles. Ponies, blinded to accustom them to the dark, suffered similarly harsh conditions. In the 18th century one miner, Azin, born Antoine Delfosse, worked from the age of seven to an incredible 63.

Although things improved during the 19th century, miners were born into and died in squalid conditions. A few of their company houses, or *corons*, which lined unmade roads – dusty in the summer, muddy in the winter – have been preserved. Emile Zola (see page 14) wrote graphically about the brutality of the times.

Seized and looted by the Germans in World War I, with miners used as forced labour, the Nord coal basin subsequently saw mass unemployment in the 1930s before the Germans were once more exploiting its miners during World War II.

In the immediate post-war era, with France short of coal, immigrants from Poland, Italy and North Africa were drafted in to help revitalise the industry. But, as in Britain, the 1960s and 1970s saw a general decline in the coal industry due to the increased use of oil, electricity, natural gas and ultimately nuclear power. On 21 December 1990 the last extraction pit in Oignies, 16km from Lens (see *Chapter 7*, page 173), closed down. Fifty years earlier, there were over 135,000 miners working in Nord-Pas de Calais.

The mining legacy now lives on through Lewarde Historic Mining Centre, the largest such museum in France, close to Douai (see *Chapter 8*, page 200). An entire mining village has likewise been superbly preserved at Wallers, close to Valenciennes.

until 1812. This backfired badly when continental Europe, harder hit than the British, indulged in semi-official cross-Channel smuggling.

20TH-CENTURY ALLIANCES For centuries power politics saw the French and English at each other's throats. But in the 20th century they stood shoulder-to-shoulder in two world wars. The loss of lives, especially in the Great War, is reflected in the hundreds of cemeteries and memorials, which now serve as places of pilgrimage for visitors worldwide.

World War I While the Battle of the Somme is remembered for the sheer loss of life – there were 60,000 British casualties, of whom 20,000 died on the first day – Nord-Pas de Calais suffered more damage in World War I than any other region of France.

The death toll for the Battle of Arras in which the Canadians played a major part was 60,000 alone, while the death toll at Loos, where Rudyard Kipling's son died, was such that the names of British soldiers killed on the opening day of the battle filled four columns of the London *Times*. Notre-Dame de Lorette National French Cemetery between Arras and Béthune contains 20,000 grave stones. The Battle of

Fromelles will long be remembered for the loss of Australian lives.

The total number of casualties in World War I, both military and civilian, was some 37 million. The 16 million dead included 9.7 million military personnel and about 6.8 million civilians. Some 21 million people were wounded. For years little was spoken on the subject, as the post-war generation, still shocked by the suffering, wished only to rebuild their shattered lives.

In recent years, however, interest in the war to end all wars has grown enormously. The death of Harry Patch, the last surviving British Tommy, at the age of 111 in July 2009 has only served to heighten this interest. (See *Practical information*, pages 19–20.)

World War II For an older generation, Hitler's raids on London were indelibly printed on their childhood minds: between June 1944 and March 1945 the deadly V1s – doodlebugs or buzz bombs, as they became known – were launched from the Pas de Calais coast (see *Chapter 4*, page 91). Basically pilotless rockets with wings, these were quickly followed by the even more lethal V2s, long-range rockets which, unlike the V1s, could not be spotted or shot down in flight. Fortunately production of the V3 at the small hamlet of Mimoyecques was halted by Allied bombing.

Details of major sites in both world wars appear under respective regions or towns in *Part Two* of the guide.

POST-WAR YEARS The immediate aftermath of war was not a good one for the region, which was desperately short of coal. Immigrants were drafted in to help revive the mining industry which, since the 1800s, had been a mainstay of the economy (see page 10). But the role of coal was fading and the following decades saw a general decline due to the increased use of alternative energy sources. In 1968 an official announcement of pit closures saw the dominance of coal mining, coupled with that of the steel industry, ended. In December 1990 the last remaining extraction pit at Oignies was closed.

The textile industry, too, was virtually finished and the image of the Black Country was wiped clean – so clean, in fact, that there was a danger of losing the very essence of an area once rich not just in 'black gold' but in close-knit mining communities.

Fortunately a far-sighted economic policy has seen the harmonious growth of a new kind of green tourism in which renovated reminders of an industrial past play footsie with eco-friendly surroundings reclaimed for sporting activities. Economic links with the powerhouses of Europe have been strengthened – Nord-Pas de Calais is a natural hub for trade between Paris, southern England, Germany, the Netherlands and northern Italy – and the ancient trade route described earlier has in effect been resurrected. This has been helped by inter-European road links and the commercial cross-Channel traffic both by ferry and through the Channel Tunnel. Lille and Arras are just two of the former industrial centres to see their fortunes flourish. It may take time to shake off the area's old image, but it looks promising. A blockbuster film *Bienvenue chez les Ch'tis* (see page 13) has played a major part in this. So, too, has a tourist campaign which has won over even some French-born cynics!

LANGUAGE

Speak French, however little, and everyone will be delighted. Speak English, especially around Calais and the coast generally, and you'll get by. The same can roughly be said for the cities, especially when talking to young people.

No visit to a town of any significance seems complete without a reference to Sébastien le Prestre de Vauban (1633–1707), who was appointed by King Louis XIV (see page 8) to design and supervise the building of a string of forts. This way, the king argued, France's northeast borderlands could never be recaptured.

You have to admire Vauban's tenacity. A brilliant young military engineer, he set about designing his now-familiar star-shaped forts with straight-sided moats, lined with walls built of local materials, mainly brick in the north. Each took advantage of natural features, such as rivers and hill slopes. He used detailed models in creating his designs, and often adapted earlier fortifications, a technique that can be seen at its most brilliant at Le Quesnoy, his first fort.

During his military career, Vauban built 33 forts and fortified walled towns, and strengthened 300 others, not just in Nord-Pas de Calais, but all round the French coast and borders. Among his fortifications were those at the coastal resort of Ambleteuse, Gravelines, Bergues (a completely walled town), and the Citadel at Lille, his so-called masterpiece.

He reached the dizzy heights of Maréchal of France in 1703, but fell from favour with Louis XIV in 1706, a year before he died. Always concerned as much with the needs of the troops as those of the king, his downfall came about because he dared to publish books on social reform. Vauban was banished from the Versailles court, and died in disgrace the following year. A century later, Napoleon recognised Vauban's military genius and had him reburied with honour in the Panthéon.

But ask '*Cha va ti?*' and you might get blank stares from those outside the region. This is 'how are you?' in Ch'ti-mi, a language said to have originated during World War I when troops from outside northern France started to call those from Nord-Pas de Calais 'the Ch'ti'. The name referred to their accent, and their pronunciation of '*c'est tu*' (it's you) and '*c'est moi*' (it's me) as '*ch'est ti*' and '*ch'est mi*'.

But it's not just an accent. Ch'ti-mi is virtually the patois language of Picardy; it's a sort of slang which, even more confusingly, differs from one city to another, both in pronunciation and in vocabulary. This makes it difficult to draw up a glossary, though the world of Ch'ti-mi is now all the rage thanks to the comedy *Bienvenue Chez les Ch'tis* (see page 13).

Ch'ti-mi also reflects a way of life, especially among the working-class of the old industrial areas. Once rather frowned upon by the cultured classes, it's now the stuff of drama and the arts.

Though still low key, it's probably spoken by far more than those who speak true Flemish, from which it derived in its slang form. National statistics show that less than 4% in Le Nord, and less than 2% in Le Pas de Calais, say they or their parents can speak Flemish. Some, however, can understand Flemish, and some French phrases have Flemish roots or are true Flemish words.

As in the UK and many other countries, various local dialects still persist. The author recalls two nature reserve wardens, one from Boulogne and the other from Arras – hardly miles apart – each of whom could still be tripped up by certain words. In Dunkirk there is a dialect which few outside the port would recognise.

CULTURE

Conflict and commerce seem to have a habit of inspiring creativity. This is certainly true of Nord-Pas de Calais where the architectural styles, still easy on the eye, have been shaped by the Flemish, and heavily influenced by the Spanish Netherlands, the French and the English.

Each has left its distinctive mark. Even the ravages of wars, including World War I – during which vast swathes of buildings were destroyed but since have been superbly restored – have failed to erase that lasting legacy.

Commercial growth in the Middle Ages stemmed from a creative instinct to produce fine lace, linen and textiles generally. From this grew the potteries and glass factories of the Industrial Age, superseded by the heavy industry fired by coal and steel. Emile Zola (see page 14) made his literary mark through his best-selling book about this period, *Germinal*. A new, more environmentally friendly era in which green tourism is playing a major role is not only revitalising the landscape but the contemporary arts scene as well. The choice of Lens as the new wing of the Louvre in Paris, is one notable example of this.

ARCHITECTURE One architectural aspect literally stands out above any other. No less than 17 Nord-Pas de Calais belfries, built as watchtowers and symbols of civic pride, were granted UNESCO World Heritage status in 2005. Visit them in Aire sur la Lys, Armentiéres, Arras, Bailleul, Bergues, Béthune, Boulogne-sur-Mer, Calais, Cambrai, Comines, Douai, Dunkirk, Gravelines, Hesdin, Lille and Loos. Most are open to the public and offer the best views in town.

Tours and a host of learned books are based on another highly visible slice of history – fortifications, dating back to Roman times. The region is positively plastered with them, the last being the ugly German blockhouses and other concrete paraphernalia of World War II.

Montreuil-sur-Mer relies on its magnificent ramparts as crowd-pullers as does

BLOCKBUSTER FILM BRINGS CH'TI TO MILLIONS

The movie *Bienvenue Chez les Ch'tis* has done great things for the image of Nord-Pas de Calais. It's not only captured the hearts of cynics who grew up on an Emile Zola image of grey skies and dingy landscapes, but has helped the hard-working tourist boards by showing the true face of a once much-maligned region.

Reviews in British broadsheets have heaped praise on the story of how a post office manager survives, and grows to love, his reassignment from Provence to 'a freezing dark place where it rains all year and people in red-bricked terrace houses dunk their Maroilles cheese in their coffee.' His gradual conversion is a hilarious account of how he warms to the down-to-earth hospitality of the locals.

'The whole world envies us the Ch'ti attitude!' joked the *Nord Éclair*, a regional newspaper. 'Long mocked for their accents, their slag heaps and their grey sky, northerners are rising up and claiming their identity.' *L'Express*, the news weekly, called the film 'an invaluable gift to Nord-Pas de Calais, a tourist brochure that the regional council could never have dreamt of'.

While the Brits may be baffled by all this fuss, the film, crudely translated as 'Welcome to the Sticks', has not only outsold *Titanic's* 20 million ticket sales in France alone, but brought the word Ch'ti and all it stands for (see page 12) to a wider European audience, especially in the Netherlands and Belgium. The town of Bergues (see *Chapter 4*, page 81), close to Dunkirk, where it was filmed, has seen visitor numbers soar.

The film is homage to French comedy actor Dany Boon's family roots. Boon both starred in and directed the film. 'I have long wanted to claim my Ch'ti identity,' he said, 'There is something poetic about the poplar trees, the smells, the very low skies and the welcome of the people.'

lesser-known Le Quesnoy whose intricate fortifications inevitably include the handiwork of the military mastermind Vauban (see page 12). A tourist leaflet provides an itinerary based entirely on fortified towns from Calais and the coast region to Arras and Lille, and beyond to Bavay and Avesnes sur Helpe. Tourist offices should have a copy.

MUSEUMS In 2010 a new extension to Greater Lille's Museum of Modern Art in Villeneuve d'Ascq was opened showing Cubist masterpieces by the likes of Picasso and major works by Miró and Modigliani; that same autumn saw the opening of the Musée de Flandre in Cassel, providing a unique insight into all things Flemish.

This is no mere coincidence, more an illustration of the affinity that Nord-Pas de Calais has with the arts generally. All, to a large degree, reflect the changing fortunes of a historically creative region from the textile industry of the Middle Ages to the lace factories and the potteries of the Victorian era.

This is evident by the choice of Lens as the site of the new wing of Paris's Louvre (see page 174). The €142 million arts centre due to open in 2012 is symbolically located on a site between the slagheaps, familiar to a generation of World War I soldiers, and the famous Bollaert football stadium.

Keen competition came from other cultural corners, including Arras where within the next decade the Fine Arts Museum will form part of the largest combined arts complex of its kind north of Paris. In 2009 the award-winning Lace Museum (Cité Internationale de la Dentelle et de la Mode) in Calais (see page 69) shone the spotlight on the historic role of the port as a major lace-making centre.

Nor was it for nothing that Valenciennes was voted the Regional Capital of Culture in 2007. The painter Antoine Watteau (1684–1721) and the sculptor Jean-Baptiste (1827–75) were both born there. Each has their work reflected in the Musée des Beaux-Arts (see page 205) which, comparable to the Louvre in size, has an astonishing collection of 16th- and 17th-century Flemish paintings.

Bringing his own artistic magic to his home town of Le Cateau Cambrésis was the master of colour Henri Matisse (1869–1954). The painter's work is recognised through the Musée Matisse in the grounds of the magnificent Palais Fénelon, former residence of the archbishops of Cambrai.

Other establishments include the Dunkirk Harbour Museum at Dunkirk (see page 78), which retraces the coast's fishing heritage, and the lesser-known Municipal Museum at Berck-sur-Mer (see page 120), which also has a fishing focus and is a real gem of a find even for a region dotted with similar examples.

Don't get the idea that Flemish art, in all its forms, dominates. Contemporary art, of the Picasso, Kandinsky and Modigliani school, are widely represented. So, too, is the work of up and coming new artists and designers in fast developing cities such as Valenciennes.

2

Practical Information

WHEN TO VISIT

It's not all about summer, sea and sand. Nord-Pas de Calais is a short-break destination, at least for the Brits, with year-round attractions. Opt for the winter and a good bet is the bevy of Christmas fairs; three of the best are those at Béthune, Calais and Arras. Lille's is another; the trip there by Eurostar being an added bonus. The December Turkey Festival at Licques, less than 40 minutes' drive from Calais, provides traditional family fun, with an excellent regional market to boot (see *Chapter 4*, page 95).

January marks the famous Dunkirk Festival (see page 80), a ring-a-ding-ding affair which, being mainly celebratory for the locals, has an added air of authenticity. February is generally a miserable month, though the Bailleul Carnival is a boisterous way to experience a truly Flemish fling.

Better still, wait for spring. Watch the kites flying at the International Festival in Berck-sur-Mer (see page 119) or enjoy a boat trip along the marshland waterways around St-Omer (see pages 130–1). But wrap up warm if you're going before early May: it can be chilly.

Plump for late spring or early summer, and the region's at its freshest, with the coastal roads delightfully traffic-free. Though this increases, congestion is never that bad and, bar the peak school-holiday season, summer is an ideal time to head for the rural peace of the Seven Valleys, behind Le Touquet, or the Avesnois, including perhaps a day or so in Lille.

Autumn, like spring, has its seasonal benefits, especially for golfers, walkers, cyclists, horseriders and the like. It is also ideal for city visits. Arras, Douai and Cambrai can all match the charm of the more obvious tourist hotspots, such as St-Omer and the coastal ports of Calais and Boulogne. So, too, can much smaller places, of which the Cassel area, around an hour's drive from Calais (even less from Dunkirk) is an all-time favourite (see *Chapter 4*, pages 134–7).

ITINERARIES

Nord-Pas de Calais is small enough for visitors to put together a mix-'n'-match collection of visits without travelling vast distances from Calais or the other ports. If you have only one day, head for a seasonally sunny day trip to Monts de Flandres, taking in Mont des Cats for the view and Bailleul for its architecture.

For something different, visit the Giants Festival in Douai in July, staying overnight and travelling there and back by Eurostar via Lille. Failing that, spend a day in St-Omer and take a boat trip on the marshland, or visit La Coupole, the former German concrete dome which now unlocks the hidden side of Hitler's World War II rocket projects.

Practical Information ITINERARIES

2

TOWNS

Cassel For embodying the essence of a French market town full of cobbled streets and medieval magic (see pages 134–7).

Arras For showing a fighting spirit which has marked it out as a place for fun, fine arts and flamboyant twin squares (see pages 159–71).

Douai For proving that Le Nord cities are far from dour but a delightful blend of old and new, with a charming canalside walkway (see pages 195–202).

Boulogne For bringing the flavour of France to day-trip Brits with a hint of more to come (see pages 98–107).

ATTRACTIONS

Calais Lace Museum For vividly showing the link between lace-making and its English heritage in a refreshing and family-friendly way (see page 69).

Historical Museum of the Second World War, Ambleteuse For showing that small can be both beautiful and highly educational (see page 90).

Berck Museum, Berck-sur-Mer For the sheer enthusiasm shown by the curator for a manageable collection of locally related exhibits (see page 120).

Fortifications at Le Quesnoy For providing a perfectly preserved setting for a delightful town on the edge of the rural Avesnois area (see pages 211–13).

ACCOMMODATION

Châtellerie de Schoebeque, Cassel For simply showing how themed rooms can be sympathetically designed without going overboard (see page 135).

La Maison d'Hotes La Corne d'Or, Arras For being a welcoming B&B conversion, with nooks, crannies and crumbling steps leading to a vaulted brick cellar three levels down (see page 165).

La Grange de Saint Hilaire, St-Hilaire-sur-Helpe For its wondrous timber-built world of stairways and shelves choc-a-bloc with garlands of dried flowers, jars of spices and old tin cans. It's a jolly place, full of warmth with big, comfortable beds (see page 217).

Les Garennes, Le Touquet For a bijou B&B built in 1892 in the style of Napoleon III,

TWO TO THREE DAYS Trips could include:

- Lille and Arras for an overall impression of the major cities of Le Nord and Pas de Calais.
- Arras, including the battlefields, and Montreuil-sur-Mer, with perhaps a trip to Desvres for its pottery or the Beussent chocolate factory in the Seven Valleys.
- Treasures of Le Nord, including Le Quesnoy for its ramparts, Maroilles for its famous cheese, and the Sars Poteries for France's top collection of contemporary glass.
- Côte d'Opale (Opal Coast), including the Lace Museum at Calais, NAUSICAA – Europe's largest exhibition of the underwater world at Boulogne, and the delightful municipal museum at Berck-sur-Mer.

ONE TO TWO WEEKS With so many outdoor activities on offer, you could easily while away a week along the coast, with or without the family, then add the short trips above to make up the second. Alternatively, simply blend a number of themes and take to the road. The region is small enough to combine say the battlefields with a short city stay at either Lille or Arras; Cambrai – or Le Cateau-Cambrésis for fans of Matisse – and the Avesnois likewise bring together the

whose rustic charm is matched by freshly bought croissants and baguettes for a breakfast featuring juice from newly squeezed oranges and homemade jams (see page 115).

RESTAURANTS

La Cour de Rémi, Bermicourt For sheer elegance without being daunting, the restaurant set in the grounds of a *château* complements the no-nonsense home cooking which is stylishly prepared and served (see page 153).

Le Farfadet (The Sprite), Cambrai For a generous sense of well being, and a greeting from a genuflecting puppet – you read that correctly – and for a great meal served with similar flair (see page 188).

Chez Tante Fauvette, St-Omer For not just being the smallest place in town (it only takes 15 diners), but also for the backdrop of paintings, old hats and hanging bunches of hops and for simple homecooked fare at its very best. Book well in advance (see page 126).

Al' Fosse 7, Avion near Lens For showing black is the colour, coal is the name, by recreating a pithead setting for a choice of menus which any self-respecting miner would have judged the finest in town (see page 179).

FESTIVALS

Giants Festival, Douai For providing the best show in town when each July the Gayant family delivers a huge three-day knees-up for the thousands who throng the streets and squares (see page 201).

Turkey Festival, Licques For bringing a genuine glow to December's seasonal festivities, when the Fellows of the Order of the Licques Turkey head a joyful procession preceded by free cups of steaming hot turkey soup ladled from a monster cauldron in the village square (see page 95).

SURPRISE FINDS

Restaurant du Channel, Calais For introducing industrial chic to this slightly out-of-town find in Le Channel, a cultural centre converted from what was once a vast abattoir (see page 64).

contrasting styles of two little-known areas. You could even cover the entire eight regions described in the guide: the coast, including the lesser-known inland villages, combined with Arras or Cambrai and Le Cateau-Cambrésis – this would create a powerful town and country combination.

TOUR OPERATORS

France has never been a mass-market country, relying instead on independent travellers or a growing slew of specialist companies. Many of these cater for outdoor and sporting activities. Others concentrate on cities, culture, food and wines. Far fewer feature northern France, focusing more on the profitable south or southwest, and when they do it's more on Brittany and Normandy. This leaves Nord-Pas de Calais relying heavily on those prepared to discover the cross-Channel attractions for themselves.

Many of the specialist companies listed below are, at the time of writing, either members of ABTA (Association of British Travel Agents; *www.abta.com*), or AITO (Association of Independent Tour Operators; *www.aito.co.uk*), or both. Most are also members of ABTOF (Association of British Travel Organisers to France; *www.franceyesyoucan.com*). NB: some booking companies have websites only.

UK TOUR OPERATORS
Short breaks and motoring

Eurostar ✆ 08432 186 186; www.eurostar.co.uk. City breaks to Lille from £94 for 1 night.

French Travel Service PO Box 563, Chichester PO19 9DZ; ✆ 0844 84 888 43; e fts@f-t-s.co.uk; www.f-t-s.co.uk. The company has 50 years' experience of high-speed train travel. Short breaks to Le Touquet & Lille from £250 to £372 for 5 days. Other destinations are available on request.

Driveline Europe 5 Brewers Yard, Ivel Rd, Shefford, Bedfordshire SG17 5GY; ✆ 0871 222 1005; e enquiries@driveline.co.uk; www.greatgetaways.co.uk, www.aagetaways.co.uk. Eurostar breaks to Lille from £155 for 3 nights, also motoring breaks to Arras, Boulogne, Calais, Le Touquet, Lille & St-Omer from £80.

Drive Alive Holidays www.drive-alive.co.uk. Tailor-made holidays created for independent motorists; routes & maps available online. Sells direct to public.

Hotels Abroad – Short Breaks 5 Worlds End Lane, Green St Green, Orpington, Kent BR6 6AA; ✆ 01689 882500; e reservations@hotelsabroad.co.uk; www.hotelsabroad.com. With a good sprinkling of hotels & B&Bs both inland & along the coast, some featured in the guide, the company began in 1978 offering overnight stops for motorists. Their main strength lies in France. Phone calls welcome.

Inntravel-Activity Nr Castle Howard, Whitwell, York YO60 7JU; ✆ 01653 617788; e brochures@inntravel.co.uk; www.inntravel.co.uk. Short 2-night breaks featured in Lille from £154, also at Les 3 Mousquetaires, Aire-sur-la-Lys from around £300 for 2 nights.

Kirker Holidays 4 Waterloo Court, 10 Theed St, London SE1 8ST; ✆ 020 7593 2288; e cities@kirkerholidays.com; www.kirkerholidays.com. Short breaks to Lille.

Leger Holidays Sunway Hse, Canklow Meadows, Rotherham S60 2XR; ✆ 0844 504 6251; e reservations@leger.co.uk; www.leger.co.uk. Includes Lille by Eurostar; 4 days from £229.

Mark Hammerton Group Spelmonden Old Oast, Goudhurst, Kent TN17 1HE; ✆ 01580 214010/4; e enquiries@alanrogers.com; www.markhammerton.com or www.bellefrance.co.uk. Walking holidays on the Côte d'Opale.

Serenity Holidays Cutter Hse, 1560 Parkway, Solent Business Park, Fareham PO15 7AG; ✆ 0845 330 2077; www.greatescapes.co.uk. Short breaks to Lille & Battlefield Breaks Arras; also self-drive breaks.

VFB PO Box 2130, Gloucester GL2 9WA; ✆ 01452 716 830; e brochures@vfbholidays.co.uk; www.vfbholidays.co.uk. Short self-drive or rail breaks to Lille & Cambrai.

FERRY BOOKINGS

Direct Ferries 2 The Quadrangle Centre, Nacton Rd, Ipswich IP3 9QR; ✆ 01473 728 118; www.directferries.com

The Travel Gateway 2 Morrow Court, Appleford Rd, Sutton Courtenay, Oxon OX14 4FH; ✆ 01235 845624 www.ttgateway.com

GOLFING HOLIDAYS/SHORT BREAKS

Driveline Golf 3 Brewers Yard, Ivel Rd, Shefford, Bedfordshire SG17 5GY; ✆ 0870 330 1056 e reservations@drivelinegolf.com; www.drivelinegolf.com. Golf holidays to Arras, Hardelot, Wimeroux, Dunkirk, St-Omer & Le Touquet.

Fields Fairway Fleurs des Champs, 433 Impasse de Cantraine, Carly, France 62830; ✆ +33 3 21 33 65 64; e golf@fieldsfairway.co.uk; www.fieldsfairway.co.uk. Golfing holidays arranged at Dunkirk, St-Omer, Wimereux, Hardelot, Le Touquet & Arras. Good selection of hotels in & around courses. Special offers.

Golfbreaks.com 2 Windsor Dials, Arthur Rd, Windsor, Berkshire SL4 1RS; ✆ 0800 2797988; e sales@golfbreaks.com; www.golfbreaks.com. Among the 100 French golf courses featured are hotel-based short breaks in Le Touquet, Arras & St-Omer from

£175; 2-night spring breaks from less than £100. Sells direct to public.

Golf in France Ltd Malvern Hse, New Rd, Solihull, West Midlands B91 3DL; ✆ 0121 713 2277; e info@golfinfrance.com; www.golfinfrance.com. Tailor-made golfing packages arranged to Dunkirk, Wimereux, Hardelot & Le Touquet. Special offers.

A Golfing Experience ✆ 01923 283 339; e enquiries@agolfingexperience; www.agolfingexperience.com. The company, which has organised tailor-made golfing breaks for 15 years, covers all the region's major courses. Its top northern France destination is Arras followed by Le Touquet. Sells direct to public.

Leisure Link Promotions Redwing Court Business Centre, Ashton Rd, Romford, Essex RM3 8QQ; ✆ 01277 247520; e reservations@

leisurelinkgolf.com; www.leisurelinkgolf.com. Tailor-made golf breaks featuring Arras, Le Touquet, Dunkirk, Hardelot, Wimereux & Lille. Special offers on golfing hotel breaks. The company is 20 years old.
Mark Hammerton Group Spelmonden Old Oast, Goudhurst, Kent TN17 1HE; ✆ 01580 214010/4; e enquiries@alanrogers.com; www.markhammerton. com or www.bellefrance.co.uk. Gourmet golfing

breaks at St-Omer, Le Touquet & Arras.
Your Golf Holidays The Green, Blackmore, Essex CM4 0RL; ✆ 01277 824100; e info@ golfplanetholidays.com; www.golfplanetholidays.com. Large selection of hotels based at Le Touquet, Hardelot, St-Omer, Arras & Lille. Special packages or tailor-made. Eurotunnel fare is included in the price.

CAMPING/CARAVANNING/CHALETS A widely used site is **La Bien Assise**, set in the parklands of a *château* on the outskirts of Guînes (see *Chapter 4*, page 93). This features chalet-style accommodation, caravanning and camping. The restaurant's menu is highly recommended; other facilities include a swimming pool with a retractable roof, water chute and a children's play area. The site is heavily used at peak periods. Traffic from the road can sometimes be heard. NB: it is wrongly described as being in Picardy on some websites. It lies in the Trois Pays area of Pas de Calais.

Canvas Holidays East Port Hse, 12 East Port, Dunfermline, Fife KY12 7JG; ✆ 0845 268 0827; e reservations@canvasholidays.co.uk; www.canvasholidays.co.uk. Features La Bien Assise; ⊕ 1 May–4 Sep. Ring for prices.
Eurocamp Hartford Manor, Greenbank Lane, Northwich, Cheshire CW8 1HW; ✆ 01606 787000; e enquiries@eurocamp.co.uk; www.eurocamp.co.uk. La Bien Assise. Tents sleeping 7. Around £300 for 7 nights in Jun.
Eurocamp Independent e independent@eurocamp.com;

www.eurocampindependent.co.uk. Caravans at La Bien Assise.
Keycamp Holidays Hartford Manor, Greenbank Lane, Northwich, Cheshire CW8 1HW; ✆ 01606 787 111; e info@keycamp.co.uk; www.keycamp.com. Features a range of tents at La Bien Assise.
Mark Hammerton Group Spelmonden Old Oast, Goudhurst, Kent TN17 1HE; ✆ 01580 214010/4; e enquiries@alanrogers.com; www.markhammerton.com or www.bellefrance.co.uk. Camping holidays in Guînes & other locations.

HOTELS/B&BS/VILLAS/*GÎTES*
Bowhills Unit 3, Furze Court, 114 Wickham Rd, Fareham, Hampshire PO16 7SH; ✆ 0844 847 1333; e enquiries@bowhills.co.uk; www.bowhills.co.uk. Villas sleeping 4–7, including at Le Touquet. Cost is around £500 for 7 nights.
French Connections Bracon Hse, High St, Etchingham, East Sussex TN19 7AJ; ✆ 01580 819303; e enquiries@frenchconnections.co.uk; www.frenchconnections.co.uk. Featuring 50 types of accommodation from B&Bs to hotels & self-catering in Pas de Calais & 6 in Le Nord, this is a valuable source of accommodation. They also provide a range of holidays activities or themes.
French Country Cottages Spring Mill, Earby, Barnoldswick, Lancashire BB94 0AA; ✆ 01282 844284; www.french-country-cottages.co.uk. Small selection of self-catering properties in rural Pas de Calais. These include Le Touquet, Montreuil-sur-Mer & Boulogne.

Holidaylettings.co.uk 2nd Floor, Barclay Hse, 242–54 Banbury Rd, Oxford, OX2 7BY; ✆ 01865 312000; e support@holidaylettings.co.uk; www.holidaylettings.co.uk. Selection of traditional & modern self-catering properties featured in the Hardelot, Le Touquet, Montreuil-sur-Mer & Hesdin areas. These sleep from 4–12. Rental is from £248–1,650 depending on size & season.
Interhome – Self Catering Properties Gemini Hse, 10–18 Putney Hill, London SW15 6AX; ✆ 020 8780 6633; e info@interhome.co.uk; www.interhome.co.uk. Self-catering holiday apartments in Lille, Le Touquet (Stella Plage), & St-Pol-sur-Ternoise.
Pierre et Vacances L'Artois – Espace Pont de Flandre, 11 rue de Cambrai, Paris, Cedex 19; ✆ 0870 026 7144; e contact@pierre-vacances.com; www.pv-holidays.com. Apartments in Le Touquet.

BATTLEFIELDS Some are merely curious, but most of those who visit the serried rows of graves that signpost the World War I carnage from Arras to Ypres in Belgium have come as children, or grandchildren, of those who perished in a

foreign field. Their aim – to discover more about those only briefly mentioned in the family tree – has led to the huge growth of battlefields tours, listed below, and individual tourist trails referred to separately in *Part Two* of the guide. These are not just geared to the Brits, but to visitors from North America and Commonwealth countries as well.

Battlefield Tours The War Research Society, 27 Courtway Av, Birmingham B14 4PP; ☎ 0121 430 5348; e info@battlefieldtours.co.uk; www.battlefieldtours.co.uk. Variety of tours including World War I sites such as Fromelles & Arras; also Dunkirk.

Ecosse Tours Limited 57 Newtongrange Av, Fullarton Park, Glasgow G32 8NE; ☎ 0141 416 1915; e contact@ecossetours.co.uk; www.ecossetours.co.uk. The Arras battlefield sites are included by this Scottish-based company whose prices include executive coach travel for the Hull crossing with P&O Ferries.

Guided Battlefield Tours ☎ 01633 258207; www.guidedbattlefieldtours.co.uk. Small company which includes Arras & Cambrai. Cost is £335 for 4-day tour.

Holts Tours Wolvers Home Farm, Ironsbottom, Sidlow, Reigate, Surrey RH2 8QG; ☎ 01293 865 000; e info@holts.co.uk; www.holts.co.uk. After 30-plus years, this is Britain's undisputed leader in battlefield tours with a good coverage of World War I as it relates to Nord-Pas de Calais.

Leger Holidays Sunway Travel (coaching) Ltd, Sunway Hse, Canklow Meadows, Rotherham S60 2XR; ☎ 0844 504 6251; e reservations@leger.co.uk; www.leger.co.uk. Northern France & Belgium Battlefield Tours by coach include Arras & Vimy Ridge from £270 for 3 days & from £329 for 4 days. Upgrade to Silver Service luxury coach; a 4-day 'Arras – Britain's Bloodiest Battle' tour is available from £369 staying at the Mercure Hotel Hotel; 'Dunkirk & Fortress Europe' includes coastal defences & rocket sites. 4 days from £359.

Poppy Travel The Royal British Legion Village, Aylesford, Kent ME20 7NX; ☎ 01622 716729; e info@poppytravel.org.uk; www.poppytravel.org.uk. Vimy Ridge, Loos & Fromelles are included in the Legion's World War I tours.

Serenity Holidays Cutter Hse, 1560 Parkway, Solent Business Park, Fareham PO15 7AG; ☎ 0845 330 2077; e holidays@corsica.co.uk; www.greatescapes.co.uk. Short breaks to Lille & Battlefield Breaks at Arras. They also offer self-drive breaks.

Specialist companies for non-UK visitors

Mat McLachlan Battlefield Tours 23 Sydney Rd, Manly, NSW 2095, Australia; ☎ + 661300 880 340; e info@battlefields.com.au; www.battlefields.com.au. Another small company whose tours cover major Australian battlefields including Fromelles.

Over the Top Tours Nieuwstraat 5, Kemmel, Belgium; ☎ 32 57 33 29 00; e info@overthetoptours-ypres.be; www.overthetoptours-ypres.be. Leslie Moores, a former history schoolmaster from England, brings his deep personal knowledge of both the French & Belgian World War I & 2 sites to bear in his 8-seater minibus tours. He takes a special interest in the Australian ANZAC & Irish involvement in World War I.

Richardson & Gray Ltd Stage Coach Cottage, 57 Broad St, Ludlow, Shropshire SY8 1NH; ☎ 01584 878914; e clive@richardsonandgray.com;

www.richardsonandgray.com. Another small UK concern specialising in groups from North America.

Somme Battlefield Tours, 9 Old Rd, Wimborne Minster, Dorset BH21 1EJ; ☎ 01202 880211; e jamespower@btinternet.com; www.battlefield-tours.com. This small award-winning company offers highly personalised bespoke self-drive or guided tours suited to overseas visitors on a family pilgrimage or a short visit, as well as catering for the British market.

Western Front Tours PO Box 4302, Balwyn East, 3103 Victoria, Australia; ☎ 06 11 26 53 82 (France) or + 33 61 0408 546 687 (Australia mid-Nov–mid-Mar); www.westernfronttours.com.au. Tours cover the battles of Arras & Fromelles at which the Aussie loss was tremendous (see *Chapter 8*, page 176).

i TOURIST OFFICES

IN FRANCE Each *département* has it own tourist office:

🛡 **Nord Tourist Board** 6 rue Gauthier de Châtillon, BP 1232, 59013 Lille cedex; ☎ 03 20 57 59 59; e contact@cdt-nord.fr; www.tourisme-nord.fr; ⏲ 10.00–12.30 & 14.00–17.00 Tue–Fri

∠ Pas de Calais Tourist Board route de la Trésorerie, Wimille; ☎ 03 21 10 34 60; e accueil@pas-de- calais.com; www.pas-de-calais.com; ⊕ 08.30–12.00 & 14.30–18.30 Mon–Sat

Both have excellent online information on where to sleep and eat, places to visit and regional events. Information on activities, such as walking and biking, can often be downloaded or is available in brochure or leaflet form. They also offer valuable online booking services.

Do sign on at either tourist board website for Nicole's Inspired Breaks – this is a regular newsletter sent by email on a variety of topics such as the best routes for motoring breaks with details of accommodation and places to visit, as well as activities to keep the children amused, cultural visits and a diary of events. It costs nothing and can be cancelled at any time.

See also **www.northernfrance-tourism.com** for an overall look at the region. All three sites include videos, photos and audio tours.

IN THE UK AND OVERSEAS For more general information on France consult the national tourist board. This is now known as **ATOUT FRANCE** which, formed in June 2009, replaces the former Maison de la France with a development agency combining public and private tourist interests. For email addresses and phone numbers log onto www.franceguide.com, select your country, and click on 'Contact us'.

ATOUT FRANCE offices include:

London office Lincoln Hse, 300 High Holborn WC1V 7JH; ☎ 090 68 244 123 (60p/min at all times); e info.uk@franceguide.com; www.franceguide.com; ⊕ 10.00–16.00 Mon–Fri. Click on to Nord-Pas de Calais; information includes last-minute accommodation availability from hotels & campsites, with links to regional & local websites.
Australia French Tourist Bureau 25 Bligh St – level 13, Sydney, NSW 2000 (also serves New Zealand)

Belgium 21 ave de la Toison d'Or, 1050 Brussels
Canada 1800 av McGill Collège, Bureau 1010 Montreal, Québec H3A 3J6
Germany Zeppelinallee 37, D-60325 Frankfurt
Ireland 30 Upper Merrion St, Dublin 2
The Netherlands Prinsengracht 670, 1017 KX Amsterdam
USA 825 Third Av, New York NY 10022 & 9454 Wilshire Bld – Suite 21, Beverley Hills, CA 90212

RED TAPE

ENTRY REQUIREMENTS European Union (EU) nationals, including those from the UK, may visit France as indefinite tourists providing they have passports valid for at least three months beyond their length of stay; visitors from some EU countries need only a national ID card. No visa is needed for visitors from Australia, Canada, New Zealand, the USA and non-European countries, who can stay for up to 90 days; visitors from non-EU countries, however, may have to justify their reason for entry and have sufficient funds to pay for a return journey.

Further information for UK visitors can be found at www.fco.gov.uk or www.worldtravelguide.net/france; non-EU visitors should consult their respective French embassies or consulates.

CUSTOMS REGULATIONS Since France is an EU country, UK visitors are entitled to buy perfume, skincare, cosmetics, champagne, wine, selected spirits, beer, fashion accessories, gifts and souvenirs – all at tax-free equivalent prices. There are no longer any allowance restrictions on such tax-free items. However, with alcohol and tobacco, you must meet the following conditions:

• You transport the goods yourself.

- The goods are for your own use or intended as a gift. If the person you give the goods to pays you in any way (including reimbursing you for any expenses or payment in kind), then it's not a gift and the goods may be seized. You are more likely to be questioned if you have more than: 3,200 cigarettes; 200 cigars; 400 cigarillos; 3kg of tobacco; 110 litres of beer; 90 litres of wine; 10 litres of spirits; 20 litres of fortified wine (for example port or sherry).
- The goods are duty and tax paid in the EU country where they were acquired.

If you don't meet these conditions, the goods (and any vehicle that transported them) may be seized. For more information visit www.hmrc.gov.uk.

As well as the fuel in your vehicle's standard tank, you can bring in reserve fuel for that vehicle without paying any Excise Duty on it. The fuel, however, must be in an appropriate container.

You must declare to customs any goods from EU countries if you think they may be banned or restricted. To do this you should use the red channel or the red-point phone.

Non-EU visitors For what you can bring home check on your country's current customs and excise regulations before leaving for France. If you are arriving from a non-EU country, the following goods may be imported into France by those over 17 years of age without incurring customs duty:

- 200 cigarettes or 50 cigars or 100 cigarillos or 250g of tobacco
- 1 litre of spirits over 22% or 2 litres of alcoholic beverage up to 22%
- 2 litres of wine
- 50g of perfume and 250ml of eau de toilette
- 500g of coffee or 200g of coffee extract
- 100g of tea or 40g of tea extract
- Medication: quantities corresponding to the needs of the patient
- Other goods up to the value of €175 (€90 per person under 15 years of age)

Restricted items Gold jewellery over 500g in weight, which is not for personal use, must be declared.

Prohibited imports Plants and plant products, meat and meat products, pharmaceutical products (except those needed for personal use), works of art, collectors' items and antiques, weapons, and obscene and immoral literature.

GETTING THERE AND AWAY

BY SEA Before the opening of the Channel Tunnel in 1994, a virtual cross-Channel cartel kept car-ferry fares fairly high. Since then keen competition, not just between major ferry companies but also with the car shuttle service through the tunnel, has seen some great deals and a wider range of fares. Online booking, which is what both the ferries and the shuttle now prefer, gives you a better chance of tracking down discounts. These can be seasonal, along with deals available for early or late bookings. Ringing first to check what's the cheapest is a good bet; you can still book online to get the discount.

Check out flat-rate fares; these include the car and up to nine passengers. Mini-breaks, too, can help cut costs. The most expensive fare period runs from early July to mid-August, also around Easter and school holidays. Weekday and night crossing fares are invariably less expensive than those at the weekends. While it's wiser to book in advance, it is also possible to turn up and wait for the next available space.

However, what ever way you buy your ticket, one thing is certain. Thanks to a sea change – literally – which saw the introduction of almost cruise-type vessels, the predicted drop, or even demise, of ferry crossings following the opening of the Channel Tunnel never happened – though one cheeky cut-price interloper went bust a few years back. Instead you have a straight choice to go under or over the Channel – the advantage of going under is that the Tunnel offers a 35-minute journey time and is not prone to bad weather, especially handy in the winter.

Unfortunately, at the time of going to press, a much-needed Dover to Boulogne service begun with such high hopes by LD Lines, was abruptly ended. This downturn in the UK ferry industry, at least on the busy cross-Channel route, cannot simply be blamed on the recession alone. As mentioned, it also stems from the price war. Huge pressure has been placed on the ferry companies to meet the challenge from the Eurotunnel which slashed its rates to win back freight and tourist traffic lost after the tunnel fire in 2008.

While aggressive pricing policies may initially help the consumer, it places a huge financial burden on the ferry companies who some admit need to rectify supply and demand to ensure the long-term survival of the vital cross-Channel options.

As for the Boulogne crossing, there is still talk of a long-promised ferry service from Ramsgate, though the LD Lines' decision hardly helps the case, especially with Calais a mere motorway drive away. For tourists, at least, use of the old town centre terminal is, I believe (albeit rather selfishly), a better bet than the new more out-of-town Hub Port Terminal, though financially this undeniably remains a crucial long-term project as an important European logistics centre. It's more a case of watch this space … even if times are currently a little choppy on the Channel!

Norfolkline (now part of DFDS) ✆ 0870 870 10 20; www.norfolkline.com. Up to 24 return sailings daily Dover–Dunkirk, from £19, 02.00–24.00. No foot passengers. Check-in: 45mins before departure; crossing: 2hrs. Journey time from ferry terminal to Dunkirk city centre is 20mins.
Capacity: 3 purpose-built ferries each taking 200 cars & 780 passengers.
Facilities: 1st-class lounge for £9.60 or £12 for on-board booking. This includes priority loading/disembarking, complimentary wine or soft drink, newspapers, coffee/tea & biscuits etc; also bistro-style menu available: 11.45–21.15.
Refreshments: the waiter service Bistro serves both breakfast 22.00–10.00 & lunch/dinner 12.00–22.00; a self-service restaurant also offers snacks, lunches & dinner.
Other: shop & children's play area.
Pets: carried for £30 each way (see page 24).
Special offers: seasonal & early booking deals; also short breaks.
P&O Ferries ✆ 08716 64 64 64; www.poferries.com. Up to 23 return sailings daily Dover–Calais, from £25 each way. Check-in: 45mins before departure (cars & foot passengers); crossing: 90mins.
Capacity: 5 ships, carrying from 1,420–2,290 passengers & 500–650 cars depending on tonnage. The first of 2 replacement ships currently being built

is due to come into service in early Jan 2011, the 2nd in Sep 2011.
Facilities: Club Class (for all passengers) is £12 pp each way or £14 pp for on-board upgrade. Add Priority Boarding for £6 each. Free newspapers, coffee/tea & biscuits. B/fast & menus. This service is unavailable on night or early-morning crossings 20.00–06.00 ex Dover & 23.00–09.00 ex Calais.
Refreshments: Langan's Brasserie is available on all ships 06.00–20.00 ex Dover & 09.00–23.00 ex Calais for lunch, afternoon tea & dinner; also lounges & self-service food courts for hot snacks, sandwiches, coffee, tea, etc.
Other: shop, games room & currency exchange.
Pets: carried for £15 each way (see page 24).
Special offers: seasonal & last-minute deals, also day & short-break offers. See online Best Search fare to Calais.
SeaFrance (UK) ✆ 0871 222 8544;
e enquiries@seafrance.fr; www.seafrance.com. Up to 15 return sailings daily Dover–Calais, from £25. Check-in: 30mins before departure (vehicles). No foot passengers. Crossing: from 75mins.
Capacity: the addition of the *Molière* in autumn 2008 completed its fleet of 3 superferries, carrying from 1,200–1,900 passengers & 480–700 cars depending on size of ship.
Refreshments: La Brasserie waiter service restaurant

offers b/fast, lunch & dinner; also Le Relais self-service restaurant; continental snacks & drinks in Le Pub, Le Parisien Café & Latitudes café bar.

Other: shop, games arcade, children's play area, baby-changing facilities & currency exchange.

Pets: carried for £35 Calais–Dover, free Dover–Calais (see below).

Special offers: seasonal & last-minute deals, also day & short-break offers. See also Ellie's blog for handy

hints & advice for in & around Nord-Pas de Calais (www.seafrance.com & click on 'inspire me').

Euroferries This 75-min fast ferry service Ramsgate–Boulogne had not begun operating at the time of writing. The ship was due to dock at Gare Maritime, pl de la République, 2000m from Boulogne town centre. For details ☎ 0844 414 5355; www.euroferries.co.uk.

BY TUNNEL

Eurotunnel UK Terminal, Ashford Rd, Folkestone, Kent CT18 8XX – follow road signs to dedicated motorway exit at junction 11A off the M20 direct to check-in booths; ☎ 08443 35 35 35; www.eurotunnel.com for online booking. There are up to 3 departures per hr during peak periods. Check-in: at least 30mins before departure. Self check-in kiosks available if tickets booked in advance. Standard pre-booked fare from £53 single journey for car & up to 9 passengers for the 35min journey.

Facilities: passengers stay with their vehicle throughout the journey in AC carriages with information screens. Those upgrading to a flexi-plus booking benefit from a dedicated check-in, exclusive lounge serving complimentary non-alcoholic drinks &

snacks as well as priority boarding on the next available shuttle. NB: passengers with vehicles over 1.85m will not have access to the lounge.

There are petrol stations at both the UK & France terminals. Both terminals offer shopping & eating facilities, also family/baby changing room. A 24-hr information desk can assist with ticketing & other queries. Facilities available for disabled passengers in both terminals. Similar facilities exist for Eurotunnel, Coquelles. Take junction 42 of the A16 motorway & use signposted slip road straight to check-in booths.

Pets: price per pet £30, charged on the Calais/Folkestone journey (see below).

Special offers: book early for the best rate. Seasonal & short stay savers are available.

✈ BY AIR

From Europe and beyond International flights, including those from the UK, fly direct to Paris's Roissy-Charles de Gaulle Airport. Of the major scheduled airlines, American Airlines (*www.americanairlines.com*), Delta Airlines (*www.delta.com*) and Continental Airlines (*www.continental.com*) offer direct flights from major US cities (New York, Boston, Chicago, Boston, Miami and Dallas among them); Air Canada (*www.aircanada.com*) likewise serves Paris from Toronto, Vancouver and Montreal. Flights from Australia and New Zealand are feasible with both QANTAS (*www.quantas.com.au*) and Air New Zealand (*www.airnewzealand.com*) respectively, with a host of handy one-night stopover flights from a huge variety of national airlines flying from mainland Asian airports. Consult the major airfare comparison websites for further details.

From Roissy-Charles de Gaulle take the 51-minute TGV train to Lille from the station at the Air France terminal; Air France (*www.airfrance.com*) sells through tickets to Lille. These run daily every 20 minutes from 06.00 to 23.00. There is a

TAKING FIDO WITH YOU

Plan well ahead if you are taking a pet on holiday. Contact **DEFRA** (Department for Environment Food and Rural Affairs; *www.defra.gov.uk*; ☎ *0870 241 1710*) for up-to-date information. It is vital you follow the instructions for the Pet Travel Scheme (PETS) as any errors could delay your travel plans either side of the Channel. Make sure the ferry companies or Eurotunnel know you are travelling with a pet; equally make sure that your French hosts will welcome Fido…

further 50-minute TGV service to Arras that runs from 06.45 to 21.00. There are connecting or direct links to other major centres in the region, including St-Omer, Calais and Boulogne.

Alternatively, international flights to Brussels airport across the border, though more limited in number, connect with a regular 42-minute TGV rail service to Lille. Tickets for this can be booked in advance.

A few flights operate to other European cities from Lille Lesquin airport which is heavily used for charter flights to the Mediterranean. This is 8km by shuttle bus or taxi from the town centre (See *Chapter 10*, page 225).

LyddAir 01797 322 207; e info@lyddair.com; www.lyddair.com. Operates scheduled w/end flights throughout the year to Le Touquet from Lydd Airport in southeast Kent. These depart 09.30 arriving 11.00 local time. There are 3 additional weekday flights in Jul & Aug. Flight time: approximately 20mins. Check in: 45mins. Return fares: from £127.14 adult, £108.90 children (2–12) & £34.02 infants. Charter offers are available for golfers & other groups. Pets, subject to regulations, charged at £30 plus £1 per kilo in excess of 10kg of the combined pet, case & passenger luggage (see website). Wheelchair assistance is provided; there is also an online hotel booking service at www.lyddair.com. Taxis meet all flights at Le Touquet for the 5min transfer downtown (€8).

BY COACH

Eurolines 4 Cardiff Rd, Luton LU1 1PP; 08717 818181; www.eurolines.co.uk. Up to 4 departures daily from London Victoria via Calais to Lille. Journey time: 6hrs 30mins–6hrs 45mins using Channel Tunnel or P&O Ferries. From around £59 depending on type of fare.

BY EUROSTAR This is the high-speed passenger train which runs at up to 300km/h on its own dedicated line from London St Pancras to Paris and Brussels via the Channel Tunnel. Some trains make intermediate stops at Ebbsfleet International and/or Ashford International in Kent and, on the French side of the Channel, in Calais Fréthun (three services per day) and Lille Europe (generally eight services per day). Journey time is one hour from London to Calais and one hour 20 minutes to Lille.

Advance booking is essential, and during busy periods the earlier you book, the greater chance you have of getting a cheap fare. Tickets can be purchased up to 120 days in advance, although this is reduced to 83 days if you are combining your Eurostar ticket with a National Rail ticket from one of over 100 UK stations.

There are three classes of travel:

- Standard: no frills but perfectly adequate, and with more legroom than you get on a plane. Snacks, hot and cold dishes and drinks are available from the buffet. Minimum check-in 30 minutes before departure.
- Leisure select: even more legroom, complimentary newspapers/magazines and a meal served at your seat. Minimum check-in 30 minutes before departure.
- Business premier: top of the range. This includes all the above plus a dedicated lounge and fast-track check-in, minimum 10 minutes before departure.

The **luggage** allowance on Eurostar is two cases and one piece of hand luggage per person. Wheelchairs and mobility scooters can be accommodated but be sure to notify the carrier or agent at the time of booking.

If you can fold or dismantle your **bicycle** and place it in a bike bag with the saddle, handlebars and wheels removed, you can carry it on board yourself as part of your luggage allowance, provided the overall size is no bigger than a normal suitcase. Failing that, you can send a bicycle as registered luggage from London to Lille. It will not necessarily go on the same train as you do, but it is guaranteed to arrive within 24 hours.

For further information and bookings see www.eurostar.com or call ☏ 08705 186 186. They can also book domestic journeys – bi-lingual staff make this a good option for non-French speakers. Another useful source is Rail Europe (*www.raileurope.co.uk;* ☏ *08448 484064*).

✚ HEALTH

EHIC CARD The standard of health care in France is good. However, the NHS recommends all travellers take out private health insurance to complement the cover given by the European Health Insurance Card. This replaces the old E111 which is no longer valid. Apply online (*www.ehic.org*) to get one within seven working days. You can apply for yourself, wife/husband/partner and up to four children in one application. The card is only available for British, EU, EEA or Swiss citizens. The main applicant must be resident in the UK and over 16 years of age. There is a £9.95 charge per application.

You can also apply by phone on ☏ 0845 606 2030 (up to 10 working days) or by post using an application form available from some post offices (up to 21 working days).

The card basically covers any accident or emergency treatment by doctors, dentists, and in public hospitals or private clinics operating within the French *sécurité sociale* (health service) framework.

EMERGENCY CALLS Emergency call stations can be found on motorways, at tourist spots and along unguarded beaches. The emergency numbers can be found on the internet, in telephone directories and on public noticeboards.

☏ **15**: national emergency number for medical aid. Be prepared to indicate exactly where you are located, and the circumstances.

☏ **18**: general emergency number which will get you connected to the most appropriate service.

☏ **112**: this is the standard European emergency number. If you are near the Belgian border, a call to 112 from a mobile phone may get directed to their emergency services.

DOCTORS France has a dense network of medical practitioners, and there are doctors' surgeries (*cabinets*) even in small towns and villages. In theory, you can go to the surgery of any doctor during opening hours.

To find a doctor, ask a local resident, or at a pharmacy. Failing that, local police stations (*gendarmeries*) can usually provide the phone number of the duty doctor (*médecin de garde*) and pharmacy (*pharmacie de garde*).

If you see a doctor, or go to a hospital, you will be given a signed statement of the treatment carried out, and possibly a prescription (*ordonnance*). These documents must be kept carefully, as you will need them in order to claim reimbursement. Take the prescription to a pharmacy, where you will have to pay for the items needed. Those with an EHIC card will be refunded at about 70% of standard doctors' and dentists' fees, and between 35% and 65% of the cost of most prescribed medicines – which may still end up costing less than in the UK.

HOSPITALS There is some kind of accident or emergency service in most medium-sized towns. Look for signs to the '*hôpital*' or '*centre hospitalier*'. In bigger towns or cities, look for signs to the 'CHR' (*centre hospitalier régional*) or 'CHU' (*centre hospitalier universitaire*).

If you are too sick to move, ask your hotel/campsite/*gîte* owners to call a local medic. The cost is slightly higher than a surgery visit, but payment and refunding are the same.

Mark Davidson

Nord-Pas de Calais is popular with tourists who go camping and enjoy the way of life of this part of the world. As with all small provincial towns, the streets of towns in the region are narrow and can be a little difficult to navigate for those in wheelchairs. However, people can get around with a little help from others.

PLANNING AND BOOKING There are a number of travel agencies offering travel to France and some cater for the needs of disabled travellers. Companies such as www.ineedaholidaytoo.com deal with holidays there and can offer further advice.

TRAVEL INSURANCE There are a few specialised companies that deal with travel to Nord-Pas de Calais. A number of operators offer cover for pre-existing medical conditions such as Travelbility (0845 338 1638; *www.travelbility.co.uk*) and Medici Travel (0845 880 0168; *www.medicitravel.com*).

GETTING THERE SeaFrance (*www.seafrance.com*) have fully accessible ferries for travel across the English Channel to Nord-Pas de Calais.
Both Eurostar and the TGV (Train à Grande Vitesse) stop at Calais-Fréthun station and both have trains fully accessible to wheelchair users and those in need of assistance.

ACCOMMODATION Most hotels and motels in the region display the *tourisme et handicap* sign to indicate accessibility. One such hotel is the Hôtel Balladins in Calais (*Zup Du Beau Marais, Angle rue Greuze et rue Salvador Allende, Calais, 62100*).

VISITING PLACES There are many historical sites in the Calais region. Unfortunately due to the age of many of the buildings, it may not be possible for people to explore the architecture unaided. It is advisable to check beforehand.
If you require a local bus service, those such as SITAC are accessible for wheelchairs, with ramps to allow easy boarding.

FURTHER INFORMATION A good website for further information on planning and booking any accessible holiday is www.able-travel.com, which provides many tips and links to travel resources worldwide.
The tourist board of Nord-Pas de Calais provides further information for travellers wishing to go there on their website, www.uk.pas-de-calais.com.
uk.franceguide.com has useful information for those in wheelchairs who wish to explore the local area.
Bradt Travel Guides' title *Access Africa – Safaris for People with Limited Mobility* is aimed at safari-goers but is full of advice and resources that will be useful for all disabled travellers.

Practical Information HEALTH

2

PHARMACIES These are plentiful in major towns, and open at the same time as other small shops; in main towns there is usually a *pharmacie de garde* or two that open each Sunday, and sometimes even at night. In towns with a number of pharmacies, a rota system usually operates: an illuminated green cross shows when a pharmacy is open. In small towns, where there are perhaps just one or two, it may be necessary to ring the bell for service, particularly in the event of a night-time emergency.

Where is there a doctor's surgery?	*Où est-ce qu'on peut trouver un cabinet médical?*
medicine	*médicament(s)*
ill, sick	*malade*
pharmacy	*une pharmacie*
We need to find a doctor urgently	*Nous avons besoin de voir un médecin au plus vite. C'est urgent.*

$ MONEY, BANKING AND BUDGETING

France forms part of the Euro-zone. Each euro (€) is made up of 100 centimes available as coins of one, two, five, ten, 20 and 50 centimes and as one or two euro coins, similar in size to their sterling counterparts. So don't get them mixed up. Remember, coins can be used anywhere within the euro area, regardless of the country of issue.

Notes are made up of five, ten, 20, 50, 100, 200 and 500 euros, though these were withdrawn by British bank wholesalers in 2010 because they were fuelling organised crime. A good mixture should include plenty of ten or 20 euro notes, a few fives and a pocketful of euros for vending machines, parking, motorway tolls (see page 30) or coffee stops. Large notes are not easy to use. Many shops and stores do not accept notes of €50 or larger. Lower denomination coins are pretty useless, too, though handy for tips.

Money can be changed at most post offices. Banks have a large minimum commission, and exchange bureaux at airports, ferry ports and train stations tend to offer poor exchange rates.

Travellers' cheques in euros, although secure, are not universally accepted. You can't always exchange them at banks or hotels, so you will probably need a trip to a post office to cash them in. A commission rate of 3% is not uncommon. The Post Office Travel Money Card and the Travelex Cash Passport are now popular ways of taking foreign money abroad. These are plastic payment cards that can be loaded with cash before departure and reloaded during the trip by phone from anywhere in the world.

In some wine and beer outlets you can pay in sterling with a credit card or cash.

CREDIT CARDS Known as *cartes de credit*, credit cards are now more or less universally accepted, though you may lose out on fluctuating exchange rate charges by the billing date. Visa and MasterCard are probably the most widely accepted, especially if you wish to withdraw money from an ATM (*guichet automatique*). Check whether your bank has sister banks in France: this way you will get a more reasonable exchange rate. Even if a bank doesn't, ATMs still often give the best exchange rates. Some banks may charge you a fee to withdraw from their ATMs.

ATMs can be found all over cities, towns and in some large villages, and are generally marked with a sign of a hand holding a card above them. The advantage of using them is that they eliminate the need to find a place to change money, and the bother of travellers' cheques.

Credit cards are widely accepted in shops, restaurants and bars in major towns. Outside of towns many small restaurants and shops do not accept cards due to high handling charges. Most bed and breakfasts do not accept credit cards so do keep cash with you just in case. The safest bet is to take a mixture of cash, travellers' cheques, a travel money card, credit and debit cards.

Store and loyalty cards are useful if you are shopping in supermarkets with Tesco or Sainsbury outlets – wine could be cheaper elsewhere, but you will have to pay in euros. French self-service petrol pumps tend to take only French credit cards although some *autoroute* stations do take foreign cards. You can, however, use most credit cards at the station kiosk.

Lost and stolen cards A few cards provide central helpline numbers to report lost cards, but it is important to keep your card provider's 24-hour helpline number handy in case you need assistance.

BANKING Opening hours vary from town to town and depend on the location and the size of branch. However, general banking hours are 09.00–17.30 Monday–Friday; some banks are open on Saturdays and certain evenings. Some banks may close on Mondays but you are likely to find at least one open in major towns. Many close for lunch from 12.00 until 14.00. Banks also close at noon on the eve of a public holiday. Depending when this falls, there is a tendency to join it to the nearest weekend and close for several days.

There are eight main banks in France: Crédit Agricole; BNP Paribus; Société Générale; Caisse d'Epargne; Banque Populaire; Credit Mutuel; La Banque Postal and LCL.

DISABLED TRAVEL

While accessibility is given high priority, travel in a wheelchair can have its difficulties. You can't, for instance, avoid the cobbled streets which add so much to the character of many towns. What you can be pretty certain of is that at least most hotels, *gîtes* and other types of accommodation (see page 35) show the '*tourisme et handicap*' label. So do many sightseeing attractions. This indicates accessibility for those with a variety of visual, oral and mental impairments. Many are old buildings so watch out for stairs, or check that a lift is available if needed. Of the seaside resorts, Berck-sur-Mer among others can provide beach-buggy type wheel-chairs.

Check on the tourist office website for both Pas de Calais and Le Nord (see pages 20–1): www.tourisme-nord.fr/UploadTIF/MEDIA_2baafdba-86ac-4d37-a80b-e48a312c5cc5.pdf has further information; it is only available in French at present. The Association des Paralysés de France website www.apf.fr can also help. See also *Notes for disabled travellers*, page 27.

GETTING AROUND

BY CAR Driving through Nord-Pas de Calais is the simplest way to see the region. Traffic on what are some of northern France's busiest roads is still relatively light compared to those across the Channel. Admittedly, driving around Lille in rush-hour can be horrendous; the same, to a far lesser extent, applies to Valenciennes. Le Touquet's grid system is interesting/confusing… take your pick. But, peak periods apart – the busiest time being around 17.00 – even those cities are less

TOILETS

Public loos can be elusive: try supermarkets, wait until you visit a museum – which may mean an admission charge – or have a coffee at a café and use the facilities there. Visitor centres, including those at major war cemeteries, generally have toilets.

daunting than some UK ones. Lunchtime, being quieter, is an ideal time to arrive, though restaurants will be busier so it is advised to book first if you can. Calais and Boulogne are ideally suited to introductory sorties, especially along the quieter coastal region roads (see *Chapter 4*).

All of this may dent the English dread of French drivers. However, if you do get hooted or flashed at, it's often not a case of Gallic gall, more simple frustration at a foreign car wobbling from lane to lane, or, worse still, hogging the middle of the road. So if someone's up your rear, let 'em go! This applies especially to lorries, which, lights flashing, head directly from often fairly short slip roads onto motorways. Slow down or move into the fast lane – rather a dodgy manoeuvre if you have no passenger to spot what's coming. An already-adjusted rear windscreen mirror is often of no great value either, so do take care.

Despite the pushy lorries, the motorways (*autoroutes*), marked 'A' on maps, are rarely busy, especially when you've well and truly cleared the port areas – statistically top danger spots for accidents whether on arrival or departure. Barriers, shrubbery and vegetation in the central reservations help against being blinded by the headlights of oncoming vehicles. There are plenty of rest stops (*aires de repos*) with toilets, picnic areas and telephones. French motorway service areas, *stations-services*, provide restaurant and shopping facilities about every 40km. Wine is served at meals, which is surprising considering that drink-drive rules are tough.

Watch out for road numbers marked 'N' on some older maps. In January 2006 the French government handed over the care of some N (national) roads to the *départements*, hence becoming 'D' roads. There is apparently no rule as regards the new numbers given to these D roads. Each *département* is free to choose. The idea is that people follow directions on the signs, and not the numbers of the roads. Most of the D roads in Nord and Pas de Calais are D9xx, eg: D943.

Traffic on the D roads, especially minor ones, is light, particularly in the Seven Valleys and the Avesnois, where driving is a doddle. It is here, too, you really need a car, though there are train links to both (see pages 146 and 212).

MOTORWAYS SHRINK THE SIGHTS

Whether using Lille, the Channel ports or the Eurotunnel, most attractions are within two hours' driving distance, using the A16, A23, A25 and A26 motorways. The A25 and A16, from Calais to Boulogne only, are toll-free. For other centres see respective chapters.

Average driving times from Calais are: Arras (1hr 5mins); Boulogne (22mins); Cambrai (1hr 35mins); Douai (1hr 20mins); Le Touquet (40mins); Lille (1hr 15mins); St-Omer (33mins). Allow, however, at least an extra 20 minutes, unless you know a centre well. Satnavs, too, are often wildly optimistic. And do make sure they're up-to-date, especially when visiting rapidly developing big cities.

Take sufficient cash to pay at motorway toll booths (*péages*) which, at some smaller exit points, are automatic. To save searching for a ticket machine that accepts coins, it is often quicker is to use a Visa or MasterCard even for a small amount. Your pin number, at the time of writing, is not required.

Check with www.bison-fute.equipment.gouv.fr (or search for 'French National Traffic Centre'; ☎ 0800 100 200) for all aspects of driving, including toll charges, weather conditions and traffic snarl-ups. NB: road works on the A25 (E42) between Lille and Bergues are continuing until 2011. An English-language leaflet that outlines diversions is available from a variety of sources, including local tourist offices, motorway outlets, tollbooths and UK AA outlets.

- Fuel prices vary, with those at supermarkets among the cheapest, so take your loyalty card just in case. The most expensive are on the motorways.
- Unleaded petrol (95 and 98 octane), diesel (*gazole*) and LPG are all available. Petrol in a can, though legal within France, is forbidden by ferry and Eurotunnel operators. A new type of fuel, the SP95-E10 (Sans Plomb 95 Octane, Ethanol 10% = Lead Free 95 Octane containing 10% of Ethanol) is sold throughout France. This is unsuitable for some cars so check before leaving. If in doubt use the standard SP95 or SP98 Octane unleaded fuel – it should still be available alongside the new fuel.
- Diesel fuel used to be about a third cheaper than unleaded, but now retails for only about 20 centimes a litre less than unleaded petrol.
- Many automatic petrol pumps are operated by credit/debit card. Not all those issued in the UK, or elsewhere, are acceptable.
- Keep topped up if visiting some of the remoter rural areas as petrol stations can be scarce. Many keep shop hours, so are shut at night, on Sunday afternoons, on Mondays or at lunchtime.
- Petrol stations on the main roads stay open longer, and those on the motorways are staffed 24 hours.

The occasional direction sign starting with the word *Bis* in italics indicates the equivalent of the British holiday route using less crowded main roads.

Driving on the right The biggest danger for UK drivers is forgetting to drive on the right, especially at roundabouts. The ideal solution is a simple transparent and non-adhesive windscreen sticker with directional arrows; this is available cheaply from Halfords and the like, as well as at the ferry or tunnel AA outlets. Roundabouts bearing the words '*Vous n'avez pas la priorité*' or '*Cédez le passage*' mean traffic on the roundabout has priority; where no such sign exists traffic entering the roundabout has priority.

Watch out for the dreaded '*priorité á droite*' sign, whereby traffic coming from streets on your right automatically has right of way. Though the tradition is gradually being phased out, especially on main roads, do take care. This applies especially at unmarked junctions, in busy town centres or villages where farm vehicles might suddenly trundle out in front of you. Otherwise it's pretty obvious, as most side streets are marked either with a stop sign and/or a thick white line meaning the same.

Signposting Signposting is pretty good: common signs include '*toutes directions*' (literally meaning 'all directions'), '*autres directions*' (other directions), with a second indicating a specific place, and '*centre ville*' (town centre). Others worth noting are: '*chaussée déformée*' (uneven road/temporary surface); '*rids de poules*' (potholes); '*déviation*' (diversion); '*gravillons*' (loose chippings); '*passage protégé*' (your right of way); and '*priorité piétons*' (give way to pedestrians).

Parking Parking presents no great problem, except during the high season summertime holidays, especially at the coast. However, restrictions are strictly enforced, particularly in major towns. You can face on-the-spot fines or have your car towed away. Parking on the left side of a street is allowed along one-way streets only. Some pay-and-display machines, common in the bigger cities, offer free parking from 12.00 to 13.30, the French lunchtime; coastal resorts may charge at

Practical Information **GETTING AROUND**

2

weekends or public holidays, though out of season there may be no charge at all. The tariff and time limit are shown on the machine.

Parking discs for 'blue zone' parking areas are obtained from police stations, tourist offices and some shops. These allow free parking for up to 90 minutes. A sign reading *fin d'interdiction de stationner* indicates the end of a no-parking zone. In villages or small towns, parking is generally free. Make sure you pull in well off the road, even if only for a brief stop.

Speed limits Speed limits are 130km/h (80mph) on motorways; 110km/h (68mph) on dual carriageways; 90km/h (55mph) on other roads; and 50km/h (31mph) in built-up areas. Lower speed limits apply in wet weather. Additionally, speed limits are reduced on stretches of motorways in built-up areas. The minimum speed limit on motorways is 80km/h (49mph).

Holders of EU driving licences exceeding the speed limit by more than 40km/h could have their licences confiscated on the spot.

Radar speed-trap detectors are illegal, though not satnav systems which show the position of fixed speed cameras, and gong you accordingly.

Seatbelts Adults and children, in both the back and front seats, must wear seatbelts at all times. Children under ten years old are not allowed to travel in the front seat of a car. The only exceptions are if there are no rear seats, the back seats are already

REMEMBER THIS...

All vehicles/drivers travelling in France must have the following:

- Original car registration certificate
- MOT certificate
- Driving licence
- Insurance certificate
- Passport
- GB (or other nationality) sticker, unless included as part of the number plate
- Headlamp beam adaptors: adhesive versions can be bought, but tend to last for only one trip. Shop around for more permanent plastic or similar convertors – they're more expensive but worth it if you're a frequent visitor to France.
- Warning triangle: have at least one in case hazard lights are inoperable. If you're involved in an accident, or suffer a breakdown, the triangle should be placed on the road 30m behind the vehicle and clearly visible from 100m.
- High visibility jackets: take at least two, one for the driver another for the main passenger. These must be kept visible and accessible, ie: not in the car boot.
- First-aid kit
- Fire extinguisher
- Spare bulbs: failure to replace a broken bulb could result in a spot fine so always carry spares for all your car lights
- Also, remember that dipped headlights must be used in the daytime when visibility is poor.

Check your **insurance policy** provides adequate cover; even if it does, still let your insurers know the dates you will be away. **Breakdown cover** is not essential, but well worth considering as repair costs are high. If you are planning a number of trips, albeit short ones, an annual cover may work out cheaper. It also saves a lot of hassle.

occupied by children under ten, or there are no seatbelts; in these circumstances they must travel in an approved child seat or a restraint adapted to their size. If in doubt, check first. Babies are allowed to travel in the front passenger seat, but only when placed in an approved rear-facing baby seat and the airbag is turned off.

A few more rules Driving **fines** are often on-the-spot. They can vary from around €135 for not wearing a seat belt up to €200 or more for speeding.

The **drink-drive limit** is lower than it is in the UK. The best advice is the same everywhere: don't drink and drive.

Using a mobile phone while driving is an offence. Hands-free use of mobile phones is not illegal. (NB: don't rely on getting a signal in some parts of the region.)

The **minimum age** for driving a car in France is 18.

Car rental Though remaining relatively expensive, French car-hire firms are now offering an increasing range of options thanks to cheaper local chains and a more competitive approach by international companies. Comparison sites, including www.carrentals.co.uk, which has received wide press coverage, have also helped.

The main contenders are:

Ada www.ada.fr
Avis www.avis.co.uk
Europcar www.europcar.co.uk

France Cars www.francecars.fr
Hertz www.hertz.co.uk

Others among the 50 or so rental outlets include:

Sixt www.sixt.co.uk
Ebookers www.ebookers.com
Opodo www.opodo.co.uk

Expedia www.expedia.co.uk
Thrifty www.thrifty.co.uk

And budget rentals are available from:

EasyCar www.easycar.com
Budget www.budget.co.uk

Holiday Autos www.holidayautos.co.uk

While car rental is available at Lille airport, it is left to major names such as Avis, Budget, Europcar and Hertz to provide a round-the-clock service at the more widely used Charles de Gaulle airport – but at a cost. A more cost-effective and comfortable choice is to book a car online in advance at a discount.

You can also find car rental at Lille International Station, handy if using Eurostar, and there are outlets at the Channel ports. Look out for special deals offered by tour operators tying in cross-Channel travel. *Yellow Pages* and Google are always useful sources. Allow from around €226 a week for a family-sized car. A reliable standard package includes third-party insurance, vehicle damage cover to a fixed amount, theft protection, unlimited mileage and 24-hour roadside assistance.

BY TRAIN *by French rail travel expert Peter Mills*
While most visitors to Nord-Pas de Calais opt to go by car, there is a lot to be said for taking the train. The combination of Eurostar, which gets you from the UK to the region in a remarkably short time, and an extensive network of local trains serving towns both large and small, makes for a relaxing way of getting around. Not only is rail travel far less polluting, but it has the added advantage of allowing you to have a drink or two with lunch. And while a little forward planning is, of course, necessary, it's easy when you know how.

There are a number of **Chemins de Fer Touristiques** (preserved railway lines) in the region which have been rescued from oblivion by groups of rail enthusiasts and where you can wallow in nostalgia to your heart's content. One example is the **Chemin de Fer de la Valléee de l'Aa**, 15km of standard-gauge line from Arques to Lambres, part of the former St-Omer–Boulogne line (*www.cftva.c.la*) – see *Chapter 5*, page 130.

Chemin de Fer de la Baie de la Somme has 27km of track, part narrow gauge, part standard gauge, running from Le Crotoy to Cayeux sur Mer via Noyelles and St-Valéry-sur-Somme (*www.chemin-fer-baie-somme.asso.fr*).

Le Petit Train de la Haute Somme runs from Froissy to Dompierre over 7km of 60cm-gauge track (*http://appeva.perso.neuf.fr/index_e.htm*), while **Chemin de Fer Touristique du Vermandois** has a standard-gauge line linking St-Quentin and Origny-St-Benoite (*www.cftv.fr*).

Don't be daunted by the names of various types of train you come across:

TGV (Train à Grande Vitesse)
Operated by SNCF (French National Railways), TGVs are long distance, high-speed trains designed, like Eurostar, to run at up to 300km/h on a dedicated track such as that linking the Channel Tunnel with Lille and Paris. That said, TGVs are compatible with the rest of the network and serve a number of stations away from the high-speed line. Thus you may occasionally encounter one in the Lille area and even in Dunkirk or Boulogne.

The main thing to remember is that you MUST book your seat before boarding the train. You can do this up to 90 days in advance or even on the day of travel, subject to availability. TGVs have first- and second-class seating and, as with all trains in France, you can take on board as much luggage as can be stored in the racks or under your seat. This includes bike bags. If you have a rigid-frame bicycle, you are advised to take a TER train (see below) which, in most cases, has a luggage van in which bikes can be stowed.

TER (Transport Express Régional)
The TER network of regional trains has benefited from a considerable amount of investment in recent years, as a result of which a lot of smart new trains and more frequent services have been introduced. They link towns and villages all over the region and are extremely easy to use. There is no need to reserve a seat; simply buy a ticket in the station and jump on. A lot of TER trains are standard class only, although you may find first-class seating (always clearly indicated) on some routes. Timetable leaflets (*fiches horaires*) are available in all stations and are invaluable in finding your way around.

Corail Intercités
Corail Intercités trains were the backbone of SNCF mainline services prior to the advent of TGV. Nowadays, they are used principally on regional services in the same way as the TER. They generally offer first- and second-class seating, and no advance booking is necessary.

For full information on all aspects of rail travel in France visit www.raileurope.co.uk or call ☏ 08448 484064.

Rail-based short breaks

French Travel Service PO Box 563, Chichester PO19 9DZ; ☏ 0844 84 888 43; e fts@f-t-s.co.uk; www.f-t-s.co.uk. The company, which has 50 years' experience of high-speed train travel, features train travel & hotel accommodation in Lille, Le Touquet or St-Omer. **Rail Europe Travel Centre** 1 Lower Regent St, London SW1Y 4XT; ☏ 08448 484 064; www.raileurope.co.uk; ⏲ 10.00–18.00 Mon–Sat & 10.00–16.00 Sun

Where you stay ultimately boils down to what suits you best, both in the pocket and whether you see your bed for the night as part of a French experience or simply as somewhere to sleep. Fortunately Nord-Pas de Calais can satisfy either requirement. But remember, this is short-break country and it's wise to plan ahead rather than face a last-minute panic to find a room. This applies particularly during the school holidays and at peak-period weekends, especially on the coast and during major festivals and Christmas markets.

It is best to book early for B&Bs and *gîtes*, especially if you're seeking a suitable base from which to explore. Popular peak summertime spots include Montreuil-sur-Mer for the Seven Valleys, or Le Quesnoy for the Avesnois. Some properties close during the off-season.

Off-season visits may not always seem ideal but late-autumn or spring city breaks see more rooms available as prices slide. This is also a good time for using B&Bs, of which there are a surprising number in the cities, often close to local eateries. However, the number of rooms can be limited.

Prices are pretty well on a par, or a little above, those in the UK, thanks to a rocky pound against the euro at the time of writing. And while this could change rapidly, France will never be as cheap as some of its Mediterranean counterparts. As in most countries, a premium is paid for the convenience of a city or coastal location. See the inside front cover for a breakdown of accommodation price codes used through the guide.

See pages 18–19 for tour operators who can assist with accommodation.

HOTELS

Touring Handy and comfortable, if a little bland and branded, are the more modern chain hotels geared to both business and leisure overnight stops. You may not want the IT extras, but the kids might – and a swimming pool is always a plus. Plenty offer free accommodation to youngsters sharing a room with adults, or add a nominal amount. Secure parking is also a boon and beats a late-night booking at a public car park or taking luggage out before reluctantly leaving your car overnight in a nearby street. Breakfast at around €9 is not generally included; if it looks too pricey head for the nearest café.

Chain brands range from the bog standard to those sporting four- to five-star facilities with fine French restaurants. The following are found in most big towns and beach resorts such as Le Touquet: **Accor** (*www.accor.com*) whose brand portfolio includes **Ibis** (*www.ibishotel.com*); **Mercure** (*www.mercure.com*); **Novotel** (*www.novotel.com*); **Etap** (*www.etaphotel.com*); **Formule1** (*www.hotelformule1.com*); **Première** (*www.premiereclasse.com*) and **Holiday Inn** (*www.holidayinn.com*). **Best Western** (*www.bestwestern.com*) offers a neat selection of character hotels, a number of which in Lille are featured by **SLIH** (*www.hotels-slih.com*).

Traditional If you fancy a bit more of a French-cum-Flemish flavour try **Logis de France** (*www.logis-de-france-nordpasdecalais.com*), the leading European hotel chain with over 300 hotel-restaurants in France. The emphasis is on comfort, culinary excellence and charm. They are mostly individual in character, often tucked away in pleasant rural towns and villages as well as occasionally being found in larger towns. They are classified with one, two or three chimney symbols graded on the price and degree of luxury. They include a healthy clutch of family-run hotels, some with more of a country house nature, others virtual *châteaux*. The same can be said of some in the Clévacances brochure (*www.clevacances.com*). A relatively small number are featured by Relais & Chateaux (*www.relaischateaux.com*).

B&B AND SELF-CATERING The two national labels are **Gîtes de France** (*www.gîtes-de-france.com*) and **Clévacances** (*www.clevacances.com*). The Gîtes de France are found more in the countryside and they're basically rural retreats. They're rated from one ear of the corn (basic facilities, which are pretty good) to five ears of corn (super-duper with private parkland and sporting facilities such as a tennis court or swimming pool). Some are B&B, others stopover properties based on a single night's stay only; camping and mobile home rentals are also offered. Some, geared to children, feature activities from theatre and dance to handicrafts and sports – kayaking, horseriding, swimming, sailing and the rest. The choice is enormous, and from 2010 the *gîtes* system extended into towns under the name City Break Gîte de France. There's a comprehensive online booking service.

The great joy of staying in properties carrying the Clévacances logo is not simply the huge diversity of B&B and rental accommodation the company offers, but the fact that Clévacances accommodation is available in top tourist spots, whether along the coast or in large and small cities and towns. A number are recommended in *Part Two* of this guide.

Look out, too, for the **'Savoir Plaire'** sign – this is a quality standard created by the Nord-Pas de Calais tourist board which exemplifies a taste for the good life, presentation of local traditions and a sense of hospitality. Spot all three and you should not go far wrong.

BUDGET If money is tight try **Accueil Paysan** (*www.accueil-paysan.com*), whose philosophy is simple: to invite visitors to share the countryside with those in the know. It offers cheaper rural accommodation of all kinds, from a simple inn (*auberge*) to a farm. Don't expect English to be widely spoken; rather, the Accueil Paysan properties offer a good way to learn about animal husbandry or wood cutting while brushing up your French at the same time.

Other sources are **Gîtes d'Étape et Refuges** (*www.gites-refuges.com*) which offer accommodation of the bunk-bed variety and simple kitchen facilities; they're often close to walking or cycling trails. These coupled with youth hostels are ideal for the young and adventurous.

Typical among the youth hostels in the region are the **Auberge de Jeunesse** (Calais: *www.auberge-jeunesse-calais.com*; Boulogne sur Mer: *www.fua.org*; La Hulotte and Montreuil-sur-Mer: *www.fuaj.org*; Le Touquet: *www.rivabella-touquet.com*).

CAMPING AND CARAVANNING Apart from the respective regional tourist offices, reliable sources include **Eurocampings** (*www.eurocampings.co.uk*), **France Voyage** (*www.france-voyage.com*) and **UK Campsites** (*www.ukcampsite.co.uk*). Some sites are suited to beginners or family groups (see *Tour operators*, page 19) but if you want a quieter place it may be better to opt for a lower-rated site. Roughly speaking a four-star rating guarantees good facilities. The tour companies' websites and brochures also provide a wealth of information.

✖ EATING AND DRINKING

The region's cuisine is a historic hotchpotch of flavours. French, English, Spanish and Dutch invaders have all played their part in creating a cuisine still strongly influenced by its Flemish, British and Picard neighbours.

But it's the culinary richness of regional produce that counts most. And this doesn't just mean meals of the hale and hearty type, however tasty; you are in France, for heaven's sake, and the Gallic flair for *haute cuisine* is there in large spoonfuls, both in swanky city restaurants and small rural inns and eateries.

One British weekend camping fan is P&O Ferries executive Chris Laming whose favourite family site has 27 pitches for tents, cars, caravans or motorhomes.

Camping Les Erables 17 rue du Château d'Eau, Escalles; ☎ 03 21 85 25 36; www.eurocampings.co.uk; ☉ 22 Mar–11 Nov; €15.40–19.80 per night per pitch. The site is located just off the D940 coast road between Calais & Boulogne.

He writes:

> This is a great little site. The neat, terraced, pitches all have their own power supply. The communal sanitary facilities are very clean. Monsieur and Madame are most welcoming with a mixed international clientele and everyone is very friendly. The village of Escalles, with a couple of reasonable restaurants, is just a ten-minute walk away, either down the main road or through the glorious local countryside. The beach takes 20 minutes to get to on foot, but is quite superb. And all this is no more than a 20-minute drive from the ferry terminal in Calais. Remarkable.

See the inside front cover for a breakdown of restaurant price codes used throughout the guide.

VEGETABLES Nord-Pas de Calais is the third-biggest vegetable-growing area in France. From fresh or smoked garlic from the Avesnois region to cauliflower from the St-Omer marshes and strawberries from a string of villages – all are as much a part of the holiday scene as the high-profile ports and the coastal resorts.

The two main varieties of potato – the *bintje*, slightly floury and protected by a thick skin, and the small but delicious *ratte du Touquet* – help provide the mouthwatering chips for which the region is famous. Nord-Pas de Calais is also the world's biggest producer of chicory, known in France as *endives* and, even more confusingly, in the local patois as *witloof*. Wild chicory (*barbe de capucin*) and curly chicory (*pissenlit blanc* and *chicorées frisées*) are among the most common varieties. Chicory is roasted and ground to make a coffee substitute, or its seeds used to bring a hint of coffee flavour to ice creams, desserts and even aperitifs. It also appears in regional menus, both in soups and salads, braised or, as endives, as a first course.

Cauliflowers, celeriac, cabbages, Brussels sprouts, leeks and garlic add to the list. Some are even celebrated through a bizarre host of festivals and events (see pages 42–4) – adding to the quirkiness in which Nord-Pas de Calais excels.

The growth of sugarbeet in the 19th century led to many types of confectionery and the *bêtises de Cambrai* (see page 188) are now very much back in fashion.

CHEESES The pasturelands of Artois, Flanders, Hainaut and Avesnois make the region an important producer of cheeses – there are over 60 varieties. These include the ubiquitous Maroilles (see page 216), which has an undeniably powerful and long-lingering stench but is still remarkably mild, and its cousin the Vieux Lille (nicknamed 'the Lille stinker'). The taste, undeniably, is often strong. The rather more discreet and less powerful hard cheeses come from Bergues, Belval Abbaye near Saint Pol sur Turnoise (see *Chapter 6*, page 156) and Mont des Cats (see *Chapter 5*, page 139).

REGIONAL DISHES Typical regional offerings, using beer or sometimes gin, include *hochepot* (pieces of beef, mutton, veal and pigs' trotters, slowly stewed with carrots, onions and potatoes), *carbonade flamande* (pieces of beef braised in a beer sauce with onions and spices) and *potjevlesch* (homemade white meat pâté of veal, chicken or rabbit in aspic decorated with bacon). Do at least try the famous Arras version of *andouillette* (a smaller version of the *andouille*), which is an offal-based sausage. If the local Brotherhood of the Andouillette, formed in 1997, has its way this will become an official label for this porky product produced in Arras since the Middle Ages (see *Chapter 7*, page 166). The *andouillete* is not to everyone's taste. It essentially consists of carefully prepared pork chitterlings cooked in milk. 'Chitterling' is the word for the small intestines of a pig in Old (or Middle) English, the language spoken between roughly 1066 and 1470. In Valenciennes *langue lucullus* (tongue garnished with *foie gras*) is the local speciality.

Others may prefer the 'sweet and sour' flavours of *coq à la bière* (chicken cooked in dark beer), *lapin aux pruneaux* (rabbit with prunes), or *canard au vin de rhubarbe* (duck cooked in wine with rhubarb) with perhaps a *flamiche au Maroilles* (Maroilles flan) or a leek pie as a first course. Further specialities include *anguilles au vert* (butter-browned eels simmered in a wine and herb sauce), red cabbage *à la Lilloise* (red cabbage seasoned with onions, cloves, grated nutmeg and pepper, ideal with roast meat), *cramique* (sweet roll with currants), *galopins* (thin slices of bread soaked in milk and beaten eggs) and *goyère* (originally white cheese with eggs, sweetened with brown sugar or honey and perfumed with orange blossom, but nowadays can be savoury flavoured as well). *Nieulles* (speciality biscuits from Armentières) come from the Spanish word *niola* meaning 'crumbs'.

Vegetarians, despite the abundance of vegetables, can sometime find Nord-Pas de Calais tough going, though open tarts, as opposed to the inevitable offer of an omelette, can provide the answer. Alternatively ask in advance: a good chef likes a challenge...

TASTE OF THE SEA With Boulogne France's largest fishing port, expect plenty of fresh fish, from traditional herring – smoked, marinated or kippered – to sole and turbot along the Côte d'Opale (see *Chapter 4*). Of the shrimps and prawns, usually sold cooked, the small brown *crevettes grises* are especially tasty. Fish dishes include *waterzooï* (a mixture of freshwater fish in a thick and spicy sauce); the same name is sometimes also used for chicken or other white meat stewed with leeks. Mussels, served in heavy black casseroles, are at their best from October to March; see them growing on wooden stakes in the sand of Wissant Bay on the Côte d'Opale.

SOMETHING SWEET For dessert try a variety of tarts; *tartes aux sucres*, topped with brown sugar, or *tartes à la rhubarb* are popular. Pancakes and waffles are a meal in themselves, while bulging brioches, called *coquilles*, are what mothers sing about to their children: 'I'll say a prayer to Jesus to bring you a *coquille* dripping in syrup,' goes the first line of a popular nursery rhyme. Cakes include *le craquelin*, a Christmas speciality in Boulogne and Étaples, consisting of a lightly sweetened flaky pastry figure-of-eight served warm with a cup of kirsch-laced hot chocolate. Coffee is consumed throughout the day, accompanied by confectionery.

Understanding the French for your favourite fish is not easy when confronted with a bewildering selection on a menu, or even on a shop or supermarket shelf. Here are some more common words: *bar* (bass); *cabillaud* (cod); *coquille St Jacques* (king scallop); *dorade* (sea bream); *hareng* (herring); *homard* (lobster); *lieu jaune* (pollack); *limande* (dab); *maquereau* (mackerel); *merlan* (whiting); *mulet cabot* (grey mullet); *plie* (plaice); *rouget barbet* (red mullet); *Saint Pierre* (John Dory); *seiche* (cuttlefish); *sole commune* (Dover sole); *tourteau* (crab); *turbot* (turbot); *buccin-bulot* (whelk).

BEER'S BIG BUSINESS No chance of sampling local wines here – Nord-Pas de Calais is beer country, and always has been, especially in the old industrial towns. This is either brewed over the border by the Belgians, past masters in the art, or increasingly by local micro-breweries whose bottles often come with the corks harnessed by champagne-style metal twists. Turn the bottle, not the cork, when opening. Some of the contents, brewed by infusion and long-maturing – at least six weeks – can be a little lively to say the least! Some beers are seasonal, others must be drunk almost immediately, and many like those from Ch'ti (brewers since 1926), can be found in supermarkets.

For the record, the word 'beer' first appeared in the region during the 15th-century reign of John the Fearless, Duke of Flanders and Burgundy. It was he, it is said, who founded the Order of the Golden Hop, which remains active today. The masters of the region are among the most important in France.

The hop growers in the Flanders region pride themselves on the aromatic varieties now available which have helped create four distinctive flavours: blond, a medal-winning popular light mellow ale (6.4% proof); amber, a copper colour with a roasted malt aroma (5.9%); white, a naturally cloudy but light beer with a fruity and spicy taste (4.5%); and brown, whose dense and full-bodied colour comes from strong roasted malts (6.4%). Variations do occur, with major breweries listed under the regions in *Part Two* of this guide.

If beer is not to your liking, then there is always *genièvre* or juniper gin distilled from locally grown rye, oats and barley by the Persyn Brewery close to St-Omer (see *Chapter 5*, page 128) with juniper berries to boost the flavour. Founded in 1812, the Houlle-based business is the sole survivor of the 132 distilleries which once served the many *estaminets*. Used by chefs in numerous dishes, it makes a great 'on the rocks' pre-dinner aperitif. You may also be offered a *bistouille*, a small cup of coffee with a large slug of gin tipped in and twirled twice with a spoon.

If all else fails, Nord-Pas de Calais cider is highly rated, while the Seven Valleys (see *Chapter 6*) produces a wide range of fruit juices from rhubarb, raspberries, redcurrants and strawberries.

RESTAURANT OPENING HOURS With restaurant opening hours tending to be 'flexible', to say the least, it is often best to wait for the 'closed' sign to go up on shop doors. This signals that lunch is being served. In most eateries it lasts roughly between 12.00 and early afternoon, around say 14.00, though this author has happily been tucking into a dessert as late as 15.30. This was in a rural area, with the ever-patient waiter locking up, by then, a deserted restaurant after he left. Dinner likewise can be anytime between 18.30 and 22.00 (or after the closing-time coffee has been served). This is all very relaxing, but can be infuriating when trying to plan a day out. As a rough rule of thumb, restaurants often close on Sunday evenings and Mondays, or on/for part of Wednesdays.

As a regular visitor to northern France, wine buff Doug Goodman suggests some of the best outlets for French wines.

For most visitors it's straight to one of the big warehouses on the edge of Calais to fill the car with cases of wine at rock-bottom prices. And despite the strength of the euro there are some amazing bargains when you buy French wine. It seems there's over production and perhaps the French are simply not drinking as much nowadays. So rule one is buy French wine and compare prices. For example the Auchan supermarket at the western end of Calais had excellent Bordeaux for well under €4 a bottle. Buy five and get one free is the usual deal during the month-long Foire aux Vins.

Possibly the most popular stopping point before heading home is the Zone Industriel just off the motorway before the ferry port. Here you'll find East Enders, Majestic, Cheers Wine and Beer and La Grande Boutique du Vin all catering for different tastes in wine and beer and providing different quality at varying prices. La Grande Boutique du Vin should be first choice for quality French wine. It's a big bright warehouse with a huge selection of champagne. East Enders is big on beer and own-brands, while Majestic has a good range of New World wines. There's also a Majestic outlet near Auchan. Cheers Wine and Beer has the best selection of wine in boxes as well as Spanish and Italian brands.

Outside Calais at the huge Cité Europe complex you'll find a number of specialist wine shops. For a good price range of French wines Le Chais, with branches at Boulogne (see page 104) and St-Omer (see page 121), is a reliable source.

But for a real treat, with not a bottle of 'foreign' wine in sight, visit Les Halles de Quercamps in the village of Quercamps on the D225 about 25 minutes from Calais off the A26. They claim to have around 3,000 different French wines and prices are the lowest I've seen for a while. With wines from every part of the country and a shop selling local produce, it's well worth a detour off the motorway.

Many cafés, or café-style or chain restaurants, stay open all day, especially along the coast and in major cities – ideal if you have hungry children in tow. Most of these keep remarkably close to regional dishes, with *moules marinières* and French fries an obvious example along the Côte d'Opale.

ESTAMINETS Do make use of the *estaminets*, which offer robust Flemish-style refreshment and are hugely popular with locals; many even sport Michelin stars. Basically bars-cum-cafés, almost little pubs, these are places to meet for a drink, a chat, and to play bar games such as 'frog' and 'hammer' – forerunners of pinball and table-top soccer.

Expect a cottage-style décor of plain wooden tables and chairs, with pots and pans and other trinkets suspended from the ceiling. These can include anything from wicker baskets, enamelled coffee pots, strings of hops and old toys to postcards and posters. Storytelling and music, both traditional and more R&B, encourage a party spirit in which weekend family groups add to a gorgeous Gallic atmosphere. *Estaminets* remain places to relax, whatever the décor, without the noise and clatter often found in bars and cafés.

In Le Nord expect a more Celtic influence of the bagpipes and fiddle kind: Scotland had strong 15th-century links with Flanders. In Pas de Calais accordionists are more to the fore.

Though the true origin of the *estaminet* is shrouded in mystery, some reckon it stems back to the Spanish occupation in Le Nord when strict alcohol laws drove the population into inviting neighbours and friends around for a drink and a knees-up. This rings true: the whole essence of the *estaminet* is one of socialising in convivial surroundings – and they were certainly the preferred choice of the working-class man in the former industrial north.

Most people agree that the word comes from *staminé* or its Flemish form *stameneeke*, meaning a place where one smoked a pipe over the *vierpot*, a pot of glowing embers. Others suggest it was the German word *stam*, a pillar used to support the main beams of a ceiling, that gave rise to the name. One last fact: it was in an *estaminet* in Lille called La Liberté that the *Internationale* was written in 1888.

SNACK OUT ON A *PLANCHE* If you're thinking snacks, try a *planche*, a kind of ploughman's lunch of ham, cheese, pâté or *andouille* served on a wooden board and garnished with salad or sometimes hot potatoes. A little more expensive, but a wonderful way to sample the local cuisine is an *assiette du pays*, a simple dish, savoury or sweet, made up of local or regional products, and accompanied by a typical drink. This can be as reasonable as €6.40 or as high as €25. A useful website, with the produce listed, is **Assiettes du Pays des Moulins de Flandre** (*www.paysdesmoulinsdeflandre.com*).

COUNTING THE COST Which neatly brings us to the question of price. With the value of the euro see-sawing against the value of sterling and other non-euroland countries, there are bound to be sudden gains and losses. Helpfully the French *table d'hôte* fixed-price menus allow for a tempting choice between a straightforward three-course meal (or sometimes four if you include the small in-between freebies) to top-of-the-range gourmet offers. Others allow for two courses only, either a starter and a main course, or a main course and dessert.

Some restaurants with a long-held reputation to maintain are by nature costly, but that is the price you pay for quality; where it goes adrift is when the meal does not quite match the price though the setting and the service does. Invariably this seems to happen more along the coast than in the country and inland cities, though some small fishing villages have excellent and unpretentious eateries. This is reflected in prices quoted in the guide, with the restaurants selected based on personal visits or recommendations.

Estaminets generally give good value; so, too, do farmhouses, with a *ferme-auberge* usually adjoining a farm and guaranteeing home-produced menus. Look out for the 'Savoir Plaire' sign: initiated in 1987 the label is a regional guarantee of quality, with an emphasis on the wealth of regional produce found on menus.

Owners of some *gîtes* (see page 36) also offer meals or provide picnic lunches for those fed up with self-catering; failing that use a high street *traiteur* (caterer) where you can buy no-hassle starters, main courses and desserts to reheat back at the *gîte*.

FESTIVALS AND EVENTS

Barely a month goes by without a festival of some kind in Nord-Pas de Calais. Some, with a sporting theme, attract worldwide attention. Others, like the giants' festivals (see page 45) have a huge family following. A few are simply local, often off-season, and are great fun to attend for their informality alone.

Below is just a sample. Dates vary.

JANUARY
Dunkirk Festival (*www.ot-dunkerque.fr*) A month of informal festivities for the Dunkirk area with carnival, dances and parades.

Serves six:

Ingredients 1.5kg braising beef, 6 onions, 50g butter, 3tbsp flour, 3tbsp wine vinegar, 75cl ale or bitter, 3tbsp vergeoise, soft brown sugar, 1 garni of fresh herbs (bay leaf, thyme, etc, plus cloves) and a few slices of *pain d'épice* (spice-bread), sometimes loosely translated as 'gingerbread'.

Cut the beef into large cubes and fry with butter in a deep pan. Add salt and pepper.
Cut the onions, cook slightly, add the flour and cook for five minutes.
Add the vinegar and the beer; add a little water to cover the meat.
When it starts boiling, add the brown sugar, the herbs and the gingerbread.
Cook for two hours on a medium heat.
This dish tastes even better re-heated so, if possible, prepare it the day before. Serve with chips.

FEBRUARY
Enduropale/Quaduro, Le Touquet (*www.enduropaledutouquet.fr*) The legendary Motorcycle and Quad Race, which takes place early in the month on the massive beach, attracts around 1,000 motorcyclists and 400 quad-bikers. Some 300,000 spectators flock into the resort by foot, bicycle, motorbike and car – even by private jet. The quad-bike race is on Saturday; the motorcycling event is on Sunday.

MARCH
Hydromel en Fête, Bouin Plumoison (*Musée de l'Abeille d'Opale – see page 155;* ℄ 03 21 81 46 24/06 81 18 19 22; e *therry.api@wanadoo.fr*) *Hydromel* is mead, or honey wine. This includes a visit to the bee museum, the cellars and *hydromel*-making demonstrations. Tasting of *hydromel*, cocktails, crêpes and other delicacies are also included.

APRIL
International Kite Festival, Berck-sur-Mer (*www.cerf-volant-berck.com*) A major meeting for kite enthusiasts from all over the world. Inventor, giant, kiddie and fighting kites all take part. So do kites pulling sand carts, and kites dancing to music. Over ten days in April each year you can learn to fly a sports kite with a professional or join the workshop to make your own to fly at home.

MAY
Museum Night Pas de Calais museums open their doors for story-telling, guided tours, concerts and many other surprises. Admission is free.

Fête de Crabbe, Audresselles (*Office de Tourisme: www.terredes2caps.com*) A truly local event at Audresselles, a small coastal resort between Calais and Boulogne, featuring music and an exhibition of *flobarts* (traditional fishing boats: see *Chapter 4*, page 99).

MAY–SEPTEMBER The summer months also see water festivals throughout Nord-Pas de Calais; processions involve pleasure boats, river cruises and an introduction to handling a boat. There is even water jousting.

JUNE
Maroilles bric-a-brac market On the third Sunday of the month the streets of the

famous Maroilles cheese-making centre in the Avesnois throng with some 500 antique and second-hand dealers, along with thousands of visitors.

Parks and gardens festival Week-long programme of local events throughout the region (see page 49).

JULY–AUGUST
Les Misérables, son et lumière, Montreuil-sur-Mer (*www.lesmiserables-montreuil. com*) Victor Hugo was inspired to write *Les Mis* while staying in Montreuil. Now Dominique Maertens directs around 250 volunteers in an impressive and moving show at the citadel. Don't forget your blanket; the show begins at nightfall.

AUGUST
'Flobart' Festival, Wissant The coastal resort celebrates the *'flobart'*, the chubby wooden fishing boat captained by one man, sometimes two. A fishing-net-raising competition, a flower-bedecked parade of *flobarts* and the chance to taste the local seafood are all part of the festive fun.

National Festival of Arts and Popular Folklore, Étaples (*www.etaples-sur-mer.com*) Every two years, hundreds of dancers from France and Europe descend on the town for a musical kaleidoscope of traditional songs, dances and gastronomic events.

Pyrosymphonic shows, Arras and Le Touquet Breathtaking firework displays to music.

Enchanted Nights, Fressin (*www.tourisme7vallees.com, www.lesnuitsenchantees.fr*) This moving *son et lumière* show involves the audience in an adventure set amid the ruins of Lady Brunehilde's castle.

SEPTEMBER
Braderie of Lille (*www.tourisme-nordpasdecalais.fr*) The first week of the month, from Saturday to Sunday, sees the craziest of annual events when 100km of pavement are taken over by 10,000 display stands. Join two million or so visitors in savouring a bowl of mussels and chips.

La Route du Poisson, from Boulogne-sur-Mer Every even-numbered year in mid-September fish wholesalers hitch up their wagons to the best Boulonnais draught horses to follow the route which took their ancestors from Boulogne-sur-Mer to Les Halles in Paris. British working horses are among those that take part.

OCTOBER
Festival of St Hubert, Bailleul-Monts des Cats Packs of hounds and horse-drawn carriages, which are traditionally blessed at a Mass held at Mont des Cats Abbey, form part of this colourful riders' festival.

The Field of the Cloth of Gold feasts, Guînes Dine medieval style in the court of François I and Henry VIII with the villagers of Guînes who are dressed for the occasion. Jesters, minstrels, dancers and peasants present an entertaining account of the historical encounter between the kings of England and France.

NOVEMBER
The Herring Festivals, Boulogne-sur-Mer and Étaples Held annually on a Sunday in November, the fishermen celebrate the coast's traditional fish – the herring.

Marinated in white wine with onions and juniper berries, grilled, smoked or fried, this was the fish that kept the coast alive for many generations. From morn till dusk the quaysides bustle with fishermen and their wives in traditional dress who grill herring and serve it to passers-by with a warming glass of Beaujolais.

DECEMBER

Turkey Festival, Licques Each year on the last weekend before Christmas, Licques, a small country town in the heart of the Boulogne–Calais–St-Omer triangle, is invaded by turkeys. Knights of the Order of the Turkey don their regalia to parade the fowl they produce through the streets, egged on by the crowds of enthusiastic visitors. There is a regional produce market, a turkey and capon competition and a dinner-dance on the Saturday evening (see *Chapter 4*, page 95).

PUBLIC HOLIDAYS The following fixed public holidays occur annually:

1 January	New Year's Day
March/April	Easter Monday
1 May	Labour Day
8 May	1945 Victory Day
May	Ascension Day (the Thursday 39 days after Easter)
	Whit Monday (Lundi de Pentecôte, the Monday 50 days after Easter)
14 July	Bastille Day
15 August	Assumption
1 November	All Saints' Day
11 November	Remembrance Day
25 December	Christmas Day

🛒 SHOPPING

Few can resist a bit of cross-Channel shopping, which is why we have devoted a large section of this guide to Calais, the leading shopping centre in northern France (see *Chapter 3*, pages 64–6). Be sure to check opening times first, even of the supermarkets, which generally stay open late but shut on Sunday afternoons. Some food shops open Sunday morning, but close between 12.00 and 14.00 daily.

Much, of course, depends on where you stay. The likes of Lille, Calais, Boulogne and Dunkirk are the major shopping centres. Others like Arras have that relaxing French feel with speciality shops, markets, cafés and bistros. Don't forget the flea markets, or *brocantes*, for which the region is renowned. The most famous is in Lille on the first weekend of September, called the Braderie. Others are held in Béthune, Maroilles and Cassel (also in September), Ardres in October, Montreuil-sur-Mer in July and Le Touquet at the end of October. A good source of information is www.pointsdeschines.com; otherwise check with respective tourist offices.

Look out, too, for weekly markets, listed in *Part Two*, especially if you're self-catering or having a picnic. Christmas markets are big attractions. Arras is one of the best, along with those in Calais and Dunkirk. Béthune and Bergues might be smaller but have delightful settings.

What to buy? Times, and exchange rates, change, but mustard, olive oil, fresh olives and detergents are a good bet.

Le Creuset remains a good buy, along with other kitchenware. Crystal and glassware bargains can be found at Arques, near St-Omer (see page 129), and Arras blue china and Desvres ceramics (see page 108) make good traditional gifts.

ONE GIANT REASON FOR CELEBRATIONS

Where they came from, no-one really knows. Each, it seems, has history, and all 300 – and growing – play a big role in local life. And when we say big, we mean big: in some case 4–6m tall. We're talking giants whose origin seems to stem from 16th-century Flanders and the surrounding areas. They first appeared around 1530 in the case of the Gayants ('Giants' in the Picard language) of Douai (see *Chapter 8*, page 201) during celebrations involving the clergy, politicians and the populace.

Why, and when, they strut their stuff is not easy to explain. Basically they are celebratory puppets that are brought out at the slightest excuse to take part in spring or summer carnivals, mid-Lenten historical processions or town and village fairs.

These huge wicker figures are often the fruits of people's whims and fancies, with roots in Biblical stories or in antiquity. In each community they represent mythical and legendary figures such as Lydéric and Phinaert in Lille, or workers like Jean the Woodcutter in Steenvoorde.

During the French Revolution they were somehow seen as symbols of the old nobility and many disappeared. But you can't keep a good giant down. Decades later they were not only back, and appearing at local festivities, but are now far greater in number than before – thanks, it seems, to marriage and plenty of children!

Much of this is due to the desire of the people of the north to keep alive their traditions – something that you will see throughout this guide. Among the most famous are the Rueze Papa and Rueze Maman in Cassel, both of whom are classified by UNESCO as masterpieces or have been classified as 'oral and non-material' heritage. Others of stature include Martin and Martine in Cambrai, Binbin in Valenciennes, Bimberlot in Le Quesnoy and Gargantua in Bailleul. For further information go to www.geants-carnival.org.

Lace also makes an excellent souvenir; the superb new lace museum at Calais has its own shop (see page 69). You can also buy lace at Caudry (see page 189), and at the delightful lace museum and shop at Bailleul (see page 143).

Antique shops are always fashionable in France; Valenciennes is among cities with a good selection. If you're buying clothes – which are not necessarily cheaper but smart and snazzy – check on comparable sizes. Charts are often available on the cross-Channel ferries or the Eurotunnel terminals. See also www.saveurs-npdc.com.

 ## ARTS AND ENTERTAINMENT

ART GALLERIES AND MUSEUMS From the Palais des Beaux Arts of Lille (see page 228) and the corresponding Musée des Beaux Arts in Valenciennes (see page 205) – reckoned two of the biggest and the best in France – the museums and galleries of Nord-Pas de Calais paint an intriguing picture of a fractured past in which different periods, schools and nations flit in and out.

While the golden age of Flemish art is represented in the Musée de la Chartreuse in Douai (see page 205) and the Musée de Cambrai, the LAAC (Lieu d'Art et d'Action Contemporaine) museum of contemporary art at Dunkirk features the likes of the early 20th-century works of Pierre Soulages to those of Andy Warhol (see page 79).

The hugely enlarged Musée Matisse in Le Cateau Cambrésis was initially established in 1952 by Henri Matisse, a native of the town. Valenciennes similarly was the birthplace of artists Jean-Baptiste Carpeaux and Jean-Antoine Watteau.

Boulogne boasts the Château Musée, housing the second-largest of Greek vases after the Louvre in Paris. Talking of which, a new wing of the Louvre will open in

Lens (see page 174) in 2012. This will be symbolically located between the coal slagheaps numbered 11/19, familiar to a generation of World War I forces and the famous Bollaert football stadium.

At Bavay (see page 214) the archaeological museum is the largest Gallo-Roman site north of the Loire. The glass museum at Sars-Poteries, also in the Avesnois (see page 219), houses a contemporary collection of glasswork created by international artists.

Some towns historically ooze with artistic interest. Arras is one in particular, whose trump card, occupying a large part of the huge St-Vaast abbey area, is the Musée des Beaux Arts. Home to an extensive range of objects of artistic and cultural interest, it will, within the next decade, form part of a giant project to combine the city's cultural elements in a single location, making it the largest centre of its kind north of Paris. This will place Arras culturally in the same league as Lens, Valenciennes and Béthune, whose own town square presents a stunning display of Art-Deco architecture (see pages 171).

Bergues (see page 81), the so-called 'other Bruges' in Flanders, is likewise a living museum, whose yellow brick façades are characteristic of the town's old buildings with over 5,000m of impressive fortifications. It is also the major setting for the movie *Bienvenue Chez les Ch'tis* (see page 13), the mickey-taking masterpiece whose box office sales outstripped those of *Titanic* and helped put the region on the tourist map.

A new kid on the block is the lace museum in Calais, known long-windedly as *Cité Internationale de la Dentelle et de la Mode Calais*. This is arguably the second-most important event in the port's lace-making history since three British weavers illicitly crossed the North Sea and sailed into Calais to set up a thriving business there (see page 69).

Museums generally open between 09.00 and 10.00 and close between 17.00 and 18.00, though they sometimes stay open longer in the summer, especially in July and August. Apart from 1 May and major events such as Christmas, they generally remain open during public holidays (*jours fériés*). See also page 14.

MUSIC AND THE PERFORMING ARTS Top spot for music and dance must go to Lille, European Capital of Culture in 2004 (see pages 221–32). Cafés resound to rock and jazz while the Opéra de Lille and the Orchestre de Lille pander to more traditional tastes. Concerts, opera and comedy are featured at the Sébastopol Theatre, a 19th-century showcase beloved by opera fans in particular. The Grand Bleu is the hip-hop and contemporary dance and drama haunt for young audiences. Benefiting from National Drama Centre status, the Théâtre du Nord operates in Tourcoing and Lille, where it stages plays in the Théâtre Roger Salengro located on the Grand'Place.

Festivals and belfries are covered separately (see pages 41 and 13), but both contribute to the rich cultural amalgam in which contemporary arts play a strong role. Arras is strong on showcase events, from the likes of concerts by the Celtic Legend and The Black Eyed Peas at the Citadel or the Gyant Expo. The city's stylish theatre, whose façade was built in a Neoclassical style with the interior in rich Italianate, is home to both traditional and modern plays and concerts.

Less well known, but deserving greater attention, is Le Channel Cultural Development Centre in Calais. Superbly converted from a vast abbatoir, this is the hub for a variety of artistic actvities, often experimental and featuring their own theatre. Puppets, a Spaghetti Western Orchestra, a contemporary opera and a Blues Festival were included in the 2010 programme. There are also student workshops and shows for primary school children. There is even a circus school. It also boasts a cracker of a restaurant (see page 64).

Exhibitions, music, dance, street and traditional theatre have also enlivened Valenciennes, a busy commercial town but voted the first regional capital of culture in 2007 (see page 203).

Bringing a showbiz concoction of classical concert, blues and jazz are the resorts of Dunkirk and Le Touquet: flip through their programmes for some of the best of each, along with folk festivals and street dancers. There are other coastal resorts not short on cultural goodies; Boulogne, Calais and Berck-sur-Mer are among them.

Don't forget the *estaminets* (see page 40). These traditional cafés-cum-bistros provide some lively, and often cutting edge, rhythm 'n' blues combos as well as more folksy offerings guaranteed to go down well with the robust Flemish fare.

SPORTS AND ACTIVITIES

For a small but heavily populated region, Nord-Pas de Calais offers a plethora of outdoor pursuits. This is thanks, in no small measure, to a massive coastline well endowed with dunes and trails as well as parks and forests (see page 4) and vast areas of reclaimed mining land now bristling with outdoor activities.

WALKING You don't need to know that part of the 5,000km E9 European Coastal Path – the signposted GR120 Littoral – cuts through the area to appreciate that the stretch from Calais to Boulogne (see *Chapter 4*) provides some of the best coastal scenery this side of Dover. But that's not all; over 4,500km of signposted paths and tracks criss-cross not just the coast but three national parks (see page 4) of which several are long distance. Nor are they all geared to keen walkers. Almost every village or town has signposted footpaths (*sentiers de randonée* or *sentiers pédestre; www.sentiersdefrance.com*), showing the way to local beauty spots. There are 281 walking itineraries in Le Nord and more than 300km of signposted trails in Pas de Calais. Both *départements* offer a varied terrain, from marshes and rivers to dunes and hills.

CYCLING The French are mad on the sport. So, too, it seems, are the Brits. If you don't own a bike, ask at tourist offices for a list of hire shops, or *location de vélos*. These are often close to railway stations (many trains, incidentally, carry bicycles free of charge) or to forests with cycling trails.

Biking trails for the family, and 44 cycling itineraries are offered in Le Nord; in Pas de Calais there 32 routes named after an historical or geographical feature. These are signposted, and each departure point indicates the distance and the difficulty of the route. Ten Logis-Vélo hotels (*www.logis-de-france-nordpasdecalais.com*) offer short-break packages based on three days/two nights in a double room.

There is a lack of organised cycling holidays to the region, but handy websites include www.bikely.com, which features a variety of routes in, or through, Nord-Pas de Calais, and www.when-in-france.com. Also useful are the regional and local tourist offices' websites.

GOLF The following that the region's coastal courses have among the Brits is evident in the number of UK companies featuring golf breaks of all kinds (see pages 18–19). Some golfers, however, prefer to travel independently. Among them is Alan Cheeseman, from Coney Hall in Kent, who has been playing golf for 36 years. He has been a regular visitor to the coastal and Arras courses. He and a group of six friends began by visiting the Le Touquet course some seven years ago for no other reason than that they knew the name, along with those of Dunkirk and Wimereux.

2

Having had a good day out, dined well and picked up some duty-free goods, they went on to try the other courses in Nord-Pas de Calais, along with one in neighbouring Picardy. Each course had its own characteristics and Alan was hard pushed to pick a favourite. In the end, he concluded, Hardelot was probably a good course to begin with.

It was cheaper back then, certainly cheaper than in England. But even with a stronger euro Alan feels that travelling to France to play golf still beats paying out £150 in fees for some English courses. This view was endorsed by a group of Essex golfers this author met at the St-Omer course, which enjoys a stunning setting plus accommodation and cuisine (see *Chapter 5*, page 133).

Taking two to three cars, Alan's group travels via the tunnel as it is quicker and they can chuck the clubs in the back of the cars. Spring and autumn are their ideal times. Only once or twice have they been given a set time to tee-off. Courses have rarely been crowded even on a Sunday – whereas at home they would have had to book three weeks in advance. French players, Alan says, often don't venture out until late afternoon – and by then he and his friends are finishing. His advice: cross the Channel around 6.30am and tee off just after nine. OK, it means an early start, but it's well worth it.

For full details, contact the respective town's tourist offices as well as those of the two *départements* (see pages 20–1). See also www.liguegolf-npc.com and www.golfencotedopale.com for details on a golf pass from €220 for nine different courses.

SADDLE UP FOR PEDALLING PLEASURES

Veteran cyclist Brian McEwan from West Wickham, Kent, offers his advice on cycling in France:

Cycling in France is a joy, even when you're soaked. There's always a *gîte* with a hot shower and a change of gear followed by French cuisine with a warming glass of *rouge* and the odd cognac or two. In other words, your Tour de France is just that – taking in the wide-open spaces, the forests, the rivers, and the sleepy villages. Indeed, you can soak up the whole culture of a magical and civilised land which, moreover, is right on your doorstep.

It really doesn't matter where you choose to go; you'll find the local tourist info totally primed to provide you with off-road cycleways whether they be centuries-old country lanes, canal tow paths, defunct railway track beds or dedicated cycle paths and, practically at every turn, there will be a village brasserie for lunch and a *gîte* where you can crash out after a stunning regional dinner washed down with superb regional wines.

In short, France has it made when you talk about provision for cyclists. Not surprising really when you realise that the Scandinavian countries, Germany, the Netherlands, Belgium, France and their immediate neighbours have recognised cycling as an integral part of leisure and transport for decades. Thanks to Sustrans, the UK is finally beginning to catch up but has a long way to go to compare with the 'off-piste' delights of northern France which make cycling such a wonderful way to see a country and its people.

Although various tour operators provide ready-made packages with cycling routes, hotels and baggage transport, the real fun is planning it yourself with the French IGN map series (*www.ign.fr*).

Probably the best way to get going on a cycling trip to France is the good old cross-Channel ferry. Depending on whether you wish to take off as soon as you land in France or get to your starting point further inland, either use car cycle racks or rail to get to your embarkation port, or carry on by car or rail at the other side to your starting point. It really is that easy, so saddle up and start pedalling.

HORSERIDING Nord-Pas de Calais also has a strong pull for British horseriders, with some exhilarating cantering along the long soft dunes. Le Touquet with its smart equestrian centre is understandably popular (see *Chapter 4*, pages 117–18) though great hacks can be had throughout the entire region, and no-one can quibble with the enormous number of horse trails (*randonées*) which are carefully documented. Bear in mind that style can be casual and Brits brought up always to wear hard hats may like to bring their own. Also take note – and I write this as a specialist writer on equestrian holidays – that a shambolic-looking stables does not necessarily mean the horses are unkempt. It's quite the reverse in many cases.

To get the best out of riding in some stunning settings, match your skills to suit the terrain and time spent in the saddle. One handy source is the Kent/Nord and Pas de Calais booklet produced by the **British Horse Society** (*www.bhs.org.uk*). Otherwise contact local and regional tourist offices. A total of 15 riding trails are available in the Flanders of Westhoek which include the Plain of Flanders between Dunkirk and the Flanders Hills and around the Mormal and 100ha Avesnois Regional Nature Park forests (see *Chapter 9*).

BIRDWATCHING Ornithologists can have a field day. There are some 170 species of nesting birds, both coastal and inland, among them rarities such as Montagu's harrier, the northern goshawk, the little owl and the spotted crake. A number of species scarcely seen across the Channel are also easier to find in Pas de Calais. These include honey buzzard, Kentish plover, little egret, spoonbill, golden oriole, crested lark, bluethroat, melodious warbler, marsh warbler and crested tit. Keep an eye out, too, for great reed warbler, bee-eater, common rosefinch and black-winged stilt. Two great areas for spotting the best in birds are Platier d'Oye for the likes of egret, avocet, teals and terns (see page 87) and the Romelaëre reserve in the heart of the Audomarois Marshlands (see pages 130–1). Look out for breeding night heron, bluethroat, golden oriole and breeding honey buzzard.

The lakes and woodland at Rumacourt/Ecourt northeast of Cambrai are recommended for spotting bluethroat, great reed warbler, black woodpecker and purple heron; likewise the forest and lake northeast of Valenciennes are home to honey buzzard, osprey and black woodpecker.

PARKS AND GARDENS

Budding artists – that's how those who annually gain floral status (*villes et villages fleuris*) for their town and village communities see themselves. Among those that have already won the coveted label are Montreuil-sur-Mer, Le Touquet and Boulogne-sur-Mer.

Keen gardeners visiting Nord-Pas de Calais cannot only follow a floral route but, in early June, enjoy an extra perk when parks and gardens throw open their doors for the National Parks and Gardens Festival. These range from the statue and sculpture public garden at St-Omer to the delightful clutch in the Seven Valleys countryside. Many are open at other times too, among them an eclectic range of styles in the Avesnois.

Each delivers a special message in a distinctive way. English-style gardens provide a rural touch whereas the French ones are laid out in a more geometrical manner and are often heavily and artistically themed. Some public gardens planted on town fortifications have become settings for walks; Boulogne-sur-Mer (see *Chapter 4*, page 98), St-Omer (see *Chapter 5*, page 121), Montreuil-sur-Mer (see *Chapter 6*, page 145) and Le Quesnoy (see *Chapter 9*, page 210) are among them. Leaflets are available from the respective tourist offices.

See www.parcsetjardins-npdc.com for the full list and calendar of events for the 32 gardens involved; it also explains how to join the Association of Parks and Gardens of Nord-Pas de Calais for a raft of benefits including trips to other gardens in France and abroad.

ℓ COMMUNICATIONS

TELEPHONE France has a ten-digit numbering system which you can dial direct if using a landline. This begins with 03, the code for the northeast, which includes Nord-Pas de Calais. If dialling from the UK, use the prefix 00 33 and drop the initial 0 from the area code. A *télécarte* (phonecard), which can be bought from a post office or tobacconist (*tabac*), is required if using a French phone box as most public phones in France do not accept coins. Calls can be received at phone boxes where the blue bell sign is shown. To call a UK number from France dial 00 44, followed by the British number but omitting the initial zero. Check on cheap rate calls on both sides of the Channel. To look up a number in a French directory you need to know in which *commune* (town or village) a person lives.

Prefixes

08: Special services, including Freephone (*numéro vert*) and premium rates.

09: Other services (*services de communications interpersonnelles*), including VoIP (such as Skype), mobile/landline grouped services, internet phone and other new technologies.

00: International dialling codes (+61 Australia; +1 Canada; +353 Republic of Ireland; +64 New Zealand; +1 United States).

00 33: If dialling France from overseas.

MOBILE PHONES The prefix 06 and more recently 07, too, is used for mobile phones, known as *portables*. Do make sure that your mobile phone can be used in France, especially with some older models: some incorrectly claim no network is available (which admittedly is sometimes the case, even along the busy coastal routes). Once in France just dial the 10 digits as normal. To call a UK home number you generally need to dial 00 44 followed by the UK number but dropping the initial 0. For other prefixes see above.

If staying for a long period of time, there are two options. Firstly, you can buy a 'disposable' mobile phone made by Bic (the same company that makes razors and pens), called the Bic phone. It costs €29 which includes 30 minutes talking time, a French phone number and a charger for the battery. The phone comes pre-charged and ready to use. You can then add credit with the standard prepaid Orange cards (*mobicartes*). The Bic is available from supermarkets, *tabac* shops, newsagents, etc. The Bic phone website (*www.bic-phone.fr*) is in French only, but has helpful information for foreign visitors.

Alternatively, you can buy a French SIM card, costing around €20 (check that your phone is not 'locked' by your operator first though, as it will not work if it is). You can top this up with the usual pre-paid cards on sale in supermarkets, *tabac* shops, phone stores, etc.

The main mobile operators in France are: Orange, Bouygues and SFR, as well as superstores such as Auchan, and Leclerc.

ⓔ INTERNET Until 2002/3 broadband access in France was limited to one supplier, France Telecom. Since then several alternative operators have sprung up offering differing levels of service.

There are many national and international internet dial-up services in France.

The majority offer free (for the cost of a local call) access. Tiscali, Wanadoo and WorldOnline are among them.

Internet cafés Internet cafés are commonplace, with at least three in Lille. They can be found in most towns throughout France. Rates vary, but you will be charged according to the amount of time spent using the computer. To find an internet café ask the local tourist office.

✉ **POST** Mail boxes in France are coloured yellow and can be found in every post office and along the street. Collection times are displayed. You can buy stamps at any post office or tobacconist, and at newsagents and souvenir shops as well. Postage costs vary according to the weight of your mail and its destination. All rates can be found at www.laposte.fr. Allow 24 to 48 hours for a letter posted in France to a destination in France, or one to five days for a letter from France to abroad.

You can arrange for letters to be sent for collection in the town you are visiting. The letter should be addressed to:

Your Name (as it appears on your identification papers)
c/o Poste Restante,
Poste Centrale,
The town the letter is to be collected,
France

There is a small fee and you will need proof of identity for collection.

Post offices are normally open weekdays from 08.00 to 17.00, and Saturday from 08.00 to 12.00; in smaller towns and villages offices may close earlier and for lunch.

BUYING PROPERTY

The closeness, and the convenience of getting there, has held the key to the continual rise in property sales along the cross-Channel coast. This accelerated with the opening of the Channel Tunnel in 1994, which brought the beaches and rural charm of the Côte d'Opale (see *Chapter 4*) – already well served by ferries – into even sharper focus as a potential setting for second, or even retirement, homes.

Lille, too, with its big city life and excellent schooling suddenly became commuter territory as the Eurostar cut the travelling time from London, and to some extent Ashford. Since 2007 and the move to St Pancras station, this has been shaved by a further 20 minutes to one hour 20 minutes. The same applies to Calais, with a limited, but handy, Eurostar stopping service at Fréthun on the outskirts of town. Living on UK salaries while enjoying the ooh-la-la residency of French life has become a reality, and is increasingly so today.

Certainly for Londoners and those living in the suburbs, house prices are considerably lower. Whether as a commuter or more likely as an expat with a French home, using Eurostar or a car, or a combination of the two, means that travel to London and other major southeastern centres is still within easy reach.

We met many retired folk, from Kent and Essex in particular, who have happily settled within what they see as striking distance from their family roots, popping back at weekends to see the grandchildren or friends. Others, living further afield, also benefit from good motorway links to Dover and the connection through the tunnel or by sea with the ferries which serve Calais, Dunkirk and Boulogne (see page 22). However, be aware that with far fewer ferries now taking foot passengers, a car is an essential item if you consider buying property in this very much home-from-home region (a region which includes the all too familiar vagaries of the English weather).

Pricewise, the more *maison* for less money incentive is strong: some properties more than match the cheaper end of, say, the coastal Kent market, and most definitely those of the London suburbs. While Le Touquet (see page 111) can be particularly expensive – though less so on the edge of town or at nearby Berck – other resorts, enticing for golf, sailing, walking and horseriding, along with a plethora of restaurants, can come up with a crop of tempting offers.

These range from late 19th-century four- to six-bedroom houses in the Calais area in the £250,000–380,000 bracket, to modest three-bedroom flats at around £150,000. The region's excellent motorway system has helped to open up the area, with the coast-hugging A16 (easily accessible from Dunkirk, Calais or the Channel Tunnel) making the entire coastline easily accessible. Moreover, the A16 easily connects to the regional road network more generally.

While apartments are available in Boulogne, they are probably only of interest to those who work in the city. But for expat Brits living in the nearby towns it remains the centre for outstandingly good shops and restaurants. So think Wimille, Wimereux and the old fishing town of Étaples; all are less than an hour's drive from Boulogne (see pages 98–106). Property is more expensive the closer you get to the coast, but there are bargains around.

Also close by is St-Omer, famed for a lively market town atmosphere (see page 121), Montreuil-sur-Mer for its sheer prettiness, or, increasingly popular Hesdin, which combines the best of both (see pages 151–2). You could be looking at £250,000 for a renovated farmhouse with four bedrooms near Hesdin, while further out in the Seven Valleys (see *Chapter 6*), a stone farmhouse in the Canche Valley with five bedrooms, vaulted ceilings and landscaped gardens went recently for £325,000. This is similar to what you would pay for a modern estate house in Kent.

Despite a less buoyant economic climate, French estate agents (*immobiliers*) still report a significant increase not just in interest but, with prices rising, a good return on your investment. But beware: the possibility of picking up a rural idyll for a song is getting more remote – unless you're prepared to fork out a considerable amount to make it habitable.

France's legal system is very different from that in Britain, so do use the services of an independent English-speaking lawyer. One such person is Dover-born Gérard Barron, MBE, a lawyer who has acted for hundreds of Brits buying property throughout France. Appointed Honorary British Consul in Boulogne over 14 years ago, he lives in nearby Wimille with his French wife and two teenage children. He also has a holiday home in the Ardeche. Contact **S C P Barron & Brun** (*28 rue Saint Jean, Boulogne-sur-Mer;* ↘ *03 21 99 05 50;* e *gerard.barron@nordnet.fr*) for more information.

The process of buying property in France may seem ponderous, he said, but there is less risk with no gazumping. Most Brits come to France to relax or retire and for the quality of life. Many choose to run a B&B to supplement pensions or investment income.

General advice if buying in Nord-Pas de Calais, of which the Pas de Calais *département*, by being closer to the UK, has the edge on sales, is don't delay, but take time to do some research – with which this guide will help no end. Learn some basic French and integrate a little with your new neighbours.

A few other top tips include:

- Have your wits about you: you'll be on your own at the start of the purchase process
- Get assistance with translations
- Make only a verbal offer
- Appoint your own lawyer (*notaire*)

- Consider a French mortgage
- Check on surveys, hidden clauses and marital status contracts
- Visit the property on, or before, the day of completion to make sure all is as it should be, particularly with fixtures and fittings

HELPFUL WEBSITES
- www.propertydefrance.com
- www.french-property.com
- www.francophiles.co.uk
- www.frenchentree.com
- www.there-4-you.co.uk (Hesdin area)
- www.AngloFrenchLaw.co.uk

TRAVELLING POSITIVELY

With much of France's charitable and environmental work already funded, it is not easy to select an overall candidate to highlight, especially for one specific region such as Nord-Pas de Calais. However, one does spring to mind: **North Nature Environment** (*Nord Nature Environnement, Maison de la Nature et de l'Environnement (MNE), 23 rue Gosselet, Lille 59000;* ↘ *03 20 88 49 33;* e *secretariat@ nord-nature.org; www.nord-nature.org;* ⊕ *09.00–12.00 & 14.00–17.00 Mon–Fri*) is a self-funded pressure group who talk tough on a variety of topics, many of common interest to UK and other overseas visitors.

The effect of a growing number of wind turbines on local flora and fauna is one such subject, which is especially topical for an area in which national parks and reserves are playing a major tourist role. They are also concerned that soil erosion is increasing the loss of hedgerows and clogging rivers in what, despite what appearances might sometimes suggest, is some 70% rural land. They have backed small coastal towns such as Ambleteuse in protecting the natural environment while still recognising the role of tourism. They have also put forward 25 measures to reform fishing and hunting.

These and similar problems close to the heart of many nature-loving fans of this all too often under-rated region are discussed on their website.

2

HOLIDAYS TO FRANCE
FOR DISCERNING TRAVELLERS

Montmartre, Paris

Tailor-made Short Break Holidays

*Luxury holidays to over 70 classic cities and relaxing rural locations
throughout Europe and beyond. We can create the perfect itinerary
using selected hotels, private transfers with travel by any combination
of air, Eurostar, rail or private car.*

Travel by Eurostar

*Eurostar's high-speed service from London means that you can now
be in Paris in little over two hours and then on your way to one of
the four corners of France on an efficient and comfortable TGV service.*
Destinations include Paris, Lille, Strasbourg and Avignon.

Unique Concierge Service

*Kirker's Concierge will arrange opera tickets, book private guided
tours, and recommend and book restaurants to ensure that you can
sit back and relax whilst Kirker takes responsibility for the smooth
running of your holiday.*

To make a booking
or request a brochure
please call us on

020 7593 2283

Kirker
FOR DISCERNING TRAVELLERS

Please quote source code SBO

ABTA
ABTA No.V5555 · AiTO · HOLIDAYS WITH 100% FINANCIAL PROTECTION

www.kirkerholidays.com

Part Two

THE GUIDE

3

Gateway Calais

Calais is not just the gateway to Nord-Pas de Calais, but to France and Europe as a whole. As such, it is too often judged on its port alone – the commercial paraphernalia provoking scathing comments both from the motorists who teem through the ferry terminal for fast motorway links to the south, and from shoppers heading to out-of-town superstores and booze outlets. In their hurry to get out, these visitors virtually give two fingers to the 75m town hall belfry that forlornly beckons visitors to follow the '*centre ville*' sign instead.

This is a pity, for while Calais's gateway role remains paramount, its town centre has much to offer. It is historically English in character, making it accessible and attractive to cross-Channel visitors. Calais is also home to some of the finest restaurants along the coast, and, for shoppers, there is a range of specialist stores (see page 64).

Getting your bearings is not always easy. Calais confusingly consists of two parts: the Old Town, home to the harbour area and the smartest restaurants, is virtually an island surrounded by canals; the southern part, meanwhile, is centred around the town hall with its landmark belfry – this is the place to shop. Neither part exactly exudes chocolate-box charm, for Calais is no beauty. But as an entrée to the surrounding coast (see pages 64–6) it deserves attention.

HISTORY

'When I am dead and opened, you shall find Calais carved in my heart,' reportedly said Mary Tudor in 1558, the year Calais returned from English to French rule. But England's queen was not just lamenting the loss of the city. She was dramatically reinforcing a symbolic cross-Channel link, which still survives today.

Calais began as the quiet 10th-century Roman fishing village of Caletum. But this quickly developed into a strategic port, whose strong ferry trade with Dover proved so irresistible to Edward III of England that he wanted the town for himself. And so in 1347, following the Battle of Crécy and an 11-month seige, by the end of which the 6,000 to 8,000 citizens were on the edge of starvation, Calais was captured by English forces. The forces numbered some 34,000 knights, archers and infantry, including 2,000 Flemish soldiers.

Far from being delighted by his troops' victory, Edward was angry about the length of time the conquest had taken. He threatened a mass execution of the townsfolk but later agreed to a reprieve on the understanding that six of the principal burghers – bareheaded, barefooted and with ropes round their necks – would give themselves up to die. Rodin's world-famous bronze statue in the town hall square, commissioned in 1880 and finished in 1888, still marks this momentous compromise. (Interestingly, one of only 12 casts of the original work permitted under French law after Rodin's death now stands close to the House of Commons in Westminster Gardens, London.)

Edward's pregnant queen, Philippa of Hainault, however, was far from happy. She feared that such a dastardly deed would prove a bad omen for their unborn child, and so implored Edward to be merciful. The burghers' lives were saved and Calais had its heroes, though, like many others, they were evicted from the town and replaced by English workers.

Edward's rule did the town some favours, though. He turned what he regarded as the 'brightest jewel in the English crown' into a commercial gateway for England's lucrative trade in lead, cloth and wool. Indeed, he was so pleased with his new acquistion that in 1360 the Treaty of Brétigny assigned Guînes, Marck and Calais – collectively the *'pale'* (occupied territory) of Calais – to English rule 'in perpetuity', though this arrangement was only loosely interpreted. Even so, its representatives sat in the English parliament for many years.

Little wonder then that Mary Tudor was so shocked when the English lost Calais over 200 years later. It happened on 1 January 1558 when, buoyed up by the then-weakened garrison and decayed fortifications, the French, under Francis, Duke of Guise, surprised the English by preventing the defensive sluice gates from being opened. This was despite a warning six years earlier by Thomas Stukley, an English adventurer formerly in the pay of the French, that a bid to recapture the town was on the cards. The region around Calais, then known as the Calaisis, was renamed the Pays Reconquis (Reconquered Country).

Calais was once again on the front line in 1805 when it hosted part of Napoleon's army and fleet prior to his aborted invasion of Britain. And in 1816, just after the end of the Napoleonic Wars, the Brits were back – this time in the shape of three skilled lace-makers who, fed up with the Luddite attitude in Nottingham, smuggled new machines to Calais (see page 69). They set up shop in the St-Pierre district where the industry grew so rapidly that practically every family was involved in lace-making one way or another. The district was eventually absorbed into Calais to create the city as we know it today. Three years later a 1,000-strong British population had launched two English-language newspapers. By the 1840s Calais was famous for lace and remains so today.

Events in Anglo–French history, including two world wars, have repeatedly brought the neighbouring coastlines closer together – and nowhere is that truer than for Calais, that most English of towns.

GETTING THERE AND AWAY

BY FERRY
From Dover

At peak-time P&O Ferries have sailings every 45 minutes, taking car and foot passengers. SeaFrance run a crossing every 60 to 90 minutes that takes cars only. The check-in times before departure for both services are: 30 minutes for cars, 45 minutes for foot passengers, 60 minutes for mobility bus. The crossing time is 90 minutes.

For full ferry details, see pages 22–4.

Getting into town from the ferry terminal

By car Follow the '*toutes directions*' sign as you leave the ferry terminal. At the roundabout take the fourth exit signposted '*centre ville*'. Turn left at the next roundabout, follow the canal and turn right at the traffic lights. This leads to the huge town hall square, which is centrally placed for shops and hotels.

By bus A shuttle bus for foot passengers (marked 'Terminal Car Ferry/Centre Ville') runs hourly from 11.00 to 19.15, seven days a week. The 7km journey to place d'Armes takes five minutes; it is 20 minutes to Gare Calais-Ville, the mainline railway station. The flat fare is €1.50 per passenger each way. The bus serves all Calais ferry arrivals, although it is not geared to connect with specific sailings (or train departures).

By foot Allow 20 minutes for the 1.5km walk to place d'Armes, which lies to the east of the ferry terminal. After the terminal gates cross a bridge and follow rue de Thermes. The route should also be signposted.

THROUGH THE CHANNEL TUNNEL The Eurotunnel from Folkestone to Coquelles takes cars only (no foot passengers), and departs every 25 minutes at peak time. The journey takes 35 minutes. To get to Calais from Coquelles, take the slip road to join the A16 at junction 42, then drive toll-free towards Calais/Dunkirk. Take exit 43 to Calais Centre via the Le Channel art centre or exit 44 via Calais St-Pierre.

The **Eurostar**'s passenger-only trains currently stop up to three times daily at Gare Calais-Fréthun (see below) *en route* from St Pancras to Paris. The journey time is 55 minutes. The station lies 10km southwest of the town. Bus route 7 runs to Calais town centre.

BY RAIL The main station for regional services on the TER network in Nord-Pas de Calais is **Gare Calais-Ville** (*ave du President Wilson; ticket office is open ⊕ 06.30–20.30 Mon–Sat; book online at www.sncf.co.uk & www.raileurope.co.uk; see also www.ter-sncf.com*). Trains to Boulogne run 17 times a day Monday–Saturday and nine times on Sunday (taking 28–48 minutes); to Dunkirk six times a day Monday–Friday and around four times Saturday–Sunday (taking 50 minutes); and to Arras 12 times a day Monday–Friday and five times Saturday–Sunday (taking 2 hours).

For Le Touquet, use the Lille–Calais–Boulogne–Amiens–Paris line, and change at Étaples station for a local bus.

A few trains on the TER Grande Vitesse (TERGV) high-speed line to Lille also stop at Gare Calais-Ville, though they stop more regularly at Calais Fréthun.

Calais Fréthun is not only used by Eurostar (see pages 25–26), but by TERGV trains on the Boulogne-Ville to Lille service. They do not stop at Calais-Ville. The regular TER trains, however, on line 12 Boulogne–Calais–St-Omer–Hazebrouck–Lille stop at both Calais Fréthun and Calais-Ville. The two stations are connected by the free Navette TER.

For details of all lines, see www.sncf.com/nord_pas_de_calais/carte horaires/index.

BY CAR Driving times are: Boulogne (22 minutes); Dunkirk (30 minutes); St-Omer (35 minutes); Le Touquet (40 minutes); Arras (1 hour 10 minutes); Lille (1 hour 20 minutes); Douai (1 hour 20 minutes); Cambrai: (1 hour 35 minutes).

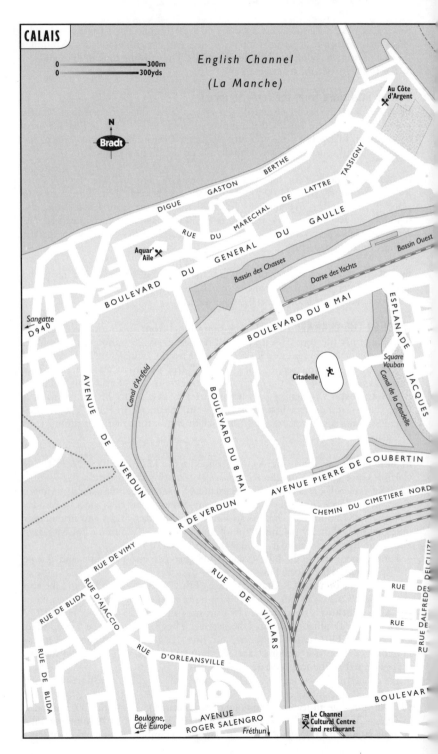

CALAIS

English Channel
(La Manche)

0 ————— 300m
0 ————— 300yds

N
Bradt

Au Côte
d'Argent

DIGUE   GASTON   BERTHE

RUE   DU   MARECHAL   DE   LATTRE   TASSIGNY

RUE   DU   GENERAL   DU   GAULLE

Aquar'
Aile

BOULEVARD   DU   GENERAL

Bassin des Chasses

Bassin Ouest

Darse des Yachts

BOULEVARD DU 8 MAI

ESPLANADE   JACQUES

Sangatte
D940

Square
Vauban

Citadelle

Canal de la Citadelle

Canal d'Arsfeld

BOULEVARD DU 8 MAI

AVENUE PIERRE DE COUBERTIN

AVENUE   DE   VERDUN

CHEMIN DU CIMETIERE NORD

R DE VERDUN

RUE DE VIMY

RUE DE BLIDA

RUE D'AJACCIO

RUE   DE   VILLARS

RUE   DES   DELCLUZE

RUE   DE

RU

RUE D'ORLEANSVILLE

RUE DE BLIDA

RUE   ALFRED   RU

Boulogne,
Cité Europe

AVENUE
ROGER SALENGRO

Fréthun

Le Channel
Cultural Centre
and restaurant

BOULEVAR

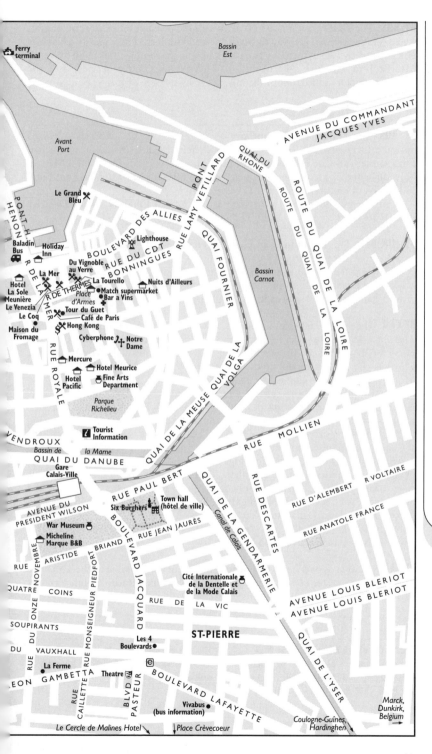

Ferry terminal

Bassin Est

AVENUE DU COMMANDANT JACQUES YVES

Avant Port

QUAI DU RHONE

PONT LAMY VETILLARD

ROUTE DU QUAI DE LA LOIRE

Le Grand Bleu

BOULEVARD DES ALLIES

PONT HENON

RUE DE LA MER

Baladin Bus

Holiday Inn

Lighthouse

RUE DU CDT BONNINGUES

Du Vignoble au Verre

QUAI FOURNIER

Bassin Carnot

ROUTE DU QUAI DE LA LOIRE

Hotel La Mer

R DE THERMES

La Sole Meunière

La Tourello

Match supermarket

Nuits d'Ailleurs

Le Venezia

Place d'Armes

Bar a Vins

Le Coq

Tour du Guet

Café de Paris

Maison du Fromage

Hong Kong

RUE ROYALE

Cyberphone

Notre Dame

QUAI DE LA VOLGA

Mercure

Hotel Meurice

Hotel Pacific

Fine Arts Department

Parque Richelieu

QUAI DE LA MEUSE

Tourist Information

VENDROUX

Bassin de la Marne

QUAI DU DANUBE

RUE MOLLIEN

Gare Calais-Ville

RUE PAUL BERT

QUAI DE LA GENDARMERIE

RUE DESCARTES

RUE D'ALEMBERT

R VOLTAIRE

AVENUE DU PRESIDENT WILSON

Six Burghers

Town hall (hôtel de ville)

RUE ANATOLE FRANCE

War Museum

BOULEVARD JACQUARD

RUE JEAN JAURÈS

Canal de Calais

Micheline Marque B&B

RUE ARISTIDE BRIAND

RUE PIEDFORT

RUE ONZE NOVEMBRE

RUE MONSEIGNEUR

Cité Internationale de la Dentelle et de la Mode Calais

AVENUE LOUIS BLERIOT

AVENUE LOUIS BLERIOT

QUATRE

COINS

RUE DE LA VIC

SOUPIRANTS

RUE DU

ST-PIERRE

QUAI DE L'YSER

DU

VAUXHALL

Les 4 Boulevards

La Ferme

GAMBETTA

RUE CAILLETTE

Theatre

BLVD PASTEUR

BOULEVARD LAFAYETTE

EON

Vivabus (bus information)

Marck, Dunkirk, Belgium

Le Cercle de Malines Hotel

Place Crèvecoeur

Coulogne-Guines, Hardinghen

BY BUS The **BCD** (☎ *0 800 62 00 59; www.ligne-bcd.com*) buses stop in front of Calais-Ville station on the way to Boulogne and Dunkirk. There are six-plus daily except Saturday (when there are two) to Boulogne (30 minutes); six daily (three on Saturday) to Dunkirk (40 minutes). There's no Sunday service. Pay the driver/conductor at the front of the bus. Leave by the side or rear.

GETTING AROUND

BY BUS The **Calais Bus Company** (☎ *03 21 19 72 72; www.mairie-calais.fr*) operates 13 regular services in and around central Calais including to Auchan supermarket and Cité Europe (except public holidays: 1 January, 1 and 8 May, 11 November and 25 December). Regular fares are €0.90 or €1 (depending on zone), and a book of ten tickets (*un carnet*) costs €30.

Complete bus guides and tickets are available from **Vivabus** (*68 bld Lafayette;* ☎ *03 21 19 72 72;* ⊕ *09.00–12.00, 13.30–18.30 Mon–Fri & 09.00–12.00 Sat*).

BY MINIBUS The **Balad'in** (a play on the French word *balade* meaning 'a stroll' or 'a drive') consists of three 22-seater minibuses serving the main shopping streets (⊕ *09.00–19.00 Mon–Sat, runs every 8–12 mins; free of charge*). Stops include la rue de la Mer, rue Royale, Calais-Ville station and l'Alhambra main square. This can also prove a handy free park-and-ride way of getting round.

BY CAR There are 50,000 parking spaces, of which only 615 are subject to a charge. The initial 15 minutes is free (simply press the green button) after which you pay €0.50 for 30 minutes, €1 for one hour, €1.50 for 90 minutes and €2 for two hours, which is the maximum duration. Charges apply 09.00–12.00 and 14.00–18.00, Monday–Saturday; parking is free on Sundays and public holidays.

Metered parking spaces can be found in boulevards Gambetta, La Fayette, Jacquard and Pasteur, the west side of place d'Armes, rue Royale and rue de la Mer, a portion of the rues des Fontinettes , Commander Mengin, Antoine Benard, and the portion of the street around the Darnel Theatre. There is also parking available at Calais-Ville train station. Additionally there is paid parking space for 720 cars on two floors at Les 4 Boulevards shopping centre (see page 66); these can be used free of charge on Wednesdays and Saturdays. There are free parking spaces on streets close to boulevards de l'Egalite, Gambetta, Jacquard and Lafayette, rues Royale and de la Mer, place Crèvecoeur, parking de la Plage, parking de la rue du Temple and parking lot boulevard Lafayette Match.

Full details of all car parking in Calais can be found at www.calais.fr/spip.php?article63.

BY TAXI Most taxis operate according to a meter, but it's advisable to check the rate before getting in. One taxi company you might try is **Taxis Radio Calais** (☎ *03 21 97 13 14*).

TOURIST INFORMATION

🛈 **Calais Côte d'Opale Tourist Information Office** 12 bld Clémenceau; ☎ 03 21 96 62 40; www.calais-cotedopale.com; ⊕ 10.00–19.00 daily (1 Apr–15 Jun); 09.00–19.00 daily (16 Jun–15 Sep); 10.00–18.00 Mon–Sat, & on Sun for special events such as festivals (16 Sep–31 Mar). The tourist office offers a hotel booking service.

Holiday Inn (17 dbl, 46 sgl, 3 suites) 6 bld des Alliés; 03 21 34 69 69; www.ichotelsgroup.com. Handy for 1 night, especially with a family, this is a typical business/tourist hotel, with smallish, but comfortable, rooms, some of which are adapted for the disabled. Centrally placed for restaurants & shops. The restaurant serves a €9 quick lunch available on w/days. B/fast is expensive. Secure parking available at €11 for 24hrs, unsecured next door. TV & AC. Special offers & child concessions. $$$$

Mercure Hotel (41 inc 2 reduced-mobility rooms) 36 rue Royale; 03 21 97 68 00; www.mercure.com. Formerly the George V, the hotel has been completely renovated in bright contemporary style with reasonably sized rooms with all mod cons. Bar only, but choice of restaurants close by & hot dishes available through room service, plus b/fast room. Central location. Private parking. TV & AC. Special offers & child concessions. $$$$

Hotel Meurice (41 en-suite rooms) 5 & 7 rue Edmond Roche; 03 21 34 57 03; e meurice@wanadoo.fr; www.hotel-meurice.fr. Originally the Le Chariot Royal, built in 1771. The owner, Charles Augustin Meurice, added luxury accommodation to attract English travellers. Sadly destroyed in World War II, it was rebuilt in 1954–55. Now, only 5mins from the beach, it blends 21st-century know-how with traditional furnishings & an elegant wrought iron staircase. A hot & cold buffet b/fast is €12; secure hotel parking is available at €8. Look out for special deals for British visitors. $$$$

Hotel Pacific (16 rooms) 40 rue du Duc de Guise; 03 21 34 50 24; www.pacifichotel-calais.com. A small but cosy hotel conveniently close to the railway station & half a mile from the beach. There are some good restaurants nearby. B/fast is €6.40, garage parking €7. $$$

Le Cercle de Malines (5 rooms) 12 rue de Malines; 03 21 96 80 65; e c.malines@gmail.com; www.lecercledemalines.com. Close to the theatre, this former family home of lacemakers, built in 1844 & now a B&B, retains a period charm that includes steepish stairs. The décor has charm too, & was described by one guest as whimsical. There is also a billiards room. Free Wi-Fi provides a nod to modern day needs. Private parking is available at €8 a day. $$$

Nuits d'Ailleurs (4 suites) 54 rue Berthois; 03 21 97 65 20; e contact@nuitdailleurs.com; www.nuit-dailleurs.com. Boasting a touch of the exotic, the themed suites are furnished with the décor & musical atmosphere of 4 different countries. B/fast included. Special w/end & other offers. $$$

Hotel La Sole Meunière (18 rooms) 1 bld de la Résistance; 03 21 96 83 66; e solemeuniere@solemeuniere.com; www.solemeuniere.com. Centrally located, near the beach & lighthouse, the hotel offers a basic cheap & cheerful priced stay with Wi-Fi facilities, garage parking at €10 or free parking close by. Handy 1-night deals include a choice from the Logis de France menu at their own widely appreciated restaurant. $$$

Micheline Marque B&B (1 sgl & 1 dbl) 101 rue du 11 Novembre; 06 07 03 63 81; e micheline_marque@yahoo.fr; www.chambres-hotes-calais.com. Tucked away in leafy location behind St-Pierre park, this rather grand-looking 1930s family home, complete with balcony & creaking stairs, comes with a welcome smile from owner Micheline Marques. The stairs take a bit of climbing, but the b/fast is spot-on with fresh croissants & freshly brewed coffee. $$

WHERE TO EAT AND DRINK

Aquar'Aile Plage de Calais, 255 rue Jean Moulin; 03 21 34 00 00; www.aquaraile.com; 11.45–14.45 & 18.30–22.00 Mon–Sat, 11.45–14.45 Sun. Uniquely located on the penthouse floor of a block of flats, with glistening décor reflecting stunning Channel views, this gastronomic restaurant specialises in fish dishes of the 'lobster casserole with crustacean coulis' kind. Dining here can be expensive so save for a special occasion. Set menu: 3 courses €30–45. $$$$$

Au Côte d'Argent 1 Digue Gaston-Berthe, Calais; 03 21 34 68 07; www.cotedargent.com; 12.00–14.00 & 19.00–21.30 Tue, Thu & Fri–Sat; closed Aug. Located on the seafront with charming nautical décor, this busy & relaxed restaurant offers a good choice of fish, seafood (including lobster specialities) & meat dishes with seasonal changes. Try their wide-ranging dessert & cheese trolleys. Menus range from €18 (w/day lunch only) to €34. A vegetarian menu is available at €18. There is a large car park opposite. $$$$

Le Grand Bleu Quai de la Colonne, 8 rue Jean-Pierre Avron; 03 21 97 97 98; www.legrandbleu-calais.com; 12.00–14.00 & 19.00–22.00 daily

Café Calais Polyglot is part of an international language movement (*www.polyglotclub.com*) whose members hold small discussion groups round café tables. English-speaking visitors wanting to practise their French (or German, Spanish or Italian) are welcome to attend the weekly Tuesday-evening meeting at the Café de Paris in Calais (see below) from 18.00 to 20.00, or the Wednesday-evening meeting, which is held at the Café Tot ou T'art in Boulogne-sur-Mer (*119 rue Faidherbe* ☎ *03 21 83 15 13*), also 18.00–20.00.

except 19.00–22.00 Tue & all day Wed. This highly rated blue-fronted restaurant with a jaunty nautical setting specialises in fish. In a touch of culinary showmanship some courses are served in differing colours to reflect the taste, from *amuse-bouche* – single, bite-sized *hors d'œuvres* served between courses – to scallops presented beside a 'green roll' of lettuce neatly wrapped in a roll of bread. It's pure panache, of course, but adds to an already well-prepared meal. Air your views: if he's not in the kichen, the chef-cum-owner likes chatting to customers at the restaurant bar. Set menus: €19 for 2 courses, €29 for 3 & €45 for a menu *dégustation*. $$$$

✕ **Du Vignoble au Verre** 43 pl d'Armes; ☎ 03 21 34 83 29; www.duvignoble-calais.com; ⏱ 12.00–14.00 & 19.00–22.00 Tue–Sat. No-nonsense Flemish fare served in a sturdy rustic setting; ideal for sampling *carbonade flamande* – the all-time favourite regional dish of beef braised in beer sauce with onions & spices. This place is perfect for an informal or family outing. Local beers available. Set menus: €14.50 entrée & main course, 3 courses €18.50–31; €7 main course & ice-cream for children under 12. $$$

✕ **Restaurant du Channel** 73 bld Gambetta; ☎ 03 21 35 30 11; www.lechannel.fr; ⏱ 12.00–14.00 Tue–Sun, 18.00–22.00 Fri–Sat. Industrial chic best describes the wood & steel setting for this slightly out-of-town find in Le Channel, a cultural centre converted from what was once a vast abattoir. A knob of butter is intriguingly borne on a heated breeze block, Brouillade eggs & black pudding are served, with a dividing biscuit, in a Kilner jar & an apple dessert gets a special squirt of gin from an 'industrial' gun. Top marks to Alexandre Gauthier from La Grenouillère, a 2-star rated restaurant near Montreuil, who devised the good-value menus. An obliging young staff adds to the relaxed atmosphere. There is a choice of a €16 2-course set menu – starter plus main course/main course plus dessert – or €20.5 for 3 courses. $$$

✕ **Café de Paris** 72 rue Royale; ☎ 03 21 34 76 84; www.cafedeparis-calais.com; ⏱ 09.00–01.00 Mon–Thu, 09.00–02.00 Fri–Sat. This lively place with plenty of nooks & crannies is ideal for day-round snacking. Menus include a good range of main dishes, with a smattering of regional specialities. It's conveniently placed for b/fast – which is often cheaper, & better, than in nearby hotels. $$

The following restaurants are recommended by the Café Calais Polyglot group, which includes Brits now living in Calais (see box above):

✕ **La Tourello** 47 pl d'Armes; ☎ 03 21 96 02 96; www.latourello.com. Call in for late-night servings of mussels, pizzas, pastas & salads.

✕ **Le Coq** 31 pl d'Armes; ☎ 03 21 34 79 05; www.aucoqdor.com. Traditional French dishes, especially grilled fish.

✕ **Le Venezia** 24 rue de la Mer; ☎ 03 21 97 80 10. Italian cuisine with budget prices.

✕ **La Mer** 30 rue de la Mer; ☎ 03 21 96 17 72. Fish dishes, 12 kinds of *moules* & paella.

✕ **Restaurant Hong Kong** 20 rue Paix; ☎ 03 21 97 80 10. Chinese & Thai specialities.

SHOPPING

OUT-OF-TOWN OUTLETS Calais is the leading shopping centre in northern France. Out-of-town outlets include **Cité Europe** (*5mins from the Eurotunnel Terminal – follow the sign to Cité Europe; 10mins from the port of Calais via A16 – follow signs for Boulogne, exit junction 41 & follow signs; number 7 bus runs regularly from Calais centre;* ☎ *03 21 46 47 48;*

www.cite-europe.com; ⏱ *10.00–20.00 Mon–Thu, 10.00–21.00 Fri, 09.00–20.00 Sat;* *restaurants, bars, bowling alley & 12-screen Gaumont cinema open daily – see www.nord-cinema for timings*), which with 147 shops and 20 restaurants as well as many leisure facilities, is by far the largest superstore. You could easily spend a day there.

Shoppers can explore a vast range of fashion for men, women and children, as well as stylish household goods toys and sports equipment. The on-site hypermarket Carrefour (the name roughly translates as a 'crossroads', 'public square' or 'plaza') stocks a wide choice of French food, wine and beer as well as clothes, garden furniture, electrical goods and kitchen equipment (⏱ *08.30–20.00 Mon–Sat*). Other favourites include Toys'R'Us, Disney Store, and four perfume shops including Sephora. English-speaking staff, free parking, cash machines and toilets are all provided.

A *cplus* loyalty card offers shopping discounts as well as special offers on accommodation, restaurants and attractions along the Côte d'Opale.

Marques Avenue (*www.marquesavenue.com;* ⏱ *10.00–20.00 Mon–Sat*), the discount designer outlet centre, is a separate building a few minutes' walk from the main car park for the entire Cité Europe complex. It has its own outside and underground parking. It will appeal to savvy shoppers who love famous names (*marques* is French for 'brands') but don't want to pay the full price.

Clothing for men, women and children, as well as sportswear and soft furnishings, are on offer in over 50 stores, all of which pledge price reductions of at least 30% although the discount is often far more. Shops display framed information certificates in the window which tell you when the company was founded, where the goods are made, how much is produced a year and what they are offering. Yes, the stock *is* from the previous season. But as new collections are produced ever faster, many designers choose to sell off their excess stock, prototypes and samples in their own outlet shops within Marques Avenue.

The building includes a coffee bar, 'La Croissanterie', and a bistro, La Fabrique à Bière; sip a reviving aperitif in the bar or eat in the brasserie where the menu includes croque monsieur, omelettes and salads as well as pasta and pizza. Most dishes are in the €6–10 range. The three-course menu (€11) includes coffee and a drink.

Also out of town are two popular, family-run outlets: **Calais Vins** (*just off the A16 at junction 44, Calais-St Pierre;* ☏ *03 21 36 40 40; pre-order by email* ℮ *contact@calais-vins.com; www.calais-vins.com;* ⏱ *09.00–19.00 Mon–Sat, 09.30–18.00 Sun*) and **Franglais** (*a distinctive white building that looks like a farmhouse, a few mins' drive from the Channel Tunnel terminal – it's easily seen from the A16 (towards Boulogne), exit Junction 40, turn left at the crossroads, follow sign 'Gare TGV' & the store is on your right;* ☏ *03 21 85 29 39; www.franglais-wine.com;* ⏱ *09.00–19.00 Mon–Sat, 09.30–18.00 Sun*), which have special offers on an extensive range of French wine, champagne and beer, spirits, liqueurs, local produce and gifts. There are free tasting bars and large parking areas.

Realising that there is no particular Calais souvenir, and that the alcohol market, like food, is moving to traditional products, Jerome Pont, the enthusiastic Anglophile who runs Calais Vins, has brought out a range of beers called Les Bourgeoises de Calais; they commemorate the Anglo–French 'incident' of 1347 (see page 57). However, the labels on these blonde (6.1% alcohol), amber and brown beers are more evocative of the Moulin Rouge than the famous siege in which the Brits captured Calais. After researching eight breweries, Jerome chose the Ch'ti Brewery in Lens (which already exports its own beers to Britain) to produce his beer. Also available at Franglais, Carrefour, Auchon and other outlets, the 75cl bottles of beer cost €2.95. In bars the 33cl size, served in elegant French stemmed glasses, costs €2.50.

Traditional and authentic blonde beer of the two coastal headlands (Cap Gris-Nez and Cap Blanc-Nez) can be purchased direct from the artisan brewer **Christopher Noyon** at Ferme de Belle Dalle (see page 92).

CENTRAL CALAIS Independent wine merchants include **Bar a Vins** (*52 pl d'Armes;* \ *03 21 96 96 31;* ⊕ *09.00–19.00 Mon–Sat, 10.00–15.00 Sun*), a long-standing British favourite owned by the charismatic Luc Gille, who visits small independent regional vineyards in his 1930s Citroën van and buys his wines direct from them. This shop sells wine *en vrac* (in bulk). Bring your own bottle – wines are priced per litre (Côtes du Rhônes, Tarn, Rosé, Sauvignon). **Les 4 Boulevards** covered shopping centre (*3 rue Neuve;* \ *03 21 97 60 06;* e *info@les4boulevards.com; www.les4boulevards.com;* ⊕ *10.00–20.00 Mon–Sat, shops stay open till 21.30 in summer; parking 07.00–21.00, first 2½ hrs free then €1 per hr, free all day Wed & Sat*) houses more than 50 shops. Stock up on basic foods as well as wines and drink at the Champion supermarket (⊕ *8.30–20.00 Mon–Sat*). Fashion, babywear and perfumeries can also be found here or in the two adjoining streets, boulevard Jacquard and boulevard Lafayette.

   Maison du Fromage (*1 rue André Gerschell;* \ *03 21 34 44 72; www.restaurant-lechannel.com*) stocks a great choice of French cheeses including Vieux Lille, the smelliest cheese in France, as well as Maroilles and Bouilette Avesne, both made in Nord. **La Ferme** (*46 bld Gambetta;* \ *03 21 97 44 53*) sells much of the produce grown locally and in the nearby region. More than 20 *boulangeries* and patisseries, ten or so butchers and charcuteries, plus a farm provision shop and cheese shop also retain their traditional identity.

Markets There are two colourful country-style markets – in place d'Armes and place Crèvecoeur – which open Wednesday and Saturday and Thursday and Saturday mornings respectively. A newer traditional market at Fort Nieulay now opens on Sundays on place du Marché, not far from rue Roger Salengro.

   Speciality foods produced in Nord-Pas de Calais are generally supported with a label attesting to their authenticity and quality.

Fish In boulevard La Fayette **Les Delices de la Mer** (*160 bld La Fayette;* \ *03 21 34 64 57*) buys daily direct from local fishermen and **Huîtrière Calaisienne** (*12 bld La Fayette;* \ *03 21 36 50 97*) is good for Brittany oysters, crabs and lobster. The 100-year-old family-run **Emile Fournier et Fils** (*53 rue Mouron;* \ *03 21 96 49 36; www.emilfournierfils.fr*) specialises in smoked fish including salmon, herring, trout and halibut. At weekends, a small fish market is held on the quayside opposite the marina.

Fine foods and wines Owned by the energetic Michel Morvan, **Le Terroir** (*29 rue des Fontinettes;* \ *03 21 36 34 66; www.leterroir-calais.com*) is well known for gastronomic products such as pâtés and foie gras. It also stocks a huge choice of wines. Ask to look downstairs: amid the dusty bottles of vintage wine in the authentic cellar is some dating back to 1876.

   Charcuterie Maffrand (*27 rue des Fontinettes;* \ *03 21 36 57 41;* ⊕ *08.30–12.45 & 14.30–19.30 Tue–Sat*), the adjoining shop, produces its own award-winning fresh meats, pâtés and terrines.

Bookshop

Place media in the commercial centre, 4B bld Jacquard; ⊕ 10.00–19.00 Tue–Sat

OTHER PRACTICALITIES

Bank Crédit Agricole (CA), 64 rue Royale; ⏰ 08.45–18.30 Thu–Wed, 08.45–12.10 Sat, closed on Mon. ATM accepts Visa, MasterCard & most other cards.
Supermarket Match, 56 pl d'Armes; ☎ 03 21 34 33 79; ⏰ 09.00–19.00 Mon–Sat, 09.00–12.00 Sun
Cyber-phone 49 rue du Seigneur de Gourdan; ☎ 03 21 96 05 02; ⏰ 09.00–22.00 daily

Pharmacy Nicodeme, 50 pl d'Armes; ☎ 03 21 96 25 88; ⏰ 09.00–19.00 Mon–Sat
Post Office pl d'Alsace; ⏰ 08.30–18.00 Mon–Fri, 09.00–12.00 Sat
Public toilet(s) av Wilson or town hall

WHAT TO SEE AND DO

Calais is not natural sightseeing territory, especially on foot. A sprawling town, it is best seen as offering two distinctive tourist areas.

OLD TOWN AREA Close to the ferry port is the 'old' centre. The fortified town dates back to 1224, but it has for centuries effectively been an island, thanks to Vauban (see page 12), the military genius who surrounded the 13th-century walls with defensive canals. These are still spanned by six bridges.

With some 80% of Calais either heavily adapted or destroyed by Allied bombing during the German occupation of World War II, only a few of the original fortifications remain. These include the **Citadelle**, near square Vauban. During the British occupation of Calais, from 1347 to 1558, English kings regularly stayed in the 13th-century castle that preceded the Citadelle. Like the old town, it was modernised by Vauban (in 1675) to form the coastal end of a second 'back-up' of defences. It now houses a sports stadium.

In **place d'Armes**, off the main rue Royale, once the bustling heart of medieval Calais, the chunky 13th-century watchtower La Tour du Guet squats somewhat forlornly in a drab setting of post-war brick buildings. Though damaged during an earthquake in 1580, it was a military post in World War I, complete with a dovecote for carrier pigeons, and remained intact during World War II. If nothing else, the square is surrounded by cafés for a coffee break. Regular weekly markets on Wednesday and Saturday add a splash of colour.

A shortish walk away via boulevard des Allies is the 51m 19th-century **lighthouse** (*le Phare, pl Henri Barbusse;* ☎ *03 21 34 33 34; www.pharedecalais.com;* ⏰ *10.00–12.00 & 14.00–17.30 Wed–Mon, 10.00–12.00 & 14.00–17.40 Sat–Sun, closed in Jan; €4.50, €2 children up to 15, under 5 free*). A climb up a rather daunting spiral staircase – 271 steps – provides a splendid view over Calais, the Channel and, on a clear day, the White Cliffs of Dover. While the waterfront area is no great shakes bar a few bobbing boats in the harbour, it does contain some of the town's top restaurants.

In 2009 the Calais Museum of Fine Arts and Lace was split into the newly opened Lace and Fashion Museum in quai du Commerce (see page 69) leaving the old site as the **Fine Arts Department** (*le Musée des Beaux Arts, 25 rue Richelieu;* ☎ *03 21 46 48 40;* e *musee@mairie-calais.fr;* ⏰ *10.00–12.00 & 14.00–17.30 Mon & Wed–Fri, 10.00–12.00 & 14.00–18.30 Sat, 14.00–18.30 Sun, closed Tue & public holidays. Entry free. Guided tours in English bookable in advance*). A cutting-edge project when it was inaugurated in 1966, the department will continue to develop its separate role; it already houses a collection of 20th-century masterpieces by painters and sculptors, including Picasso and Dubuffet. Works by Rodin provide an insight into how the famous bronze of the *Six Burghers* developed.

SOUTHERN PART It was not until the 19th century that the old town extended southwards from its canal-locked location into what is now the main town centre.

3

Tucked between rue de Seigneur de Gourdan and rue Notre Dame in the Old Town is the church of Notre Dame (*Eglise Notre Dame, 500m northeast of the tourist office in bld Clemenceau;* ⊕ *14.30–15.30 daily Jul & Aug, though the hrs could be extended as rebuilding work continues*). It was here, in 1921, following the civil ceremony at the town hall, that the then Captain Charles de Gaulle married a young Calais woman, Yvonne Vendroux, who had been christened in the church 21 years previously. 'I shall look ridiculous, because he is 40cm taller than I am,' she is reported to have said at the wedding, which is commemorated by a special plaque in the church. Sadly, on 26 September 1944 – only a few days before the Liberation of Calais – Notre Dame was mistakenly bombed by the Allies. This destroyed most of the building, with the bell-tower collapsing onto the northern transept.

The interior, left largely neglected for years, is currently undergoing a massive €8-million facelift in line with its claim to be the only church built in English perpendicular style in continental Europe. This includes renovation of the chancel with its magnificent 17th-century 17m altar and the 17th-century Lady Chapel whose French Classical-style stucco blue decorations are at long last emerging from the dirt and the dust.

The original church was started in 1214 and completed in 1224. The nave dates back to the 13th century and during the English occupation of Calais was enlarged by Flemish craftsmen to such an extent that, by the late 15th century, Notre Dame – by then part of the archdiocese of Canterbury – became the most important religious building in town.

During the French Revolution, the building was turned into a Temple de la Raison (temple dedicated to the Goddess Reason). Later it was used as a warehouse, before being returned to the Church in 1802.

Both Flemish and English styles are represented, the latter partially by the bell-tower at the transept crossing as well as the wood-panelled vaults and Tudor-style basket-handled arches. The 58m bell tower consists of a square base topped with a two-level octagonal spire. Watchmen lived on the first level until 1846. Water from the church roof runs into a huge reservoir built on the order of Louis XIV by Vauban in order to provide the garrison and the population with water. The church's walls are 2–4m thick.

It became a listed building in 1927. Other features include works by major Flemish painters, including *The Assumption of the Virgin* by Gérard Seghers (Antwerp, 1591–1651). This dates from 1629 and underwent a €88,000 renovation in 2006. The stained-glass windows made in 1976 by the famous glassmaker and sculptor Gérard Lardeur represent man through the symbol of the circle. The previous windows were destroyed in 1915 by a Zeppelin bomber. Though some guidebooks are sniffy about Notre Dame's worth, the restoration could well see the building become a major Calais attraction.

To the right lies the old St-Pierre quarter (see map) which was incorporated into Calais in 1885. In many ways, this is the far more fascinating part of the town. Head first via rue Royale for Calais-Ville railway station: to the south of this the 800m boulevard Jacquard leads to the **town hall** (*l'hôtel de ville;* ⊕ *08.00–12.00 & 13.30–17.30 Mon–Fri*), a red-brick and decidedly Flemish-style set piece designed to impress. The equally ornate 75m belfry was an easily recognisable landmark for British pilots in World War II. Work on the building began in 1911 and ended in 1925; curiously, the exotic exterior hides a reinforced concrete structure. Do drop in, if only to admire the superb stained glass windows showing the liberation of the city from the British.

In front of the huge town hall square stands Rodin's impressive bronze statue of the *Six Burghers of Calais*. This commemorates their willingness to sacrifice their lives in order to save the citizens from being slain by England's Edward III at the end of the 11-month siege by British forces (see *History*, page 57). A painting by

LACE IS THREADED THROUGH THE TOWN'S HISTORY

In 1816, newly invented – and closely guarded – machinery, smuggled in by three skilled English workers from Nottingham, brought fame to Calais, which was at the time struggling to cope with a renewed demand for lace. Their aim was to escape bitter opposition at home to machine-made lace over traditional handmade methods. By the 1820s workshops, using the English Leavers-style loom ideally suited for mass production, were flourishing; in 1830 St-Pierre and Calais, then separate towns, boasted 113 manufacturers of which a large majority were English.

Other workers went to Caudry, near Cambrai (see page 189) to open lace factories there around the same time. Competition between the two remains as keen as ever. People in the Calais region still eat Christmas puddings and a local version of Welsh rarebit (cheese on toast), just two traditional dishes English lace-makers brought to the region.

These historical events explain why the opening in June 2009 of the **Cité Internationale de la Dentelle et de la Mode Calais** (*135 quai du Commerce;* ◤ *03 21 00 42 30;* e *cite-dentelle@mairie-calais.fr; www.cite-dentelle.fr;* ⊕ *1 Apr–31 Oct 10.00–18.00 & 2 Nov–31 Mar 10.00–17.00, both daily except Tue; adult/child €5/2.50, under 5 yrs free*) – the rather long-winded name for the International City of Lace and Fashion Museum – was arguably the second-most important event in Calais's lace-making history since Clark, Webster and Bonnington, the three Brits involved, crossed the North Sea and sailed into Calais with their illicit cargo.

Not only is the museum's opening a timely reminder of how Calais became world famous for producing lace, but it brings home in a powerfully contemporary setting just what this meant to the economic and social development of this oh-so-English town.

Today two lace factories with some 700 looms still employ 3,000 workers, many descendants of expats who built rows of terraced houses in the St-Pierre district of Calais with space for their workshops. The sharp social division created by the growing prosperity of this once working-class area can still be seen today: north of the main railway station the road is the grandly named rue Royale while on the other side it becomes boulevard Jacquard, named after Lyons-born Joseph Marie Jacquard who devised the perforated cards used for transferring complicated designs ready for production.

His work on these is reflected in the undulating glass façade at the imposing entrance to the museum, while a statue of him stands outside the town's 19th-century theatre at the corner of boulevard Jacquard.

Mere curiosity, if nothing else, makes the museum a not-to-miss-attraction. Four fully operational Leavers looms bring back the sound and complexity of producing machine-made lace; there is even the chance to chat with operators. A large screen shows how the thread is passed through the loom.

The same permanent collection gallery also illustrates how handmade lace influenced French production and fashion from the 16th to the 19th centuries. Good use of multi-media techniques throughout bring a strong hands-on family appeal to exhibits.

Built on the canalside site of the old Boulart factory, one of the largest of the great factories from the 1870s, the museum holds lace-making workshops and fashion shows. There is also a restaurant and library and a shop opens daily except Tuesday (⊕ *Apr–Oct 10.30–18.30, Nov–Mar 10.30–17.30*).

Jeanne Thil illustrating their dedication hangs in the town hall.

Also not to be missed is the creeper-covered **War Museum** (*Le Musée de la Guerre; situated in the middle of Parc St-Pierre, facing the town hall;* ☏ *03 21 34 21 57; www.museeguerrecalais.free.fr;* ⊕ *Feb–Apr & Oct–Nov 11.00–17.00 Wed–Mon, May–Sep 10.00–18.00 daily – these timings are subject to change; adult/child €6/5, 2 adults/2 children €14 inc audio-guide*). A former German Navy bunker and command post, the 194m-long building survived the extensive bombings of the last war thanks to being cleverly camouflaged under the cover of trees. Rooms display objects and photographs, mostly with English captions, depicting the World War II occupation of Calais. An entire room is devoted to World War I. There are interactive displays, and an audio guide in English. The surrounding park is an idyllic setting for a picnic lunch.

The construction and style of the **theatre** (*corner of bld Jacquard & bld Gambetta;* ☏ *03 21 36 58 65; www calais.fr;* ⊕ *14.00–18.00 Tue–Sat for tickets & information*) was decided on – as were the town hall and the railway station – when Calais and St-Pierre fused to become just one town. Built in 1903 the first floor of the façade is decorated with statues symbolising poetry, comedy, dance and music.

BEACHES Calais's sandy beach, just 1km from place d'Armes and linked by a cycle path, plays second fiddle to the town centre attractions. It's not that it is underrated, just that the albeit long stretches of yellow sands with the almost obligatory white beach huts can be found in prettier settings elsewhere along the coast. But the beach does at least provide light relief from sight-seeing, especially for children. This takes the form of funfairs and a mini-golf course, as well as plenty of seafront snack bars and ice-cream stalls. Oh yes, and bags of opportunities for building sandcastles or playing beachball. Summer festivals bring about a further splash of colour, along with the seasonal crowds.

Take a stroll to the 16th-century **Fort Risban**, once a strategic part of the Calais defences held in turn by the English, French and Spanish. It was subsequently used as a shelter during World War II, but is now little more than a ruin.

4

Coastal Country

This is Nord-Pas de Calais in a nutshell. Straddling 120km of the Côte d'Opale (Opal Coast), which runs easterly from the Belgian border to the estuary of the Somme, the coast and hinterland embrace the strong Flemish flavour of Dunkirk, the essential Englishness of Calais and the Edwardian glitz of Le Touquet. It also includes Boulogne, beloved by the British and vouched for by Charles Dickens.

Once the stuff of history, from where invasions were planned and sea battles fought, this rolling region of often-windswept sand dunes now acts as the familiar, almost reassuring, face of France to thousands of cross-Channel visitors.

Some get no further than Calais. Other braver souls take longer sorties. The imposing heights of Cap Blanc-Nez and Cap Gris-Nez can easily be tied in with a shopping expedition; so, too, can Guînes or Ardres, two French charmers just inland from the coast. It was here, between the two towns, that Henry VIII vied for attention with François I at the Field of the Cloth of Gold.

Yet these are mere starters on a surf-and-turf combo where coast and country merge naturally. Almost all of the places described in this chapter are within 90 minutes of Calais, and even closer to the Boulogne or Dunkirk areas.

Golfers, walkers, cyclists and horseriders are all catered for; fly surfing is the latest of the white-knuckle sports to join sailing, sand yachting and speed sailing. Nature-lovers and birdwatchers are likewise spoilt for choice. The Calais and Boulogne coasts take the lion's share in reliable family resorts, Wissant and Wimereux being traditionally the more obvious; Audreselles provides a sleepier, fishing-village alternative. Others, many child-friendly, also deserve consideration.

An older generation will recall the coast for the War World II evacuation of Dunkirk and the Allied bombing around Calais. Bleak German bunkers still riddle the region, while wartime museums and monuments help bring home the closeness of this now peaceful playground to the British coast.

DUNKIRK

For a town virtually destroyed in World War II, Dunkirk has made a remarkable recovery. Looking at photos of rubble-ridden streets and shattered buildings taken in 1940, the year of the Dunkirk evacuation, it's understandable that the French government originally deemed the port scarcely worth repairing. But Dunkirk is now France's third-largest port and its vast industrial approach is frankly off-putting. This is a pity, for while Dunkirk suffers from an image problem similar to that of Calais this flamboyantly and proudly Flemish centre is once more buzzing with confidence, and is eager to show off its array of shops and fine eating places.

The town's huge urban regeneration, together with the Dover–Dunkirk ferry link, has brought about renewed tourist interest in a town which only 12 years ago many would not have given tuppence for. Now a fresh-faced town centre packs considerable tourist punch, with an excellent Port Museum (see page 78) alongside

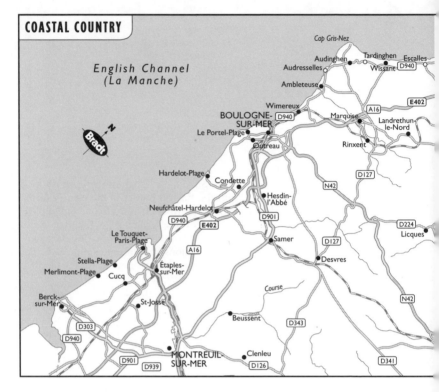

*English Channel
(La Manche)*

Cap Gris-Nez

Audinghen Tardinghen Escalles
Audresselles Wissant D940
Ambleteuse

Wimereux A16
BOULOGNE- D940 Marquise Landrethun-
SUR-MER le-Nord
Le Portel-Plage Rinxent
Outreau

Hardelot-Plage D127
Condette N42
Hesdin-
l'Abbé
Neufchâtel-Hardelot
D940 E402 D901 D224
Le Touquet- Licques
Paris-Plage Samer D127
A16
Stella-Plage Desvres
Merlimont-Plage Cucq Étaples-
sur-Mer
Berck- Course N42
sur-Mer St-Josse
Beussent D343
D303
D940
MONTREUIL- Clenleu
SUR-MER
D901 D939 D126 D341

the quay that, on a sunny day, positively sparkles with rows of bobbing yachts.
It is also the gateway to the inland villages whose flavour, both culinary and
architecturally, reflects the true nature of French Flanders.

HISTORY Back in 1067, a handful of fishermen lived in a hamlet among the dunes.
Deeply religious, they built a church on the top of one of them – hence the name
Dunkerque (as per the French spelling), 'The Church of the Dunes'. Herring was
their main catch and they sold it, alongside prawns caught by their wives, at the local
fish market – in those days a small concern. By 1360, however, the town's port,
known as West Dunkirk, was flourishing.

Dunkirk's strategic position at the entrance to the North Sea was not lost
on the English, Dutch, French and Spanish, all of whom were eager for a slice
of the action. There followed a mixture of treaties, alliances and general carve-ups.
Dunkirk was handed over to the English in 1659 in exchange for Cromwellian
troops who helped fight off the Spanish; it was bought by back by Louis XIV in
1662. A sustained period of prosperity followed, thanks largely to fortifications
created by the military mastermind and architect Vauban. These transformed the
thriving port, which by now was favoured over Bergues.

Growth was later undermined when, in 1713, the Treaty of Utrecht obliged the
town to give up its military port, with locals turning instead to cod-fishing off Iceland.
Happily the 19th century saw a large increase in commerce and wealth, reflected in
new Art-Nouveau villas in the seaside suburb of Malo-les-Bains (see page 80).

All this ended when Dunkirk was damaged first in World War I, and then all but
totally destroyed in World War II. Due to heavy German resistance, it remained the
last French town to be liberated, with freedom finally arriving on 10 May 1945.

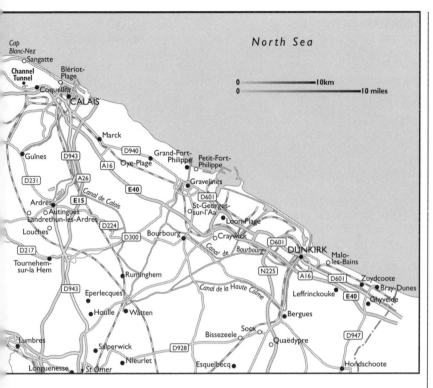

GETTING THERE AND AWAY

By car From Calais (40km) take A16/exit 54–62; the road is toll-free and the journey takes 30 minutes. From Norfolkline ferry port (12km) take the slip road to A16/exit 53 for Dunkirk.

By rail There is a regular 30-minute service from Lille Europe station, or it's one hour by TER from Lille Flandres station (see page 224). For those travelling from Calais, the train service is more limited. There's only one direct (45-minute) early-morning train service from Calais; later trains are routed via Hazebruck and take from 90 minutes to two hours. It is therefore advisable to take the bus; see below.

By bus Buses from Calais take about 30–40 minutes from Calais-Ville Station (*BCD; www.ligne-bcd.com*); see page 59.

GETTING AROUND Many **local buses** operate from the bus station (*DK Bus Marine, pl de la Gare;* \ *03 28 59 00 78;* ⊕ *08.30–12.30 & 13.30–18.00 Mon–Sat; www.dkbus.com*). Get a €3 day pass, which covers the centre, main beaches and suburbs; bus line A operates hourly to Gravelines and bus line 2 travels to the Belgian border. There is a regular service to Bergues (see page 81).

Parking Dunkirk has some 4,600 spaces. Try **Pôle Marine** (⊕ *09.30–13.00*); **Centre Marine** (⊕ *08.30–20.00; free parking*) or **Vinci Park** multi-storey car park (*Jean Bart pl;* \ *03 28 66 22 40; www.vincipark.com;* ⊕ *07.30–20.30 Mon–Sat, closed Sun & public holidays;* €7 *daily*).

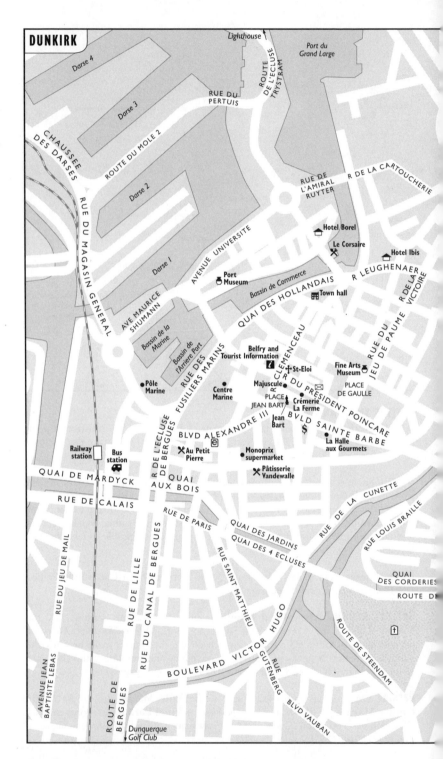

DUNKIRK

Lighthouse

Port du Grand Large

Darse 4

ROUTE DE L'ECLUSE TRYSTRAM

RUE DU PERTUIS

Darse 3

ROUTE DU MOLE 2

CHAUSSEE DES DARSES

RUE DE L'AMIRAL RUYTER

R DE LA CARTOUCHERIE

Darse 2

RUE DU MAGASIN GENERAL

Hotel Borel

Le Corsaire

Hotel Ibis

R LEUGHENAER

R DE LA VICTOIRE

AVENUE UNIVERSITE

Darse 1

AVE MAURICE SHUMANN

Port Museum

Bassin de Commerce

QUAI DES HOLLANDAIS

Town hall

RUE DU JEU DE PAUME

Bassin de la Marine

Bassin de l'Arriere Port

RUE DES FUSILIERS MARINS

Belfry and Tourist Information

CLEMENCEAU

St-Eloi

Fine Arts Museum

Pôle Marine

Centre Marine

Majuscule

R DU PRESIDENT POINCARE

PLACE JEAN BART

Crémerie La Ferme

PLACE DE GAULLE

Jean Bart

BVLD SAINTE BARBE

RUE DE L'ECLUSE DE BERGUES

BLVD ALEXANDRE III

Au Petit Pierre

Monoprix supermarket

La Halle aux Gourmets

Railway station

Bus station

QUAI DE MARDYCK

QUAI AUX BOIS

Pâtisserie Vandewalle

RUE DE CALAIS

RUE DE PARIS

QUAI DES JARDINS

RUE DE LA CUNETTE

RUE LOUIS BRAILLE

RUE DU JEU DE MAIL

RUE DE LILLE

RUE DU CANAL DE BERGUES

QUAI DES 4 ECLUSES

QUAI DES CORDERIES

ROUTE DE

RUE SAINT MATTHIEU

AVENUE JEAN BAPTISTE LEBAS

ROUTE DE BERGUES

BOULEVARD VICTOR HUGO

RUE GUTENBERG

BLVD VAUBAN

ROUTE DE STEENDAM

Dunquerque Golf Club

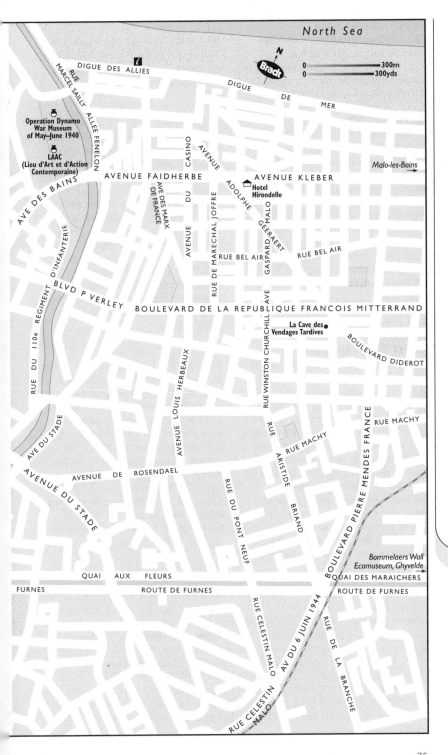

TOURIST INFORMATION

 Dunkirk Dunes de Flandre Tourist Information Centre The Belfry, rue de l'Amiral Ronarc'h; ℡ 03 28 66 79 21; e accueil.dunesdeflandre@ot-dunkerque.fr; www.ot-dukerque.fr; 🕐 09.30–12.30 & 13.30–18.30 Mon–Fri, 09.30–18.30 Sat, 10.00–12.00 & 14.00–16.00 Sun & public holidays. 3-day city pass includes 3 or 4 free visits to major sights, free public transport, a €5 shopping voucher & other special offers; adult/child aged 5–12 €12/6.

WHERE TO STAY

🏠 **Hotel Borel** (48 rooms) 6 rue l'Hermite; ℡ 03 28 66 51 80; e borel@hotelborel.fr; www.hotelborel.fr. With wooden panelling & leather chairs in the drawing room, the sense of traditional reliability is continued in the bedrooms with subdued colours & furnishings more in line with an ocean liner. Though built in the 1950s, it keeps up with the now almost obligatory 3-star fitness & Wi-Fi requirements. It is also handy for the city centre & golf course. Wheelchair access to disabled car-parking spaces; parking €5. B/fast €10. $$$

🏠 **Hotel Hirondelle** (50 rooms) 46/48 av Faidherbe; ℡ 03 28 63 17 65; e info@hotelhirondelle.com; www.hirondelle.com. Within walking distance of the beach at Malo-les-Bains, this is a homely base with English widely spoken — not surprising as the lady of the house once worked for a British company. A restaurant is available with a good selection of regional menus from €14–25 to a €27–32 Sunday gourmet & a €11 children's menu. B/fast is worthwhile at €8. Useful FB off-season deals. Parking is in the street or nearby. Avoid pl Turenne on Mon night — the Tue market starts early & you may find your car has been clamped. $$$

🏠 **Hotel Ibis** (88 rooms) 13 rue du Leughenaer; ℡ 03 28 66 29 07; e h6546@accor.com; www.ibishotel.com. This is a convenient, straightforward chain hotel with special deals & w/end prices. Close to centre with pasta café & parking. $$

WHERE TO EAT AND DRINK

✕ **Le Corsaire** 97 entreé du Port; ℡ 03 28 59 03 61; e contact@lecorsaire-dk.com; www.lecorsaire-dk.com; 🕐 09.30–23.00 Mon–Sat & 09.30–16.00 Sun. Some may remember Arnaud Tétart as the chef who cooked Princess Di & Dodi Fayed's favourite dish at The Ritz in Paris before the fatal subway crash in 1997; many more will recall dining at his original quayside restaurant before he switched his undoubted talents to the current spanking-new glass-fronted 75-seater property symbolising the commercial confidence of the quayside area. Expect the best: choices range from the €20 market menu served Mon–Sat afternoons to the smooth €35 menu, which uses the subtle blend of local & international specialities for which Tétart is noted. $$$$

✕ **Au Petit Pierre** 4 rue Dampierre; ℡ 03 28 66 28 36, www.aupetitpierre.com; 🕐 12.00–14.00 except Sat & 17.00–21.00 except Sun. The décor & ambience of this charming 18th-century house draws a loyal local clientele & regular praise from the French press. Tuck into a fine selection of classic French meat & fish dishes from €12, as well as Flemish & regional specialities including the famous *Waterzoï de poissons* (a delectable fish casserole; €14.50). Set menus €18.50–25.00 & €8.82 for children. Look out for Petit Pierre, the boss. Pierre Neuville is now a tall, lanky chap but his red-bricked restaurant is named with a tongue-in-cheek nod to his childhood shortness. $$$

SHOPPING With 400 town-centre outlets, Dunkirk is a captivating temptress for those with a weakness for a spot of shopping. Downtown, **Crémerie La Ferme** (*22 rue Poincare;* ℡ *03 28 59 22 55;* 🕐 *05.00–12.15 Tue–Fri, 13.30–19.00 Mon & 05.00–19.00 Sat*) offers a choice of 300–plus cheeses, including Bergues, Maroilles and other local varieties. Buy wine at **La Cave des Vendages Tardives** (*21 pl Voltaire;* ℡ *03 28 21 60 82;* e *vendagestardives@wanadoo.fr;* 🕐 *09.30–12.30 & 14.30–19.30 Tue–Sat*). For other regional produce try **La Halle aux Gourmets** (*24 bld Sainte Barbe;* ℡ *03 28 63 66 20;* 🕐 *09.30–12.30 & 13.30–19.00 Tue–Sat*).

You can't mistake **Centre Marine** (*close to pl Jean Bart; www.centremarine.com;* 🕐 *10.00–19.00 Mon–Sat; free parking*). With 23 shops, it ties in nicely with a visit to the regular Wednesday and Saturday **market** in the place de Gaulle area (🕐 *09.00–16.00*).

There are two out-of-town hypermarkets: **Auchan** (*A16/exit 54 for route Nationale 40 Grande Synthe;* ☏ *03 28 58 55 55; www.auchan.fr;* ⏱ *08.30–21.30 Mon–Thu & Sat, 08.30–22.00 Fri; closed Sun*); and **Carrefour** (*A16/exit 58 for St-Pol-sur-Mer;* ☏ *03 28 58 58 58; www.carrefour.fr;* ⏱ *08.30–21.00 Mon–Sat*).

Bookshops

Majuscule 47 pl Jean Bart; ☏ 03 28 59 26 83; ⏱ 09.00–19.00

Virgin Dunkirk Pôle Marine, Quai des Fusiliers; ☏ 03 28 51 85 85; ⏱ 10.00–20.00 Mon–Sat & 11.00–19.00 Sun

OTHER PRACTICALITIES

Bank Société Générale, 2 bld Sainte Barbe; ☏ 03 28 58 57 00; ⏱ 10.00–13.00 & 15.00–17.00 Tue–Sat. ATM takes most cards.

Supermarket Monoprix, pl de la République; ☏ 03 28 59 01 11; www.sitedesmarques.com/dunkerque; ⏱ 08.30–20.00 Mon–Sat

Internet Café Micro Point, 5 pl Jeanne d'Arc; ☏ 03 28 26 61 12; www.pagesjaunes.fr/activites/dunkerque/cyber-cafe.html; ⏱ 12.30–20.00

Mon–Sat. 19 PCs available.

Pharmacy Pharmacie du Beffroi, rue Amiral Ronarc'h (in front of the belfry); ☏ 03 28 66 89 86; ⏱ 09.00–19.00 Mon–Sat

Post Office 55 rue du Président Poincaré; ☏ 08 00 00 90 42; ⏱ 08.30–18.00 Mon–Fri, 09.00–12.00 Sat

Public toilet(s) pl du minck, pl roger salengro, or in the town hall (pl Charles Valentin)

WHAT TO SEE AND DO There's no better place to get an overview of the town than at the tourist office. It's located on the ground floor of **the belfry** (*Beffroi St-Éloi, rue de l'Amiral Ronarc'h;* ☏ *03 28 66 79 21; www.ot-dunkerque.fr;* ⏱ *09.00–12.30 & 13.30–18.30 Mon–Sat, 14.00–16.00 Sun; adult/child €2.90/2*). Now a World Heritage Site, this free-standing belfry soars to 58m and dates back to the 13th century. Finely decorated with Gothic-style arches, it once served as the bell tower to St-Éloi Church, which burnt down in 1558. In World War II it was one of the few buildings to survive the massive bombing. It remains the oldest monument in town. The belfry houses a peal of 48 bells which ring out Jean Bart tunes every quarter hour. Take the lift to the chimes, and then climb the 60 steps for a bird's-eye view. At 16.00 on Saturdays, concerts are performed by the peal player. Further information from the tourist office.

FINGER-BITING RECIPE

Take a bite out of Jean Bart's fingers when dropping in for a coffee at **Pâtisserie Vandewalle** (*6 rue du Sud;* ☏ *03 28 66 72 78; www.auxdoigtsdejeanbart.com;* ⏱ *08.00–12.30 & 14.00–19.15 Wed–Sat, 08.00–14.00 Sun & public holidays*). The delicious gateau, Aux Doigts de Jean Bart, is named after the town's prized privateer (see page 79). It's made from a secret recipe involving coffee cream and almond biscuit covered in crunchy milk chocolate.

Nowadays the sweet is made by Jean-Daniel Vandewalle, the fourth generation of the family of pastry-makers; the speciality was first created by his grandfather and the name, Jean Bart's Fingers, dreamt up by his grandmother. Vandewalle owns just the one shop, though the fingers, which he hopes will eventually carry a trademark, are known nationwide.

Vandewalle also sells ice-cream, handmade chocolates and a mouth-watering selection of cakes, mousses and fruit cocktails. His shop is well worth a shopping and a coffee stopover. Better still try breakfast here for €5.80. The shop also runs cookery courses.

Allow plenty of time to explore the **Port Museum** (*9 quai de la Citadelle;* ℘ *03 28 63 33 39;* e *museeportuaire@nordnet.fr; www.museeportuaire.com;* ⊕ *10.00–12.45 & 13.30–18.00 daily except Tue, 10.00–18.00 Jul & Aug; adult €4–7.50 (museum & ships) or €10–22 family ticket*). The interactive multi-media exhibition, housed within a former 19th-century tobacco warehouse, has the happy knack of bringing the already bustling quayside to life. Through an easily digestible series of galleries and family-friendly presentations, it offers a fascinating glimpse of the town's thousand years of history. The second floor contains a huge collection of model liners, schooners, frigates and troop-carrying ships. Though badly damaged in World War II, the tobacco warehouse reopened in 1949, but was bought by the town in 1974. In 1992 it opened as a museum.

Outside, tied up alongside the quay, are some real examples of seafaring ships (⊕ *Jul–Aug daily & every Sun in Apr–Jun & Sep–Oct*). These include *The Duchesse Anne*, a square-rigged three-masted tall ship, launched by the German Merchant Navy for training purposes in 1901. The only one in France, it was handed over by

DUNKIRK SPIRIT STILL LIVES ON

It was the biggest wartime evacuation in history. In a matter of nine days between 25 May and 4 June 1940, some 340,000 men, mainly British, were rescued by a motley group of around 1,000 quickly assembled vessels. Among them were Winston Churchill's 'little ships' made up of a co-ordinated collection of merchant marine and fishing boats, as well as pleasure craft and Royal National Lifeboat Institution lifeboats. The 'Dunkirk Spirit' they evoked has since become the stuff of legend. A number of them returned to the port in May 2010, amid a blaze of media interest, to mark the 70th anniversary of the evacuation.

The full story of this epic World War II evacuation is depicted at the **Operation Dynamo War Museum of May–June 1940** (*Mémorial du Souvenir, rue des Chantiers de France;* ℘ *03 28 26 27 81;* e *production@ot-dunkerque.fr; www.dynamo-dunkerque.com;* ⊕ *Apr–Sep 10.00–12.00 & 14.00–17.00; adult/child under 12 €3.50/free*). The museum, inaugurated in June 2000, is installed in the casemate of bastion 32 which, in 1939, was the headquarters of the French Army. Volunteers now keep alive memories of those incredible days when British, French and Belgian troops were, despite limpet mines, torpedoes, bombs and heavy German shelling, snatched from the 15km of Dunkirk beaches.

Like similarly aging wartime museums, this one lacks the latest gizmos, though retains an authenticity that will appeal to a wartime generation. It is also a reminder of how the Allied troops, cut off by the advancing German army, were forced down a narrow corridor of land as the ferocious battle for Dunkirk began. The evacuation was achieved in stages, with 64,000 Allied soldiers departing on 1 June before German air attacks prevented further daylight attempts. The British rearguard left on 2 June, along with 60,000 French soldiers. Two French divisions, who remained to protect the evacuation, were soon captured. It is estimated that around 61,000 troops were killed, wounded or taken prisoner.

A ten-minute black-and-white film, screened alternately in French and English, vividly illustrates much of this. The remainder of the exhibition relies largely on wartime memorabilia; old newspaper cuttings capture the audacity of the operation. Black-and-white photos, mostly captioned in English, bring additional starkness. The strong role played by the French and the heavy toll in lives taken is emphasised, answering resentment felt by some over the allegedly small number taken aboard the ships – a feeling no doubt fostered by the then pro-German Vichy government.

He was arguably the most celebrated corsair in France with the citizens of Dunkirk proclaiming themselves 'the children of Jean Bart'. His statue stands proudly in place Jean-Bart. Jean Bart tunes are played on the belfry bells. There is even a chocolate delicacy named after him (see page 79).

The people of Dunkirk celebrate Jean Bart with good reason: as a famous privateer it was he who in 1694, during the Franco–Dutch War, saved the French from famine by capturing 130 ships loaded with wheat – just one in a long line of exploits which earned him the rank of Commodore from a grateful Louis XIV.

Born into a poor seafaring family in Dunkirk, then part of the Spanish Netherlands, his path to glory began ironically when, aged only 12, he joined the Dutch Navy in order to fight the English who by then had taken over Dunkirk. Armed with skills learnt from the formidable Admiral Michel de Ruyter, he returned home to fight for the French, who were now in charge of the town. He commanded a fleet of privateers who, during the Anglo–Dutch War, proved the scourge of the North Sea trade routes, destroying and capturing some 3,000 ships.

Described as a simple but plain-speaking man, Jean Bart married a local innkeeper's daughter, had a son, François, and by the end of the war was Dunkirk's most celebrated privateer. Unlike lawless pirates, privateers were granted 'letters patent' from the monarch – much like Sir Francis Drake in Elizabethan England – allowing them legitimately to harass warships and merchant vessels. He died in 1702 and is buried in the church of St-Éloi.

Some 30 French Navy ships have since borne the name of Jean Bart. In World War II his statue was spared from destruction by the occupying Germans. This was due, so the story goes, to his sword-waving defiance of the English by whom he was once taken prisoner – and from whom he promptly escaped!

the Germans in 1946 as part of war reparations. After large-scale restoration it was opened in 2001 to the public, who now have a unique chance to explore the primitive conditions of the crew compared with the captain's quarters, and to gawp at the web of ropes, masts, yards and shrouds needed to sail such a magnificent vessel.

Others exhibits include the *Sandette* (1949), the last French light-ship, and the *Guilde* (1929), which demonstrates the important role played by barges.

Within walking distance of the quay is the **Fine Arts Museum** (*Musée des Beaux Arts, pl de Général de Gaulle;* \ *03 28 59 21 65;* e *musees@ville-dunkerque.fr;* ⊕ *10.00–12.15 & 14.00–18.00 daily except Tue & public holidays; adult/students €4.50/1.50, children free*). Founded in the 19th century, the museum features important Flemish, Dutch, French and Italian paintings and sculptures from the 14th to the 20th centuries. Works include those by Synders, Jean de Reyn and Van Dyk, as well as Corot – his painting *A Dune at Dunkirk* is here – and Vernet and Carrier-Belleuse. The modern art gallery, with exhibits dating from 1950, includes works by Cesar, Arman and Hartung.

One room, dedicated to Jean Bart, contains a 17th-century moneybox in the shape of a chained captive; it once held money to buy back slaves. Look out, too, for a death mask of James II, the English king who died in 1701 after living in exile in France. The mask wears a lace bonnet made by nuns from an English convent that once stood close by. The basement contains a collection of butterflies, birds, insects and minerals.

Other sights include **LAAC** (*Lieu d'Art et d'Action Contemporaine, Pont Lucien;* ⊕ *14.00–17.30 Tue & Fri, 14.00–20.30 Thu, 10.00–12.30 & 14.00–17.30 Sat–Sun mid-Sep–mid-May & 1hr later Sat–Sun mid-May–mid-Sep*), a modern art and sculpture

Coastal Country **DUNKIRK**

4

It began as a lively feast before the 19th-century *visscherbende* ('groups of fishermen' in Flemish) set off to catch cod in the freezing Icelandic waters. Now the Dunkirk Carnival is one of the most popular in northern France. It's held for several winter weeks with Shrove Tuesday as the highpoint, but be warned: the celebrations are not so much a money-spinning tourist attraction as a simple way of symbolising the soul of Dunkirk. This means merry-making revolves round local fishing lore and games in which teams from Dunkirk and the surrounding villages take part. Street theatre plays a strong role, though performances which incorporate sea shanties and stirring tales of Jean Bart are often lost on bewildered visitors. So brush up your French, and Flemish, before joining this joyous private party.

garden which brings together works from 1950 onwards, including those of Andy Warhol. **St-Éloi Church** (*12 rue Clemenceau*), badly damaged in both world wars, is where Jean Bart is buried. In the same road is the **town hall** in which an equestrian statue of Louis XIV recalls the return of Dunkirk to France. The **lighthouse**, at 55m, is the highest building of its kind in France. **Harbour tours** (*daily in the summer at 14.30 & 16.00 plus 15.00 in Jul & Aug; for other months consult the tourist office; adult/child aged 3–12 €8.50/6.50*).

Golf Particularly popular with the Brits is **Dunkerque Golf Club** (*Coudekerque-Village;* ✆ *03 28 61 07 43; www.golf-dk.com*). The Le Vauban 6,579m 18-hole course was built in the early 1990s, with the French architect Robert Berthet invited back in 2006 to create a further nine holes for the Le Fort-Vallières course (2,966m). The course is often windswept, so you need to know your shots. Other distractions include superb views of the Flemish countryside, the water features on many holes and, above all, the nine 'fortified' holes, based on the designs of Vauban, the military mastermind behind Dunkirk's own fortifications. Advance booking recommended; look out for special deals. Many golfers view the course as a contrasting challenge to those at Le Touquet (see page 117).

Beaches Getting to Dunkirk's beaches can be confusing. Dunkirk is a sprawling town, with numerous suburbs. The best bet is to catch a bus or to follow the signs, via the avenue Faidherbe, to **Malo-les-Bains**, 3km east of the city centre (*Malo-les-Bains tourist information office; 48 digue de Mer;* ✆ *03 28 58 10 10;* e *eole.dunesdeflandre@ot-dunkerque.fr;* ⊕ *mid-Jun–mid-Sep 10.00–12.30 & 14.00–18.00*). A once-fashionable 19th-century resort, Malo-les-Bains still retains a family ambience. Its 7km of sloping beaches dotted with beach huts stretch to the Belgian border. The Digue des Alliés beachfront bristles with cafés and seafood restaurants; drop in for a giant bowl of mussels and fries at **Le Bistro de la Plage** (✆ *03 28 65 01 11; $$$*). A less cluttered seafront, but lying in the industrial shadow to the west, is Digue de Mer.

While their delights may now seem old-hat, the beaches' blustery charms – and boy, can it blow – suit the current vogue for surfing, sand-yachting and similar adrenaline-driven pursuits, especially in off-season autumn. There are also special areas for sand and beach volleyball.

On the western end of the linking promenade, perfect for a slow sunny-day saunter, is a monument commemorating the soldiers who fought on until 4 June 1940 and the 250 boats destroyed in the evacuation of Dunkirk. Beyond Malo-les-Bains in the residential roads that pan out from the coastal drag are a few remaining grand villas reminiscent of the resort's Belle Epoque heyday. Excellent patisseries, *boulangeries* and charcuteries are a feature of avenue Faidherbe and avenue Kléber, with place Turenne, a shady green square, squeezed in between them.

From Malo-les-Bains, and 6km from Dunkirk, the Flanders Dunes drift languidly along the coast to **Leffrinckouke**, where around 100 Allied soldiers were killed during Operation Dynamo and eight members of the local resistance were executed in September 1944. **Fort des Dunes**, built between 1878 and 1880 and occupied by the Germans during World War II, was restored and reopened to the public in 1988. There are unspecified guided visits on Saturday and Sunday afternoons during July and August; ask at the tourist office for times.

Less than 5km on, **Zuydcoote** was the setting for a film based on the award-winning novel by Robert Merle, *Week-end à Zuydcoote*, which provides a harrowingly realistic portrayal of the evacuation of Dunkirk.

Finally, 20km northeast of Dunkirk and 2.8km from Zuydcoote lies **Bray-Dunes**. It is famous today for its 5km beach, which is particularly favoured for sand yachting. Seaside villas act as a reminder that this was an important 19th-century resort which, by 1928, was enjoying a property boom. It is here that the Côte d'Opale ends, sliding rather unceremoniously into Belgium, with the border marked both on the beach and in town. If you miss both, a large 225ha camping site, **Le Perroquet** (*rue des Dunes;* ↘ *03 28 58 37 37;* e *contact@campingleperroquet; www.campingleperroquet; adult/children €5/2.50 per night*), shares the border.

Bray-Dunes, unusually for French towns, has its own flag. This is made of three horizontal blue, yellow and green stripes, which probably stand for the sky, the sand and the surrounding land.

Close to the beach A short distance from Bray-Dunes, and 12km east of Dunkirk (*off the A16 near junctions 34 & 35*), **Ghyvelde** is home to **Bommelaers Wall Ecomuseum** (*20 route de Furnes, opposite the dunes factory;* ↘ *03 28 20 11 03;* ⊕ *Apr–Oct 10.00–18.00 Mon–Sat & 14.00–18.00 Sun & public holidays; adult/child over 12 €5/3, children 4–12 free*), housed in the 18th-century barns of an arable farm. The museum tells the history of farming of the Franco-Flemish coast in a highly entertaining way, even for non-French speakers. There is both a Flemish farm kitchen and surgery and even a reconstructed schoolroom. Old photos add an air of authenticity; so, too, do a selection of traditional bar games.

AROUND DUNKIRK

BERGUES You could easily be excused for calling this sleepy market town – whose official name is Bergues Saint-Winoc – the other Bruges. Lying 9km southeast of Dunkirk, its canals, bridges, cobbled streets and gates give an air of picture-postcard perfection. This has paid off handsomely – especially since the town was chosen as the setting for *Bienvenue Chez les Ch'tis*, a French comedy which in France has outstripped *Titantic* in ticket sales. Tourist figures, already healthy, have quadrupled since the film came out in 2008 while the number visiting the magnificent belfry has climbed from around 1,000 to 36,000 in one year.

You don't have to see the film to appreciate why French comedy star and director Dany Boon saw the chance to explode the image of Nord-Pas de Calais as an industrial rain-soaked wasteland stuck in the sticks. Even a trundle round town in the tourist tram quickly paints a different picture.

Tourist information

🏛 **Office de Tourisme** pl de la République (also called pl Henri Billiaert); ↘ 03 28 68 71 06; e tourisme@bergues.fr; www.bergues-tourisme.fr;

⊕ Nov–Mar 10.00–12.00 & 14.00–18.00 Mon–Sat, Apr–Oct 10.00–12.00 & 14.00–18.00 Mon–Sat, 10.00–13.00 & 15.00–18.00 Sun & public holidays

⌂ Where to stay

⌂ **De Vast Brug** (2 rooms) 10 quai Maçons; ☏ 03 28 20 70 08; www.devastbrug.com. If you want a cosy atmosphere, with the chance to unwind with a coffee, or local beer, in front of the fire, then look no further. This short-break B&B, run by the genial Mme Wolniick, is a home-from-home in a historic townhouse close to the town centre & the market. $$$

⌂ **Hotel le Tonnelier** (25 rooms inc 1 for disabled) 4 rue du Mont Piété; ☏ 03 28 68 70 05; www.autonelier.com. A friendly 2-star hotel, already known to many Brits. There is a convivial bar serving local beers & a restaurant, open for lunch & dinner, featuring Flemish-style dishes. Try the Welcome to the Sticks menu, which includes meatballs & sugar pie! HB available. B/fast is served in your room. $$$

✗ Where to eat

✗ **La Taverne du Bruegel** 1 marché aux Fromages; ☏ 03 28 68 19 19; www.lebruegel.fr; ⊕ 12.15–14.00 & 19.15–22.00. Constructed in 1597, this is one of the oldest buildings in town. Not surprisingly, it's heavily Flemish both in cuisine & décor with long wooden tables & even costumed staff. Slightly kitsch, perhaps, but all very jolly & with hearty meals to match. Choose between a 2-course lunch & dinner Mon–Sat (€13.50), or 3 courses including the ubiquitous *carbonade Flemish* (beef stew) or *potjevlesch* (a combination of white meats); avoid, suggests one otherwise satisfied customer, the steak spoiled by a somewhat chewy cheese. There's a €7.20 menu for the children. Do try the local beers. They go far better with the Flemish food than those softy southern wines! $$$

What to see and do There are many ways to explore Bergues and its surroundings, either on foot or by car, depending on time and specific interests. Some sites cannot be ignored, of which the 54m sand-coloured brick built **belfry** (⊕ *10.00–11.30 & 14.00–17.30 Mon–Sat, 10.00–12.30 Sun & public holidays & 15.00–17.30 Mar–Oct*) is the most obvious. Home to the tourist office, it was built in 1112, and was twice destroyed – first by the French and secondly, after being rebuilt in the 19th century, by the Germans who blew it up in 1944. Restored in 1961, the belfry, with 193 steps to the top of the tower, is now classified as a World Heritage Site by UNESCO.

Nine of the bells automatically chime every quarter of an hour, except at 11.00 during the Monday market when Jacques Martel, who doubles up as tourist director and official bell-ringer, hurries off to provide a concert on the full carillon of 50 bells. This is played by striking a keyboard called a 'baton' with the fists and by pressing the keys of a pedal keyboard with the feet, thus allowing the *carillonneur* to vary the volume of the note according to the force applied.

Another must-see is the **Town Museum** (*Museé de Bergues, 1 rue du Mont Piété;* ☏ *03 28 68 13 30;* ⊕ *mid-Apr–Oct 10.00–12.00 & 14.00–17.00 daily except Tue, Jul–Aug 10.00–12.00 & 14.00–18.00; adult/child under 14 €3.90/1.30*). Works include *Le vielleur au chien*, a delightful canvas of a hurdy-gurdy player and dog by Georges de la Tour, along with fine collections of Flemish and Italian paintings. Most of these works came from St Winoc's Abbey, the ancient Benedictine abbey perched on the hill of St-Winoc Bergues that gave the town its name. There are also works by Jan de Rey, a pupil of Van Dyck, and Mathieu, from the school of Dunkirk painters. The ornate 17th-century Baroque building was originally conceived as a state-controlled pawnshop to help the poor.

From here you are virtually lost for choice among Bergues's centuries-old jumble of pilasters and yellow-brick façades, strange sculpted heads and faces (*mascarons*), anchors, small chapel windows, holy statues and huge chimneys on red-tiled roofs.

For starters head for the **town hall**, on place de la République, a scaled-down version of the grandiose pile that stood from the 17th to the end of the 19th century when it was dismantled. This at least provides a central point from which to explore, either through a guided tour from the tourist office or simply by going with the flow.

Let the walls, the bare bones of history – from Flemish, Burgundian, Austrian, Spanish and finally French occupations – set the scene. Likewise the streets, where the Marchés aux Chevaux, aux Fromages and aux Poissons, lend reminders that the surrounding flat marshlands provided rich pastures for medieval farmer monks who took their goods to market – markets whose successors are still well stocked with local products. Cafés, restaurants and specialist shops reflect life today, with the underwear in **La Lingerie** in place Gambetta receiving special attention for its role in *Bienvenue Chez les Ch'tis*. Other locations also played their part, including the canal side where the drunken stars enjoyed a welcome pee. This will no doubt go down in history too…

Beyond Bergues At **Quaëdypre**, or Bad Elm, one of a spiderweb of 11 villages best reached off the E42/A25 (Lille direction), look out for the graves topped by skulls and crossed bones at the 16th-century St-Sylvestre Church; they were used to show death in an explicit way. Then head for **Socx** and on to **Bissezeele**, one of the first flower villages (*villages fleuris*) in the area (see page 49).

HONDSCHOOTE On the Belgian border, just 10km from Bergues via the D916/916A and D110, Hondschoote epitomises the Flemish rural scene with gabled houses, canals and windmills.

Tourist information

🛈 **Tourist Information Office au Pays du Lin (Land of Linen)** 5 pl de Gaulle, Hondschoote; ☎ 03 28 62 53 00; www.otpaysdulin.over-blog.fr (in French only); ⊕ 10.00–12.30 & 14.00–17.30 Tue–Fri, 10.00–12.00 & 14.00–16.00 Sat Jun–Aug & 10.00–12.00 Sat Sep–May

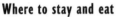

Where to stay and eat

🏠 **La Meunerie Hotel & Restaurant** (9 rooms & studio flat) 174 rue des Pierres, Teteghem; ☎ 03 28 26 1439; e contact@lameunerie; www.lameunerie.fr. 5mins from the A16/exit 63 or a 10-min drive from either Dunkirk or Bergues, this is handy for the whole area. Located on a bend in the road with a somewhat unprepossessing exterior but with a pretty garden, this is a beautifully appointed hotel built on the site of a 19th-century steam mill. It has a range of individually themed rooms & a gourmet restaurant. A €54 menu includes a glass of wine to complement each course. Special packages are available to include meals for FB, gourmand & golf w/ends. **$$$$**

For a handy half-way lunchtime, or even an overnight, stop, turn off for the D110 from Hondschoote for Warhem and **Ferme Auberge de la Becque** (*2 rooms; 520 rue Est;* ☎ *03 28 62 05 01; www.bievenue-a-la-ferme.com;* **$$$**). It has a rustic setting with great Flemish farmhouse dishes. The €25 menu includes chicken terrine with juniper, guinea fowl and homemade pies. Book in advance.

What to see and do The **Moulin Noord-Meulen**, on rue Coppens, is said to be the oldest windmill in Europe, its foundations dating back to 1127. The surrounding area is also known as Au Pays du Lin (In the Land of Linen) as the soil is particularly well suited to the traditional crop of flax. The small blue flowers in bloom are an enchanting sight should you have the good fortune to see them – sown in March, they apparently last for just a day. These days the flax is sent to China for processing and weaving into linen as all the local workshops have closed. However, there are linen items for sale at **Le Grenier du Lin** (*1101 Chemin de Roesbrugge;* ☎ *03 28 62 64 61; e vvr@legrenierdulin.fr; www.blog.legrenierdulin.com;* ⊕ *14.00–18.00 Mon, 10.00–12.00 & 14.00–18.00 Tue–Sat*). Signposted down a series of small lanes, the showroom is housed in an atmospheric old granary. Apart from clothes for men, women and children, there are household goods and linen by the metre (not cheap but worth bringing measurements from home); craft items, organic soaps and unusual jewellery also feature.

GRAVELINES You could be forgiven for thinking of Gravelines as another suburban backwater as you turn off the A16 (*exit 52/53 if coming from Dunkirk or exit 51 from Calais*). The town centre proves otherwise with the Friday open-air market adding a sparkling French frisson. So, too, do the fortfications which are so well embedded that you forget that this pleasant town, 16km southwest of Dunkirk, developed from being a major 16th-century stronghold to a triple fortress designed in his familiar star-shape by Vauban, Louis XIV's military mastermind (see page 12). In 1950 Gravelines was awarded the Croix de Guerre for the part it played in the evacuation of Dunkirk.

Tourist information

🛈 **Office de Tourisme Gravelines** les Rives de l'Aa, 11 rue de la République; ☏ 03 28 51 94 00; e gravelines.cote.opale@wanadoo.fr; www.tourisme-gravelines.fr; ⊕ Apr–May 09.00–12.00 & 14.00–18.00 Mon–Sat, 10.00–13.00 Sun & public holidays, Jun–Sep 09.00–12.30 & 14.00–18.00 Mon–Sat, 10.00–13.00 Sun & public holidays,

Oct–Mar 14.00–18.00 Mon, 09.00–12.00 & 14.00–18.00 Tue–Sat. A tourist pass, reviewed annually, provides free or reduced fees to a number of sites & activities; dining out family offers are also available. Allow around €7.50 or €15 for family pass, but check current price with tourist office.

Where to stay

🏠 **Hostellerie du Beffroi** (24 dbl, 10 twin, 6 sgl) 2 pl Charles Valentin; ☏ 03 28 23 24 25; e contact.hoteldubeffroi@wanadoo.fr; www.hoteldubeffroi.com. Located centrally in the main market square, the Best Western hotel ticks the boxes in terms of comfort & convenience. It's a good place to enjoy a beer & people watch from

the covered terrace. Unpretentious traditional cuisine (€16–40), with a handy €12.70 lunch, is served in the adjacent but rather plain restaurant; closed for Sat lunch/Sun dinner. A €9.15 b/fast is served. Parking is allowed in the square, but kept clear on Thu night ready for the Fri market at 07.00; this means other nearby streets are likewise busy. $$$

Where to eat

✕ **Restaurant le Turbot** 26 rue de Dunkerque; ☏ 03 28 23 08 54; www.leturbot.com; ⊕ 12.00–14.00 except Sun & 18.00–21.00 except Thu, closed Mon. A reliable & often busy 50-seater restaurant conveniently close to the town centre. Specialities

include turbot with creamed leeks, coquille St Jacques, duck foie gras seared with calvados & fillets of sole with champagne. Menus €16–31 with à la carte dishes from €18 $$$$

What to see and do Gravelines has more relics than you can shake a shovel at. One option for viewing them is to take a map and rent an English-language audio-guide from the tourist office (€4). Allow between 90 minutes and two hours for this self-guided tour. Less daunting is the audio-visual version provided by the splendid **Museum of Gravelines** (*Museé de Gravelines, Château de Gravelines Arsenal;* ☏ *03 28 51 81 00;* e *conservation.musee@ville-gravelines.fr; www.ville-gravelines.fr;* ⊕ *Sep–Jun 14.00–17.00 Mon–Fri, 15.00–18.00 w/end & public holidays, Jul–Aug 14.00–18.00 Mon–Fri, 10.00–12.00 & 15.00–18.00 w/end & public holidays, closed Tue; adult/under 18 €2/free*), commonly known as the Arsenal. The five historical halls include an interactive terminal that allows visitors to hone in on ten virtual itineraries; a complementary scale model of the town, with trees sculpted in ironwork and silk, helps you pick your preference. The halls are housed in the so-called Château, which Charles Quint started to build in 1528. It was later revamped and restored at the end of the 20th century.

In 1985, Christian Cardin, an amateur underwater historian, was diving off the coast of Cherbourg when he discovered six 17th-century ships wrecked and lying on the seabed. The discovery sparked an idea: Cardin would reconstruct a full-scale version of a Louis XIV man-of-war armed with 84 cannons. And what would he call the vessel? *Jean Bart*, of course, after the Sun King's all-time favourite privateer/buccaneer (see page 79). By 1991 Cardin had launched The Tourville Association, and construction of the ship started the following year. Work continues today on the 57m vessel at the **boatyard site** (*rue de Calais;* ✆ *03 28 21 22 40; www.tourville.asso.fr;* ☉ *14.00–17.00 Mon, 10.00–12.00 & 14.00–17.00 Tue–Fri, 10.00–12.00 Sat; adult/child €6/3, under 6 free*).

A scale model of the ship can also be seen at the **Port Royale Museum** in the former powder store of the Arsenal (see opposite). This relives the swashbuckling days of buccaneers and great sea battles while model sheep, pigs and poultry illustrate how on-board animals helped provide fresh food. The opening hours and entrance fee listed above cover both attractions, which are three minutes by car or a 15-minute walk from each other.

There is also an excellent printmaking exhibition beneath the arched brick roof of the Arsenal's 18th-century powder store. This shows techniques used for reproduction, from wood cuts to silk screen printing and lithography. Prints on show include some by Goya and Piccaso. It's well worth a rainy-day visit for the family.

Close by, in the gardens, are contemporary bronze sculptures, including works by Charles Gadenne from Roubaix, close to Lille (see page 232). You can't miss *The Conversation*, depicting a group of five gossiping women.

Petit-Fort-Philippe and Grand-Fort-Philippe

Gravelines's seaside resort of **Petit-Fort-Philippe** lies 2km northwest at the mouth of the River Aa. During Napoleon's trade blockade on the English, goods became so scarce for both sides that France allowed *smogglers* to operate, leaving the village to become a sort of semi-official smuggling centre. The blockade was lifted in 1812, but not until the Brits had paid a hefty duty for the privilege.

Street names reveal the port's fishing heritage: rues du Cabillaud (cod), Merlan (whiting) and Saumon (salmon) are among them. The **lighthouse** (☉ *peak season except Mon; adult/child aged 8–12 €1.50/1*), with 104 steps, is another example. It was painted white when it was built in 1843, but a stripe was added in 1931 to make it stand out against the cloudy sky.

The North Sea-facing beach is great for kids but, remember, low tide means a long walk across the sands. Nautical activities include sailing and windsurfing. To the east lies a nuclear power station, one of Europe's biggest, supplying power to England just across the Channel. Part of the warm process water is used for hatching bass and sea bream.

To save any back-tracking, use the *canote*, a free ferry, to cross to **Grand-Fort-Philippe** on the other side of the River Aa. Times depend on the tides. Boat trips and fishing in the Aa, sea-fishing, tennis and **Sportica** (*pl du Polder;* ✆ *03 28 65 35 00; www.sportica.fr;* ☉ *daily, see website for times*), whose attractions include a swimming pool, bowling alley and cinema, all add interest to this under-rated resort.

There is no beach as such, but do drop in at **The Smokery** (*Saurisserie, 20 rue Félix Faure;* ✆ *03 28 65 34 05;* e *nathaliedutriaux@wanadoo.fr;* ☉ *09.00–12.00 &*

14.00–18.00 daily; free guided tours by arrangement). In an era when an original flotilla of 140 local fishing boats has been reduced to one, this family-run business may appear an anachronism. But it has been thriving since 1888, with Nathalie Dutriaux as keen to carry on the family tradition as her father Charles was before her. She has even gone one step further by opening an *estaminet* (bar-cum-restaurant; see page 40) specialising in fish dishes a few doors away, a perfect foil to the huge range of smoked products on sale at The Smokery. These may no longer feature the herring catch of yesteryear, but extend to salmon, mackerel and halibut, which arrive freshly packed from Iceland and Norway.

The smoking process, using sawdust from beeches, is still very much in line with that employed by the original *saurisseries* for which the fishing port became famous. There are still a few other smokeries operating today – some even older than the Dutriaux smokery – but they work on an industrial basis only; the Dutriaux smokery is now the only one open to the public.

Grand-Fort-Phillipe also has two museums. Built where the old fishing school stood, **The House of the Sea** (*Maison de la Mer, bld Carnot;* ↘ *03 28 23 98 39;* ☼ *Apr–Jun 14.00–17.00 Wed & Sat, 15.00–18.00 Sun, Jul–Aug 14.00–17.00 Mon, Wed–Thur & Sat, 15.00–18.00 Sun & school holidays; adult/child under 12 €2/free*) helps safeguard maritime traditions. Model fishing boats, newspaper clippings, photos, bells, payroll and paintings are all part of the package.

The House of Rescue (*Maison de la Mer, bd de la République;* ↘ *03 28 23 10 12;* ☼ *14.00–18.00 Mon–Sat & 15.00–18.00 Sun & public holidays, closed Tue, Easter Sun–mid-Sep; adult/child under 12 with parent €10/free for both museums*) concentrates on rescues at sea. Jutting out into the Channel, the brick-built former lifeboat centre, with its stepped gables, spans the work of the volunteer crews as well as the dangers of deep-sea cod-fishing expeditions to the stormy waters off Iceland.

Further references to the fishermen who once spent six months of each year catching cod off the Icelandic coast (often taking along a 12-year-old ship's boy as one of their crew) can be found elsewhere in Gravelines, including The Icelanders' Walk. This refers to the nickname 'Icelanders' given to those who fished in the region between 1830 and 1938.

SURROUNDING DISTRICTS Gravelines is one of seven districts on the banks of the Aa. Strung along the Cote d'Opale between Dunkirk and Calais, they are known collectively as the Rives de l'Aa. Of these **Oye-Plage**, whose wild beach stretches over 10km, is the only one located in Pas de Calais. In 879 invading Vikings used it as an island, sheltering here during the high spring tides.

Look out in Oye-Plage for **La Tour Penchée** (The Leaning Tower), built in 1942 to fool Allied pilots into believing that it was the Loon-Plage church further along the coast. In 1944 the retreating Germans made a hash of blowing it up, leaving the tower leaning sideways at about 20 degrees.

The small town has a few other historical points of interest. Its former castle hosted a peace conference between France and England in 1439. Its church was dedicated to Saint-Médard, and contains the remains of many English killed during the siege of Calais of 1346, and the dead of the French army killed while taking Calais at the Battle of Gravelines. The church tower was originally built by the English in 1523 during the reign of Mary Tudor; it was restored in 1953.

Though heavily bombed in World War II **Loon-Plage** is now rated as a four-flower town for its blooms; it is also home to the Tourelles Park and the Galamé wooded area, which are worth a visit. Also lying on the coast side of the A16 is **St-Georges-sur-l'Aa**. The village church features a massive square tower dating back to the 14th century; not far away at 88 Route de Gravelines is a café-theatre, formerly a farm.

You don't need to be a keen twitcher to enjoy a few hours exploring Oye-Plage nature reserve (*from Grand-Fort-Philippe follow route des Dunes which runs parallel to the D119; from Calais take the A16 Dunkirk direction & turn off at exit 49; look out for the extended visitor centre, Maison dans la Dune, which is easily missed in the maze of tiny lanes that lace the windswept dunes;* ✆ *03 28 51 94 00/03 21 82 65 50, groups* ✆ *03 21 36 13 82; English-language pamphlets are available*), 400ha of dunes that were set aside in 1987 for the preservation of the natural ecosystem.

So what's to see? There are some 250 species of migratory birds including little egret, oystercatcher and shelduck; also wild roses and *argousier* (sea buckthorn) whose berries contain 30 times more vitamin C than oranges and are used for making cordial and jam. Children will love the flocks of geese and ducks, as well as the bizarre sight of wild Scottish highland cattle which, along with selected breeds of horses and sheep, are used to mow the meadows in a natural way. Guided tours (*first Sun of each month 09.00–12.00, €3/free for children*) not only let you get your bearings, but take in the main viewpoints including a colony of little terns and the main feeding grounds – which the wardens nickname the 'bird supermarket'.

Craywick (The Raven's Spot), the final Aa district, dates back to the 12th century and is known for its peculiar shape – the commune spreads over 7km in length but is only 700m wide. It is framed by two ditches, from Loon-Plage in the north and Bourborg in the south.

Bourbourg Lying to the north of the motorway, equidistant inland from Dunkirk and Calais (*15km from both on the A16; take exit 52*) the small Aa town of Bourbourg is now a not-to-be-missed destination for anyone interested in contemporary sculpture. This is thanks to the creation of *Le Choeur de Lumiere* (Choir of Light), known as the 'Chapel of Light' in English, by British Sculptor Sir Anthony Caro, which was inaugurated in October 2008 (*Reception Centre, Le Choeur de Lumiere/ The Choir of Light, 1 rue de Dunkerque;* ✆ *03 28 22 01 42; www.lechoeurdelumiere.fr;* ⏰ *09.00–12.00 & 14.00–18.00 Mon–Sat, 10.00–13.00 & 14.00–18.00 Sun & public holidays; guided tours every last Sun of the month at 15.00 €3/children under 12 free; no visits permitted during religious services*). In 1940 a plane crash-landed on the roof of the town's Church of St-Jean-Baptiste; the foundations of which dated from Roman times, the choir from the 13th century, and the nave from the 15th century. Repairs were carried out on the body of the church after World War II, but the ruined choir was bricked up and sealed off – until 2000 when the arts council for Nord-Pas de Calais commissioned Caro to inject new life with sculptural and architectural installations. After years of work, and inevitable controversy, the undamaged arched niches are now filled with steel, wood and terracotta sculptures that depict the theme of The Creation. These include fascinating sea creatures and a large stoneware representation of Adam and Eve entitled *Paradise Garden*. Twin 5.84m oak towers, called *Morning* and *Evening*, house enclosures for meditation and short flights of stairs leading to vantage points from which to view the installations at different levels. The Chapel of Light can be approached through the nave of the church, or through an atmospheric threshold sculpture on the street.

Originally built in 1539 under Spanish rule, the three-storey **18th-century prison** building in Bourbourg's main square includes several dungeons and strongrooms. Above the entrance door is a sundial with the motto: *qua hora non putatis* – 'no-one knows the time'. The old **fishmarket** hall (*halle au poisson*) dates from 1587 and holds a fish market every Tuesday.

Coastal Country **AROUND DUNKIRK**

4

Where to stay

La Villa Blanc Marine (2 rooms) 25 rue Gustave Meesemaecker; ℄ 03 28 62 50 57; e villablancmarine@yahoo.fr; www.villablancmarine.com. An unobtrusive front door opens onto a surprisingly large 18th-century house decorated in Flemish style. There is a nice homely ambience, with reception rooms & bedrooms furnished with antiques. B/fast served in the beautiful garden. A typical Flemish dinner (€12 by pre-arrangement) includes main course, dessert & wine. $$$

From Bourbourg to Sangatte Westwards off the A16 lies Calais and its beach (see *Chapter 3*, page 70). From Calais Plage pick up the D940 to Boulogne; you could alternatively do a quick 20-minute or so dash along the A16, but why miss out on what is arguably the most scenic drive of the Côte d'Opale? First stop is **Blériot-Plage**, a rather sprawling village just off the A16 at junction 43, remembered mainly for the first-ever successful flight across the Channel. This was achieved by French aviator Louis Blériot in 1909, and is marked by a monument near the town centre.

With a smattering of cafés and restaurants centred round the place de la République, the resort is basically a residential town of retirement villas and holiday homes. However, it does have a decent beach with water-skiing and sand-yachting available, while windsurfing and sailing fans are catered for at the **Yacht Club of Calais** (℄ *03 21 97 73 81;* e *elenoir@club.fr; www.calais-voile.fr*). The club has two sites, one at a gravel pit between neighbouring Sangatte and Blériot-Plage, the other on the beach at Blériot-Plage.

Where to stay, eat and drink

Les Dunes Restaurant-Hotel (9 rooms) 48 route Nationale; ℄ 03 21 34 54 30; www.les-dunes.com. Conveniently located near the beach, the hotel has enjoyed mixed, but generally good, reviews. The rooms, though smallish, are comfortable. While restaurant prices rightly reflect the owner's undoubted culinary skills, wine is expensive – so stick to beer in what are attractive surroundings. You are in beer country after all. Look out for special deals. Pets are welcome. Free parking is available. $$$

Sangatte Further down the D940 lies Sangatte, too often remembered as the site of a huge refugee centre. It is, however, a pleasant enough town, identified in the 19th century as the French terminal for a proposed Channel Tunnel. Work actually began, but the project was abandoned in May 1882, when Britain claimed it would compromise its national defence. The existing Channel Tunnel, not that far away at Coquelles, opened in 1994.

At the western end of town, a striking statue to another aviator and popular French adventurer, Hubert Latham, looks almost forlornly across the Channel. He reportedly met his death not flying but at the hands, or rather horns, of a wounded buffalo in Equatorial Africa.

Where to eat

✕ **Le Blanc Nez** 2281 route Nationale, Sangatte; 📞 03 21 82 00 53; www.blancnez-restaurant.com; 🕐 12.00–15.00 & 18.00–21.00 Mon–Thu, 12.00–21.00 Fri–Sat; closed 3 wks mid-Dec–1st week of Jan. This delightfully unpretentious eaterie offers a real sense of being beside the sea. Though the front-of-house tables are quite basic, those at the rear are more formal & brighter. Be warned: the reliable range of 4 set-price menus €15–32 are of generous proportions. $$$

LES DEUX CAPS

Sangatte is also the gateway to **Les Deux Caps**, with the D940 twisting and turning from **Escalles** – an ideal village coffee stop – as it climbs dramatically to the 151m-high white-chalk cliffs of **Cap Blanc-Nez** (White Nose). From here on a clear day you can gaze across the Channel to the corresponding White Cliffs of Dover. A monument to the Dover Patrol, high on the hill, celebrates the co-operation between the French and British navies in World War I. A large parking area and a good network of cliff paths encourage walkers to explore the area (see pages 90–1).

The more southerly **Cap Gris-Nez** (Grey Nose) gets its name from its grey clay and, as the closest point to England, is the arrival point for those brave enough to swim the Channel.

Between them Les Deux Caps help defy the notion that the region is flat and dull. Not only do they simply provide some stunning seascapes in which the distant ferries are reduced to mere model size but they also reflect a rural landscape rich in local produce, including beer (see page 92), fish, meat, cheeses and jams.

Between them, Les Deux Caps encompass some of the prettiest resorts along the Côte d'Opale. **Wissant**, 20km southwest of Calais and hence easily accessible even on a day trip, lies neatly between the two. The 12km stretch of sand (Wissant means 'White Sands') is a natural home to windsurfing, sand-yachting and fly-surfing. Charles de Gaulle was a fan of the resort, as are the French generally, so book in advance at peak season weekends.

Families will love the child-friendly seafront with the usual bars and cafés; the village reached via the parish church is intriguingly French with a winning mixture of small shops, cafés and restaurants. Look out for the sight of a tractor hauling the small open fishing boats, or *flobarts*, onto the beach (see page 99). There is an example of one in the village square where you can also buy fresh fish.

WHERE TO EAT

✕ **Le Thome de Gamond** Mont Hubert, Cap Blanc-Nez, nr Escalles; 📞 03 21 82 32 03; 📧 restaurant@capblancnez.com; www.capblancnez.com; 🕐 12.00–15.30 & 18.00–21.00 daily; closed 3 wks in Jan. Worth a visit for lovely views over the countryside, with food, once variable, now receiving good reports again. Staff is friendly & helpful. Menus €23–30.50, €8 children. $$$

LES DEUX CAPS TO AMBLETEUSE

Audresselles Lying slightly off the D940, Audresselles is probably the most charming stop in terms of picture-postcard prettiness. It's a bit of a detour but this sleepy fishing village is well worth a visit.

Where to eat

✕ **Restaurant Au P'tit Bonheur** 2 rue Jeanne d'Arc, Audresselles; 📞 03 21 83 12 54; www.resto.fr/restaurant/audresselles/au_p'tit_bonheur; 🕐 12.00–15.00 & 18.00–21.00 except Mon & Tue in Jul & Aug. It is advisable to book first for this cosy, if somewhat cramped, family-run restaurant. Its emphasis is on good homespun dishes, mainly fish. A no-nonsense blackboard menu attracts both locals & those there either on recommendation or because they've simply stumbled upon it near the main square. $$$

Ambleteuse   Some 2km further on, *flobarts* are again a feature at Ambleteuse, a quiet seaside resort where fishermen's houses lie alongside decaying villas from the 1900s. Fortified by the Romans, English, French and Germans, it was well placed to protect Boulogne, only 11km away. Henry VIII had two forts built here, while Fort d'Ambleteuse, a sombre building dramatically lashed by the sea, was built to protect the harbour at the estuary of the River Slack. It was modified by Napoleon to create a harbour ready for what proved to be an aborted invasion of England. It later served as a World War II German look-out point. The estuary is now a nature reserve with small explanatory signs marking the reeds, grasses and delicate wild flowers that have colonised the dunes.

   To the north of the village on the D940 or from the A6/exit 36, is the **Historical Museum of the Second World War** (*Musée 39–45: Historique de la Seconde Guerre Mondiale;* ☏ *03 21 87 33 01;* e *musee.39-45@wanadoo.fr; www.musee3945.com;* ⏲ *Apr–Oct 10.00–18.00; Jul & Aug 10.00–19.00; Mar–Nov 10.00–18.00 w/end; closed Dec–Feb; adult/child aged 7–14 €6.50/4.50*). It took 35 years for collectors Denis Barbe and Christophe Deschodt to create this cracker of a museum. Relying solely on glass-fronted showcases – in which tableaux of uniformed waxwork figures appear remarkably human – this chronologically correct collection not just traces the course of the war but takes an impartial look at the roles played by the protagonists. This and the use of thousands of items in the way of uniforms and backdrops, brings the wartime story to a new generation in an understandable and informative way.

CALAIS TO BOULOGNE ON FOOT: 40KM

The route, based on one taken by Kent walker Noel Wills, takes two to three days, depending on which sights you visit. The terrain is fairly flat, with the obvious exceptions of Cap Blanc-Nez and Cap Gris-Nez. Walking on sand, however, can be tough work unless you keep close to the wet sand near the water's edge. Overnight accommodation is available either in small hotels or in campsites. The relevant IGN topo 1:25,000 maps are *2103ET Calais* and *2104ET Boulogne-sur-Mer*, available from Stanfords (*12–14 Long Acre, Covent Garden, London WC2E 9LP;* ☏ *020 7836 1321; www.standfords.co.uk*). These show clifftop paths if you choose to leave the beach. It is essential to check on the times of the tides, obtainable from Admiralty Easytide at http://easytide.ukho.gov.uk.

THE ROUTE *Noel Wills*

Finding your way from the Calais ferry terminal can be the trickiest part. Head for the boulevard des Alliés, turning right when it becomes the boulevard de la Resistance to cross the Bassin Ouest. At the roundabout continue across avenue Raymond Poincare and continue to the next roundabout, turn right and then left into Jetée. You should now be standing on the beach. There is only way to go – west towards Boulogne.

   The fine sand provides good walking, past beach chalets and the remains of concrete World War II bunkers and gun emplacements. These continue until you approach **Cap Blanc-Nez**, visible from some distance and marked with an obelisk commemorating the Dover Patrol which kept the Channel free from U-boats during World War I.

   At **Sangatte** you need to decide, depending on the tide, whether to continue along the beach or take the clifftop path. Provided the tide is starting to recede, it should be safe to continue along the beach to **Wissant**. Steer clear of possible falling stones by not walking too close to the chalk cliffs at **Cap Blanc-Nez**. If the tide is in, or about to come in, take the coast path through the **Dunes du Fort Mahon**, a conservation area west of Sangatte, and across Cap Blanc-Nez until you're able to return to the beach. The ancient fishing village of Wissant is a good refreshment stop on a hot day. From here head along the beach

Take time to stand and stare: look behind the German defences along the Channel coast, the fighter pilots of the Battle of Britain or the often forgotten Pacific War, which dragged on after victory in Europe. Allow time, too, to watch a 40-minute video in a typical 1940s' cinema. It might increase your visit by at least two hours, but it's well worth it. You can't miss the museum: there's a collection of military hardware outside along with a colourful collection of flags.

CAP GRIS-NEZ TO LANDRETHUN-LE-NORD At **Audinghen**, reached via Audresselles but accessed just as quickly from Ambleteuse, lies an ugly gun turret, which housed 21 German soldiers whose job was to pound the coast of Kent with 35m-long cannons. The building and the guns remain, along with German memorabilia at the **Museum of the Atlantic Wall** (*Musée du Mur de L'Atlantique;* ↘ *03 21 32 97 33;* e *musee-audighen@wanadoo.fr; www.battereriedt.com;* ◔ *Feb–May & Sep–Nov 09.00–12.00 & 14.00–17.00 daily, Jul & Aug 09.00–19.00 daily; adult/child aged 8–14 €5.50/2.50*).

In spring 1943 the commune of Landrethun-le-Nord (*7km northeast of Marquise off the A16 at junction 37*) was the site of a secret German installation designed to house the V3 which, unlike the V1 and V2, was a fixed super gun. The plan was to unleash 350 shells a day on London 150km away. Thanks to local information and aerial reconnaissance, Allied bombs put paid to the site before a single rocket was fired.

towards **Cap Gris-Nez**, which is surmounted by an obelisk. The walking here is good, though keep to the water's edge as the soft sand makes for hard going – especially if you wander into the dunes!

If the tide is favourable, stay on the beach until you reach **La Sirène**, possibly stopping here for lunch; alternatively take the clifftop route at Pont de la Coute Dune to La Sirène, another stiff climb, and continue to the top of Cap Gris-Nez for a view of the White Cliffs of Dover on a clear day. A hotel or campsite at La Sirène can provide handy overnight accommodation. (NB: it might be possible to stay on the beach below the Cap if the tide is completely out; however, with boulders on the west side, walking would be time-consuming and hard work.)

You now turn south as you head for Boulogne, following the path to the beach at **Cran-aux-Oeufs**. Then either continue along the path or take to the beach to **Audresselles** (see page 89), a delightful old fishing village with limited accommodation and camping facilities. It lies on the left bank of the estuary of the River Slack whose tendency to silt up eventually ended its strategic role. This still presents a problem as the estuary floods when the tide is in. This means taking a detour via the town – an interesting diversion anyway – to cross the river higher up. If the tide is out, cross from the fort using the groyne. Beware: the exposed boards are slippery when wet. You could, of course, wade across...

Once past the resort of **Ambleteuse**, make for **Wimereux** (see page 97), a family resort with good restaurants. The **Dunes de la Slack** to your left are both towering and tiring, though interesting from a bird-spotting point of view. If pushed for time, you would be well advised to walk at the water's edge.

You are now only 4km from your destination. Continue along the beach towards **Pointe de la Crèche**, which you will see jutting out. If the tide is completely in you may be forced to take the coast path; it depends on just how high the water is. As you approach the corner of the cliff before the Pointe juts out, look for a stairway which takes you to the top. From here take the path south leading to a road. It is now just a short walk downhill into Boulogne!

Coastal Country **LES DEUX CAPS**

4

In 2010 La Coupole (see page 126) took charge of the site, converting it into a museum. The refurbished site will reveal the action of the famous 617 Squadron RAF Bomber Command and his wing commander Leonard Cheshire. Full details were unavailable at the time of writing.

DAY-TRIP COUNTRY

Some of these sights, and resorts, can easily be seen on a day trip to Calais; stay for a longer break and you're spoilt for choice – and not just along the coast but also in the rural surroundings just across the motorway.

NO USE WHINING – BEER'S THE WINNER!

France may be known for fine cheese and wine, but Nord-Pas de Calais is strictly beer country, with the one small wine-producing project near Guines eventually fizzling out. Christophe Noyen's award-winning brewery **Brasserie Artinsanale des 2 Caps** (*Ferme de Belle Dalle, Tardinghen – on the D249 between the D940 & the D238;* ✆ *03 21 10 56 53;* e *noyon.brasseur@wanadoo.fr; www.bieredes2caps.com;* ✆ *for guided tours: Jul & Aug 15.00 Fri, 11.00 Sat; all year for private groups by appointment; €4 or €3.50 for groups, minimum of 15*) promotes the idea of beer complementing certain varieties of cheese (as well as main courses). And in a shrewd move, his four distinctive brands are now sold in conjunction with Phillipe Olivier, whose famous *fromageries* in nearby Boulogne and Lille reflect 100-plus years (and four generations) of producing cheese (see page 103).

Located in delightful rural surroundings at Tardinghen, lying between Cap Gris-Nez and Cap Blanc-Nez, the craft brewery is a throwback to the beginning of the 20th century when there were just over 1,000 breweries in Nord-Pas de Calais, of which seven were based locally.

Nowadays a more scientific approach to beer-making is adopted by Christophe, who originally opened the brewery in 2003 using a Belgian brewer, before investing in his own equipment. Born in 1964, he came from rural stock. His father farmed on the site, and his grandfather, who ran a now-defunct alcohol distillery at nearby Audembert, fuelled his idea for a brewery.

But it was not until Christophe was 37 – after working with the giant Dupont company – that he took an eight-month beer-making course at a Belgian university. Gaining experience with small Belgian breweries, he created his own brands which were brewed first in Belgium to test the market. Now with his own equipment, he uses barley from the farm for his four labels. These include: La 2 Caps (6%), a flavoured pure-malt beer for use as an aperitif or to accompany country-style cooking such as mussels, herrings, poultry or stews; La Blanche de Wissant, at 4.5% a weaker white light beer, brewed with soft winter beer and malted barley, ideal for drinking cold in summer and year round with fish, shrimps and shellfish; La Noire de Slack (5.4%), a black beer made from roasted barley with a slight but distinctive taste – it goes well with smoked fish (it is exported to the Danes), oysters and red meat dishes. Finally La Belle Dalle, bearing the farm's own mark, rates 8%. A high-quality single-malt limited-vintage beer with a unique recipe and brewing method, it is ideal as an aperitif or after-dinner drink and goes well with cheeses, including the ubiquitous Maroilles (see page 216). This can be stored as an investment in a light-free cellar with the vintage recognised in much the same way as wine.

Christophe's guided tours provide not just the taste – literally at the end of the visit – but an insight into the character of the Deux Caps countryside.

Henry VIII not only brought along his favourite tipple, Hyprocas, to Guînes but also filled two pillars of his castle with the fortified wine so that his courtiers might enjoy it at will. But it needs drinking in moderation. Look carefully at the giant portrait in the Clocktower: you'll see one self-indulgent drinker is a little the worse for wear. Buy a bottle of Hypocras, or Hipocras in English, at the shop. Basically a mixture of white or red wine, sugar or honey, cinnamon, ginger, spices and black pepper, it makes a tasty souvenir.

GUÎNES Guînes is a good example of day-trip territory – it is less than half an hour's drive from the Calais ferry port, closer still from the Channel Tunnel. This is rural France all dressed up in its toy-town prettiness.

Don't miss the highly imaginative interpretive centre at the **Clocktower** (*La Tour de l'Horlage; rue de Château;* ✆ *03 21 19 59 00;* e *tour-horlage@wanadoo.fr; www.tour-horlage-guines.com;* ⊕ *Jul–Aug 10.30–18.30 daily, Apr–mid-Sep 14.00–18.00 Sun–Fri & on Saints Days & during Feb & Oct school holidays, times can vary annually so call ahead; adult/child aged 5–16 €6/3.50*). Though hardly 21st-century high-tech, the presentation of the town's history is pure joy. One moment you are sitting in a recreated *drakkar* (a Viking longboat) gently swaying while watching a 15-minute film on how a conquering Dane called Sifrid helped create the town's fenced mound and double ditch. The next you are an onlooker as a multi-media presentation focuses on The Field of the Cloth of Gold held over 7–24 June 1520. Swivelling figures represent England's Henry VIII and France's François I whose bids to outshine each other virtually bankrupted their respective countries. The aim was to forge a military alliance to outwit the Holy Roman Emperor Charles V, or Charles Quint, as the French know him, but nothing came of it other than the chance for each of the then-young kings to show off their sporting prowess. Henry also pitched his own palace of glass and wood, which was specially shipped across. This is best illustrated through an enormous painting hung in the centre.

The actual site was diplomatically sited mid-way between French-held Ardres (see page 94) and English-held Guînes. A plinth stuck alongside the D231 2km southeast of Guînes is all that marks the spot. Far better, then, to let events unfold inside the centre, during which you learn that François's wife had once been engaged to Charles V who, in turn, was the nephew of Henry VIII's wife Catherine of Aragon. Presented in a far from stuffy manner, it sheds light on the strong links the region has with its cross-Channel English counterpart.

Kids will love rummaging through drawers and opening flaps, each revealing some new nugget of historic interest; there's brass-rubbing, too, and a chance to finger fabrics of the time. You can even play traditional games, or try on chainmail, an offer the author could not resist. It's a touch-and-try-for-yourself philosophy that pays off well.

A similar 'living museum' approach applies to the marshland setting of **Saint-Joseph Village** (*2450 1er 'Le Marais;* ✆ *03 21 35 64 05;* e *e.baclez.stjo@wanadoo.fr; www.st-joseph-village.com;* ⊕ *Feb–mid-Nov 10.00–18.00 Sat–Sun & Tue–Thu, closed Mon & Fri; w/ends only mid-Nov–Feb but dates can change so call ahead; adult/child aged 7–16 €10/5, other discounts available*). This bewildering array of 20th-century memorabilia has been brought together by businessman Daniel Beclez, who began by building a small wooden chapel in memory of his late father. Now the 'village', run by his son, provides a blast from the past, with sized-down shops including a pre-1950s grocery store whose shelves are stuffed with some still-familiar names, a garage and a clockmaker's shop sporting a range of genuine tools. There is also a bike shop, a real find for cyclists – as indeed for all those for whom the 1950s have not yet become the dust of history.

Allow a good two to three hours: it's a real family fun day out. The children will enjoy setting the small-scale windmill in motion, the fairground or peeping behind the scenes of an old school. Saint-Joseph Village also has its own *estaminet* (bar-cum-restaurant: see page 40) a handy introduction to the specialities of the region – of which *potjevlesch* (basically white meats in aspic) and *carbonade flamande* (beef braised in beer with onion and spices) are just two. Allow from €12 or €8 for a child's menu.

Lying between Guînes and Ardres (see below), **Guînes Forest** is laced with cycling and hiking trails. Extending some 785ha, and densely covered with oak, beech, hornbeam and birch, it is also home to **Passion d'Adventure** (*signposted off D231 3km southeast of Guînes;* ✆ *03 21 25 15 53; www.passiondaventure.com;* ⊙ *Mar–Nov 09.30–19.30 Wed–Mon, Jul–Aug 09.30–19.30 daily; €23 for 2–3hrs of activities, family & other discounts available*). Wannabe Tarzans of ten years old or more will love the treetop trail; bridges and swinging logs are strung out among the branches ranging 4–15m above ground. Colour-coded flyways, from easy to extreme, feature a 120m-zip line. A nine-hole mini golf course caters for those preferring to keep their feet on the ground. Bike rental is available.

Guînes is part of Les Trois Pays which also includes Licques, famous for its turkey festival (see opposite).

Tourist information

🇮 **Office de Tourisme des 3 Pays** 14 rue Clemenceau Guînes; ✆ 03 21 35 73 73; www.tourisme-3pays.fr; ⊙ Oct–Mar 10.00–12.30 & 14.00–17.00 Mon–Fri, Apr–Sep 09.30–12.30 & 14.00–18.00 Mon–Fri, 10.00–13.00 Sat, Jul–Aug 09.30–18.00 Mon–Fri

ARDRES With its outskirts of lime trees and parkland Ardres, 11km from Guînes via the D231, is natural day-trip territory. Criss-crossed by roads and only 14km southeast of Calais, it offers an instant image of a French market town, complete with cobbled streets and a respectable clutch of ancient buildings.

History Way back in 1060 Arnoul d'Ardres, whose son fought with William the Conqueror, founded the market which is still held each Thursday. Ardres quickly became, along with Guînes and Licques, one of the three towns known as the Les Trois Pays. As the first town in the French king's land, it retained a rich and vibrant history as a military and trading post for the English from 1347 to 1558. François I stayed here and later Louis XIV came here twice.

Tourist information

🇮 **Office de Tourisme** Chapelle des Carmes, pl d'Armes; ✆ 03 21 35 28 51; e ardres.officedetourisme@wanadoo.fr; www.ardres-tourisme.fr; ⊙ 2 May–30 Sep 10.00–12.30 & 15.00–18.00 Tue–Fri, 10.00–12.30 & 15.00–17.00 Sat, 10.00–12.30 Sun, 1 Oct–1 May 10.00–12.30 & 15.00–17.00 Tue–Sat, closed Sat in Jan. An English-language leaflet on the town's history is available.

Where to stay

⌂ **Auberge du Moulin d'Audenfort** (13 rooms) Impasse ford, Audenfort; ✆ 03 21 00 13 16; e catherinecadet3@wanadoo.fr; www.lemoulindaudenfort.com. This highly recommended overnight stop in the tiny hamlet of Audenfort lies off the A26/E15 on the D217 between Tournehem & Licques, or 10km via the D224 from Ardres. Room numbers 7 & 8 overlook the mill race used to channel the water. Short & long distance footpaths begin outside the *auberge*. Take a drink on the veranda before a €24 3-course menu with local specialities (**$$$**). Parking is plentiful. **$$$**

When it comes to talking turkey, the good folk of Licques, which is less than an hour's drive from Calais, are in a league apart. Each year, two weeks before Christmas, the Confrérie de l'Ordre de la Dinde de Licques (Fellows of the Order of the Licques Turkey) hold a three-day weekend festival, the Fête de la Dinde, devoted to this bastion of festive fowl. And be it fine or, dare we say it, foul, the small community of some 1,500 souls swells to several thousand who, flushed with Christmas spirit, bring a genuine glow to the seasonal festivities.

Feel free to join in: the rip-roaring slice of rural tradition starts in earnest on Sunday morning with free cups of steaming hot turkey soup ladled from a monster cauldron heated by an open log fire in the village square. This heralds not just the arrival of the turkeys, a gobbling group of around a hundred who spill from a lorry to strut their stuff on the cobbled street; it introduces, too, the joint stars of the show – the Confrérie, dressed in all their finery. Joining them is a colourful cast of brothers and sisters from the Confrérie de Chou-fleur de St-Omer, whose green cauliflower costumes mingle with the equivalent purple and white of their hosts. Watch out, too, for the Confrérie des Amis de la Tête de Veau de Licques bearing a cow's head – not a real one, we hasten to add…

Headed by musicians from the local Licques band and girl majorettes – the turkeys ambling with little or no coercion, close behind – the whole joyful procession climbs slowly but surely up the main street. Families wave and cheer, while an accordionist regales them with regional songs in Ch'ti or Ch'timi.

It ends as suddenly as it began. The crowds rapidly disperse. Some head for neighbouring bars and cafés, others attend the grand lunch, where guests sit down to a pre-paid meal and general jollity in a massive heated marquee. The slumbering hills of the Parc Naturel Regional des Caps et Marais d'Opale provide a suitably sleepy background.

Some (mainly les jeunes) are nursing hangovers from the Saturday dance which goes on until dawn. Many more will have earlier snapped up local and seasonal fare – including the much sought-after Licques turkeys – sold in a similar heated marquee opposite the church in place d'Église during Saturday.

This whole festival is one big community booze-up, organised by the Coopérative de Licques, in which young and old play an equal part, along with a flurry of English visitors. Around 4,000 turkey meals are served over the weekend.

On the Monday, Licques – dubbed 'Turkey Capital of France' – takes on a more serious atmosphere. This is when farmers from other poultry-producing areas, including Perigord where the Licques turkey's distinctive black feathers stem from, mull over the merits of the best in breed, while local celebrity chefs prepare more culinary delights.

The turkeys were first introduced by 17th-century monks of the Abbaye of Licques who led them along paths to reach the meadows. In doing so, the turkeys ate grass, berries, herbs and other vegetation. The abbey farmers quickly realised they were on to a winning flavour.

Nowadays, with the abbaye long gone, the birds, a slow-growing breed reared in the summer to capture the flavour, have festive nuts and berries added to their 100% vegetarian diet.

PRACTICALITIES Licques is a 40-minute drive from Calais; a little less from Boulogne. Create your own lunch from produce at the indoor Christmas market; alternatively eat at the accompanying restaurant or at the dinner-dance on Saturday evening or Sunday lunch. Tickets for the dinner-dance can be bought at the door.

Coastal Country **DAY-TRIP COUNTRY**

4

✖ Where to eat

See page 94.

✖ **La Taverne de Kate** 40 rue St André; ☎ 03 21 82 53 91; e latavernedekate@wanadoo.fr; ⏰ 10.30–14.30 & 18.30–22.00 Thu–Sun, 10.30–14.30 Tue & Wed; closed Mon. Pop in to this jolly pizzeria-cum-brasserie for anything from a French-style Welsh rarebit to regional fish or meat dishes. Set menus €9.90–12.90. Popular with the locals, who include some expat English, it's smack next door to its sister shop selling tempting cakes & tarts. **$$$**

Shopping The **Épicerie Fine Dumont** at 8 rue Parent Réal (☎ 03 21 35 47 67; ⏰ 08.30–12.30 & 14.30–19.30 Tue–Sat, 09.00–12.30 Sun) is a great place for regional products, especially cheeses. It is one of a number of local outlets listed on the tourist office website www.ardres.com.

What to see and do The tourist office is uniquely housed in the Chapelle des Carmes, originally a 17th-century Carmelite convent. The building was subsequently used as a market hall – a clue to this is provided by the cobbled street that runs straight through the reception area. It also houses one of the town's giants, Francis, who, at 4.8m high, honours François I who stayed within the town's walls during his encounter with Henry VIII at the time of the Field of the Cloth of Gold (see page 94).

Though now hidden by vegetation, the remains of the medieval fortifications were where the Bastion de Festin once stood. It was at this spot, while escaping a storm raging between Ardres and Guînes, that the two kings came to feast.

Close by in the main square, spot the bullet holes in the tower of Notre Dame church. The oldest parts of the church, in flamboyant Gothic style, date back to 1503. The bullet marks were left when the Rambures, a rebel group from Picardy who, during a plot to return the town to the Spanish, began firing at locals who took refuge in the tower on 1 July 1653.

A second giant, Belle Rose, 4.5m high, represents a local heroine who escaped the Spanish occupation in the 17th century.

While you're at the tourist office ask to see **Les Poires**. These so-called pears of Ardres are a series of nine underground grain silos. Originally built in 1530, they were designed to store 1,000 tons of grain, sufficient to feed the heavily fortified town of 500 people, plus their animals, for a year. By the 17th century they had fallen into disuse.

It was not until 1962, during road works in the vicinity of the old corn market, that the silos, sealed off by the Germans in World War II, were rediscovered beneath a recently purchased house long suspected of holding the secret store. There is no admission fee, but you should arrange your visit with the tourist office 15 days before. This gives them time to contact the owner of the house, or to get someone from the tourist office to show you round.

Around Ardres Head 1.5km northwest for 64 acres of recreational lakes and marshland: le Lac d'Ardres is the largest area of natural water in this part of northern France. The area is home to **Eurolac** (av du Lac; ☎ 03 21 35 13 91; www.eurolac-ardres.com; ⏰ 11.00–19.30 daily (Jul–Aug & school holidays); 13.30–19.00 Sun (Mar & Apr) & daily from mid-Jun; 14.00–18.30 & from 13.00 Sat–Sun & public holidays (selected days only spring & autumn), check dates to avoid disappointment; adult/child €1.90 & €10 day pass), where youngsters will revel in the range of electric boats from tugs and ferries to a lightship and a Mississippi steamboat. Competent over nines can sail their own boat. A bouncy castle and an obstacle course cater for 7–12 year olds. You certainly won't go hungry: there is a fully fledged restaurant serving freshwater fish dishes, as well as a pancake stall, a burger bar and an Italian ice-cream stall.

Close by lies **Maison de la Flore** (rue des Rainettes; ☎ 03 21 82 89 27; ⏰ 1 Apr–30 Jun 10.00–12.00 & 14.00–17.30 Mon–Fri, 1 Jul–30 Sep 09.00–12.00 &

14.00–17.00 Tue–Fri, 15.00–18.00 Sun) where you can learn a little about the 250-plus medicinal plants grown by André Coudron, owner of this small but intriguing natural garden. He provides advice and gives talks on selected days.

Other villages scattered throughout the Ardrésis-Vallée de la Hem include: **Autingues** with 17th- and 18th-century white Guemy stone buildings; **Landrethun-lés-Ardres** famed for its strawberries; **Louches** with typical rural buildings from the area and **Tournehem-sur-Hem**. Comprising the villages of Tournehem and Guémy the latter is an ideal coffee stop on the Route of the Cloth of Gold.

Youngsters under 11 can also unwind at nearby **Bal Parc** (*291 rue de Vieux-Chateau;* ✎ *03 21 35 97 26; www.balparc.com;* ⊕ *Apr–Sep 10.30–19.00 or 10.30–18.30 (varies on a daily basis so check first);* €*10, children under 1m free*). Expect circus-style fun, with bouncy castles and pedaloes, swings and traditional roundabouts. A bit tame for some perhaps, but with a small farmyard, mini-golf and picnic areas it's ideal for a family day out.

WIMEREUX Excursions along the River Hem take in magnificent views of the region before heading back to the coast and Wimereux, a real Edwardian charmer from the belle époque era. This is reached either directly off the A16/exit 33 or on the D940 only 6km north of Boulogne. Once dubbed somewhat optimistically as the 'Nice of the North' it retains a slightly raffish air, compared to some of its quieter neighbours. It's none the worse for that, and its jolly family atmosphere draws a fair number of day-tripping Brits.

The town gets its Flemish-sounding name from the river running through it to the sea; in the 13th century it was written as Wimmerrewe or Wimerreuwe.

Tourist information

🇮 **L'Office de Tourisme Quai Giard** ✎ 03 21 83 27 17; e info@wimeroux-tourisme.fr; www.wimeroux-tourisme.com; ⊕ Apr–Sep 09.00–12.00 & 14.00–18.30 Mon–Sat, 10.00–12.00 & 14.00–18.30 Sun, Oct–Mar 09.00–12.00 & 14.00–17.00 Mon–Sat, closed Sun

Where to stay and eat

🏠 **Hotel Atlantic** (18 rooms, facing the sea) Digue de Mer; ✎ 03 21 32 41 01; e alain.delpierre@wanadoo.fr; www.atlantic-depiere.com. This has been a long-time favourite with short-stay Brits due to its relaxed ambience. But do book early: the dbl rooms, some with balconies or terraces, are quickly snapped up. B/fast is €13. There is a free car park opposite the main entrance. $$$$

✗ **Restaurant La Liegeoise, Hotel Atlantic** (see above) ⊕ 12.00–14.00 Tue–Sun & 19.30–21.00 Mon–Sat.

The Hotel Atlantic's 1st-floor gourmet restaurant is well patronised by guests & non-residents alike. It has a glamorous Art Deco ambience & extensive sea views. Chef Alain Delpierre specialises in fish, shellfish & superb local produce including foie gras plus complimentary appetisers, & *petits fours* with coffee. Gourmet 3-course menus €36–65. A la carte dishes are available from €30. For more casual dining **L'Aloze** on the ground floor overlooks the promenade (⊕ 12.00–13.45 Tue–Sun & 19.30–21.00 Tue–Sat; $$$$). $$$$$

BALLOONISTS DIE IN CROSS-CHANNEL BID

Forget Blériot for one moment – what about Jean-François Pilâtre de Rozier? De Rozier and his co-pilot Pierre Romain were killed near Wimereux when their balloon crashed in flames while they attempted to cross the Channel on 15 June 1785. They thus became the first victims of an aviation crash.

A none-too-impressive monument on the D940 stands where they crashed. This is located on the corner of rue Pilatre de Rozier and rue René Cassin in Wimereux.

What to see and do The seafront is set against a backdrop of fine façades and ornate Anglo-Norman architecture with the occasional turreted house appearing between rue Carnot and the seafront's long promenade. Even the wooden huts, huddled against the sea wall, are an odd mixture of pointed and flat roofs.

The beach, a blend of flat sand, shingle and rock pools is gently shelving. Beware: the tide goes out a long way so avoid the high-tide rush for car parking spaces. Supervised games for youngsters under 12 are arranged on weekday afternoons during July and August.

Strong on sailing and sand-gliding, the resort is also home to Golf de Wimereux, an 18-hole 6,150m par 72 course, which, established in 1907, is the region's oldest (*ave François Mitterrand;* ☎ *03 21 32 43 20;* e *accueil@golf-wimereux.com; www.golf-wimereux.com; green fees €25–60*). Set above the cliffs directly overlooking the English Channel, views of the white cliffs of Dover can be seen from the course on a clear day. The clubhouse, although small, offers a good menu and range of wines.

Apart from attracting walkers, nature-lovers and surfers, the dunes around Pointe aux Oies are home to prehistoric dolmen.

BOULOGNE-SUR-MER

Boulogne has long been Britain's best-loved picture-postcard port. 'My French watering hole', is how Charles Dickens dubbed it. Hugged by the harbour walls, its Gallic charms quickly win you over with an eye-catching view of the three distinctive upper and lower town districts that characterise France's largest fishing port.

Forget the faded post-war blocks that face you on arrival. Focus instead on the splendid dome of Notre-Dame Cathedral, reached by the Grande Rue (the main thoroughfare) which threads the three areas together.

Its hilltop position pinpoints the medieval Old Town, one of the best-preserved in France, a Montmartre-like magnet for those who have a craving for ramparts, cobbled streets, craft shops and pavement cafés. Explore the City Heights before succumbing to the lower town temptations – both along and off the Grande Rue – of individual pâtisseries, charcuteries, delicatessens, and cheese and chocolate shops.

The huge fish market on quai Gambetta, near the harbour entrance, dominates this salty district of shrieking gulls and bobbing boats. Glistening heaps of sole and mounds of shellfish naturally inspire thoughts of lunch. Indeed many cross the Channel just to dine at the enticing choice of restaurants. Bear in mind the French start lunch early so it's always best to book ahead, especially at peak periods. Boulogne has traditionally been popular day-trip territory with coach trips and the like arriving via Calais providing an instant snapshot of France in your face – in the nicest possible way, of course! No wonder Graham Greene, in the first line of *Travels with My Aunt*, admitted: 'Strangely enough I felt almost at home in Boulogne'. *Mais oui...*

HISTORY Boulogne has historically been the base for bids to bash the British. First Portus Itius – the fortified town's Roman name which was later to become Bononia – was used by Julius Caesar, then by Napoleon Bonaparte. More recently, Hitler was desperate to take the town for strategic purposes. All attempts were flawed to some degree.

In his 55BC campaign, Caesar's back-up force was hampered by a storm, limiting any large-scale action and forcing a withdrawal. It was not until the following year, in 54BC, with an increased force of 2,000 cavalry and five legions, that his forces dug deeper into English soil, only to be warned of pressing problems back in Gaul (present-day France). By September the troops had left. Both attempts were launched from Boulogne, though some say the second was from nearby Wissant.

England, too, had its troubles – in defending the port. Six years after taking Boulogne by siege in 1544, Henry VIII's army marched out again, finding it too difficult to defend. The port was returned to France in 1550.

In 1803, a year after being proclaimed Emperor of France, Napoleon Bonaparte based himself in Boulogne for two years training a Grande Armée of 200,000 men; there was even a flotilla of 2,000 flat-bottomed boats ready in the harbour. 'Let us be masters of the Channel for six hours and we are masters of the world,' is his much-quoted challenge. But the planned invasion of Britain never took place – instead Napoleon headed off to his triumphal victory over the Russians and Austrians at the Battle of Austerlitz.

Hitler, likewise, thought twice about attacking Britain from Boulogne when he failed to gain air supremacy. The town, however, was bombed 487 times during World War II, destroying over 5,000 buildings, hence the rather grim post-war edifices facing the harbour entrance.

GETTING THERE AND AWAY

By car If driving from Calais (35km) or Dunkirk (75km) or continuing elsewhere by car, a dual carriageway autoroute link connects Boulogne with the A16 at exit 29. If using the former, take care to follow closely the directions off the various roundabouts to Boulogne when you leave the Calais ferry port or you could find yourself on the A16 alright, but heading east towards Dunkirk. Even heading correctly west, watch for the overhead sign for Boulogne, as the road, a vital link to the entire regional road network, is busy at this point with signs to other major destinations. It is probably less complicated from the Channel Tunnel.

VIKING-STYLE DESIGN PROVED QUITE A CATCH

The descendants of Viking ships, *flobarts* (small open fishing boats) can often be seen along the Côte d'Opale. They can float in less than a foot of water and, until the 1950s, were powered by oars or sails. Their versatile flat-bottomed and bulbous shape makes them easy to haul ashore in shallow water.

Once built of entirely of elm, but since the 1970s made with polyester moulds, they are now almost universally owned by fishing associations. They are used to catch herring, from November to December, as well as bass and mackerel; crabs and lobsters are also caught, especially around Audresselles.

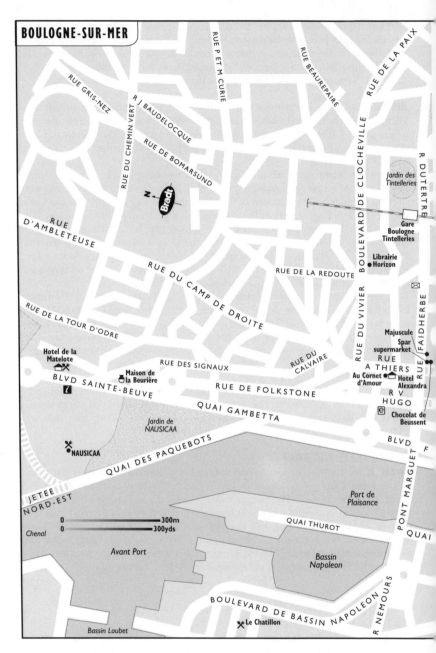

BOULOGNE-SUR-MER

RUE P ET M CURIE

RUE BEAUREPAIRE

RUE DE LA PAIX

RUE GRIS-NEZ

R J BAUDELOCQUE

RUE DU CHEMIN VERT

RUE DE BOMARSUND

BOULEVARD DE CLOCHEVILLE

R DUTERTRE

Jardin des Tintelleries

N

Brad

RUE D'AMBLETEUSE

RUE DU CAMP DE DROITE

RUE DE LA REDOUTE

Gare
**Boulogne
Tintelleries**

Librairie
● **Horizon**

RUE DE LA TOUR D'ODRE

RUE DU VIVIER

RUE FAIDHERBE

Majuscule
Spar
supermarket

Hotel de la
Matelote

RUE DES SIGNAUX

**Maison de
la Beurière**

RUE DU
CALVAIRE

R U E
A THIERS

Au Cornet ●📮 **Hotel
d'Amour Alexandra**

BLVD SAINTE-BEUVE

RUE DE FOLKSTONE

R V
HUGO

QUAI GAMBETTA

● **Chocolat de
Beussent**

*Jardin de
NAUSICAA*

BLVD

PONT MARGUET

F

NAUSICAA

QUAI DES PAQUEBOTS

QUAI

JETEE
NORD-EST

*Port de
Plaisance*

| 0 | ━━━━300m |
| 0 | ━━━━300yds |

QUAI THUROT

Chenal

Avant Port

*Bassin
Napoleon*

R NEMOURS

BOULEVARD DE BASSIN NAPOLEON

✕ Le Chatillon

Bassin Loubet

The alternative, and less frenetic, route is to pick up the scenic D940 coastal road (see page 88) at Bleriot Plage, and take a lunch break along the way, returning, if on a day trip to Boulogne, via the A16 where there are plenty of signs for the tunnel and car-ferry ports. The motorway is also clearly indicated from Boulogne town centre.

Driving times: Le Touquet 30 minutes (30km via the coast, 40km via the A1); Berck-sur-Mer 35 minutes (50km via the A16) or 50 minutes (40km via the

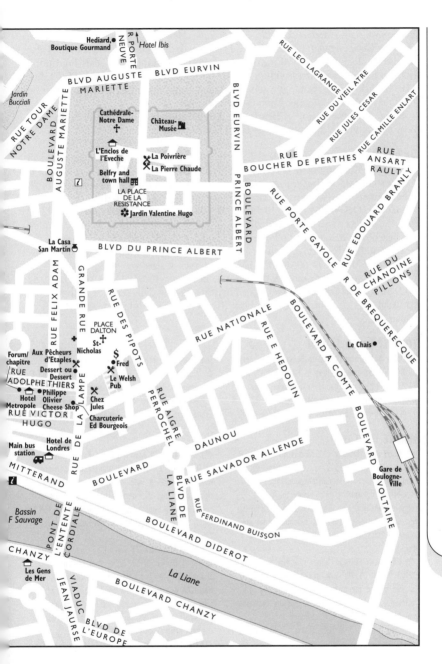

coast); St-Omer 40 minutes (50km).

By train There are two SNCF railway stations. Around 15 TER trains run daily to **Gare Calais-Ville** (*line 12; 30–40mins; see page 59*) from **Gare de Boulogne-Ville** (*bld Voltaire, 1–1.5km or 15–20 mins' walk from the town centre;* ☎ *08 91 67 10 59 in French only*). The station also serves the Calais–Hazebrouck–Lille route (*line 12:*

Boulogne–Calais–Hazebrouck–Lille; 2hrs to Lille Mon–Sat) and Dunkirk (*line 10, change at Calais; around 4 trains Mon–Sat taking up to 1hr 40mins*). The station is also on the Boulogne–Calais (20 minutes) and Boulogne–Lille (via Calais Frethun; 1 hour) TER Grande Vitesse (High Speed) routes as well as the regular TER Lille–Hazebrouck–Calais–Boulogne services. Line 11 also serves Étaples-Le Touquet on the Lille–Calais–Boulogne–Amiens–Paris service.

Some TER trains stop at **Boulogne Tintelleries station**, on rue de Belterre near the university, but not on the fast TERGV services.

By bus The **bus station** for local TRCB services is on place de France, by the main post office. You can buy tickets from the ticket office (*20 pl de France, next to rue de la Lampe which leads to Grande Rue;* ℡ *03 21 83 51 51*), direct from the driver or through other outlets; see www.trcb.fr/tarifs-depositaires.asp or www.tcrb.fr. TRCB also operates to Desvres (℡ *03 21 10 34 34*); Berck-sur-Mer via Étaples (℡ *03 21 32 42 98*); Calais via coastal towns and villages, or via Marquise (℡ *03 21 36 91 23*) and to the beaches at Wimereux, Le Portel and Hardelot (℡ *03 21 83 51 51*).

Yet another company, Colvert (℡ *03 21 36 91 23; www.colvert-littoral.com;* ⏰ *08.00–12.00 & 14.00–18.00 Mon–Fri*), serves Calais via Wissant line 44 or Marquise line 03. For Dunkirk use the Line Boulogne–Calais–Dunkirk (℡ *08 00 62 00 59; www.ligne-bcd.com/horaires.php*). There are six-plus daily services, with reduced Saturday service, which take one hour 40 minutes to Dunkirk or 40 minutes to Calais.

TOURIST INFORMATION

🛈 **Office du Tourisme** bld Sainte Beuve, on the parvis de NAUSICAA (the square next to NAUSICAA); ℡ 03 21 10 88 10; e info@tourisme-bolougnesurmer.com; www.tourisme-boulognesurmer.com; ⏰ 09.30–12.30 & 13.45–18.30 Mon–Sat, 10.00–13.00 & 15.00–18.00 Sun. There is a second office called Jean Noel on quai de la Poste in front of the main post office in bld F Mitterrand. A third, open in the high season is simply a kiosk in the square Mariette Pacha, at the top of Grande Rue, next to Porte des Dunes.

WHERE TO STAY

🏠 **Hotel de la Matelote** (35 rooms) 80 bld Sainte-Beuve; ℡ 03 21 30 33 33; e tony.lestienne@la-matelote.com; www.la-matelote.com. This well-established, high-quality hotel facing the sea (opposite NAUSICAA) is also home to a Michelin-star restaurant. Business facilities & swimming pool are available; b/fast is €15; private parking is €12 a day. $$$$

🏠 **L'Enclos de l'Eveche** (5 rooms) 6 rue de Pressy; ℡ 03 91 90 05 90; www.enclosdeleveche.com. Located behind the cathedral, this delightfully restored townhouse B&B hotel is enjoying increasing popularity. Each of the high-ceilinged rooms, furnished in traditional style, sports a different decorative theme. $$$

🏠 **Hotel Metropole** (26 rooms) 51 rue Thiers; ℡ 03 21 31 54 30; e hotel.metropole@wanadoo.fr; www.hotel-metropole-boulogne.com. While not winning a wow factor, it is clean, comfortable & friendly. In the town centre close to the ramparts; English TV, minibar & business facilities are featured. B/fast is €10 is served in the lounge. Parking available at €9. $$$

🏠 **Hotel Ibis** (79 rooms) 62 rue Porte Neuve; ℡ 03 21 31 21 01; www.ibishotel.com. Functional, with basic smallish hotel-chain-style rooms, it lies close to a range of eateries. There is free outdoor public parking opposite or secure parking for €8. Handy for overnight stop with possible Ibis deals. $$$

🏠 **Hotel Alexandra** (18 rooms) 93 rue Adolphe Thiers; ℡ 03 21 30 52 22; e contact@hotel-alexandra.fr; www.hotel-alexandra.fr. Close to NAUSICAA & the shops, the hotel offers a useful selection of adequate rooms, including 4 family ones. Buffet b/fast is €7; parking from €5. Look out for seasonal offers. $$$

🏠 **Hotel de Londres** (20 rooms) 22 pl de France; ℡ 03 21 31 35 63; www.hoteldelondres.net. Nicely located in the heart of town, though it is within the bus station area. If worried, park the car at the nearest pay & display. The rooms, renovated & redecorated, come recommended for a comfortable & friendly overnight stop. Bags of restaurants nearby to choose from. B/fast is €6.50. $$$

🏠 **Les Gens de Mer** (44 rooms) Quai Chanzy; 📞 03 21 31 73 20; e agismarineboulogne@wanadoo.fr; www.lesgensdemer.fr. This is part of the 2-star Houses of Seafarers group which, created in 1946 to accommodate seafarers, opened to the public in 2000. The Boulogne hotel is largely regarded as basic, convenient for town & has a plentiful b/fast at €7.50. There is also free parking. $$

✖ WHERE TO EAT

✖ **La Matelote** (see *Where to Stay*, opposite) 80 bld Sainte Beuve (opposite NAUSICAA); 📞 03 21 30 17 97; www.la-matelote.com; 🕐 12.00–14.00 daily except Thu, 19.30–21.30 daily. A 1-Michelin-star fish restaurant with elaborate décor, menus are €25–71. These include surprise complimentary extras such as little appetisers, soup tasters in tiny glasses, tempting pre-desserts, *petits fours* & chocolates. Knowing this can help you pace your appetite. Gourmets will relish Saveurs de la Mer (Tastes of the Sea). The food is served on a delightful collection of plates, many with fish designs, from ultra-modern triangular glass to exquisite Limoges porcelain. $$$$$
✖ **Aux Pêcheurs d'Étaples** Brasserie de la Mer, 31 Grande Rue; 📞 03 21 30 29 29;

www.auxpecheursdetaples.fr; 🕐 12.00–14.30 & 19.00–21.30, oyster bar open all day. Walk through the fish shop to both Le Carré oyster bar & brasserie as well as the buzzy main restaurant with its nautical décor. Menus from €13 to €24 include speciality herrings marinated in oil & spices served in little brown earthenware-lidded dishes. Seafood comes in decorative model boats. Welsh de la Mer (Seafood Rarebit) is a favourite ('Le Welsh' dishes topped with melted cheese are a feature of Boulogne cuisine). This is 1 of 3 restaurants with fish shops run by a ship owners' co-operative which guarantees the freshness, quality & taste of their catch (the others are in Étaples & Lille; see page 109). $$$$

Bars and restaurants around the market place in place Dalton include:

✖ **Chez Jules** 8–10 pl Dalton; 📞 03 21 31 54 12; 🕐 from 12.00 for lunch & 18.30–22.00. Ground-floor pizzeria with upstairs brasserie/restaurant. Specialities include huge brochettes of seafood or meat supported on stands & *blanquette de poisson* which comes with mushroom cream sauce & a ladle. Set menus from €18.50–40. $$$

✖ **Le Welsh Pub** 26–28 pl Dalton; 📞 03 21 31 51 31. Virtually non-stop eatery from 12.00 with lively atmosphere. Menus from €24 to €34. $$$
✖ **Restaurant at NAUSICAA** bld Sainte Beuve; 📞 03 21 33 24 24. Situated in the Sea Life Centre. Traditional & regional cooking complements an excellent sea view. Menus €19.50–23.50. $$$

In the port area **Le Chatillon** (*6 rue Charles Tellier;* 🕐 *lunchtime only* $$) offers the opportunity to eat fish with the port workers. In rue de Lille several reasonably priced bistros and pavement cafés include **La Poivrière** (*15 rue de Lille;* 📞 *03 21 80 18 18; menus €14–35*) and **La Pierre Chaude** (*19 rue de Lille;* 📞 *03 21 80 30 32; menus from €14 –31.50*), which serve traditional dishes.

SHOPPING

Food and wine The **Philippe Olivier Cheese Shop** (*43 rue Thiers;* 📞 *03 21 94 74; www.phillipeolivier.fr;* 🕐 *09.00–19.00 Tue–Sat*) stocks the largest choice of cheese in northern France, beautifully displayed on straw mats. They include some 30 from Nord-Pas de Calais. One of the most famous is the tasty (and strong) '*fromage de la ville*': Vieux Boulogne. The Cremet du Cap Blanc, a white creamy-yet-crumbly mound, reflects the landmark Cap Blanc-Nez cliff on the coast. **Chocolat de Beussent**'s (*56 rue Thiers;* 📞 *03 21 92 44 00; www.choco-france.com;* 🕐 *09.00–18.00*) delectable chocolates are made at the chocolate factory at Chocolaterie de Beussent-Lachelle, 60 rue de Desvres (see page 155). **Fred** (*30 pl Dalton;* 📞 *03 21 30 95 95*) stocks such mouth-watering favourites as *tartes framboises*; Boulonnaise speciality *tarte campagne* is a delicious version of prunes and custard and the splendid range of breads includes *pain noisette*. Other recommended pâtisseries are **Dessert ou Dessert** (*35 Grande Rue;* 📞 *03 21 92 57 02*) and **Au Cornet d'Amour** (*91 rue Thiers;* 📞 *03 21 31 65 89*).

Coastal Country BOULOGNE-SUR-MER

4

At **Charcuterie Ed Bourgeois** (*1 Grande Rue;* ⤫ *03 21 31 53 57*) you can buy ready-to-eat vegetable dishes, croissants stuffed with cheese or shellfish, pâtés, hams, sausages, black and white puddings and *rillettes* (similar to pâté).

Le Chais (*49 rue des Deux Ponts/30 rue Brequerecque;* ⤫ *03 21 31 65 42;* e *le-chais@wanadoo.fr; www.lechais.com;* ⊕ *09.00–12.00 & 14.30–19.00 Tue–Fri, 09.00–12.30 & 14.30–18.30 Sat*) is tricky to find but it's worth persevering: head out from the town centre via the rue Nationale. Follow the sign for Brequereque, go under a railway bridge and turn left immediately. Parking is free. The stock of 50,000 bottles ranges from table wine at prices similar to supermarkets to rare vintages and famous *marques*. Denis Lengaigne, the charismatic owner, will happily open bottles for tastings.

Opposite the Old Town ramparts **Hediard, Boutique Gourmand** (*7 rue Porte Neuve;* ⤫ *03 21 31 65 47; www.hediard.com*) is a vibrant-red, but unobtrusive, branch of a Paris-based chain store stocking exquisitely packaged gourmet treats and hampers.

There is a **fish market** daily on quai Gambetta and traditional French markets are held on **place Dalton** (⊕ *08.30–12.00 Wed & Sat*). A vast range of local produce (organic too) is sold by local farmers from stalls and open-sided vans.

Bookshops

Majuscule 48 rue Faidherbe; ⤫ 03 21 87 43 44; ⊕ 14.00–19.00 Mon, 09.30–12.30 & 13.30–19.00 Tue–Sat
Librairie Horizon 6 bld Clocheville; ⤫ 03 21 83 57
87; ⊕ 10.00–12.30 & 14.00–19.00 Tue–Sat
Forum/chapitre 57 rue Adolphe Tiers; ⤫ 03 21 10 28 70; ⊕ 14.00–19.00 Mon & 10.00–19.00 Tue–Sat

OTHER PRACTICALITIES

Bank Banque CIC; 32 pl Dalton; ⤫ 03 21 30 87 93; ⊕ 09.00–12.30 & 14.00–18.00 Tue–Fri, 09.00–13.00 Sat. Most cards accepted.
Supermarket Spar; 40–54 rue Victor Hugo; ⤫ 03 21 10 81 01; ⊕ 08.00–20.00 Mon–Sat, 09.00–12.30 Sun
Internet café Photographe art et image; 87 rue Victor Hugo; ⤫ 03 21 30 54 99; ⊕ 09.30–18.45 Tue–Sat
Pharmacy Pharmacie Centrale; 41 Grand Rue; ⤫ 03 21 31 64 51; ⊕ 09.00–12.30 & 13.45–19.00 Mon, 08.45–12.30 & 13.45–19.00

Tue–Fri, 10.30–12.30 & 13.45–19.00 Sat
Post Office La Poste Boulogne Sur Mer Faidherbe; 135 rue Louis Faidherbe; ⊕ 13.30–17.00 Mon, 09.30–12.00 & 13.30–17.00 Tue–Fri, 08.30–12.00 Sat
Public toilet(s) Town hall in the Old Town; quai Gambetta, promenade Jean Muselet (next to the fish stalls); pl Dalton, next to St-Nicolas Church & a bus stop facing aux Pêcheurs d'Étaples; next to the Theatre Monsigny; Carrefour shopping centre bld Daunou & at NAUSICAA

WHAT TO SEE AND DO Sightseeing is simplicity itself: the sheer compactness of the town means you can stroll round the major sites with ease – and even shop on the way. Bear in mind, however, that Boulogne is hilly and walking can involve some steep climbs, so pick those places which suit you best. An ideal way to tour the town is to hire an audio guide with headphones (€3) from the tourist office or the

Château-Musée where the tour starts. It provides a 30-minute commentary on the town ramparts and inside the old walled town. Each of the 17 recognised stops triggers a brief commentary. This allows you to walk at your own pace, or even retrace your footsteps.

Four gates, barely changed since ancient times, lead to the pathway for an easy stroll round the **ramparts**. From here you get the best views of the town and the well-tended gardens at the foot of the walls. Then head for the **Château-Musée** (*rue de Bernet;* ☎ *03 21 10 02 20;* ✆ *10.00–12.30 & 14.00–17.00 Mon & Wed–Sat, 10.00–12.30 & 14.30–17.30 Sun; adult €2, under 18 free*). The stylish and subtly lit 21st-century presentation is totally in sympathy with the ancient walls of the castle, which was built at the same time as the ramparts. Exhibits include the largest collection of Greek and Etruscan vases outside of the Louvre; the paintings and sculpture section includes works by Corot, Fantin-Latour and Rodin. The Egyptian collection includes a mummy, sarcophagi and amulets donated by Auguste Mariette, the Boulonnais who became an eminent Egyptologist and founded Cairo's famous Egyptian Museum. See his fez-topped statue on the top of a large pyramid in front of the ramparts alongside statues of other famous Boulannais citizens.

Virtually next door in rue de Lille, the familiar 101m dome of **Cathédrale-Notre Dame** (✆ *1 Sep–1 Mar 10.00–12.00 & 14.00–17.00 daily, 1 Apr–31 Aug 10.00–12.00 & 14.00–18.00*) was undoubtedly inspired by St Paul's Cathedral, as well as St Peter's in Rome, the Panthéon and Les Invalides in Paris. With an earlier Romanesque building destroyed during the Revolution, it was left to Agathon Haffreingue Benedict, a young priest from the Boulogne countryside who had become a professor at a college nearby, to buy the ruined site around 1820.

Redeveloped between 1827 and 1866, the centre-piece is the High Altar of the Princes of Torlonia, a masterpiece of 19th-century Italian mosaic inlaid with 145 different sorts of marble. The medieval crypt (*La Crypte Notre Dame;* ☎ *03 21 99 75 98;* ✆ *14.00–17.00 daily except Mon; adult/child aged 5–12 €2/1*) is the second-largest in France. It houses objects of holy art, including a 14th-century gold reliquary said to contain Christ's blood sent back from Jerusalem in 1100 by Godefroy de Bouillon, Earl of Boulogne and Commander of the First Crusade. In 1308 it was given as wedding present by the French king Phillipe le Bel to his daughter Isabelle on her marriage to Edward II of England.

Walk down rue de Lille to **La Place de la Résistance**, the heart the Upper Town. You can't miss seeing the 47m **belfry** (☎ *03 21 87 80 80; limited number of guided tours;* ✆ *see town hall below*). This was once the Roman-style keep of an earlier medieval castle; it became one of the region's famous belfries (see page 13) at the beginning of the 13th century. The **town hall** (*hôtel de ville;* ☎ *03 21 87 80 80;* ✆ *08.00–18.00 Mon–Fri, 08.00–12.00 Sat; admission free*), which seemingly embraces the belfry, was completed in 1735 under Louis XV. Though altered six times, it is the only building in the Old Town to be made of brick and stone, all the others being in stone only. Opposite, next to porte des Dunes, is the **Palais de Justice**, built in the Greek Revival style in 1852, and the former nunnery of **Annonciades**. This is now the town's main library housing a collection of rare manuscripts.

A bit further along, on the main square, place Godefroy de Bouillon, is **Napoleon's Palace**, where the First Consul, then Emperor, stayed between 1801 and 1805. Look out for rue Guyale, once home to the merchants' guilds, which leads to the leafy oasis that is **Jardin Valentine Hugo**.

Pause at 113 Grande Rue for a quick look at **La Casa San Martín** (☎ *03 21 31 54 65;* ✆ *10.00–12.00 & 14.00–17.00 Tue–Sat except public holidays*). This was the home of the Argentine general José de San Martín, who liberated his country as well as Chile and Peru from from Spanish colonial rule. Also somewhat overlooked is **St-Nicholas** (*L'Eglise Saint-Nicholas;* ⊕ *09.15–11.15 Mon & Wed, 14.00–17.00 Sat*), a lovely 12th-century church with lit candles standing before wooden statues of the saints and pigeons fluttering beneath the vaulted ceiling.

Highlight of the harbour area is **NAUSICAA, Centre National de la Mer** (*bld Sainte Beuve;* ↘ *03 21 30 99 99; www.nausicaa.fr;* ⊕ *Sep–Jun 09.30–18.30 daily, Jul–Aug 09.30–19.30 daily, 14.00–18.30 daily, other months subject to change so check first; adult/child 3–12/disabled €17.40/11.20/9.50 (wheelchairs available free of charge); family of 2 adults & 2 children aged 3–12 €8.70, mini groups of 4 adults €14.90; audio guides €3.20 with tours in English (passport needed). Check on special events*). Don't be put off by the name, which refers to a Greek heroine in Homer's *Odyssey*. As a home to sharks, sea lions and thousands of other sea creatures, this is ideal for a half- or even a full-day family outing. Recognised as a major European venue for putting marine life in a broad environmental context, it includes a serious 'wake-up' call portrayed in a far-from-pompous mànner. The kids will love the interactive gadgets and the touch tanks, in which turbot and other fish take turns to have their tummies tickled, that are guaranteed all-round family winners.

In 2006 Steer South! added a Jean-Michel Cousteau-style journey to meet African penguins; two years later the World Ocean exhibition provided the chance to peer into the world of plankton life. In Spaceship Earth, visitors get a cabin's eye view of the North Sea. Underwater observation tanks, including ever-popular sharks, add to the marine thrills as does a three-dimensional virtual submarine trip to discover what lies at the bottom of the sea.

Look out for the joint promotion with the Boulogne-sur-Mer Association for the Promotion of Sea Products, a nourishing way of explaining man's stake in protecting the sea resources; visitors can also sample seafood delicacies in the Bistro du Port. Video booths likewise take a serious look at the changes in fishing techniques; elsewhere you learn how modern medicine draws on the sea's resources to develop drugs, the use of marine shells in buildings or how the food industry uses seaweed. The central message, of preserving the Blue Planet, is enhanced by the good use of electronic music.

In complete contrast is **Maison de la Beurière** (↘ *03 21 30 14 52;* ⊕ *15 Jun–15 Sep 10.00–13.00 & 15.00–18.00, closed Mon; 16 Sep–14 Jun 10.00–12.00, 14.00–19.00 Wed & Sat–Sun; adult/child under 12 €2.50/€1*). This lies on rue du Mâchicoulis, which is basically a flight of 120 steps on the side of the cliff opposite NAUSICAA. La Beurière's houses, built around 1870, are typical of those lived in by a once 10,000-strong fishing community. One of them has now been converted into this museum, with the interior reconstructed to show how a sailor's family lived in 1900. The furniture, costumes and other objects starkly portray the harsh life of what Charles Dickens called 'the most picturesque people we have ever encountered'. Around eight people lived here; children were put to bed in a cupboard in the kitchen.

From Boulogne you have a couple of options for further exploration: either continue from Boulogne along the D940, which at this point runs almost parallel with the A16 towards Le Touquet (see page 111) or follow the coast by using the D119, a twisting and little-used road. Take the latter and it will bring you neatly into Hardelot-Plage, 11km from Boulogne via the D113e (see opposite).

LE PORTEL-PLAGE South of Boulogne, between the port and the Cape of Alprech lies Le Portel-Plage, a small but lively family resort with bags of activities and with one of the cleanest of the Boulonnais beaches. It is also widely known for being disability-friendly. Boat owners seeking a cheaper berth than Boulogne use the small harbour. Tuesday and Friday morning markets are held on the square near the church.

Tourist information

What to see and do Look out for Fort de l'Heurt. Though located on the beach, this stone building, built by Napoleon in 1803 to protect Boulogne, is only accessible at low tide. It was used by German machine-gunners in World War II during which time the town was badly damaged.

The 17ha **Parc de la Falaise**, overlooking the sea, is a paradise for bird lovers and children alike. The former can spot migratory species; the latter can pat the ponies, goats and donkeys, or try out the slides, swings and pirate ships. It's a great place for a picnic, with a drinks and ice cream stall near the main entrance, right next to the mini-golf. There is free parking around the two entrances.

HARDELOT-PLAGE

Less frenetic than Le Touquet, but similarly surrounded by woods and dunes, and well-upholstered homes, Hardelot-Plage is fast developing as a centre for holiday homes and flats. This is scarcely surprising. Ideal for youngsters, it has a gently sloping beach of fine sand, and a string of leisure activities. These include cycling, horseriding and walking trails, also sailing, kite-flying and a country club with tennis courts and a swimming pool.

HISTORY Much of the town's history is down to developer John Whitley who, in 1905, followed up his success in Le Touquet by creating a similar sports-orientated centre at Hardelot-Plage, drawing wealthy clientele from Britain and Paris. Villas mushroomed, among them a 32-room home owned by Louis Blériot (Blériot was credited with the invention of sand-yachting on Hardelot's beach). Although the town took a hammering during World War II, this sporty image remains intact.

Tourist information

Where to stay

What to see and do Hardelot-Plage's sporting attractions include two well-known **golf courses**: the 18-hole 5,926m par 72 Les Pins and the 8-hole 5,193m par 69 Les Dunes designed by Paul Rollin in 1990 (*Golf d'Hardelot, ave du Golf;* 03 21 83 73 10; *e hardelot@opengolfclub.com; www.opengolfclub.com/hardelot; green fees from €48, with special w/end hotel B&B deals*). Both feature as part of hotel breaks in Hardelot and Le Touquet (see page 18).

Hardelot also has a **castle** – the resort's name stems from several Saxon words meaning 'a stronghold'. Originally planned to defend the village from the Normans, but restored in the 13th century by the Count of Boulogne, Château d'Hardelot, as it is known locally, has now been renamed the **Centre Culturel de l'Entente Cordiale – Château d'Hardelot** (*1 rue de la Source Condette;* ✆ *03 21 21 73 65;* e *chateau-hardelot@cg62.fr; www.chateau-hardelot.fr;* ⊕ *the yard is open to the public year-round, the chateau only during exhibitions – for dates see website*). Located at Condette, a short 5.8km drive away, this will strengthen the already strong links between Pas de Calais and the county of Kent.

Less than 5km away on the D119 (Boulogne direction) lies **Aréna** (*World of Dunes, Ecault–St Etienne au Mont;* ✆ *03 21 10 84 30;* e *arena@agglo-boulonnais.fr; www.arena.agglo-boulonnais.fr;* ⊕ *Mar–Oct 08.30–12.30 & 13.30–17.30 Mon–Fri, 10.00–12.30 & 14.00–18.00 Sat–Sun on 1st w/end of the month, also 10.00–12.30 & 14.00–18.00 Tue–Sun in school holidays; adult/child aged 7–16 €4/3 or 2 adults & 2 children €11*). Managed by Eden 62 (see page 5), Arena, the Latin word for sand, is one huge interpretation centre providing a fascinating glimpse into the fragility of the coastal dunes. The Sunday discovery weekends, in particular, feature a range of activities and workshops. A boutique stocks a large selection of handy souvenirs, including seasonal homemade jams made from the fruits of wild rose bushes and sea buckthorn in the surrounding dunes, and sea buckthorn candles. There is also free audiovisual access to some 60 nature films.

DESVRES AND THE INLAND VILLAGES

Desvres's delightful earthenware pottery is known worldwide. While it suffers from being the centre for eight intersecting roads, and has a mind-blowing one-way system, it's a pleasant enough town, if dingy in parts.

GETTING THERE AND AWAY Desvres is located 16km southeast of Boulogne, via the D341 or just over 18km from Hardelot, via the D215/52.

TOURIST INFORMATION

🏢 **Office de Tourisme de Desvres-Samer** 41 rue des Potters; ✆ 03 21 92 09 09 (Desvres) or ✆ 03 21 87 10 42 (Samer); e ot@cc-regiondesvres.fr (Desvres) or officetourisme.samer@orange.fr (Samer); www.paysfaiencedesvres.fr; ⊕ Nov–Mar 10.00–12.30 & 14.00–17.00 Tue–Fri, Apr–Jun & Sep 10.00–12.30 & 14.00–17.00 Mon–Fri, 10.00–12.30 Sat, Jul–Aug 10.00–12.30 & 14.00–18.00 Mon–Sat

WHAT TO SEE AND DO Ceramic work on the main square clock bears testament to Desvres's nickname 'City of Potters', as do public buildings decorated with geometric tiles or murals. Local shops, cafés and restaurants likewise sport the one-off decorative wall tiles for which the town is particularly noted. Since 1993 artists in residence have collaborated with local potters in enriching and encouraging new lines in the Desvres tradition.

These are seen to their best at the **Museum of Ceramics** (*Maison de la Faïence, rue Jean Macé;* ✆ *03 21 83 23 23;* e *desvresmuseum@wanadoo.fr; www.desvresmuseum.org;* ⊕ *Apr–Jun & Sep 09.30–12.30 & 14.00–18.30 daily except Sun & Mon am, Jul–Aug 09.30–12.30 & 14.00–18.30 Tue–Sun, Oct–Mar 14.00–17.30 Tue–Sun; adult/child €4.6/3.90, under 8 free*) where a 15-minute audio-visual shows the history of pottery, and how Desvres diversified from rustic figurines to the intricate and colourful porcelain it still produces today. The museum visit includes a guided tour of the workshops. Another tour organised by the museum includes a nature day combining hiking with the history of the pottery.

AROUND DESVRES Desvres is the centre of the Pays de la Faïence (the Land of Earthenware and Pottery), comprising 32 communes. Of these, **Samer** is noted for St-Martin's, which uniquely retains the medieval habit of building shops and homes around churches. The village, 8km southwest of Desvres, was also the home of the 19th-century artist Jean-Charles Cazin. A **town hall museum** contains some of his paintings and drawings (*Musée Jean-Charles Cazin, Mairie, Grand Place;* ✆ *03 21 33 50 64;* ⏰ *09.00–11.30 & 14.00–17.00 Mon–Fri; free*).

Famous, too, for strawberries, it joins others in the region in arranging tours to local producers. Walking, fishing, cycling and horseriding trails also fall within the scope of this little known region, which like so much of the coastal inland has woken up to its rich rural potential.

ÉTAPLES

When it comes to fish, **Étaples** is historically the place to be. Its name stems from *stapal*, the Old Dutch for a medieval staple port. Having survived fire, plague and even the excesses of the French Revolution, it grew into a popular late-19th and early-20th-century resort attracting from across the world artists eager to capture its herring fleet heritage on canvas (see page 120).

Though the silting of the Canche estuary has now meant the famous smacks are moored at Boulogne, the port's net income still revolves around fishing. Two museums, one housing the tourist office, are devoted to the subject. Quayside stalls sell freshly caught fish and restaurants attract a healthy haul of diners.

Don't be put off by the inevitable commercial clutter on the outskirts: Étaples remains a working port whose cleverly marketed maritime past makes it well worth visiting.

GETTING THERE AND AWAY Étaples lies 14km further along the D940 from Hardelot.

TOURIST INFORMATION
🛈 **Office Municipal de Tourisme** La Coderie (The Rope Factory), bd Bigot Descelers; ✆ 03 21 09 76 96; e contact@etaples-tourisme.com; www.etaples-tourisme.com; ⏰ Oct–Mar 10.00–12.30 & 14.00–18.00, closed Sun am, Apr–Sep 10.00–13.00 & 14.00–18.30. Tourist passes for 4 museums adult/child €9/6.50.

✕ WHERE TO EAT
✕ **Aux Pêcheurs d'Étaples** Quai de la Canche; ✆ 03 21 94 06 90; e etaples@auxpecheursdetaples.fr; www.auxpecheursdetaples.fr; ⏰ 12.00–14.30 & 19.00–21.30. This is not just another seafood restaurant. Everything from mussels & oysters to turbot & skate have been freshly caught by the fishermen's co-operative. They're either for sale on the stalls outside or served in the smart 1st-floor restaurant. The menu is enormous. Fish soup at €8 is filling enough, let alone other such tempters as smoked salmon, lemon cream & warm toast at €13. A €30 seafood platter or grilled sole at €27 are typical of the main courses. A children's menu is available at €9. This is the place to lash out on a virtually guaranteed taste of the town. $$$$

✕ **Planète Océan** Quai de la Canche; ✆ 08 11 09 22 12; e contact@planetocean.fr; www.planeteocean.fr; ⏰ 12.00–14.30 & 19.00–22.00; closed Mon evening. This is a cheaper, more simple, & hence often more crowded alternative to the above. It's great for familiar family fare, with fish & chips (€12), marine pizza (€16) & fisherman's pie (€10) all providing value for money. 2–3 course menus cost €10–15; there is a 1 dish & drink offer at €9. With a reasonable-sized jug of red wine priced at €7, beer €4–6, & soft drinks & coffee/tea at €3 this is a far from costly meal out. $$$

WHAT TO SEE AND DO In the same building as the tourist office, and formerly a rope factory, is **Maréis** (*La Coderie, bld Bigot Descelers;* ✆ *03 21 09 04 00;* e *contact@mareis.fr; www.mareis.fr;* ⏰ *Apr–Sep 10.00–13.00 & 14.00–18.30, Oct–Mar 10.00–12.30 & 14.00–18.00, closed Sun am; adult/child aged 4–12 €6/4.50; discount with tourist pass/over 60*). Allow two hours to explore this indoor high-tech interpretation

The vast **British Cemetery** (*Cimetière Britannique; 2km northwest of Étaples off the D940; ⊕ year round; free of charge*) epitomises more than most the massive loss of life in two world wars. Terraced rows of white gravestones fan out before you, a grim reminder that, of 11,500 interred here, 10,773 died in or around Étaples during World War I alone.

These included soldiers not only from the UK (among them Victoria Cross recipient Major Douglas Reynolds of the Royal Field Artillery) but others from Canada, Australia, New Zealand, South Africa and India.

With a further 119 buried from World War II – of which 38 remain unidentified – this is the largest Commonwealth cemetery in France. It also contains 658 German burials. The towering white stone arches at the entrance were designed by Sir Edwin Lutyens.

Étaples was chosen by the British Army for a vast World War I training camp due to its safety from attack by land forces. It also had good rail links with both the northern and southern battlefields. But according to many destined for the Western Front, Étaples – or 'Eat Apples' as it was inevitably called – was reckoned to be about the most detested base camp ever. In 1917, 100,000 troops were camped among the sand dunes with a variety of hospitals able to deal with 22,000 wounded or sick. Ten months after the Armistice, three hospitals and a convalescent depot still remained.

Conditions at the camp were atrocious, and both recruits and battle-weary veterans were subjected to intensive training at the notorious Bull Ring training camp set among the sand dunes. This involved training in gas warfare, bayonet drill and long sessions of marching at the double across the dunes. After two weeks, many of the wounded were only too glad to return to the front with unhealed wounds. There were even clashes between patients and the Military Police.

Hospitals were again stationed at Étaples in World War II with the cemetery used for burials from January 1940 until the evacuation at the end of May 1940. After the war, a number of graves were brought into the cemetery from other French burial grounds. Étaples, heavily bombed with 70 civilians killed, received the Croix de Guerre in 1949 in recognition of 'the courage of its people'.

Nowadays the cemetery is a place of quiet reflection, even among the school and other groups who visit by the coachload. Like all Commonwealth war cemeteries, there is a visitors' book you can sign: 'So sad I never met you, dad,' and 'At last I meet you granddad,' are typical of many of the comments. A register shows the location of each grave. Both books are kept in a recess in one of the walls, behind a small bronze door.

centre on the fishing industry: it is not simply a wet-day experience, but an enthusiastic bid to win a family audience. The kids will love tickling turbots in a touch tank and testing their sea legs in a simulated storm.

Elsewhere a genuine 'on-board' feeling is portrayed as you are plunged into the often-dangerous lives of the fishing folk, as they cast their nets, clean the fish and snatch a few hours' sleep. You will leave with a greater knowledge of trawling, dragging for scallops or looking for lobsters than you ever thought possible. Apart from an introductory film in French, English translations are to hand. The staff, too, are helpful.

Also showing what makes the port tick is the **Maritime Museum** (*Musée de la Marine Halle à la Criée, bld de lmpératrice;* ✆ *03 21 09 77 21;* e *museemarineetaples@wanadoo.fr; www.2p2m.org;* ⊕ *Oct–Apr 10.00–12.00 & 15.00–18.00 Mon, Wed–Sat & Sun am, May–Sep 10.00–12.00 & 14.00–19.00, closed Sun am; adult/child €2/1, discount with tourist pass*). Housed in what was once the town's 19th-century fish market, this takes around an hour's concentrated look at the port's fishing heritage. Social life is explored through traditional costumes, including the lace headdresses worn along this stretch of the coast by the often hard-pressed fishermen's wives. On one floor models of *flobarts*, the famous flat-bottomed boats (see page 99) join those of an early steam-powered Channel ferry. Local crafts, from boat-building to coopers and carpenters, also get a showing. Tie this in with a visit to the **Maréis**.

A far more formal, but still fascinating, look at the origins of Étaples is provided by the **Museum of Archaeology** (*Musée d'Archéologie Quentovic; 8 pl du Général de Gaulle;* ☎ *03 21 09 76 20;* e *musee-quentovic@etaples-sur-mer.com; www.musenor.com;* ⊕ *Sep–Jun 14.00–17.00 Mon–Sat, 14.30–17.30 Sun, Jul–Aug 10.00–12.00 & 14.00–18.00 Mon–Sat, 10.00–12.00 & 14.30–18.30 Sun; adult/child aged 6–12 €2.50/1.50; discount with tourist pass, free first Sun of each month*). Lying off the main square, the museum gets its name from Quentovic, from where the Romans planned their invasion of Britain. Tracing the formation of the English Channel, it houses a remarkable collection of geological finds, including flint tools, fossilised fish and bronze- and iron-age pottery, both from the region and beyond. It also devotes space to the role played by Étaples in World War I (see opposite). Special panels are set aside for children.

A world of scaled-down boats, tanks and German bunkers are housed in the **Miniature Workshop and Museum** (*Atelier et Maison de la Miniature La Coderie, bld Bigot Descelers;* ☎ *03 21 09 78 24;* e *preuvost@aol.com; www.modelisme-naval-etaples.fr;* ⊕ *10.00–12.00 & 14.30–18.00 Tue–Sat, 09.30–12.30 & 14.30–18.30 Sun during school holidays; adult/child €3/1.50, discount with tourist pass*). The centre-piece is a 32m² scale model representing the port as it was in 1991–93. This rather splendidly brings to life the sights and sounds of the time – from a fire engine racing to put out a fire in one of the 54 fishermen's houses to the sound of seagulls as the tide ebbs and flows. You also see the gendarmes on the Rose Bridge roundabout, no doubt keeping an eye on the traffic that so often blocks the town in summer.

LE TOUQUET-PARIS-PLAGE

Some say the old girl's lost it. She's old hat, a fading star – suburban even – superseded by swanky jetset resorts where the showbiz rich top up their tans. Statistics prove otherwise. Forget the lack of sun, the windswept dunes and the sometimes long haul to reach the receding seashore: Le Touquet has been, still is – and probably always will be – the place where it all happens. It has everything from sporting activities, of which there are now around 40, to a legacy of unashamed opulence symbolised by the tree-lined avenues of oh-so-British style villas and the four-star splendour of the Westminster Hotel. Portraits of the glitterati of the 1920s, the glory years, hang here alongside those of the new moneyed of the post-war era. A young Sean Connery signed up to his first James Bond film at the Westminster. Winston Churchill was another guest; so, too, were Marlene Dietrich and Edward and Mrs Simpson.

And though the faces may change, Le Touquet retains a swagger which still attracts those bent on seeking, if not quite the hedonistic lifestyle of the early 20th century, at least a highly passable alternative. British drivers predominate at the resort's golf courses, while their fellow compatriots – quite often their wives! – head for the generous selection of specialist food and clothes shops, indulge in watersports or simply stroll along the prom with its usual family-friendly paraphernalia. Le Touquet is a lucky dip of a place, not perhaps to everyone's taste – too English, some say, too racy, even raucous, argue others – but, with 1,200 rooms and some 60 restaurants, her pulling power is as strong as ever.

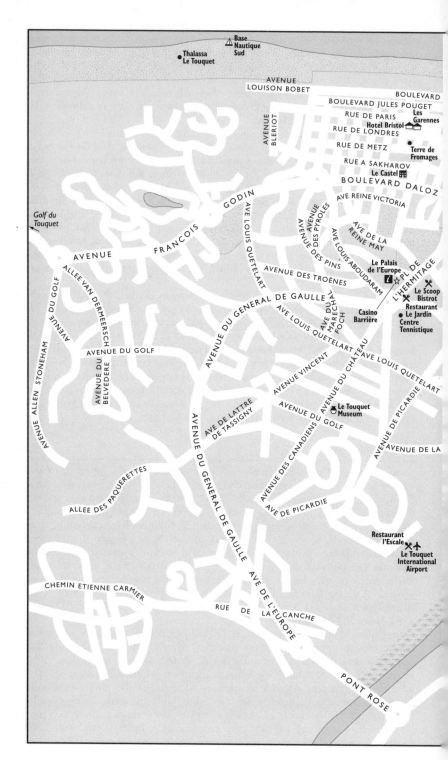

Base
Nautique
Sud

Thalassa
Le Touquet

AVENUE
LOUISON BOBET

BOULEVARD
BOULEVARD JULES POUGET
RUE DE PARIS   Les
Garennes
Hotel Bristol
RUE DE LONDRES
RUE DE METZ   Terre de
Fromages
RUE A SAKHAROV
Le Castel
BOULEVARD DALOZ

AVE REINE VICTORIA

AVENUE
BLERIOT

AVENUE
GODIN

FRANCOIS

Golf du
Touquet

AVENUE

ALLEE VAN DERMEERSCH

AVENUE DU GOLF

AVENUE DU GOLF

AVENUE DU BELVEDERE

AVENUE ALLEN STONEHAM

AVE LOUIS QUETELART

AVENUE
DES PYROLES

AVENUE
DES PINS

AVENUE DES TROÈNES

AVE DE LA
REINE MAY

AVE LOUIS ABOUDARAM

Le Palais
de l'Europe

L'HERMITAGE

PL. DE

Le Scoop
Bistrot
Restaurant
Le Jardin
Centre
Tennistique

AVENUE DU GENERAL DE GAULLE

AVE DU MARECHAL FOCH

Casino
Barrière

AVE LOUIS QUETELART

AVENUE LOUIS QUETELART

AVENUE VINCENT

AVENUE DU CHÂTEAU

AVE LOUIS QUETELART

AVENUE DU GOLF

Le Touquet
Museum

AVE DE LATTRE
DE TASSIGNY

AVENUE DE PICARDIE

AVENUE DU GENERAL DE GAULLE

AVENUE DES CANADIENS

ALLEE DES PAQUERETTES

AVE DE PICARDIE

AVENUE

AVENUE DE LA

Restaurant
l'Escale
Le Touquet
International
Airport

CHEMIN ETIENNE CARMIER

RUE DE LA EUCANCHE

AVE DE L'EUCANCHE

PONT ROSE

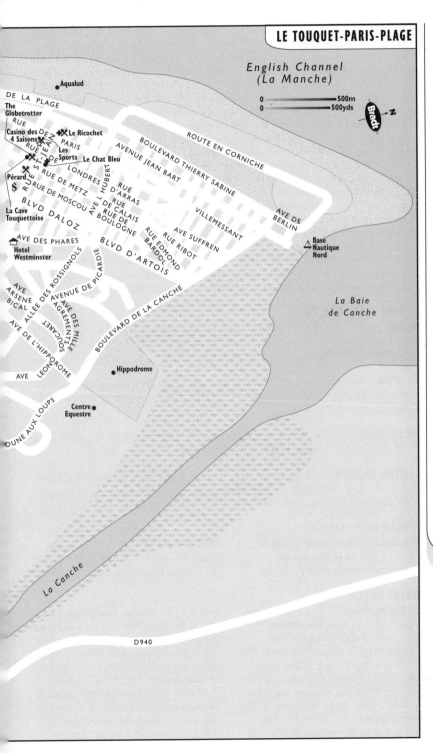

LE TOUQUET-PARIS-PLAGE

**English Channel
(La Manche)**

0 — 500m
0 — 500yds

Bradt N

Aqualud

DE LA PLAGE

The Globetrotter

RUE

Casino des 4 Saisons

Le Ricochet

ROUTE EN CORNICHE

RUE DE S T JEAN

PARIS
Les Sports

Le Chat Bleu

BOULEVARD THIERRY SABINE

AVENUE JEAN BART

Pérard $

RUE DE METZ

LONDRES

RUE DE MOSCOU

RUE D'ARRAS

AVE L DE CALAIS

RUE DE BOULOGNE

VILLEMESSANT

AVE SUFFREN

AVE DE BERLIN

La Cave Touquettoise

BLVD DALOZ

AVE L HUBERT

RUE DE

RUE EDMOND BARDOL

RUE RIBOT

Base Nautique Nord

AVE DES PHARES

Hotel Westminster

BLVD D'ARTOIS

AVE DES ROSSIGNOLS

AVENUE DE PICARDIE

La Baie de Canche

AVE ARSENE BICAL

ALLÉE DES MILLE

AVE DES AGREMENTS

SOUCARET

AVE DE L'HIPPODROME

BOULEVARD DE LA CANCHE

AVE LEONARD

Hippodrome

DUNE AUX LOUPS

Centre Equestre

La Canche

D 940

Coastal Country **LE TOUQUET-PARIS-PLAGE**

4

113

HISTORY Put away the history book: Le Touquet was a simple, and, as it turned out, wise piece of land speculation. In 1837 two French entrepreneurs, Daloz and Alyon, bought 1,600ha of wild and arid land south of the estuary of the River Canche. And though an initial agricultural project failed miserably, and Alyon dropped out, Daloz pressed on with planting pine, poplar, elm and alder trees. By the end of the century, the site had become an attractive wooded enclave by the sea, favoured by the sporting set for its game. Among them was the owner of *Le Figaro* newspaper, who coined the phrase 'Paris-Plage'. By 1894 there were around 170 houses and hotels.

However it was the enthusiasm of two turn-of-the-20th-century English businessmen, John Whitley and Allen Stoneham, which gave rise to Le Touquet Syndicate Ltd – and the targeting of a wealthy British clientele with tempting facilities for golf, tennis, polo and horse racing. Parisians, too, fell under its spell. Even World War I only briefly curtailed the languid way of life. By the 1920s the glory days were in full swing as grandiose villas, often Hollywood in size but frightfully British in character, sprang up to cater for a gaggle of writers, royalty, film stars and politicians all clamouring to be seen in this most trendy of resorts. Vast hotels catered for their every need – they even stretched, it is said, to having separate rooms for wives and mistresses! Some, Noël Coward and P G Wodehouse among them, bought property. The latter was later held by the invading Germans who built the familiar blockhouses along the coast, and left Le Touquet one of the most mined towns in France.

GETTING THERE AND AWAY
By car From Calais or Boulogne take the A16 to Étaples, then follow signs for the 3km journey to Le Touquet. Driving time is 45 minutes from Calais and 30 minutes from Boulogne.

By train Although there are trains from both Calais-Ville and Boulogne-Ville stations to Étaples station, you will have to take a bus or taxi from Étaples to Le Touquet.

By air Approximately 20-minutes' flight with LyddAir from Lydd, Kent departing 09.30, arriving Le Touquet 11.00 local time (see page 25).

GETTING AROUND Le Touquet operates three free-of-charge mini electric buses. These run daily during the holiday season and, throughout the rest of the year, every weekend and on market days, Thursday and Friday, in the morning.

TOURIST INFORMATION
☑ Le Touquet-Paris-Plage Tourisme Le Palais de l'Europe; ☎ 03 21 06 72 00; e contact@ letouquet.com; www.letouquet.com; ⏰ Oct–Mar 09.00–18.00 Mon–Sat, 10.00–18.00 Sun & public holidays, Apr–Sep 09.00–19.00 Mon–Sat, 10.00–19.00 Sun. Free maps & help with accommodation/activities.

🏠 WHERE TO STAY
🏠 **Hotel Westminster** (115 rooms & suites) ave du Verger; ☎ 03 21 05 48 48; www.westminster.fr. Offering oodles of 1930s old-style charm, the impressive red-brick building was built between 1925 & 1928 in the Anglo-Normandy Art Deco style & named after the Duchess of Westminster. Lying just 500m from the beach, it's the sort of place to lash out on for a special occasion. It's not cheap: an off-season double starts at €160 with b/fast from €18 pp. Look out for special gourmet – the hotel sports 2 top-class restaurants – or golf short-break offers or promotions. A new luxury spa, opened at the beginning of 2009, offers a wide choice of treatments: a great pampering experience in a wonderfully calm, relaxing atmosphere, reported one guest. $$$$
🏠 **Hotel Bristol** (49 rooms) 17 rue Jean Monnet; ☎ 03 21 05 49 95; e reservations@hotelbristol.fr; www.hotelbristol.fr. Long-established family-owned hotel just 2mins from Market Square & shops, with a short stroll to the beach. 2 floors of refurbished

rooms in cool, neutral colours, with great shower-rooms rather than bathrooms & a couple of family suites. There is a conservatory-style b/fast room & a comfy bar area with sunken fireplace for cosy winter evenings. Parking at the rear. $$$$

🏠 **Les Garennes** (1 suite, 2 rooms with shower/toilet) 16 rue de la Paix; ✆ 03 21 05 90 49; e lesgarennestouquet@wanadoo.fr. You can't fail to miss one of the oldest houses in town: built in 1892 in the style of Napoleon III the rustic balconied exterior is matched inside by twisting wooden stairs (check if suitable for those unsteady on their feet) & bedrooms reflecting the watercolour talents of artist owner Alexandra Gaillard. It's quiet, comfortable & quaint. With freshly bought croissants & baguettes for a b/fast featuring juice from newly squeezed oranges (always a good sign) & homemade jams, this a place to bag for a short break — or as home to a w/end workshop run by fellow artist Gerard Viret. $$

✖ WHERE TO EAT AND DRINK

✖ **Restaurant Le Jardin** pl de l'Hermitage; ✆ 03 21 05 16 34; www.restaurant-lejardin-letouquet.com; ◷ 12.30–14.00 & 19.00–22.00 daily. Another trusted favourite with traditional décor, & a pleasant garden area for lazy summer lunches & people watching. Excellent fish dishes, great choice of dinner menus with main courses from €10. Set menus from €25.50, for children €10. The superb chocolate puddings will please any chocoholic. They also do a fine crème brûlée. $$$$

✖ **Le Ricochet** 49 rue de la Paris; ✆ 03 21 06 41 36; e contact@ricochet-letouquet.com; www.ricochet-letouquet.com; ◷ 12.30–14.30 & 19.30–23.00 Mon–Tue & Fri–Sun. Following extensive experience in the Caribbean & the US, chef Jean-Marc Carelle returned with his wife Christelle to his hometown in 2004 to set up this popular little restaurant offering a personal twist on French- & Asian-style cuisine with a deli & cookery school opposite. Set menus €12–28. Jean-Marc, who speaks excellent English, also offers a 2hr demonstration on an easily achievable 3-course menu. $$$$

✖ **Restaurant l'Escale** Aéroport du Touquet; ✆ 03 21 05 23 22; e contact@escale-letouquet.com; www.escale-letouquet.com; ◷ 09.00–23.00 daily except Tue. Watch the planes land from this bright open-plan new restaurant: the locals like it & it makes a handy out-of-town midday stop. There's a tasty €10 2-course choice of entrée/main course or main course/dessert with a €7.50 menu for children up to 12. $$$$$

✖ **Le Scoop Bistrot** 1 pl de l'Hermitage; ✆ 03 21 06 30 11; www.le-scoop.fr; ◷ daily 08.30 for b/fast & 11.30–14.30 & 19.00–22.30. An unassuming but friendly bistro perfect for a quick bite. Recommended by its popularity with the locals, this is a solid choice for classic dishes at very reasonable prices (€10–22.50). There are no set menus. A lively Sun lunchtime sees a real mix of customers from families & student types to wealthy dowagers with lapdogs! $$$

✖ **Les Sports** 22 rue St-Jean; ✆ 03 21 05 05 22; www.brasserieslesports.fr; ◷ 07.00–04.00 daily. A popular no-nonsense café & brasserie with a basic but good-value menu: try fish with *ratte*, the town's famous potato, rather than chips. This early variety of spud is similar in shape to a mouse, hence its name. $$$

✖ **Pérard** 67 rue de Metz; ✆ 03 21 34 44 72; www.restaurantperard.com; ◷ 09.00–23.00 daily. Drop in at this restaurant & shop whose famous fish, crab or lobster soup stems from 1940 when a hungry war-torn Serge Pérard, aged 20, concocted a dish of cooked fish heads from Boulogne, potatoes, thyme, bay & garlic croutons. In 1963 he opened his own restaurant & by 1970 was producing the best-selling soup; sample some at the Oyster Bar for €7.50–8.50 or as part of a set menu for €23–34. $$$

✖ **The Globetrotter** 66 rue de Metz; ✆ 03 21 05 12 54; www.leglobetrotter.com; ◷ 08.00–01.00 Mon–Fri, 08.00–02.00 at w/ends. This is the place for UK Premier League footie fans. Man Utd & other shirts decorate the traditional wooden-panelled walls of this great little hang-out for sports lovers of all kinds. Expect a noisy night out with the lads... $$

SHOPPING The streets near the seafront present an entirely different picture. Gone are the wide boulevards and squares of the town centre. Instead, a huddle of shops and a maze of alleyways, within a close-knit grid, is dominated by the horseshoe-shaped market hall, its moon-shaped entrance framed by wooden gables. This listed building offers that colourful pallet of fresh veg, cheese and fish that the French manage so well. Look out for **Elizabeth's**, a stall run by Yorkshire-born Elizabeth Green-Vellissariou. Married to a Frenchman, she started the stall selling English products some 17 years ago. The market, held on Saturday

4

Pause for a moment. **Le Chat Bleu** (*47 rue St-Jean;* \ *03 21 05 03 86; www.letouquet.com*), a chocolaterie whose branches include Paris and Lille, proved popular with children when it was opened in 1912 by two elderly sisters – thanks largely to their two blue Persian cats. By 1920, Le Chat Bleu, as it became known, was also a fashionable tearoom, with the cats attracting the cream of society. In 1929 it moved to its present location, and until 1939 a delivery boy cycled though the woods with boxes of chocolates for the private villas and grand hotels. Today the expression *faire un chat bleu* means 'give yourself a treat'.

mornings year round and on Thursday mornings from mid-May to September, lies at the southern end of rue de Metz, which is itself a magnet for shoppers, or those simply eyeing up the wares.

Just as intriguing is **La Cave Touquettoise** (*72 rue de Metz;* \ *03 21 05 63 40;* e *lacavetouquettoise@wanadoo.fr; www.cavetouquettoise.fr*), which stocks not just trendy rosé wines and a cellar full of others, but over 200 whiskies and a great selection of regional beers. Cheese? Just seek advice from Vincent Vermesse at **Terre de Fromages** (*118 rue de Metz, pl du Marché;* \ *03 21 90 61 59; www.terr-de-fromages.com*).

OTHER PRACTICALITIES

Bank Crédit Agricole (CA), 39 bld Daloz; ⊕ 09.15–12.15 & 13.45–18.00 Tue–Fri, 08.30–12.30 Sat. ATM accepts the majority of cards.

Supermarkets 4 in the town centre accepting credit cards; ⊕ 08.00–13.00 & 15.00–19.00, 08.00–13.00 Sun

Pharmacies *Pharmacie des 4 Saisons* 17 rue St Jean; \ 03 21 05 04 66; ⊕ 09.00–13.00 & 14.00–19.30 Mon–Sat; *Pharmacie de la Côte d'Opale* 45 rue St Jean; \ 03 21 05 13 42; ⊕ 09.00–12.30 & 14.00–19.30 Mon–Sat. These 2 pharmacies also open on alternate Sun at the times stated above.

Post Office rue Royale; ⊕ 08.30–12.00 & 13.30–17.00 Mon–Fri, 08.30–12.30 Sat

Public toilet (s) 1 by market, 3 on the seafront

WHAT TO SEE AND DO No sooner have you reached the outskirts of town than neatly signposted avenues gracefully guide you past the sporting enclaves towards the big bouncing boulevards where the rich rub shoulders with short-break visitors. You can't miss the tourist office. It forms part of the **Le Palais de l'Europe** – no address, just a snazzy building dominating a vast garden. The congresses, concerts and shows that it hosts are proof of Le Touquet's enduring attraction. Grab a handy bunch of English-language leaflets from the tourist office, which illustrate how a pot-pourri of unrestrained architectural styles created the town's sometimes outrageous, but certainly innovative, villas. 'Cathedrals on toast' my late father affectionately called them.

Either use these to do your own thing, or make use of the **Promenades and Decouvertes**, a programme of different ways to discover the town. These are bookable at the tourist office for selected dates (*45mins by horse-drawn carriage dep 10.00 year round, adult/child €6/3.50 or €2.50 under 5; 90mins by cycle using marked tracks, with parking, for seasonal architectural, historic & maritime themes dep 14.30 adult/child €5/2.50, under 5 free; also 1–4hrs walking tours on network of paths*). Some of the main buildings are shown on the town map (page 113).

Don't miss **Le Castel** on rue Jean Monnet, built in 1904 and initially called La Tourelle, near the town hall – itself a rather splendid 1931 building with a very eclectic architectural style. With its spiralling tower reminiscent of that of Rapunzel, this is as much Disney as Art Nouveau. Other villas such as **Villa Sunny Corner** in avenue du Général de Gaulle, built in 1927 and inspired by the

English arts and crafts movement, provide a perfect backcloth for the social manners of the Noël Coward era. There is even a bit of Czech cubism at **Tata Ice**, on avenue de la Paix, built in 1926.

Le Touquet Museum (*Musée du Touquet, ave du Golf;* ⟍ *03 21 05 62 62;* e *musee@letouquet.com; www.letouquet.com;* ⊕ *10.00–12.00 & 14.00–18.00 Mon–Sat, 10.00–1200 & 14.30–18.00 Sun; adult/child €3.80/1 & €2 concessions, free 1st Sun of each month*) is housed in a handsome forest villa, Wayside, built for a doctor in 1925. Exhibits include the works of around 200 painters who flocked to the Étaples region from Britain, the USA, Norway and Australia between 1880 and 1914 (see page 120). A seascape by actress Sarah Bernhardt is kept close to the neo-impressionist paintings of Henri Le Sidaner, Iso Rae's religious scenes and the famous representation of *La Plage de Berck* by Eugène Boudin. Signed photos taken by Parisian art editor Edouard Champion between 1880 and 1938, of presidents, sportsmen, writers and other celebrities, paint a picture of the resort's golden era.

Recognised as one of France's best-known thalassotherapy centres, **Thalassa Le Touquet** (⟍ *03 21 09 85 30;* e *H0449-Sb@accor.com; www.accorthalassa.com;* ⊕ *daily 08.30–18.30 except Sun afternoon*) ties in with short stays at the sea-front Novotel and Ibis hotels, as well as the Mercure Grand Hotel which, overlooking the Bay of the Canche, has its own swimming pool and aqua and spa fitness facilities. A one-day discovery visit costs €139.

Le Touquet has two casinos: **Casino Barrière** (*Palais de l'Europe;* ⟍ *03 21 05 01 05; www.lucienbarriere.com;* ⊕ *slot machines 10.00–03.00 Mon–Fri, 10.00–04.00 Sat & evenings before public holiday, tables 22.00–03.00 Mon–Fri, 22.00–04.00 Sat & evening of public holidays*) which also features shows, bars and restaurants, and **Casino des 4 Saisons** (*rue St-Jean;* ⟍ *03 20 05 16 99;* ⊕ *09.00–03.00 & 04.00 Sat & public holidays*).

ACTIVITIES

Walking The forests and the dunes around Le Touquet offer year-round hiking trails: La Pomme de Pin (*from ave de l'hippodrome, 6km along forest paths, 2–3hrs*); La Daphné (*from ave du Château, 9km forest paths & villa gardens, 3–4hrs*); Le Feuille de Chêne (*from ave J L Sanguet, 10km pines & sea & the Ypres Garden, 4hrs 30mins*); and L'Argousier (*from ave A Bical, 16km dune plants mudflats & birdwatching, whole day*).

Golf With its dune and pineland setting, **Golf du Touquet** (*ave du Golf;* ⟍ *03 21 06 28 00;* e *letouquet@opengolfclu.com; www.opengolfclub.com; green fees from €36/120 depending on course & season*) ranks high in France with two 18-hole and one nine-hole courses, as well as a driving range. La Fôret (18-hole 5,827m par 71) is set in a pine grove; La Mer (18-hole 6,407m par 72) was inaugurated in 1931. Mainly sculpted around the rugged and windswept dunes, it has been likened to a Scottish links and has hosted the French Open. Le Manoir (9-hole 2,817m par 35 and opened in 1994) is suited to beginners, or those who wish to perfect their swing. It is used for teaching and to help golfers to gain their green card.

Tennis The **Centre Tennistique** (*Rond point des Sports;* ⟍ *03 21 05 02 97;* e *tennis@letouquet.com; www.letouquet.com;* ⊕ *year round; from €17 for off-peak hr, €210 for carnet of tickets (2 per hr), to €346 weekly for couple with 2 or more children*) has 25 clay and 8 indoor courts. The tennis school offers individual and group tuition and school holiday courses. There's also a swimming pool.

Horseriding Forest dunes and beach hacking for all levels, including sunset and sunrise rides, is on offer in La Canche International Park (see page 118). France takes horseriding seriously, and Le Touquet offers the chance to take lessons or top up your skills. Contact **Centre Equestre** (*ave de al Dune Aux Loups;* ⟍ *03 21 05 15 25;*

e accueil.centreequestre@letouquet.com; www.letouquet.com; ⊕ *year round with riding school, competition & coaching; adult/child €13.40/9.20 under 16 for 1hr & €9 for pony ride for children over 3. Easter & summer beach rides for children; also rides for disabled, birthday & stag/hen night groups)* for further information.

Sailing and water sports
At least call in at the **Base Nautique Nord** (*1 ave Jean Ruet;* ℡ *03 21 05 59 77; e basenautiquenord@letouquet.com; www.letouquet.com*), if only for a snack or to watch the yachts bobbing in the superb estuary setting of the Bay of La Canche. Apart from courses held at the sailing school, instruction is given in windsurfing, kayaking, canoeing and sailing a catamaran. The bay is also home to a huge range of wildlife, from birds to seals, and the surrounding coastline offers trails through pine groves and salt marshes.

Land yachting
From 1910, Louis Bleriot (see page 192) was criss-crossing the beach at the controls of his *aeroplage* or 'beach plane'. By the 1930s, Henry Demoury was building and hiring out sand yachts. Nowadays this fast-growing sport can be practised at **Base Nautique Sud** (*bd Pouget;* ℡ *03 21 05 33 51; e charavoile@ letouquet.com; courses inc 5 days, 2hrs yachting daily, at €161 for youngsters 8–12*).

Family fun
A water world of twisting rivers is created at **Aqualud** (*Front de mer;* ℡ *03 21 90 07 07; e contact@aqualud.com; www.aqualud.com;* ⊕ *Apr–Jun & Sep–Nov 10.15–17.45 but not every day so check first; Jul–Aug 10.00–19.00 or 10.00–23.00 at peak times; adult/child from €15.50 in low season to €17.50 high season; under 1m tall free, €23.50/25.50 with snacks*), in an indoor pyramid of glass. The braver try the Black Hole and the Twister, which dramatically finish in a spinning centrifuge; most rides, reported one young enthusiast, are just big slides with the water kept at a year-round 27 degrees. The outdoor section, open in summer, with a large terrace with loungers overlooking the sea, has three more pools, flumes and rides. English is spoken widely with lifeguards providing guidance on rides.

ENJOY A DREAM OF A GALLOP!

Regular rider and horse owner Ellie Philpott, an executive with SeaFrance, gets to gallop at long last…

If, like me, you happen to live in a part of the UK where stony beaches prevail, you'll love the undulating dunes and long, wide sandy beaches at Le Touquet. And they're great for more than just building sandcastles. There's an amazing variety of fun sports available including horseriding along the beach. I've ridden horses for years, but never had the chance to gallop along a beach, until my last visit to Le Touquet fulfilled that dream. I pitched up at the Centre Equestre (see page 117). It caters for riders of all abilities and with 45km of forest bridleways, dunes, estuary and long sandy beaches on its doorstep the choice of riding is fantastic. I joined a small group of experienced riders and followed a little track leading down from the centre to the beach – we didn't have to go on the road once. We had the opportunity for a couple of canters on the way down, and then two lovely flat-out gallops along the edge of the sea. The staff were very friendly and competent and the horses were nicely turned out and well mannered. If you're not very experienced, it doesn't matter at all. The centre has treks for adult and child beginners and some bombproof trekking ponies that are perfect for the job. Smaller children can enjoy a pony ride on a leading rein. There's a lot to tempt me back – dawn and dusk rides, swimming with the horses, polo lessons and carriage riding to name but a few.

It is at Berck that the Côte d'Opale leaves Pas de Calais to cross into Picardy and eventually the basin of the Somme. Berck may seem at first glance to consist of little more than a typical, somewhat garish seafront. Behind this candy-floss façade, however, lies a fascinating history: from the late 19th century its traditional reliance on fishing gave way to sanatoriums and a new life as a bright, and certainly breezy, resort known for its curative qualities. It's also a wow with kite fliers – the town holds its own annual spring festival – while kite buggies and sand yachts hurtle along the northern edge of the 12km sands.

HISTORY Originally on the mouth of the Arche, a small coastal river, the town, which appeared first as Berc in 1215, became the centre of maritime activities as the river silted up. By 1301 it was officially known as Berk (derived from *berg* in German or *bekrr* in Scandinavian) and had 150 homesteads and nearly 800 inhabitants.

St John the Baptist's Church was built around this time. Its roofless steeple was used as a lighthouse and watchtower: it's now a major site at Berck-Ville, some 1.5km inland, and reminds visitors how the medieval harbour gradually fell victim to the shifting sands with the village separated from the sea by wide expanses of dunes and water-meadows.

Despite the loss of the harbour, new-style fishing vessels allowed the locals not only to continue trading but, towards the end of the 19th century, to have the highest number of fishing smacks on a French beach. Eventually, with only the bay of the River Authie suitable for sheltering ships, the wharf at La Madelon became the last mooring place for the smacks, or *flobarts*, which are still a traditional sight along the Côte d'Opale (see page 99). Life became hard for a fishing population now stuck in a landlocked village.

But the changing scenery was to prove their saviour: the water meadows, dotted with windmills, looked pretty good as a rural idyll in harmony with the coast. And first one doctor, then another, noticed Berck's healing properties – especially for children. One nurse nicknamed Marion-Tout-Seule (a statue of whom is seen by the seafront) demonstrated particular success with the healing waters – her 72 young charges showed vast improvement. By 1861 a small wooden hospital had been built by architect Emile Lavezzari. It was Lavezzari's artist son, Jan, who later captured perfectly the opal colour which gave the entire coastline its name. Interest in the town was accelerated when in May 1864 the Empress Eugénie, worried by her son's health, came to Berck. In 1869 the Grand Hospital Maritime was inaugurated and, following alterations in 1887, nearly 1,000 patients were accommodated in Berck.

Swimmers, too, flocked to the beach. Berck's first hotel was built in 1858, and, in the following decade, chalets and shops began to fill each side of the funnel-like Entonnier at the end of the present rue de Impératrice. In 1896 the local train brought more than 77,000 passengers to the beach station inaugurated five years earlier. Berck-Plage was born – and from then on it was plain sailing as it became associated with society life where the Parisian bourgeoisie rubbed shoulders with regular visitors from Russia and Latin America. Among those who had villas at Berck was La Baronne James de Rothschild; he became a great benefactor of the town.

But it was not casino thrills they sought. They preferred racing in sand yachts, or joining early attempts at flying in which Cambrai-born Bleriot (see page 192) took part. Bathing huts could be found amid the hulls of smacks hauled up on the beach and were suddenly shared by fishermen, patients and tourists alike.

By the 1930s the iodine-laden sea air began drawing seasonal crowds when the first paid-for holidays hailed the arrival of hordes of workers from the region's industrial north. This and bombing in World War II, in which many fine villas

Berck-sur-Mer also became famous for its aerial photographs from high-flying kites. The first, it seems, were taken with the help of E D Archibald, a British meteorologist, in 1887. The following year a French enthusiast, Arthur Batut, used a 4.3m^2 kite to take aerial photos with a 8x10cm camera. This was controlled by a wick which lit up when he released the kite. From 1889–91 Emile Wenz improved the technique by using electricity to start the camera, photographing Berck using glass plates. From then on the resort became the most photographed place from the air prior to 1914.

See www.carnetdevol.org/siteCVang/kiteaero.swf for a brief history of the technique in France.

were destroyed, changed the once upper-class character for ever. But, as with family resorts Europewide, times are changing with greater emphasis now placed on the get-up-and-go activities in which the resort revels.

WHAT TO SEE AND DO The Berck painters were undoubtedly the last chroniclers of the fishing fleets for which the town was famed. Edouard Manet who, in 1873, portrayed Berck in one of his most famous canvases *On the Beach*, and Eugéne Boudin are the most representative. But it was arguably the artist Jan Lavezzari (1876–1947), a seafarer to the core, who captured with the most terrifying accuracy the fishermen's daily and nightly struggle with heaving seas and often sullen skies. Lavezzari's grey-green canvasses are seen at their best in the surprisingly unsung **Berck Museum** (*60 rue de Impératrice;* ❧ *03 21 84 07 80;* e *musee@berck-sur-mer.com; www.opale-sud.com;* ⊕ *1 Jan–30 Jun & 1 Sep–31 Dec 10.00–12.00 & 15.00–18.00 daily except Mon am & Tue, 1 Jul–31 Aug 10.00–12.00 & 14.00–19.00 except Tue; free).*

The museum, a converted police station, is also home to a captivating collection of fishing memorabilia, including a traditionally furnished family room, and a collection of character-catching miniatures of fishermen and their wives by two more of the artistic fraternity, Francis Tattegrain and Charles Roussel. Contemporary work includes a highly tactile shoal of fish made of tinkling glass by Marcoville. Upstairs, in a bright and air-conditioned setting, is the only exhibition of underwater archaeology in northern France. Some of the 2nd-century treasures have been – and are still being – found by André l'Hoer from the museum, a diver himself. The museum is a real find if ever there was one.

For families On the seafront, **Agora** (*Esplanade Parentier;* ❧ *03 21 89 87 00;* e *info@agora-berck.com; www.agora-berck.com*) is an all-things-to-all-ages centre. It has a 25m eight-lane pool with a wave machine and a 30m slide, as well as ten-pin bowling and kite flying. There's also horseriding and a chance to learn to speed sail with classes for beginners.

Close by, between Le Touquet and Berck at Merriment, **Parc Bagatelle** (*off the A16 motorway at junction 25;* ❧ *08 26 30 20 30;* e *contact@parcbagatelle.com; www.parcbagatelle.com;* ⊕ *Apr–Jun & Sep selected dates, Jul–Aug 05.00–19.00 daily; adult/child from €19.50/€16.50, children under 1m tall free & concessions €12 for disabled*) likewise splashes out on thrills and spills. These range from the more sedate Monorail, seeing the park from above, to a stomach-churning water ride aboard big wooden logs. It's real family stuff, with a string of fast-food eateries.

Families may also like to go **seal-spotting** at the lifeguards' or first-aid stations located at the Base Nautique at the end of the paved walk alongside the beach starting from the huge Hôpital Maritime.

5

St-Omer and the Flemish Hinterland

This is the area where day trip familiarity gives way to the rural heart of the region, a place to dip your toe into a pot-pourri of tall tales, even taller giants, and a plethora of local dishes designed to bring out the flavour of Flemish culture and heritage. Scenically, too, it is one of the most fascinating. From the market gardens of the St-Omer marshland, where the postman delivers by boat, to the cheese-making monks at Cassel, this is France as we imagine it. Walkers, cyclists, horseriders and birdwatchers are all catered for. So, too, are campers and self-caterers. Sit back in the rustic surroundings of an *estaminet*, sip a locally brewed beer and, with the coast still not that far way, revel in the best of surf and turf.

ST-OMER

Squatting almost smugly in a network of roads St-Omer, a mere 45-minute drive from Calais or the Channel Tunnel, represents for many the first real taste of France. In fact, previously ruled by the Spanish, it only became French in 1678, later than any other part of the Artois region in which it lies.

But why nitpick when there's so much to drool over? There's the massive cathedral for starters, which presides over a flamboyant Flemish central square and has sufficient sculpted bays and gables to seal St-Omer's position as a religious and historic cornerstone in northern France. It also has some fine shops, a string of cafés and restaurants and a superbly landscaped golf course. It is furthermore a major beer-brewing centre.

St-Omer does admittedly get crowded, however, especially in the peak season. Parking can be a problem and the often odd blend of old and new buildings could grate, although in practice it seldom does. So don't bypass it, as so many do. It's worth at least a day's detour, if not more, and is an ideal base for visiting other parts of Nord-Pas de Calais.

HISTORY Opportunity, it is said, rather than a reasoned choice drove Audomar (otherwise known as St-Omer) and three other missionary monks to establish a marshland abbey on the bend of the Aa River in AD651.

By the 12th century St-Omer had become a coveted commercial port, which fell, in turn, to the Earl of Flanders, the King of France, the Earl of Artois, the Duke of Burgundy and the Emperor of Spain. In 1678 it was returned to France.

By the end of the 17th century it was a flourishing religious centre, surviving the excesses of both the French and, later, the industrial revolutions. Though largely spared from major battles, it did witness the building of some of Hitler's most daunting weapons in World War II (see page 126).

Now housing many educational centres and the Assizes of Pas de Calais, St-Omer has become the intellectual and administrative capital of the region. It is also

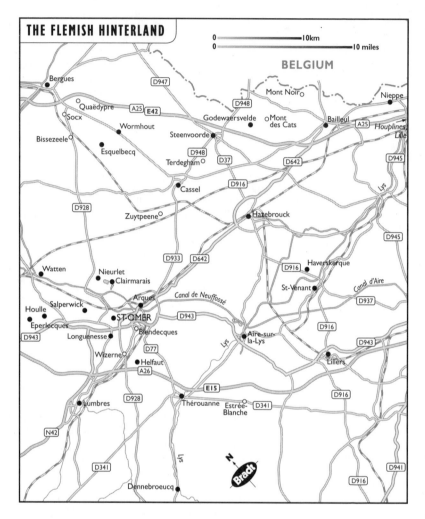

THE FLEMISH HINTERLAND

BELGIUM

one of five Nord-Pas de Calais towns recognised as being of artistic and historic significance. The others are Boulogne-sur-Mer, Cambrai, Lille and Roubaix.

GETTING THERE AND AWAY
By car From Calais take the A26/E15 motorway. After 31km take exit 3 (St-Omer–Arques) then follow the D942 (St-Omer–Tatinghem through Saint-Martin-au-Laërt). Motorway toll: €2.30.

By rail To get to St-Omer take TER Line 12 (Calais–St-Omer–Lille) for the 30-minute journey from Calais-Ville (see page 59). There are around 25 trains a day. From St-Omer, train Line 12, serves Lille (50 minutes) and Hazebrouck (15 minutes). From Hazebrouck there are connections to Dunkirk (30 minutes), Béthune (30 minutes), Lens (45 minutes) and Arras (1 hour). Line 6 trains serve Arras–Hazebrouck–Dunkirk. There are around 20 trains a day, with stops at Vimy, Bergues and Cassel.

Getting into town From St-Omer station, place du 8 Mai 1945, you can walk to the town centre, which takes around 15 minutes, or take a bus. Buy the €1 ticket from the driver or at the railway station; 10 tickets are available for €8. Lines A and B (St-Omer to Helfaut via Arques) run to place Victor Hugo, the main square, and Line D (Clairmarais–St-Omer–Arques) to the public garden. Timetables (*horaires*) are available at the train station or at www.casobus.com, or can be obtained by phoning ⬩ 0 800 510 232 free of charge or calling in at 3 place Foch on the main square.

By bus There is no direct bus link from Calais or Boulogne; rail (opposite) is the only public means of transport between the ports. There are four buses daily via Arques to Aire-sur-la-Lys (see page 133) from the railway station, with a stop at the public garden (*Cars Merlier 17 rue Jules Verne;* ⬩ *03 21 98 44 12; or ask at railway station or tourist office;* €3.40 *1-way for the 45min journey; dep: 08.02, 12.33, 13.58 & 17.46*).

There are no direct buses to attractions. NB: Though Lines A and B go to Helfaut, the town for La Coupole (see page 126), the bus stop is some distance away.

TOURIST INFORMATION

🔲 **Office de Tourisme de la Région de Saint-Omer** 4 rue du Lion d'Or; ⬩ 03 21 98 08 51; e contact@ tourisme-saintomer.com; www.tourisme-saintomer.com; ⏰ Jan–10 Apr & Oct–Dec 09.00–12.30 & 14.00–18.00 Mon–Sat, 11 Apr–Sep 09.00–18.00 Mon–Sat, 10.00–13.00 Sun & public holidays. Located in a modern cinema & leisure complex, the office offers a wide range of tours & sightseeing tickets. A €5 audio-guided tour of St-Omer centre narrated by the monk Audomar lasts 1hr 20mins.

WHERE TO STAY

🏠 **Hôtel Bretagne** (70 rooms) 2 pl du Vainquai; ⬩ 03 21 38 25 78; e acceuil@hotelbretagne.com; www.hotelbretagne.com. Nicely located near the town centre, & conveniently laid back from the main road, this red-bricked 3-star hotel provides a handy & comfortable overnight stop. It has plenty of parking. A buffet-style b/fast costs €9. Extensively refurbished, it is now part of the Inter-Hotel group. $$$

🏠 **Hôtel Le Saint-Louis** (30 rooms) 25 rue d'Arras; ⬩ 03 21 38 35 21; e contact@hotel-saintlouis.com; www.hotel-saintlouis.com. Close to the city centre, this is a good place to hang up your hat, leave the car for €9 in the locked yard & settle down for a quiet overnight stop. The rooms in what was formerly a coaching inn are small, but comfortable. B/fast at €9 is good value. There is a comfortable bar & the Le Flaubert restaurant provides a handy €15.90–30 set menu ($$). $$$

🏠 **Hotel Ibis** (65 rooms) 2–4 rue Henri Dupois; ⬩ 03 21 93 11 11; e h0723@accor.com; www.ibishotel.com. In line with others in the chain, it provides reasonable rooms, a restaurant & round-the-clock snacks, all useful if you have made a last-minute booking. $$

WHERE TO EAT

✖ **Le Cygne** 8 rue Caventou; ⬩ 03 21 98 20 52; www.restaurantlecygne.fr; ⏰ 11.45–13.45 & 18.30–21.15 Mon–Sat, closed Sun evening. Said by one reviewer to be unpretentious yet providing great food, the restaurant is highly regarded by British day-trippers, many from cross-Channel Kent. $$$$

✖ **Le Vainquai** (Hotel Bretagne: see above) ⏰ 12.00–14.00 & 19.15–21.30. With pleasant surroundings & reasonably priced menus, the restaurant is ideally placed if staying overnight. The emphasis is on fish dishes, from fishermen's stew (€13) to fried scallops Provençale style (€18.50) & sea bass in olive oil at slightly less. Set menus, €14.50–35 for 2 courses up to a full-blown gastronomic affair with ½ bottle of wine, include meat courses. $$$

✖ **Au Vieux Marché** 2 pl Pierre Bonhomme; ⬩ 03 21 29 39; ⏰ 12.00–14.00 & 19.00–22.00 Mon–Sat. Recommended for its speciality food & friendly atmosphere. $$$

✖ **De Drie Kalders** 18 pl du Maréchal Foch; ⬩ 03 21 39 72 52; ⏰ 12.00–14.00 & 19.00–22/23.00, closed Mon & Wed; e contact@restaurant3caves.fr; www.restaurant3caves.fr. Located in a cellar, this busy, bustling & cheery place is as much a part of the square as the more stately surroundings. Even better is the daily blackboard menu, or the mind-boggling standard one, which between them bring together the essential flavours of the Nord. A €20.50 regional menu will provide pâté cooked with beer or Maroilles cheese, *carbonade flamande* (beef stew made with

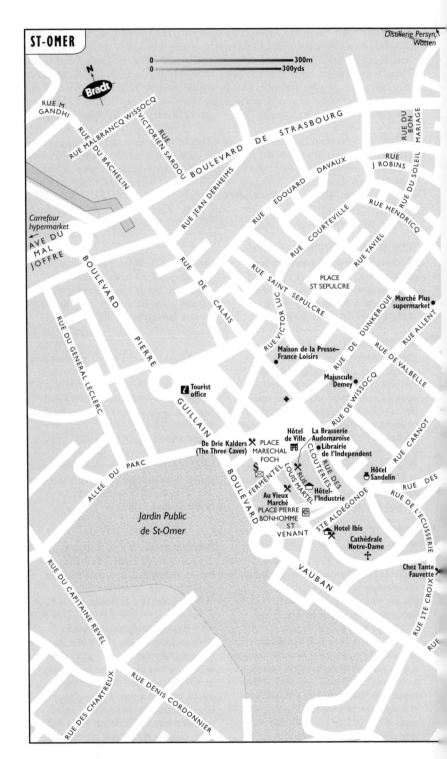

ST-OMER

Distillerie Persyn,
Watten

N

Bradt

0 ———————— 300m
0 ———————— 300yds

RUE M GANDHI

RUE MALBRANCQ WISSOCQ

RUE DU BACHELIN

RUE VICTORIEN SARDOU

BOULEVARD DE STRASBOURG

RUE DU BON MARIAGE

Carrefour hypermarket

AVE DU MAL JOFFRE

RUE JEAN DERHEIMS

RUE EDOUARD DAVAUX

RUE J ROBINS

RUE DU SOLEIL MARIAGE

RUE COURTEVILLE

RUE HENDRICQ

RUE TAVIEL

BOULEVARD PIERRE

RUE DE CALAIS

RUE SAINT SEPULCRE

PLACE ST SEPULCRE

RUE VICTOR LUC

RUE DU DUNKERQUE

Marché Plus supermarket

RUE ALLENT

RUE DU GENERAL LECLERC

Maison de la Presse– France Loisirs

RUE DE VALBELLE

Majuscule Demey

RUE DE WISSOCQ

Tourist office

RUE CARNOT

GUILLAIN

Hôtel de Ville

La Brasserie Audomaroise

De Drie Kalders (The Three Caves)

PLACE MARECHAL FOCH

Librairie de l'Independant

Hôtel Sandelin

RUE DES

RUE DE L'ECUSSERIE

BOULEVARD FERMENTEL

RUE LOUIS MARTEL

RUE DES CLOUTERIES

Hôtel- l'Industrie

ALLEE DU PARC

Au Vieux Marché

PLACE PIERRE BONHOMME

ST VENANT

STE ALDEGONDE

Hotel Ibis

Jardin Public de St-Omer

Cathédrale Notre-Dame

Chez Tante Fauvette

VAUBAN

RUE STE CROIX

RUE DU CAPITAINE REVEL

RUE DES CHARTREUX

RUE DENIS CORDONNIER

RUE

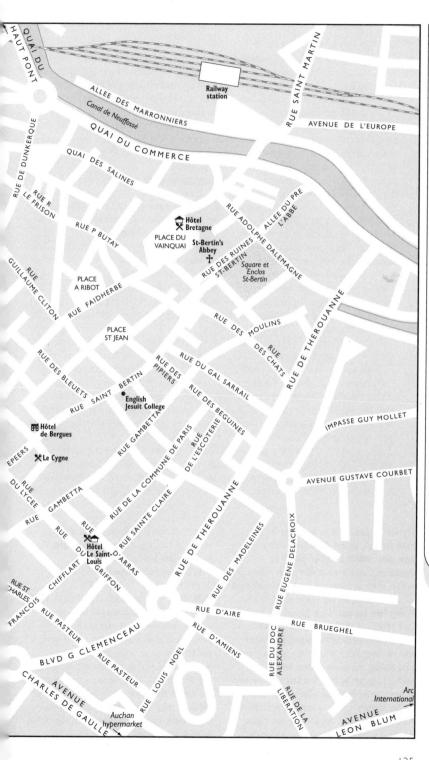

Railway
station

QUAI DU HAUT PONT

ALLEE DES MARRONNIERS

Canal de Neuffossé

RUE SAINT MARTIN

AVENUE DE L'EUROPE

QUAI DU COMMERCE

QUAI DES SALINES

RUE DE DUNKERQUE

RUE R LE FRISON

RUE P BUTAY

RUE ADOLPHE DALEMAGNE

ALLEE DU PRE L'ABBE

Hôtel
Bretagne

PLACE DU
VAINQUAI

St-Bertin's
Abbey

RUE DES RUINES
ST-BERTIN

Square et
Enclos
St-Bertin

RUE GUILLAUME CLITON

PLACE
A RIBOT

RUE FAIDHERBE

PLACE
ST JEAN

RUE DES MOULINS

RUE DES CHATS

RUE DE THEROUANNE

RUE DES BLEUETS

RUE SAINT BERTIN

RUE DES
PIPIERS

RUE DU GAL SARRAIL

English
Jesuit College

RUE DES BEGUINES

IMPASSE GUY MOLLET

Hôtel
de Bergues

RUE GAMBETTA

RUE DE LA COMMUNE DE PARIS

RUE DE L'ESCOTERIE

EPEERS

Le Cygne

RUE DU LYCEE

GAMBETTA

RUE SAINTE CLAIRE

RUE DE THEROUANNE

AVENUE GUSTAVE COURBET

RUE

RUE

Hôtel
Le Saint-
Louis

RUE D'ARRAS

RUE DU GRIFFON

RUE DES MADELEINES

RUE EUGENE DELACROIX

RUE ST CHARLES

CHIFFLART

FRANCOIS

RUE PASTEUR

RUE D'AIRE

RUE BRUEGHEL

BLVD G CLEMENCEAU

RUE PASTEUR

RUE D'AMIENS

RUE DU DOC ALEXANDRE

AVENUE CHARLES DE GAULLE

AVENUE

RUE LOUIS NOEL

RUE DE LA LIBERATION

Arc
International

Auchan
hypermarket

AVENUE
LEON BLUM

There's nothing quite like **La Coupole**. Planned, but never used by Hitler, as one immense bunker for German V2 rockets it was abandoned in 1944 following the D-Day landings. Now this tour de force is the **History and Remembrance Centre of Northern France** (*rue du Mont a Car, Helfaut, 8kms from St-Omer & 17km from Aire-sur-la-Lys;* ✆ *03 21 12 27 27;* e *lacoupole@lacoupole.com; www.lacoupole-france.com;* ⊕ *Jul–Aug 09.00–18.00 & 10.00–19.00 daily, closed 21 Dec–3 Jan; adult/child aged 5–16 €9/6*). It is not so much a museum, more a 21st-century interpretation showing how the development of German rockets in occupied France led to the exploration of space from 1945–69. Since opening in 1997, La Coupole has welcomed 1.5 million visitors.

In spring 2010, and in line with contemporary thinking, the entire exhibition was made even more interactive with the introduction of advanced audio-visual equipment. Galleries were better signposted, and increased use made of lighting. Films used in temporary exhibitions along with 3D videos were introduced. A memorial, dedicated to those sent to the Nazi death camps from Nord-Pas de Calais was also unveiled.

For an older generation it will recall the random rocket raids on Britain; the first Vergultungswaffen (vengeance weapon) or VI was fired on 13 June 1944. Many of these doodlebugs, as they were called, fired from ramps in France and Belgium, fell on London. Although called rockets, these winged weapons were basically pilotless planes set to dive steeply onto a target. In practice this generally caused the engine to cut out. The ominous silence that followed helped alert many a wartime family to the inevitable explosion as the VI hit the ground.

The second wave of weapons, the V2s, which looked like any other rocket, were stored in vast concrete bunkers such as those at Eperlecques (see opposite) and Helfaut.

The sheer size of the bunker, constructed from 55,000 tons of reinforced concrete 72m in diameter and 5.5.m thick is impressive enough. The fact it shelters an underground city of more than 7km of galleries shows why it attracts more than 100,000 visitors annually. Even for younger generations, the high-tech and audio-visual approach with two cinemas, rare archive film footage and an animated model showing the arrival of the V2s, makes for a thoughtful family day out. There is even a genuine V2, the only one on show in France.

Take a journey through the silence of 300m of underground tunnels dug out by harshly treated Allied prisoners. Elsewhere a reconstruction of a wartime shop front in Calais and the dining-room of a worker's cottage shows the conditions endured by large sections of the French population. On a replica of the 'execution wall' in the Citadel at Lille is a letter

---

local beer) **&** *pain crotté au caramel au lait* (hot bread with milk, caramel & vanilla ice-cream); other staple dishes include the typical *planche de charcuteries* (ham platter) or *waterzoi de poissons* (3 varieties of fish in a vegetable stew). A children's menu (€10) is available. Regional beer is €4.40. $$$
✖ **Chez Tante Fauvette** 10 rue Sainte-Croix; ✆ 03 2111 26 08; ⊕ 19.00–21.00 & 12.00–14.00 Wed–Sat; www.cheztantefauvette.com. Some places have the happy knack of combining quirkiness with great cooking. This is one of them. Dubbed the smallest restaurant in town – it only takes 15 diners – there's no set menu, just what's on the board for the day. A typical cost for 3 courses is €27, for 4 €34. Cooked to order, this is simple homecooked fare at its very best. While you wait, admire the

eclectic collection of paintings, old hats & hanging bunches of hops; it's intimate, homely &, above all, great fun. Book well in advance. $$$
✖ **La Brasserie Audomaroise** 6 rue Louis Martel; ✆ 03 21 88 08 80; ⊕ 11.00–14.30 & 18.30–01.00 Mon–Thu, 11.00–14.30 & 18.30–02.00 Fri, 10.00–02.00 Sat & from 11.00 Sun; e brasserie-audomoroise@wandadoo.fr; www.brasserie-audomoroise.fr. Fancy a noisy night out? You need go no further than this popular big-time boozer. Real ale fans take note: it's got its own micro-brewery. Owner Emmanuel Bee will guide you through the flavours. Better still, the bistro-style restaurant serves a bumper range of easy-on-the-pocket dishes, from Welsh Rarebit, French style, to hot dishes & pizzas. Snacks range from €4.50. $$

from a 21-year-old teacher declaring his belief in a future Franco–German reconciliation. Panels on the lower-level walls show the devastation of the region generally, as do the films shown at the Rex and Cineac cinemas.

Allow at least three hours; this is a remarkably lucid portrayal of recent history. Free audio-guides are in English as are the information panels. Wheelchair access is good. The centre is unusual in marketing its own short break packages – these include Land of Discovery from €190 which includes passes to La Coupole and Arc International (see page 129), a mini cruise in the Audomarois marshes (see pages 130–2) and B&B at one of four hotels in St-Omer.

Some 18km away, southwest via the D195/928/943 and 219, lies another potential V2 launching pad: the 22m high **Blockhaus d'Éperlecques** (*rue du Sart;* ✆ *03 21 88 44 22; www.leblockhaus.com;* ⊕ *Mar 14.15–17.00, Apr–Oct 10.00–12.00 & 14.15–18.00, May–Sep 10.00–19.00 & Nov 14.15–17.00; closed Dec–Feb; adult/child €9/5, 2 adults & 2 children €25).* Opened to the public in 1974, this looming concrete structure was intended to shelter a factory for assembling, fuelling and launching V2 rockets as well as making liquid oxygen. Neither plan succeeded. Outside, a V1 flying bomb can be seen on its 45m-long launch pad ready for firing.

The Germans told locals the site was simply a power station, but undercover intelligence led to Allied bombing in August 1943. This went on for almost a year, culminating in the use of the five-ton Tailboy bombs designed by Barnes Wallis to pierce 5m-thick concrete. The impact of one is still visible on the north side.

Allow around 1½ hours; youngsters may get bored but small trolleys for pulling them around the giant site – the dimensions of which are truly awe-inspiring – helps keep them interested. There are special sound effects and audio-guides are available in English.

Finally, and a touch ironically considering the region is best known for the German rocket sites, is the **British Air Services Memorial** dedicated to those who gave their lives in World War I. This is located at the St-Omer airfield which, in sight of La Coupole, played a major role in supplying the Western Front. It was also an important headquarters; those based here included Major General Hugh Trenchard of the Royal Flying Corps, considered to be the founding figure of the infant Royal Air Force on 1 April 1918.

On Remembrance Day 2006 the late Henry Allingham, then aged 110, placed his poppy wreath at the memorial, which is designed in the shape of a canvas aircraft hangar. It was erected by Cross and Cockade International, the World War I Aviation Historical Society, on land provided in perpetuity by St-Omer.

SHOPPING The main shops are mostly clustered in **rue de Dunkerque**, and **rue de Calais**, the town's busiest thoroughfares. Alternatively try those in the old alleyways; **rue des Clouteries** (Nailmakers Street) and **rue des Cuisiniers** (Cook Street) are just two. Shopping hours are 14.00–19.00 Monday and 09.00–12.00 and 14.00–19.00 Tuesday–Saturday.

There are four hypermarkets in the vicinity: **Auchan/Rives de l'Aa** (*ave des Frais Fonds;* ✆ *03 21 98 78 00*); two branches of **Carrefour** (*46 ave Maréchal;* ✆ *03 21 88 79 00 & rue du Bois, Aire sur la-Lys (see page 133)* ✆ *03 21 38 89 00*); **Centre Leclerc** (*ZAC des sar, route d'Acquin,* ✆ *03 21 12 29 29*). Opening times are roughly 08.30/09.00–20.00. They are generally shut on Sundays and on public holidays, but check first.

Bookshops

Librairie de l'Independent 14 rue des Clouteries; ✆ 03 21 38 24 10
Maison de la Presse–France Loisirs 17 rue de Calais;

✆ 03 21 98 71 14
Majuscule Demey 45 rue de Dunkerque; ✆ 03 21 98 94 00

TASTE A SIP OF JUNIPER GIN

Said to contain the scents of the northern French countryside, juniper gin, or *genièvre*, has been distilled in the village of Houlle (*12km northwest of St-Omer via the D943*) since 1812. **Distillerie Persyn** (*19 route de Watten;* ☎ *03 21 93 01 71; e distilleriepersyn@orange.fr; www.genievredehoulle.com; 90-min tours Mon–Sat €5 or €4 for larger groups (20–50 people); book in advance*) offers tours that begin with a video presentation and end with a tasting. Run by the Persyn family since 1944, it is one of the last two of what were 100-plus distilleries supplying *estaminets* in the northern countryside. Using age-old traditional methods, the spirit is prepared from a blend of rye, oat and barley. The addition of juniper berries provides the extra kick.

Favoured by chefs and gourmets alike, the Flemish tipple can be served on the rocks as a pre-dinner aperitif, as a *trou flamand* as a mid-meal digestive, or as a sorbet. It can also be served ice-cold from the freezer at –18°C or in a glass chilled to –10°C.

OTHER PRACTICALITIES

Bank Le Credit Agricole, 26 pl Maréchal Foch; ☎ 08 10 81 08 42; [open:] 09.00–12.00 & 13.30–18.30 Tue–Fri, 09.00–12.45 Sat. This is the most convenient of 9 banks.

Supermarket Marche Plus, rue de Dunkerque; ⏰ 07.00–21.00 Mon–Sat, 09.00–12.45 Sun

Internet café 4 rue du Minck; ⏰ 10.00–21.00 Mon–Sat

Pharmacy Pharmacie Silvie, 51 pl Maréchal Foch; ☎ 03 21 38 22 53; ⏰ 08.00–19.30 Mon–Sat. There are 6 others in & around the centre.

Post Office pl Foch; ⏰ 14.00–18.00 Mon, 09.00–12.00 & 14.00–18.00 Tue–Fri, 08.30–12.00 & 14.00–16.30 Sat; also pl A Ribot; ⏰ 08.30–18.00 Mon–Fri, 08.30–12.00 Sat

Public toilet bld Pierre Guillain; ⏰ 10.00–17.30 Mon–Sun

WHAT TO SEE AND DO The tourist office's audio guide (see page 123) and a handful of leaflets are sufficient to enjoy this most walkable city. Start with a stroll in the **Jardin Public de St-Omer**, a 20ha park created in 1899 and home to an impressive arboretum boasting some 100-year-old species. A leaflet, obtainable from the tourist office close by, guides you round the former Vauban fortifications of the western side of the city. At the foot of the walls lies a formal French garden with familiar clipped box hedges, as well as an English-style park (⏰ *daily year round; admission free*) complete with grandstand and a mini zoo for children.

The 50m cathedral tower which faces the park is reached via five narrow lanes. It is crowned with 15th-century turrets, some of which still bear the marks of the city gates that were once closed at night.

The 800-year-old **Cathédrale Notre-Dame** (*Enclos Notre-Dame;* ⏰ *08.30–18.00, or until 17.00 Oct–Mar; 1hr audio-guided tours, €3, available from the tourist office*) replaced the original cathedral destroyed by Charles V (Charles Quint) at Thérouanne (see page 133). Started in the 13th century and completed in 1561, the building is now regarded as one of the finest Gothic monuments in the region. By all means marvel at the Rubens painting of the *Descent from the Cross*, or the astronomical clock which has been telling the time, day, month, sunrise, sunset and phases of the moon since its completion in 1558. The huge 18th-century church organ, the masterpiece of a family of local sculptors and carpenters, likewise holds strong appeal. But please don't miss the extraordinary shrine to St Erkembode, patron saint of children with walking difficulties. It is covered with tiny shoes of all shapes and sizes, left by parents to aid recovery. A nearby plaque recalls various miraculous cures.

Considerable compassion was shown by this Irish monk who lived during the late 7th and early 8th centuries. As the fourth bishop of St-Omer, he constantly walked his huge diocese, stretching from Ypres to the River Somme, looking for land he could give to the poor. He died in 723 crippled and almost paralysed.

St Erkembode was previously an abbot at **St-Bertin's Abbey**, built between 1325 and 1520 to replace St-Audomar's first abbey. Closed during the French Revolution (when the saints on the façade had their heads knocked off) the remains show how the abbey was organised. The abbey stands in a small park and is floodlit nightly in different colours.

The ruins are reached from the cathedral via **rue St-Bertin**, the town's oldest street. Look out for the Jesuit buildings on the south side, including the **English Jesuit College** that dates from 1726; on the other side a small courtyard contains the simple 13th-century St-Denis church. Stay within the area to see the crow-step and Flemish girders of the 17th-century Episcopal seminar in neighbouring rue Gambetta, as well as the old market square in place Victor Hugo – this was the first square to develop at the foot of the cathedral cloisters.

The elegant **Hôtel de Bergues** (the word hotel in this context means mansion) at 20 rue St-Bertin accommodated George V and the future Edward VIII on their visits to the front during World War I (⊕ *briefly during Jul & Sept; €3; book through the tourist office*). The finest mansion by far, though, is the **Hotel Sandelin** (*Museé de l'Hôtel, 14 rue Carnot;* ☏ *03 21 38 00 94;* e *contact@musees-ville-saint-omer.com; www.musees-ville-saint-omer.com;* ⊕ *10.00–12.00 & 14.00–18.00 Wed–Sun; adult/child €4.50/3, free on 1st Sun of the month*). Built in 1777 as the winter residence of the Viscount of Fruges, bought by the city in 1899 and completely renovated in 2004, the 18th-century townhouse is elegantly set between a courtyard and a garden. A portal with an impressive Louis XV gate makes a highly appropriate entrance for a monumental trawl through one of the finest art collections in northern France, referred to by locals as 'the little Louvre'. While the fine arts collection from the late 16th to the early 19th century is undoubtedly magnificent, local interest is centred on items from the ruined abbey of St-Bertin. These include not only stone carvings of exotic animals and mosaics, but also the *Foot of The Cross* (*Pied de Croix de Bertin*), a priceless 12th-century crucifix stand made of copper. A collection of ceramics contains a number of items from St-Omer, including clay pipes for which the town became famous in the 18th and 19th centuries when tobacco was an important crop. Downstairs, overlooking the gardens, are three adjoining rooms whose wood panelling is listed under the Historic Monuments scheme. Finely carved wainscoting and 18th-century fireplaces complete the picture of grandeur on a lavish scale.

Need to chill out? Then make for **place Maréchal Foch**, the central 13th-century square. This is dominated by the 19th-century **hôtel de ville** (town hall) whose neo-Classical architecture conceals a brightly coloured Italianate theatre.

CRYSTAL-GAZING AT A FAMOUS FACTORY

Visiting a factory is not everyone's idea of a fun day out, but the famous crystal glassware factory **Arc International** (*Zone industrielle – RN 43 Industrial Zone, Arques (4km southeast of St-Omer);* ☏ *03 21 12 74 74;* e *visite-usine@arc-intl.com; www.arc-intl.com;* ⊕ *09.00–12.30 & 13.30–17.30 Mon–Sat except for public holidays; adult/student €6.50/4.20 for 90min tour at 09.30, 11.00, 14.00 & 15.30. Booking is recommended*) is special. The factory in Arques first opened in 1988 to meet demand from curious tourists; it now welcomes 50,000 visitors annually. And if the magic of watching molten glass being transformed into goblets, champagne flutes or smart stemmed wine glasses all proves too much, there's always the factory shop. Discounts are available on a wide range of handy souvenirs, from snazzy crystal to tableware, including plates and cutlery. One pricewise British customer left with blue-and-white-striped tumblers and a set of glass plates in the shape of fish. There's also a huge range of Pyrex products.

A grandiose affair, it replaced a smaller 16th-century city hall, which was on the verge of collapse.

Pavement cafés and bars on the south side provide a splendid place for a brief sit down. Parking is easy, with plenty of pay-and-display spaces, except for Saturday mornings when the market's eye-catching stalls are crammed with equally colourful local goodies, notably vegetables. These are freshly dug from the fertile soil of Marais, the drained marshlands that were once worked by the medieval monks (see below). Look out for tasty souvenirs, from Maroilles cheese (see page 216) to homemade produce from the market gardeners. For lunch, or an evening out, join the locals at the **De Drie Kalders** (see page 123).

AROUND ST-OMER Inextricably linked with St-Omer is **Arques**, site of the giant glass factory (see page 129) a mere 4km away. If the factory is not your scene, or you have time for both, visit the **boatlift** (*L'Ascenseur à Bateaux des Fontinettes; 21 rue Denis Papin,* \ *03 21 88 59 00;* e *arques.tourisme@wanadoo.fr; www.ville-arques.fr;* ⏲ *10.00–12.00 & 14.00–18.00 Mon–Fri, 14.00–18.00 Sat–Sun & public holidays; adult/child aged 5–11 €4/2.50*). Originally built to help some 300 fully loaded barges cope with the 30m drop between the Aa and the Lys canals, this 1887 feat of engineering remained in operation until 1967. It is now a museum, with scale models showing the changing world of canal workers and a video of the lift in operation.

Alternatively take a relaxing 45-minute journey aboard *Le Picasso* – an old-fashioned diesel train with red-and-white 1950s-style wagons. Operated by the Chemin de Fer de la Vallée de l'Aa, the lovingly preserved line runs from rue de la Gare in Arques to **Lumbres** (*Tourist Office Lumbres;* \ *03 21 93 45 46; or at Arques* \ *03 21 88 59 00; www.cftva.c.la; train times: May–Jun & Sep 14.00 & 16.00, Jul–Aug 10.15, 14.30 & 16.30 from Arques, or 46 mins later from Lumbres; adult/child aged 4–14 €7/4.50*). Using standard gauge track on what was once part of the old St-Omer to Boulogne line, the train winds 15km through the Aa Valley countryside; stops include **Wizerne** for La Coupole (see page 126) and the old station at **Blendeques** with its collection of railway memorabilia. Staffed by volunteers, the line takes groups, including cyclists. Seasonal offers include a Santa Special.

Lumbres is also home to another form of transport. The difference here is that you provide the pedal power for the blue flatbed wagons that run from Nielles-lès-Bléquinon. **Rando-Rail**'s (*rue de la Gare;* \ *03 21 88 33 89;* e *rando-rail@rando-rail.com; www.rando-rail.com;* ⏲ *Apr–Sep daily, closed Mon Apr–Jun & Sep except public holidays; departures hourly 10.00–15.00 Apr–Jun & Sep & hourly 10.00–17.00 Jul–Aug; €23 4 adults or 2 adults & 3 children; advance booking is essential*) wagons each have two bicycle-style saddles for those doing the pedalling. The passengers sit comfortably in a sort of deckchair in the middle. Child seat-type vehicles are available; wheelchairs can also be taken.

You have a choice of two different round trips. Either follow the Chevalier de la Chapelle (the west side) through a wooded trail where you can swap pedalling for a short walk, or the Course of the Adelhur, through the valleys and hills of the Artois. NB: wear trainers and be prepared for a 20-minute wait before departure.

Barge cruises featuring the Audomarois leave from Arques (*1hr 40mins;* ⏲ *Mar–Oct, times vary so check with tourist office; adult/child aged 5–11 €9.50/9*).

MARSHLANDS It's easy to forget that St-Omer owed its growth as a medieval trading town to its privileged position on the edge of a vast marshland whose rivers led straight to the sea. Originally a salt estuary, reclaimed first by the 7th-century monks and in the 15th century drained and developed as ditches by the Dutch, there are now two main parts to the marshlands: the market gardening area of the Audomarois and the Romelaëre Nature Reserve. There is also an eastern arm.

The Audomarois St-Omer's commercial history is evident if you follow either the rue de Calais or the rue de Dunkerque to the port through which the goods once passed. From here follow the Salines River through the quayside, perhaps picking up some warehouse bargains such as fish, cheese and antiques on the way, before you reach the splendid château-style St-Omer railway station. Cross the canal bridge and follow the towpath to the market garden suburbs of Lyzel and Haut-Pont where marsh water washes around traditional homes.

Behind them lies the biggest surprise of all: the Audomarois, 3,500ha of the River Aa marshlands, were the last to be cultivated in France. Named after Audomar, St-Omer's much-loved patron saint, Audomarois now sports a flourishing market-gardening industry. Some five to seven million cauliflowers alone are cut annually and taken to St-Omer by traditional black-tarred boats called *bacoves*. There are also carrots galore, likewise leeks and chicory, each vegetable sporting its own fellowship or order whose colourful costumes are worn at many a regional festival (see page 37).

Romelaëre Nature Reserve Midway between Clairmarais and Nieurlet, and sandwiched between the market gardening area east of the railway line and the eastern arm, lies Romelaëre Nature Reserve. Preserved for private shooting, this is now home to 200 species of birds, 300 species of plants, 17 species of fish and 11 species of bats. Walking trails include a number geared to the disabled, including plaques in Braille and studded paths. Walks start from the **Clairmarais Nature Centre or Grange Nature** (*Maison du Romelaëre, rue du Romelaëre;* ↘ *03 21 38 52 95;* e *masiondelaromelaëre@parc-opale.fr; www.parc-opale.fr;* ⊕ *Jul–Aug 14.00–18.00 Tue–Sat, 15.00–18.00 Sun; reserve only* ⊕ *mid-Mar–Sep 08.00–20.00, Oct–mid-Dec 08.00–17.30; admission free; guided tours in French adult/child under 14 €3/free);* don't forget your binoculars. A massively long boardwalk, perfect for prams and wheelchairs, meanders round the marshes and leads to hides highly praised by birdwatchers. You may even spot Marie Grouette, a wicked witch of the water ready to snatch unwary children from the riverbank.

Boating trips The best way to appreciate this *Wind in the Willows* landscape is to do what the postman does daily except on Sundays, and take to the waterways, or *watergangs*, by boat. The choice is wide: there are canoes, rowing boats and launches offering guided tours to the market gardening area, the nature reserve, or a combination of both. For a more original mode of transport, hire a surf bike and pedal across the water. Travelling by water offers a unique chance to wave at the islanders as the boat glides by, or buy flowers from the market gardeners, one of whom is now in his eighties.

There are two big boat-hire companies: the first is **Société Isnor** (*near Clairmarais church, 4km from St-Omer via the D209; 3 rue du Marais, Clairmarais;* ↘ *03 21 12 30 10;* e *fluvial@isnor.fr; www.isnor.fr;* ⊕ *Apr–Jun & Sep 10.00–18.00 Mon–Sat, Jul–Aug 10.00–18.00 daily, Oct–Mar 10.00–17.00 Mon–Sat, prior booking advisable w/days; adult/child aged 4–14 €6.60/5.60 for 1hr boat trip departing 11.00 (Jul–Aug) 15.00, 16.00 & 17.00; adult/child €13.40/10.40 2hr wildlife tour Apr–Sep, check departure dates & times; also electric boats for 6 from €35 1–3 hrs, rowing boats for 6 from €20 1hr–all day, with boats for disabled due in 2010).* Check the weather forecast – I recall shivering on a cold wet day in May, despite the loan of a heavy condom-shaped plastic cape. (It was, however, still worth it for the unique views and the hot chocolate and brandy back at base.)

You can also tuck into traditional Flemish fare at the company's waterside restaurant **La Baguernette** ($$). The name refers to a boat used to remove silt from the ditches, while the menu features dishes such as sausage stuffed with chicory and leeks, served with red cabbage and chips, that pay homage to the local vegetables. For dessert, speciality bread cooked French-style and served with brown sugar and a scoop of ice-cream vies with homemade chocolate mousse. And do try the country-style bread *au gratin*.

Operating from Salperwick, 8km away from Clairmarais via the D209/928, is **Au Bon Accueil** (*9 rue du Rivage Boitel;* ❧ *03 21 38 35 14; www.bonaccueil.info;* ⊕ *tours Apr–May, Jun & Sep 14.30, Jul–Aug 11.00, 14.30 & 16.00; 1hr tours with commentary on 36-seater covered boats adult/child €7/6. Canoes, rowing & motor boats are also available for hire at similar prices to those at Clairmarais*) which also has a popular and long established 160-seater café with a bar and terrace.

Other methods of exploring the wetlands There's still one more option open: go round by car. Not in yours, but a 2CV, that most quintessentially French of vehicles, rented out by Deux Chevaux buff Bruno Delforge from his huge converted barn in Clairmarais. It's from here that he runs his quirky vehicle hire firm **Les Belles Echappées** (*Ferme de l'Abbaye;* ❧ *03 21 98 11 72;* **e** *bruno@les-belles-echappees.com; www.les-belles-echappees.com;* ⊕ *Jun–Sep 09.00–12.00 & 14.00–19.00 Tue–Sun & w/ends & public holidays in May*). Bruno, who began the business in 2007, can boast of at least two original 2CVs among his multi-coloured collection of cars and bikes, one with a mere 35,000km on the clock. Each car takes two to four people, for a €90/160 half-/full-day country spin.

Alternatively opt for a bike; there are tandems (*€10–14 h/day*) or Solex electric bikes (*€18 half day*) which silently whizz round the Clairmarais forest and marshes with speeds up to 35kph. Three-seater and family models are also available.

If all else fails, there's always Bruno's golf course. But watch out for the cows! This is no ordinary course, but a farm one, where you whack a large leather ball through the thistles and molehills. It's daft but more difficult than you think. At least the abbey, dating back to 1720, provides a dignified backdrop! And it's a snip at adult/child €6.50/4.50 a go.

Walks in the marshlands Walkers are well catered for in the **Fauquembergues Canton**. Characterised by watermills at Renty, Dennebroeucq and Enquin-les-Mines, the rolling countryside 24km southwest of St-Omer on the D928 to Hesdin (see page 151) is riddled with footpaths. Summertime guided walks, conducted in French, end with afternoon snacks; led by the 'Guides Nature de l'Audomarois', a non-profit organisation, they must be booked in advanced (❧ 03 21 98 05 79; **e** *guidesnatureau@yahoo.fr; www.guidesnaureau.chez-alice.fr; adult/child under 12 €4/free*). Take sturdy shoes and binoculars. Many are of the walking itineraries are available free from the tourist office.

Other activities The 8ha amusement park, **Dennlys Parc** (*Parc du Moulin de la Tour; Dennebroeucq;* ❧ *03 21 95 11 39;* **e** *dennlys-parc@wanadoo.fr; www.dennlys-parc.com;* ⊕ *see website*) has around 200 attractions including hot air ballooning.

🏠 Where to stay, eat and play golf

🏠 **Best Western AA Saint Omer Hotel du Golf** (54 rooms inc 8 suites) Chemin des Bois, Lumbres; ❧ 03 21 11 42 42; **e** aagolf@najeti.com; www.stomer-hoteldugolf.com. The hotel is part of the Najeti group, created in 1999 with the aim of developing 9 hotels & 3 golf courses in France; among them is the Best Western Hotel de l'Univers in Arras (see page 165). The St-Omer hotel is the latest addition, 8km away from Tilques. You can't fault this swish hotel when it comes to style. The use of brick & stone for the ground floor, along with subtle hints of wood in the bedrooms, cleverly continues the architectural vein set by the clubhouse itself. With a stunning backdrop of rolling countryside it's little wonder the 18- & 9-hole courses are popular among golfing Brits. Room rates are €120–215 a night; 1 night stays with B&B & green fees included cost from €90 pp. There are 2 restaurants: **Le Ristandèl** at the clubhouse serving a €12.30 2-course menu, & the open-plan **Le Lodge** located near the central bar. The latter's gourmet menu is thoughtfully crafted. Expect small but delicious portions of the red mullet in a puff pastry with green anise sauce kind; choice is good with set 2-course meals €21–24 & 3 courses €28. A 4-course menu gourmand is €39. The restaurant shuts at 21.00 ($$$$). Standard green fees for the championship golf course vary from €18–22 for the 9-hole off-season, €20–25 high season (Apr–Jun, Sep & Oct) & €44–60 & €58–83 for the 18-hole 6,294m par 73. Golf buggy hire is extra. $$$$$ (or $$$$ if using introductory off-season packages) 🏠 **Château Tilques** (53 rooms) rue de Chateau; 📞 03 21 88 99 99; e www.chateautilques.com; chateautilques.hotel@najeti.com. Some 10km away from Clairmarais, via the D209, this Flemish-style 19th-century *château* offers country chic in 5ha of parkland close to the marshland boats & other major attractions. 29 rooms, lavishly fitted out with fine fabrics & furniture, are in the turreted *château*. A more contemporary look is given to the 24 more expensive rooms with terrace or balcony in the conservatory. A buffet b/fast at €19 has been highly praised for its scope. As at many hotels of its kind, guests' comments are mixed but won over our reviewers on location alone. Golfing, culture/heritage & off-season B&B offers are available. The hotel's restaurant, **Le Vert Mesnil** (🕐 *12.00–14.00*), lavishly converted from an old 17th-century stable block, was likewise praised by our reviewers for its imaginative use of locally sourced produce. But with starters at €14–24 & main courses around €30 it is expensive; book a cheaper €35–40 3-course set menu in advance if money is tight. Alternatively have lunch instead at the hotel's Café du Parc for €20, less in the off-season, or €13.50 for 1 course & a *café gourmand* ($$$$$). $$$$

FROM ST-OMER TO CASSEL

Sadly, too few visitors leave the confines of St-Omer, wrapping themselves up instead in a cosy cloak of familiarity. This is understandable: St-Omer is a great base from which to explore, and Calais is comfortably close. But don't miss out. Beyond lies foreign territory – certainly to most Brits and to many French as well. It's a patchwork of forgotten towns and villages, which beg to be discovered.

You have a choice: either head directly for Cassel (see page 134) or take a little time and swing round in an arc beginning first at Thérouanne, 16km away from St-Omer via the D97 and 341.

THÉROUANNE The town, once one of the wealthiest bishoprics in northern France, was famed for its 12th-century cathedral. This was razed to the ground in 1553 by the Spanish Emperor Charles Quint who was convinced that it was a French stronghold. Some items were salvaged, including the *Grand Dieu de Thérouanne,* a group of sculpted figures, which now take pride of place at St-Omer cathedral (see page 128). The last remaining vestige of the ancient city, the **Chapelle de Nielles-de-Thérouanne**, is worth a visit (🕐 *Apr–Oct 09.00–18.00 daily; admission free*). There is also a small **archaeological museum** (🕐 *09.00–12.00 & 14.00–17.30 Mon–Fri; admission free*).

AIRE-SUR-LA-LYS Lying 10km southeast between the Flemish mounts and the Artois hills, **Aire-sur-la-Lys**, reached from Thérouanne via the D341/D157, is a quiet, almost unassuming, town, whose gloriously endowed Grand'Place quickly catches the eye. And so it should. The hub of an historic market town fought over by the French and Spanish for its strategic location on two canals and the River Lys, the square contains some real gems. Not least is **the Baillage**, the glittering guardhouse originally built for the town's militia in 1600. This splendid Flemish-style edifice, with its gloriously decorative themes largely inspired by the Italian Renaissance, is now home to the **Tourist Office** (*Office de Tourisme d'Aire-sur-la-Lys; Le Baillage, Grand'Place;* 📞 *03 21 39 65 66;* e *tourisme.airlys@wandoo.fr; www.ville-airesurlalys.fr;* 🕐 *mid-Jan–Mar 14.00–18.00 Tue–Thu & Sat, 09.00–12.00 & 14.00–18.00 Fri, Apr–Sep 14.00–18.00 Mon, 09.00–12.00 & 14.00–18.00 Tue–Sat, 10.00–12.00 Sun, Oct–Dec 09.00–12.00 & 14.00–18.00, closed public holidays*).

Almost as eye-catching is the **town hall**, completed in 1724 with a façade of ten pilasters and a statue-strewn balustrade. This replaced the old one, which was regarded by the conquering French king Louis XIV as not being prestigious enough. Two central doors, guarded by the town's giants Lydéric and Chrymilde, take you either to the grand staircase or to the Halletes, an arcade leading to the rear and the foot of the 45m belfry, which was reconstructed in the 18th century.

A few steps away is the former Baroque-style **Jesuit Chapel of Saint-Jacques** (*rue de Saint-Omer;* ⊕ *Jul–Aug 15.00–18.00, closed on Mon*); it was classified an historic monument in 1942. The suppression of the Jesuits in 1761 led to the chapel being converted into a riding school for the militia. The building's return to a cultural role is commemorated with the locally crafted sculpture, which stands at the back of the apse and dates to 1858.

Sadly the 11th-century **Collegiate Church of St-Pierre** (*pl St Pierre;* ⊕ *09.00– 18.00 daily*) fell foul of two 17th-century sieges and the French Revolution. Though extensively restored thanks to a wealthy 19th-century dean, it was bombed during an Allied raid in August 1944. This left the eastern end in rubble. Surviving relics still housed beneath the splendid giant nave include the 17th-century organ case from the Clairmarais Abbey. Of the remaining 16th-century paintings, the fresco of Saint-Jacques, restored in 1995, is found in the sacristy.

Also worth a visit are the **17th century fortifications**, masterminded by the indefatigable Vauban, which used sluices capable of flooding the surrounding countryside in case of siege; the **town quays**, which show the unprecedented development of 19th-century breweries, tanning mills and basket-makers, and the **wetlands**, where huge lakes provide a haven for birdwatchers and fishermen.

AROUND AIRE-SUR-LA-LYS Also in the vicinity is **Château de Créminil** at **Estrée-Blanche**, 10km west of Aire by Witternesse. Its reconstructed medieval gardens are open on Heritage Days (see page 49) and in mid-September. **Lillers**, 12km southeast via the D188/185, was once one of France's shoe-making centres; it sports a small museum of the trade, **Maison de la Chaussure** (*pl Captain Ansart*), which is free to visit. The town giants are the shoe-maker Ovide, his wife Marie and their daughter Lilia who, christened on 1 May 2000, symbolises the cultivation of watercress. All three take part in the Lillierades festival, held annually on 1 May.

CASSEL

Perched perkily on the top of Mont Cassel, the fortified town of Cassel is the embodiment of rural France – a theatrical set piece of cobbled streets, ridiculously ornate architecture and a reassuring sense of old world charm. Order a beer in the Grand'Place, sit back and soak up a scene of picture-postcard perfection.

HISTORY Legend has it that Mont Cassel, at 176m the highest point in the Flanders Hills, was created by three giants (see page 137). The truth is that by sticking high above the fertile plains it was a foregone haven, first for the Celts and later for the Romans who used it as a starting point for seven arrow-straight roads.

It has also been besieged, demolished and even restored 13 times. Three major battles were fought here: the first was in 1071 over succession to the throne of Flanders, the second in 1328 when Philip VI squashed the peasant revolt in Flanders and the third in 1677 when the French army, under the younger brother of Louis XIV (The Sun King), defeated the Spanish-Dutch army on the plain west of the town. Instrumental in the third was the battlefield at Noordpeene, a small village 7km west of Cassel. A scale model, along with an introductory description, now features in the small Maison de la Bataille museum (see page 136).

According to various sources Frederick Augustus Duke of York, second son to George III of England, led two unsuccessful campaigns in the French Revolutionary Wars. And it was in Cassel in 1793 that, according to the nursery rhyme, the Grand Old Duke of York marched his 10,000 men to the top of the hill and back. Whether it was the same duke is a matter of conjecture...

During World War I Cassel's fame for its fine-day ability to view Five Kingdoms – France, Belgium, Holland, England and, of course, heaven – led Marshal Foch, Supreme Commander of the Allied Forces, to set up headquarters here. The town still pays homage to him with a statue (see page 137).

GETTING AROUND Reaching Cassel by public transport is not easy: the railway station, though served by a regular service on the Dunkirk–Lille line, lies more in Oxelaëre, 3km west of town. This means a walk to the town centre as there are no taxis. A better bet is to change at Hazebrouck (*Lines 6 & 7: Arras–Hazebrouck–Dunkerque–Calais; Line 8: Dunkerque–Hazebrouck–Armentières–Lille; Line 12: Boulogne–Calais–(St-Omer)–Hazebrouck–Lille*) then take a bus to Cassel. Tickets cost €1.50, which covers all zones, and are available from the driver. The service, which currently runs from the train station at Hazebrouck, is Line 202: Hazebrouck–Cassel–Oudezeele (*www.icars-vivacar.com/horaires_liste_lignes.php*). The journey takes 25 to 40 minutes depending on the time of the day. At the time of writing two bus companies were reorganising under the name Arc en Ciel (meaning Rainbow), so details may change.

TOURIST INFORMATION

🛈 Office of Tourism 20 Grand Place; ☏ 03 28 40 52 55; e contact@ot-cassel.fr; www.cassel-horizons.com; ⏲ Nov–Mar 08.30–12.00 & 13.30–17.30 Mon–Fri, 09.00–12.00 Sat, closed Sun, Apr–May & Sep–Oct

08.30–12.00 & 13.30–17.45 Mon–Sat, 14.00–17.45 Sun, Jun 08.45–12.00 & 13.30–17.45 Mon–Sat, 14.00–18.30 Sun, Jul–Aug 08.45–12.00 & 13.30–18.00 Mon–Sat, 14.00–18.30 Sun

WHERE TO STAY

🏠 Châtellerie de Schoebeque (15 rooms) 32 rue Foch; ☏ 03 28 42 42 67; e contact@schoebeque.com; www.schoebeque.com. This is a cracker of a conversion from an 18th-century *château* and is where Marshal Foch welcomed England's George V in World War I; his role as supreme commander of the Allied forces is recognised in La Suite Foch, one of the themed rooms which make a stay at this prestigious hotel memorable. They could easily be naff but, thanks to the interior designing skills of the owners, are both tasteful & in line with the overall ambience – which has won praise from many a guest. The wisteria-laden courtyard can accommodate a number of cars. It's expensive, but nice for that special occasion. The view from the dining-room terrace is stunning. $$$$$

🏠 La Maison des Sources 326 rue d'Aire; ☏ 03 28 42 42 67; e contact@schoebeque.com. Now run by the Châtellerie de Schoebeque, this peaceful B&B, still superbly equipped, lies peacefully tucked away in the fold of the hills. The Grand'Place is within 10mins' walk, but you may want to take the car as the climb is a tough one. Parking in Cassel is pretty good. Treat yourself to a slap-up €12 b/fast at the hotel. It's money well spent. $$$

🏠 **La Gourgandine** 72 rue de Bergues; ☎ 06 67 66 63 46; ✉ chombart.stephane@neuf.fr; www.chambresdhotes-peintre.com. This slightly surrealist B&B will appeal to those of an artistic nature. Choosing The Trollop (the English translation) means colour, bags of it, with psychedelic paintings from the owner Stéphane Chomb'art boldly displayed in the themed guest-rooms. Depending on your tastes, you'll either love it or loathe it. What you can't fault it on is originality nor the comfort & furnishings of the 4 dbl rooms. $$$

✖ WHERE TO EAT

✖ **La Table du Meunier** 25 Grand'Place; ☎ 06 84 64 64 04 or 03 28 42 48 57; ⏱ 08.30–23.00 Tue–Sun. Packed to the gills even at lunchtime, this popular revamped eaterie, with its snazzy black-&-white décor, offers regional specialities at reasonable prices. Try the Welsh rarebit, a French-style version guaranteed to keep you going for the rest of the day. The view across the square is terrific. $$$

✖ **Kasteel Hof** 8 rue St Nicholas; ☎ 03 28 40 59 29; ✉ estaminetkastheelhof@orange.fr; www.ot-cassel.fr. An archetypal *estaminet* full of rustic charm, it provides the instant flavour of Flanders, both through its robust Flemish dishes & its beers. You can't miss it: it's signposted close to the windmill, enjoys the best views in town & has a shop stuffed full of regional products. With baskets & pots hanging from the ceiling, traditional games & a storyteller to boot, this is the place for a lively night out. $$$

SHOPPING Pick up some tasty souvenirs at **Traditions en Nord** (*32 Grand'Place – Hotel d'Halluin;* ☎ *03 28 48 10 53;* ✉ *h.lysiane@alicedsl.fr;* ⏱ *09.30–12.30 & 14.30–19.00 daily except Tue & Sun, also open Tue morn Jun–Aug*). Products range from local cheeses, beers and pâtés to Flemish waffles.

WHAT TO SEE AND DO OK, I am biased: I love Cassel. But then most writers rate it highly on their must-see lists. Even one grump who suggested it was a little shabby on the edges admitted to being bowled over by the 'picturesque and photogenic' Grand'Place, which correctly plays centre stage.

Strangely, however, Cassel lacks any big-time buildings of the formal kind: even the 11th-century **Collegiate Notre-Dame de la Crypte**, rebuilt and restored during the 16th, 17th and 19th centuries, is relatively low key.

Instead, history unfolds quite naturally, beginning with a visit to the **Cassel Horizons Heritage Centre** (⏱ *08.30–12.00 & 13.30–17.30 Mon–Sat off-season & 08.30–12.00 & 13.30–17.45 Mon–Sat, 14.00–18.30 Sun in season; adult/child aged 6–14 €3/2.50*), housed in a former 18th-century mansion attached to the similar 17th-century home of the tourist office. This permanent audio-visual exhibition delves into the history and legends surrounding the town.

It will be joined in October 2010 by the **Musée de Flandre** (*opening times & admission price unavailable at the time of writing*) on the site of the former Hotel de la Noble Court, or Lanhuss. This was, in the 11th century, Cassel's financial and administrative centre and later the Court of Justice. The first ever multi-media museum representing Flemish cultural life, it will feature both paintings by the Flemish masters and contemporary works by worldwide artists. Major collections of rare and original religious, historical, ethnographic and geographical works are also shown. An ambitious schedule of temporary exhibitions up to the year 2014 will highlight the feminine form in the 15th and 16th centuries, 17th-century Flemish painting, animals in Flemish art and Flemish festivals and fairs.

The **Maison de la Bataille** (*200 rue de la Mairie;* ☎ *03 28 40 67 36;* ✉ *maisondelabataille-noorpeene.fr; www.noordpeene.com;* ⏱ *Feb–Nov 10.00–12.30 & 14.00–18.00 Wed–Sun; adult/child €5/3, under 7 free. Audio guides available in English*) offers a scale model and introductory description of the battle at Noordpeene in 1667. Modern panels spotlight famous locals, such as Joseph Duvat, a local mayor who died aged 103, and an itinerant salesman nicknamed Tisje Tasfe, well-known for his storytelling and now the village giant. A small garden outside grows old-fashioned strains of fruit, vegetables and flowers. You can also walk to the battlefield from the neighbouring village of **Zuytpeene**.

As for Marshal Foch, a statue of him mounted on his horse stands high above the town in the place du Chateau close to **Le Moulin de Cassel** (↘ *03 28 40 52 55 (tourist office);* ⊕ *1 Apr–Sep 10.00–18.00 daily (times may vary so check first); adult/child €3/2.50*). This imposing wooden mill replaced the original 16th-century one, destroyed in a horrendous fire on 30 October 1911, with the flames, whipped by strong winds, reportedly seen as far away as Dunkirk, Calais and even Arras. A 1947 replacement was the first windmill, of which there were once 20 or so locally, to open to the public in 1949.

Be warned: it's a bit of a grind getting there. Some 30 steep and rocky steps lead to the public gardens, set in the former *château* grounds, and you need to climb a further 12 wooden steps to watch the milling process. You do at least get a souvenir bag of freshly ground flour, using locally grown corn and rye.

The *château*, now likely to be converted to flats, was originally planned as a spa hotel for the rich from Lille and Paris but the project never materialised. It has in its time, however, been a turn-of-the-20th-century family centre with games for children, and a dancehall-café. It was also a radio station which in 1953 reported on the coronation of the current British Queen Elizabeth.

To avoid the steps, follow instead the signposted alleys leading past the viewpoint indicators and the *estaminet*. These will eventually bring you back to the Grand'Place via the rue Constant Moeneclaey. Take time to admire the wooden carvings by **Stéphane Lemaire** (*68 rue Constant Moeneclaey;* ↘ *03 28 40 52 90;* ⊕ *09.00–12.00 & 14.00–18.00; Sat by prior appointment*). Working largely in oak, Stéphane concentrates on providing intricate restorations for historic monuments. Among them is the current font at the Church of Notre-Dame in Calais (see page 68) where the wife of Charles de Gaulle was baptised. Take a 20-minute guided tour of the workshop and watch him at work (€1). It provides a unique insight into Flemish culture.

NOW FOR A GIANT-SIZED LEGEND

Once upon a time, a couple of giants were carrying a huge mound of earth to fill in a ravine. One, a woman, was exhausted by the task and let go meaning the mound tipped over. And that, dear reader, is how the hill at Cassel was formed. But the story doesn't end here. A second tale tells of how a huge creature disembarked from a boat to create the Flanders Hills with his bare hands, promising he would be back soon. And he was, along with his wife. Everyone was so pleased that they danced with gratitude.

The third account is even better. A rampaging ogre was on the loose, striking fear throughout the region. There was only one solution: get him drunk by placing an enormous barrel of beer in his path. He duly downed it in one swallow, falling to the ground in a giant stupor. To bury him, the people brought so much earth that a mountain was created. It is said that when he turns over in his sleep once a year the whole of Mont Cassel dances... Take your pick – they all make good party pieces.

Now, around Easter each year, Reuze Papa, sometimes referred to as 'Le Reuze' (Flemish for 'giant'), joins Reuze Maman, nicknamed 'La Reuzaine', for general high jinks. Like the Gayants of Douai (see page 201) these two heavyweights, 94kg and 82kg in weight and 6.25m and 5.80m in height respectively, are officially classified as UNESCO heritage treasures.

Papa wears the costume of a Roman legionnaire, with the crest of his helmet adorned with a sphinx. Maman, who once took the form of a shrimper with a basket on her back, now wears a diadem, a red robe and a golden shawl. They're a dashing couple, indeed, but do book accommodation early if you want to meet them in person.

For many this is 'foreign' territory, but it features some of the most intriguing parts of the whole Nord-Pas de Calais region. It also offers some of the finest examples of Flemish rural fare and traditions.

FROM CASSEL TO STEENVOORDE Head for Steenvoorde, 7km from Cassel via the D948, centrally located for exploring the surrounding villages and hamlets with unpronounceable names.

Tourist information

Steenvoorde Tourist Office pl Jean-Marie Ryckewaert; ☎ 03 28 42 97 98; e si.steenvoorde@ wanadoo.fr; www.pay-des-geants.com; ⏰ 09.00– 12.00 & 14.00–17.30 Tue–Fri, 09.00–12.00 & 14.00–17.00 Sat. Offers information on the area, including accommodation, camping & local events.

✖ Where to eat Close to Steenvoorde is **Auprès de mon Arbre** (*932 route d'Eeck, Terdeghem;* ☎ *03 28 49 79 49; www.aupresdemonarbre.fr;* ⏰ *12.00–14.00 daily & 19.30–21.00 Fri & Sat*) which offers a frank and honest approach, hence a great selection of homemade food. Set menus €12–44; €12 menus for children are competitively priced. A pleasant rustic décor rounds off this rural find.

What to see and do Close to Steenvoorde is **Le Steenmeulen** (*55 route d'Eecke;* ☎ *03 28 48 16 10; www.steenmeulen.com;* ⏰ *09.00–12.00 & 14.00–18.00 Sat–Thu, closed Fri & last Sun of every month; adult €3 for the mill & €3 for the museum or €5 for combined visit*), probably the only fully operational stone mill left in Europe. This and a rural museum, in former farm buildings, are the pride and joy of Joseph Markey, a fifth-generation miller.

Joseph was originally an engineer, but his enthusiasm for repairing everything from vintage water wheels to an old Lancia car led to a his retirement dream – to restore the family mill built in 1864, which continued to produce bread until 1965. Special events range from mill days where you can learn bread making to bean thrashing and hop-picking. Children will love the chance to ride on a tractor.

GODEWAERSVELDE Back on the road, you find yourself in Roald Dahl-type territory full of tales of the unexpected. Take the border village of Godewaersvelde

IT SHOWS WHAT CAN-CAN BE DONE

To spot one leggy showgirl in a rural field is surprising; to meet an entire sequinned troop is, to say the least, surreal. But then that's precisely what **Le Grand Cabaret**, brainchild of 'crazy man' (his words not ours) Patrice Chevalier aims for. **Kent & Kim Derrick Productions** (*1095 route d'Estaire, Vieux-Berguin;* ☎ *03 28 42 75 75; e reservations@legrancabaret.com; www.legrandcabaret.com;* ⏰ *19.30–03.00 or 21.00–02.45 show without dinner; €40–100 ranging from show only to champagne dinner with show*) is plonked in what appears to be the middle of nowhere in the village of Vieux-Berquin, yet the glitzy indoor cabaret brings a slice of Parisian panache to this quiet corner of Flanders. The costumes, designed by Patrice's wife, add a Montmartre sparkle to a floor show guaranteed to keep the family, and especially dad, happy. Gloriously bizzare, but fulfilling the dreams of Patrice, ex-sword swallower, dancer and singer, it adds yet another new dimension to this extraordinary region. Don't be surprised by a stable full of horses and camels – they're also part of the show.

right Azincourt battlefield — learn about the battle at the Medieval Centre just down the road (SS) page 150

below The Historic Mining Centre at Lewarde, near Douai, is a reminder of Nord-Pas de Calais's industrial past (SS) page 200

bottom The vast British Cemetery at Étaples epitomises more than most the massive loss of life during the two world wars (JR) page 110

left Le Moulin de Cassel is a good viewpoint over the picture-postcard market town of Cassel, perched high in the Flemish hills (SS) page 137

below The rolling landscape of the Côte d'Opale (WD) page 71

bottom The activity resort of ValJoly has a stunning setting in the Avesnois countryside (JR) page 218

right   Plants for sale in the Seven Valleys, an area rich in colour and country crafts (JR) page 151

below   Montreuil-sur-Mer has inspired artists and visitors alike with its cobbled streets, half-timbered houses and 3km of ramparts (SS) page 145

bottom   Ski run on a former slag heap — the industrial area around Béthune and Lens has been transformed into a centre for outdoor activities (SS) page 171

above right The origin of Maroilles cheese goes back 800 years to when the Abbey of Maroilles collected cheese instead of dues from local peasants (JR) page 216

above left No chance of sampling local wines here – Nord-Pas de Calais is beer country, and always has been (JR) page 39

below left Look out for weekly markets, especially if you're self-catering or having a picnic (JR) page 44

below right The *andouillette* is an offal-based sausage that is only produced in Arras, and can be found in local shops such as this one (JR) page 166

above Some restaurants in Nord-Pas de Calais boast unusual features, such as the gourmet restaurant in Cambrai where you can shake hands with this genuflecting puppet (JR) page 188

right Production of Bêtises de Cambrai — these famous sweets were the result of an apprentice's mistake (JR) page 188

below Watch the world go by from a restaurant on Lille's Grand'Place (SS) page 230

above   The 7km of sloping beaches at Malo-les-Bains stretch to the Belgian border and are dotted with beach huts (SS) page 80

left   *Flobarts* like this one can be seen as working boats along the Côte d'Opale (WD) page 99

below   The beach at Le Touquet-Paris-Plage offers memorable horseriding opportunities (SS) page 118

right Cap Blanc-Nez — from here on a clear day you can gaze across the Channel to the corresponding White Cliffs of Dover
(SS) page 89

bottom The quiet seaside resort of Ambleteuse has a surprisingly action-packed history — it was fortified by the Romans, English, French and Germans
(SS) page 90

left   Each year, two weeks before Christmas, the
           Confrérie de l'Ordre de la Dinde de Licques
           (Fellows of the Order of the Licques Turkey)
           hold a festival devoted to this bastion of
           festive fowl (JR) page 95

below right The breezy town of Berck-sur-Mer is popular
           with kite fliers, and holds its own annual
           spring kite festival (SS) page 119

bottom   Sculptures et Jardin in Bergueneuse is one of
           the many parks and gardens in the region
           that throw open their doors for the National
           Parks and Gardens Festival in June
           (JR) page 157

If indoor bowls is your bag, try the traditional game played on a concave runway with convex cylinders which wobble like mad. Join the locals at either the **Bowls Club** (*rue St Jacques, Bailleul;* ✆ *03 28 42 21 91;* ⊕ *14.30–18.00 Tue & Thu–Sat; adult €2 by reservation, initiation free*) or the **Bowling Hall** (*rue de Godewaersvelde:* ✆ *03 28 49 45 04;* ⊕ *every day by reservation; adult/€2 for 1hr 30mins, free under 12*).

Ask, too, about vertical archery. The idea is to fire a rubber-tipped arrow to a height of 25 or 30m, hopefully to hit 'birds' perched above you. The sport goes back to the Middle Ages when archers formed guilds and fraternities. Some towns still have them.

– now there's a name to conjure with – where smuggling was once a way of life. The village, with its winding streets and lace-curtained brick-and-tile houses, is undeniably Flemish. It is also great for local food, served with gusto at two gorgeously rustic *estaminets*: see below.

✕ Where to eat

✕ **Het Blauwershof** 9 rue d'Eecke; ✆ 03 28 49 45 11; www.audomarois-online.com; ⊕ all day from 11.30, except Mon, early Jan & 3 wks in summer. With authentic 1900–20s décor, chunky wooden tables & a bar bristling with Flemish beers from France & Belgium, this popular watering-hole is Flemish to the core. Even Christian, the bearded boss, wears a T-shirt emblazoned with the rampant black lion of Flanders. Take time to join in traditional bar-top & other games. Robust Flemish *carbonade*, beef stew cooked in beer, with bags of French, or should it be Flemish, fries, washed down with *hommelbier*, a local brew, sets the tone for a moderately priced menu. $$$

✕ **Estaminet Du Centre** 11 route de Steenvoorde; ✆ 03 28 42 21 72; www.estaminetducentre.com; ⊕ 12.00 –14.00 Thu–Mon, 17.00–22.00 Fri–Sun. Long-associated with the cuisine of the flamboyant Pierrot de Lille, this well-established tavern now has a new chef, Julien Caron, to carry on the tradition of producing great Flemish fare. Think *flamiche au Maroilles*, derived from the region's famous cheese, along with meat delicacies & homemade rhubarb tart & you've got the picture. Set 2–3 courses €19.50–27 are available; so, too, are afternoon snacks, from terrines & tarts to crêpes. $$$

What to see and do A wry take on the wily ways of smuggling is on show at the quirky **Border Life Museum** (*Musée de la Vie Frontalière; 98 rue de Callicanes;* ✆ *03 28 42 08 52;* e *contact@musee-godewaersvelde.fr; www.musee-godewaersvelde.fr;* ⊕ *14.00–17.00 Wed–Sat & 1st & 2nd Sun of each month; adult/child €3, accompanied under 12 free*). Sorting out the goodies from the baddies is not always easy. Everyone in the village, it seems, was in some way involved in a giant pre-EU game of smuggling everything from pigs, horses, hens and eggs to chocolate, wines and lace across the then-manned Belgian border 5km away. So much so that in 1994, when the border was removed, a local giant weighing 70kg was symbolically created in way of celebration. He now welcomes visitors at the museum entrance; with him are Dick, a customs' dog, and Tom, a smuggler's dog.

There is, of course, a serious side. Along with a fascinating look into methods used by locals to trick the customs officials are reminders of the present-day fight being waged against drugs and illegal weapons.

Just over the Belgian border, the old customs' house in Poperinge has since 1998 been **'t Kommiezenkot**, a café-cum-museum stocking 30 local beers.

Around Godewaersvelde Just over 2km southeast of Godewaersvelde lies **Mont des Cats**, the steepest of the Monts de Flandre, reached via a narrow lane that winds through wooded hills to the hilltop village. The name has nothing to do with cats, but was the stronghold of the Catti – a fifth-century tribe of Germanic origin.

Drive further on to the peak which, at 158m, provides a panoramic view of pastoral perfection, where undulating waves of fields and woods roll gently into Belgium. Proving the ultimate backdrop is the massive red-brick **Abbaye du Mont des Cats**, a Cistercian abbey established in 1826 following the Revolution. This is a warm, welcoming place where visitors are invited to take part in monastic activities or even stay as guests. Its prize-winning cheese, processed from locally sourced milk, provides the main livelihood of the Trappist monks. They also have their own bakery, turning out a delicious brioche. This, along with the deceptively smooth cheese with a bite, is sold at the bright and airy store (⊕ *Apr–Sep, 14.00–18.30 Sun, 14.00–18.30 Mon, 10.00–12.00 & 14.00–18.30 Wed– Sat, closed Tue, Oct–Mar 14.30–17.30 Sun–Mon & Wed–Sat, closed Easter, Christmas & other religious festivals plus New Year's Day*). Stock up on some unusual gifts, or buy a selection of Trappist beers. A series of documentaries on monastic life are shown in the shop.

Chill out with a beer or coffee and a Flemish cheeseboard (€7.90) on the terrace of **l'Auberge du Mont Cats**. It has one of the best views in town. Then head back either to Steenvoorde, for Bergues and the coast (see *Chapter 4, page 81*) or direct to Bailleul and eastwards towards Lille (see pages 221–32).

TOWARDS BERGUES AND DUNKIRK Join the E42/A25 and continue to Bergues, or turn off at **Wormhout**. Look out for the memorial marking the infamous Wormhout Massacre, **La Plaine au Bois** (*rue des Dunkerque, off the Wormhout road*) 1km southwest of **Esquelbecq**. This took place during the British retreat to Dunkirk (see page 78) in May 1940 when an estimated 100 prisoners of war, mainly British but some French, were herded by the advancing Germans into a small cowshed in an isolated farming area. Grenades were then thrown in, killing many of the men instantly. Those still alive were led outside and shot one by one. Of two men who managed to escape, one was caught by the SS and shot in the head. The other survived by playing dead after being shot in the neck.

The site remained unknown until the 1960s – and it was not until 2000 that the meadow area was bought and a memorial built amid the beeches and oaks planted in memory of the victims.

Esquelbecq
Tourist information
🄴 **Office de Tourisme** The House of Westhoek, 9 pl Alphonse Bergerot, Esquelbecq; ☎ 03 28 62 88 57; e maison.westhoek@wanadoo.fr; www.esquelbecq.com; ⊕ Apr–Oct 10.00–12.00 & 15.00–18.00 daily except Mon, Nov–Mar 10.00– 12.00 & 15.00–18.00 Mon–Wed & Fri–Sat,

10.00–12.00 Thu, closed Sun. The tourist office building is also home to **Maison du Westhoek**, (adult/child aged 12–16/child aged 6–11 €2/1.5/1), where regular exhibitions between Easter & Oct provide a unique insight into Flemish culture & life.

MAKE AN ASS OF YOURSELF

Fancy something to bray about? Well why not walk the Flemish countryside with a donkey? It knows the route and will help you carry your bag. An 11km tour takes you past the 17th-century castle and the River Yser. Contact the tourist office or La Flânerie d'Esquelbecq (2 pl Alphonse Bergerot; ☎ 03 28 65 71 61; e la-flanerie-esquelbecq@club-internet.fr; €20–45 for day, lunch included, guide available at €5; so, too, is an extra donkey).

Richly endowed with trails for walkers and cyclists, the region also caters for horseriders, as Gillian Thornton a specialist writer on France, discovered when she rode with a stables at Saint Jans Cappel near Bailleul.

I was introduced to Bony, a dun-and-white mare, who was to carry me round the tracks and lanes of Mont Noir, one of the several modest hills which rise out of the Flanders Flatlands. This is great country for riding, with a network of broad dirt tracks and quiet country lanes, which pass hop fields and windmills, small villages and farms.

We rode hard and fast up the tracks, the horses loving every minute, then slowly and calmly along the lanes, allowing everyone to get their breath back. After some 30 minutes, we crossed from France into Belgium, clopping over the cobbles of a small town with traditional Flemish architecture and a café advertising *saucisse de cheval a l'ancienne*, a dire warning to horses who misbehave.

After two hours we arrived back at the farm to the comfort of the owners' two well-equipped *gîtes* and a long soak in the bath before sampling traditional Flemish nightlife – the *estaminet*. These old-fashioned pubs have simple furniture, wooden tables and rib-sticking local cuisine, plus a substantial list of locally brewed beers (see page 40).

Details from **Ferme Equestre de la Rose des Vents** (*280 route de Bailleul;* \ *03 28 49 00 10;* e *larosedesvents@free.fr; www.larosedesvents.free.fr; rides €13.50–48, 1hr to full day*). Owned by Nicole and Guy Terrier, the yard has 50-plus horses and ponies, with rides organised according to ability. They also arrange outings in an open horse-drawn cart or *caleche* carriage for 10 people (*€98–275 90mins–1 day*).

Where to eat

✕ La Table des Géants 9 bis pl Bergerot, Esquelbecq; \ 03 28 62 95 84; e contact@restaurant-latabledesgeants.com; www.restaurant-latabledesgeants.com; ⊕ 12.00–14.00 & 17.00–22.00 Thu–Sun; open by request if more than 8 people. This appropriately named hostelry does just what it says. Not only is it high-ceilinged enough to accommodate the average giant, but also serves fair-sized portions of the best in local cuisine. No wonder the giant on the wall is smiling… it's a jolly place for lunch or dinner. $$$

What to see and do The village is crossed by the River Yser, a small coastal river lined with oak trees, from which derived the Flemish name Ekelsbeke, or 'stream with acorns.' The church of **St Folquin**, dating back to the 10th century, was destroyed by fire on Palm Sunday in 1976. It reopened after being restored in 16th–17th-century Flemish style on Christmas Eve 1978 (*guided tours by prior arrangement;* \ *03 28 62 88 57; €2; the 75-step tower – great for a photo shot – can also be visited for €2; €3 for both*).

ONWARDS TO BAILLEUL AND LILLE If going direct from Esquelbecq take the D17 to A25/E42 for the 30km drive of around 30 minutes. From Cassel either head northwest following the D16 and D933 direct to Bailleul, 10km away, or take a detour to **Mont Noir**, 8km via the D10. Characterised by fir trees, this was the childhood home of French author Marguerite Yourcenar, the first female member of the Académie Française. The *château* where she lived was destroyed in World War I, but a wooded park in her memory is great for walkers. Rejoin the D10 for **Bailleul**, a big-hearted town, virtually rebuilt after World War I with an even bigger square and a fine-looking belfry.

St-Omer and the Flemish Hinterland **FLEMISH HEARTLAND**

5

Bailleul From 1713, Bailleul was the centre of the judicial centre of western Flanders, and this lively market town still exudes an industrious air. Its Flemish brick-stepped façades bring an extra flourish.

Tourist information

⚡ Monts des Flandres Tourist Office 3 Grand'Place; ✆ 03 28 43 81 00; e tourisme@montsdeflandre.fr; www.montsdeflandres.fr; ⏲ 14.00–17.30 Mon, 10.00–12.00 & 14.30–17.30 Tue–Fri, 10.00–12.00 & 14.30–17.30 Sat. A shop stocks a wide range of Flemish goods.

What to see and do This is the place to both shop and explore. Pop into Le Petit Fournil Flamand (*Maison Marone, 36 pl Charles de Gaulle;* ✆ *03 28 49 02 34;* ⏲ *closed on Wed*) for a freshly-cooked pastry or bread for a lunchtime snack before tackling the top attractions. Thanks to a wealthy 19th-century collector the **Museum of Benoît-Puydt** (*rue de Musée;* ✆ *03 28 49 12 70;* e *musee@ville-bailleul.fr;* ⏲ *14.00–17.30 Wed–Mon, closed on public holidays; adult/child under 18 €3.60/free*) contains an eclectic collection of all things Flemish from the 15th to the 19th centuries. This includes paintings by Brueghel and local artist Pharaon de Winter. A portrait of De Puydt by Cassel artist Alexis Bafcop hangs on the first floor. Nose around his collection of furniture. His cabinets of curiosities with their secret drawers are fascinating. A new lace museum adds rather than detracts from Benoît-De-Puydt's original works.

The museum makes a handy introduction to the **Lace Museum** (*La Maison de la Dentelle, 6 rue du College;* ✆ *03 28 41 25 72;* e *ecole-dentelle@ville-bailleul.fr; www.ville-bailleul.fr;* ⏲ *13.30–17.00 Tue, Fri & Sat on alternate weeks, 13.30–19.30 Thu, closed public holidays & Christmas/New Year period; adult €1.50, under 12 free*). Offering beginner and advanced techniques, the college is a unique throwback to the 17th century before mechanisation put paid to the art of fine tailor-made lace. Now a small group of all-female students are once again happily bobbin' away at the looms. One has worked here 25 years. All are capable of creating super

JUST A FEW HOPS AWAY...

Given that beer-brewing Flemish monks introduced hops to Kent in medieval times, it's no wonder French Flanders has won the praise of real ale fans. Top tipple for many is *hommelpap*, a brawny 7% alcohol beer brewed at **Ferme Beck** (*118 Eeckelstraete, Bailleul;* ✆ *03 28 49 03 90; www.fermebeck.com;* ⏲ *19.00 Sat & from 17.00 Mar–Nov for pre-arranged visits; €2.80 to include tasting; there is also a shop*). The distinctive flavour comes not just from the farm's own 3ha of hop fields but also from the barley grain, which is sent to a nearby malthouse for roasting and soaking. Even the water is drawn from a well on the 60ha farm, which opened the microbrewery in 1994, providing *hommelpap* (meaning 'hop juice' or 'hop porridge') every few weeks or as needed, says Dany Beck who, with his brother Thierry, now runs the farm. It was thanks, however, to the enthusiasm of their father Denis, that this strangely opaque-looking beer sprang to prominence as part of a general resurgence of artisan beers in Nord-Pas de Calais.

Due to its characteristic flavour and aroma, *hommelpap* does not benefit from ageing and should be drunk as soon as possible and certainly by its 'best before' date. What better excuse can a beer buff ask than that ? The farm also has two *gîtes* and a brasserie serving a €10.50 brewer's platter.

Hoofnote: the Becks also keep tradtional Chevaux Flamands, enormous chestnut horses with flaxen manes and tails. These are used during a hop-picking festival on the first Sunday of September of even years.

Campers and self caterers take note: a co-operative of three farmers has not only brought the diversity of regional and national products under one roof, but also prepares oven-ready dishes at its headquarters at Strazeele, 8km from Bailleul off the D642. **La Ferme des Flandres** (*573 route d'Hazebrouck;* ✆ *03 28 44 32 70;* e *lafermedesflandres.fr; www.keldelice.com;* ⊕ *09.30–12.30 & 15.00–19.00 Wed–Sat, 10.00–13.00 Sun; online service is planned*) sells over 400 products, from dairy and meat products to vegetables, jams, chocolates and beer.

handcrafted lacework for special occasions, from an anniversary of a sports club to an engagement or wedding. An open doors policy in June, with workshops, is held to commemorate St Ann, patron saint of lacemakers.

You can't fail to miss the magnificent **Belfry** (*Le Beffroi, Grand'Place; guided 1½hr tour adult/child aged 6–12 €3.50/2.50, free under 6, tickets from tourist office, see opposite*). Climb the 200 steps to the top where the 35 bells of the carillon chime out local ditties. Look out over the best view of Les Monts des Flandres, the Rivet Lys plain and the Artois hills.

Around Bailleul Some 2km away, via the D23 Ypres road, is **The Botanical Conservatory** (*Conservatoire Botanique National de Bailleul, Hameau de Haendries;* ✆ *03 28 49 00 83; www.cbnbl.org;* ⊕ *08.30–12.00 & 13.30–18.00 Mon–Fri; adult/child €3*). It's both educational and great fun, with winding paths and small ponds. An open or semi-guided tour introduces the collection of 850 species of wild plants.

Before leaving the region meet the energetic Jean-Francois Brigant – a real waffler, but in the nicest possible way. He creates the finest in Flemish waffles at his shop and museum at **Houplines**, on the outskirts of Lille, which is a veritable shrine to the traditional thin version of the region.

Watch him at work at **La Gaufre du Pays Flamand** (*4 rue Victor Hugo;* ✆ *03 20 77 40 19;* e *gaufrehouplines@aol.com; www.gaufrehouplines.com;* ⊕ *08.00–19.00 Mon–Fri, 09.00–12.00 Sat*). Taste one of the rum or grand marnier classics, or a speciality flavour such as chicory. His latest is the *speculoos* waffle based on the cinnamon taste of this regional biscuit.

Learn more about the origins of waffles during a 45-minute tour, bookable in advance, around his renovated Flemish fires complete with waffle irons. The visit ends with a tasting, bringing a final flavour to this most Flemish of the regions.

St-Omer and the Flemish Hinterland **FLEMISH HEARTLAND**

5

6

Montreuil-sur-Mer and the Seven Valleys

There is a distinctive Camelot ring to this region. Dominated by Montreuil-sur-Mer, an Arthurian-style fortress in everything but name, it appears little more than a tranquil landscape of rippling rivers and lowing cows. But scratch the surface and you'll find it's not quite a land of bygone legends, rather one in which contemporary boutique businesses, fiercely proud of their pastoral heritage, are carving out cottage industries free from a world of big-brand blandness. Many are young entrepreneurs; others now have outlets in fashionable French cities.

All are fiercely individual, fearful of trendy projects. One government accountant, convinced the Seven Valleys would wither and die without big-time rural tourism, reportedly made the mistake of suggesting a leisure park. He was promptly sent packing. Rightly so: the Seven Valleys is not a playground, but a working community in which country pursuits come naturally, and not as part of some grand eco design. It does have historic links, of which the Battle of Agincourt ('Azincourt' in French), is a glaring example, but above all the region still provides a chance to sit back, enjoy the countryside and soak up some stunning scenery.

Most visitors will need a car, though the roads and lanes are ideal for motorcyclists, cyclists and walkers. Buses are few and far between; however, there is a train service to the bigger towns via Montreuil.

MONTREUIL-SUR-MER

Once located on the coast, until the River Canche silted up, Montreuil-sur-Mer – as it still officially called – has inspired artists and visitors alike with its cobbled streets, half-timbered houses and 3km of ramparts, stunningly captured in a setting summer sun. Even the rain cannot dampen this delightful setting, particularly popular in the peak season and probably seen at its pastel-coloured best on an off-season short break. Shopping, sightseeing and some splendid restaurants complete the blissful scene.

HISTORY Having already repelled a Viking attack in 898, the fortified town of Montreuil (probably derived from the Latin *monasteriolum* or 'small monastery') in 987 became the only seaport of the royal domain. It even had a castle, long since gone. By the 13th and 14th centuries the prosperity of the port, one of the wealthiest for cloth, grain and wine in northern Europe, brought about the construction of the first of many gates to guard the town. In the 15th century, the White Tower, part of the city wall, was said to predate the great Renaissance buildings in the richness of its architecture.

By the 16th century the river had silted up, leaving present-day Montreuil 15km inland on a rocky spur, ideally suited to defending France's northern frontier with the Spanish-ruled Artois and Flanders regions. Even a siege by the combined forces of Henry VIII and Charles V (Charles Quint) of Spain in 1522 was repelled.

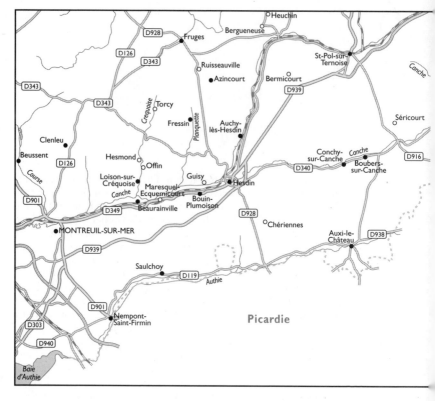

A second, however, in 1537 succeeded. Montreuil was sacked, leaving the town and the Abbey Church of Saint-Saulve partly ruined. It was all change again when François I recaptured the town which, with a new citadel and generally updated, remained intact until a century later when Vauban, Louis XIV's military mastermind (see page 13), completed the fortifications by adding a new arsenal and gunpowder store.

From then on Montreuil reverted to a sleepy town on the coaching road from Calais to Paris. In World War I, it was headquarters of the British Army; General Haig stayed in a *château* close by.

GETTING THERE
By car Either join the A16 at Calais and leave at exit 29 for the D901 for the 75km journey, which is toll free, or continue on the A16 and leave at exit 26 for the D939/D901, which might be slightly quicker but is subject to a €2.70 toll each way on the Boulogne stretch of the motorway.

By train If arriving at **Calais**, take the frequent TER service from Calais-Ville station to Boulogne-Ville and change to the TER Line 14 (Arras via Étaples and St-Pol) for Montreuil-sur-Mer station which is just a few hundred metres down from the ramparts. There are nine trains daily from 04.00 to around 18.30 and the journey takes between 30 and 50 minutes.

If travelling from **Lille Flandres** take the TER Line 15 (Boulogne via St-Pol and Béthune). Trains are less frequent but the journey time is around the same.

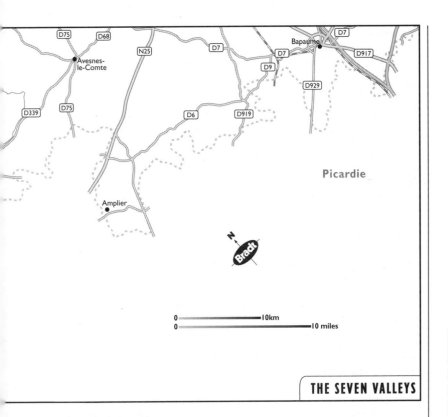

THE SEVEN VALLEYS

TOURIST INFORMATION

Tourist Office Office de Tourisme, 21 rue Carnot; 03 21 06 04 27; e accueil@tourisme-montreullios.com; www.tourisme-montreuillois.com; Jan–Mar, & some days early Nov–24 Dec 10.00–12.30 & 14.00–17.00 Mon–Sat, Apr–Jun & Sep–early Nov 10.00–12.30 & 14.00–18.00 Mon–Sat, 10.00–12.30 Sun & public holidays, Jul–Aug 10.00–18.00 Mon–Sat, 10.00–12.30 & 15.00–17.00 Sun, 10.00–12.30 public holidays. Information is available on bus & other tours, including 'In the footsteps of Victor Hugo & the surrounding valleys'.

WHERE TO STAY

Hotel Château de Montreuil (12 rooms, 4 suites) 4 Chaussée des Capucins, Montreuil-sur-Mer; 03 21 81 53 04; e reservations@chateaudemontreuil.com; www.chateaudemontreuil.com. Supremely comfortable & with well-appointed bedrooms this is top-drawer material, complete with antiques & charming artefacts. Built in 1933 with an almost Gatsby-esque ambience & lovely gardens, this cries out to mark a special occasion. An outdoor swimming pool opens in summer. Hotel closed on Mon (except Jul & Aug); annual closing in Jan. B/fast is €18; private parking €12 a day. $$$$$

Hotel Hermitage (57 rooms, inc suites) pl Gambetta; 03 21 06 74 74; e contact@hermitage-montreuil.com; www.hermitage-montreuil.com. Located within the walls of an ancient 11th-century hospital, restored under Napoléon III, the 3-star Best Western Hotel blends historic interest with the whims of the 21st century. These include free Wi-Fi & a spa & fitness centre. Private parking is €10 a day. Watch out for seasonal offers, including golfing breaks. $$$$

L'Auberge de la Grenouillère (4 rooms) Rue de la Grenouillère, La Madelaine-sous-Montreuil; 03 21 06 07 22; e auberge.de.la.grenouillere@wanadoo.fr; www.lagrenouillere.fr. The small rooms built into the eaves reflect the romantic feel of the restaurant. B/fast is €10. $$$$

🏠 **Le Darnétal** (4 rooms) pl Darnétal; ☎ 03 21 06 04 87; www.darnetal-montreuil.com. Cosy rooms & the warm & unpretentious atmosphere appeal. The check-in system, whereby you have to tie in with the restaurant hours, has, however, come in for criticism. $$$

✗ WHERE TO EAT

✗ **L'Auberge de la Grenouillère** rue de la Grenouillère, La Madelaine-sous-Montreuil; ☎ 03 21 06 07 22; ✉ auberge.de.la.grenouillere@wanadoo.fr; www.lagrenouillere.fr; ⏰ 12.00–13.45 & 19.00–21.30 Thu–Mon, open daily Jul–Aug. Tucked away in a small village, this unashamedly gourmet restaurant is where chef Alexandre Gauthier gained his first Michelin star at the age of 27. His father Roland Gauthie, who once worked at the Connaught Hotel in London, ran the business before then. With the highly creative menus hovering around the €80–90 mark expect the best from creative & strictly seasonal menus based on local produce. The illustrations on the wall of froggy-like characters relate to La Fontaine's fable of the frog who ate until he exploded. This also explains the model frog in the most atmospheric part of the main room. $$$$$

✗ **Restaurant de Château de Montreuil** ⏰ 12.00–14.00 & 19.30–21.30 Tues–Sun & Mon Jun–Aug. Flavour first is what chef-patron Christian Germaine seeks for his Michelin-star gourmet restaurant with its elegant setting & friendly, yet faultless, service. To achieve this he uses fresh local produce, including vegetables & herbs from the *château* garden as well as locally sourced fish & meat. Cheeses come from Philippe Oliver's famous shop in Boulogne (see page 103). A 3-course set lunch is €38; 3 courses from à-la-carte menu for lunch or dinner €75 & a 7-course tasting menu €90. This is top-drawer dining out at a price. $$$$$

✗ **Le Jeroboam** (linked to Hotel Hermitage) 1 rue des Juifs; ⏰ 12.00–14.00 & 19.00–21.30 Tue–Sat, closed Sun–Mon & Jan. Proving you don't have to be stuffy to be stylish, this is a restaurant where exposed red-brick walls & contemporary black tables complement a menu of traditional fare with a modern twist. Expect the best. Owner/manager Céline Germain, comes from a family famed for its cooking. Try *marmite de poisson des petits bateaux* (€18) on the à-la-carte menu: the black-lidded casserole brims with a mouth-watering blend of fish & chunks of vegetables in an aromatic creamy sauce. There's enough for 2. Finish with a *café gourmand* (coffee with a selection of mini-desserts). A set lunch at €17, 3-course set menus (except Sat) & the 3-course €66 set menu for 2 all provide good value in this most pleasing of places. If you fancy some champers there are a few Jeroboams stacked on the wine racks that cover an entire wall. $$$$

✗ **Le Darnétal** ⏰ 12.00–14.00 & 19.00–21.15 Wed–Sun. This restaurant with olde-worlde charm has been cited as a popular best-to-book bet for lunch or dinner. The décor is cosy with red tablecloths, a colourful array of pictures, flower arrangements & soft lighting. The extensive collection of caps hanging from the ceiling belongs to Jean-Paul Vernay, the 'patron' who is an avid rugby fan. His daughter is an England supporter! Prawns in an orange sauce or duck with a blackcurrant sauce come highly recommended. The Menu Spécialités for €25 includes such delights as *escargots et grenouilles à la crème d'ail* & *magret de canard* or *rognons de veau*. The €34 Menu Gastronomique includes warm oysters in

---

CALLING ALL *LES MIS* FANS

On 4 September 1837 *Les Miserables* author Victor Hugo stopped over in Montreuil-sur-Mer on his way back to Paris. So impressed was he that Cavée-Saint-Firmin, a steeped cobbled-stoned alleyway, became the spot where the reformed convict-turned-hero, Jean Valjean, rescued Fauchelevent after he was run down by a cart in Hugo's subsequent novel.

Les Mis fans will love the two-hour *son-et-lumière* show based on the novel that runs during July and August. This includes fireworks and displays by re-enactment groups and horses (☎ 03 21 06 72 45; www.lesmiserables-montreuil.com for online booking; adult/child aged 5–12 €15/9; show starts at 22.30 & lasts 1hr 30mins).

champagne (a house specialty) & *cote de boeuf* sur le grill with a sauce Béarnaise for 2. Never had a duff meal, said our reviewer, but don't wipe your hands on the red curtains as one diner mistakenly did! Moral: always take a good supply of hand towels. $$$$

WHAT TO SEE AND DO There's only one way to explore Montreuil: by foot. And, though tremendous, the views alone are lost without an audio or guided tour of the major sites.

Foremost of Montreuil's attractions is **the citadel** (*La citadelle;* ☎ *03 21 06 10 83;* ⏱ *mid-Oct–mid-Apr 14.00–17.00 daily except Tue, mid-Apr–mid-Oct 10.00–12.00 & 14.00–18.00 daily except Tue, closed Dec–Jan & during Les Miserables Son-et-Lumière; adult/child €3/1.50*). Constructed on a promontory some 40m above the Canche Valley, the citadel, built in 1585, has seen plenty of action – not least during World War I when the casements were used as the communications centre for the 5,000-strong British general headquarters. An equestrian statue of Field Marshal Douglas Haig in the Grand'Place is a replacement of the original one knocked down by the occupying Germans in World War II. Be warned, some of the steep stone steps may be unsuitable for children or those less steady on their feet. If that's the case head instead for the **Roger Rodière Museum** (*Musée de France Roger Rodière;* ☎ *03 21 86 90 83;* ⏱ *Sep–Jun 14.00–17.00 Tue–Sun, Jul–Aug 10.00–12.00 & 14.00–18.00 Tue–Sun, closed certain weeks in Nov & over Christmas period; adult/child €3/1.50*). Displays show the influence of the Church through the ages, as well as paintings of the town and the surrounding area by the Étaples School of Painting (see page 120).

Much of Montreuil's religious wealth is stored in the remaining major sites. First is **St-Saulve Abbey Church** (*L'abbatiale Saint-Saulve, pl Gambetta*) where many of a growing number of relics were destroyed during the French Revolution in 1793. Despite this, treasures from the 13th and 17th centuries are still stored here, largely from the old St-Austrebertha Abbey which dates back to Viking times. Between them they make up one of the richest collections of religious art in northern France. The most prestigious item is the Crosier of St Austreberthe, carved in oak and dating from the end of the 7th century. The magnificent organ, built in 1806, was restored in the 1970s. The casework, in flamboyant Louis XV style, is a protected historical monument.

The **Hotel-Dieu Chapel**'s (*La Chapelle de l'Hotel-Dieu, pl Gambetta;* ⏱ *Jul–Sep 15.00–18.00; adult/child under 14 €1.5/free*) superb 19th-century stained-glass windows contribute enormously to its already-rich 17th- and 18th-century furnishings. It began as a hospital around 1200 and was used as such until 1992.

If you can't go in, simply stroll round the ramparts. On the west side you'll pass five 13th-century towers encircling the citadel; there are a further two on the southern front. On the north flank is the imposing Boulogne Gateway which, widened in 1955, is the town's surviving gate – the rest were sacrificed in the name of traffic improvement. A by-pass built in the 1970s has eased traffic congestion but parking can be difficult in peak season. At least the ramparts let you stretch your legs for a short while. So, too, do the cobbled streets and alleyways wending their way past the craft shops in **rue Clape-en-Bas**; other shops are around **Grand'Place** and **place Darnétal**.

For more serious walking, there are 16 loops covering about 150km in the Montreuil municipalities. Approved by the French Federation of Hiking, they range from 4km to 30km. Most are accessible by bike, though there are four specific tracks for cyclists. Bikes are available to hire; details can be obtained from the tourist office.

BATTLE FOR AZINCOURT STILL CONTINUES

Who would have thought that a battle, anathema to French ears and a clarion call to Brits everywhere, would still be hotly discussed some 600 years on?

This is mainly due to Christophe Gillot, the genial director of **The Medieval Centre** (*Centre Historique Medieval, rue Charles VI;* ↘ *03 21 47 27 53;* e *office.de. tourisme.azincourt@wanadoo.fr or of-azincourt@nordnet.fr; www.azincourt-medieval. com;* ⏲ *09.00–18.00 Mon–Sat; adult/child aged 5–16 €7.5/5).* He stirred up a veritable hornet's nest in the UK press by suggesting the story of the English victory was, to put it mildly, a little distorted. Historians, including one from England, he argued, now disputed the claim that the French outnumbered the brave Brits by 20 to one. It could even be as low as two to one. Even worse, the English were an apparently barbarous lot.

The coverage no doubt boosted the centre's tourist figures, of which a huge number are British, many of them schoolchildren. It also encouraged this most enthusiastic of men in his mission to shed new light on the story of how on 25 October 1415, St Crispin's Day, the best in English bowmen trounced the cream of French nobility. So much so that the centre was, at the time of writing, due for a total revamp with even greater emphasis on historical interpretation, along with workshops, and what has always been a lively, but straightforward, multi-media reconstruction of the fatal day. There were also plans for archaeological digs in the field where the battle was fought.

All of this is a far cry from 2000 when, after years of understandably bruised pride, a local initiative finally acknowledged that, like it or not, the village had huge historical tourism potential. What was a small token museum was replaced by its contemporary counterpart and it has grown from there.

Now animated models and dual-language headsets allow English- and French-speaking visitors alike to listen to their team captains, Henry V and Constable d'Albret, give rousing pre-battle addresses – with Shakespearean-style prose in the case of the Brits.

It could all be a bit crass, but this blend of history, medieval weaponry and magic portrays this turbulent time with aplomb. It certainly impressed a group of young English schoolchildren when we visited, though their teacher was a little unsure whether they quite understood what was going on. Nevertheless they loved the gizmos, which include some great hands-on chances to wave a broadsword, feel the weight of chainmail or, best of all, heave on a rope to judge the force needed by the mainly Welsh archers as they let rip with the longbows. There are also 11 talking video screens which spring into action when you face them; allow at least two hours to see it all.

Do visit the battlefield itself. A compact site, it illustrates, even today, how a small English army came to defeat a large French army of heavily armoured knights. The forest of trees which helped hem in the French horsemen has long since gone, but the track at the bottom of the sloping battlefield, along which trundled carts keeping the English archers well supplied with arrows, is still recognisable. It was from here and both sides of the rain-soaked field that they let rip with a hail of arrows as the French knights slithered downhill in the mud to meet their death.

Whether this was at the hands of the dastardly/brave British (make up your own mind) the arguments will continue, much to the delight of Christophe.

✕ WHERE TO EAT

✕ **Le Charles VI** 12 rue Charles VI, ↘ 03 2141 53 00; e restaurantcharles6@wandadoo.fr; www.azincourt-medieval.com; ⏲ May–Aug 09.00–20.00 daily, closed Wed. With its traditional décor of beams, plants & tapestries, this is a good spot to relax after touring the centre of which the restaurant forms an integral part. A €24 medieval menu or €28 with ¼ carafe of red wine is tempting. Otherwise choose from an entrée & main course or dessert at €13, or €28–37 3- to 4-course set menus. $$$

If anywhere is guaranteed to explode the myth of Nord-Pas de Calais as being flat, boring and bleak, then this is it. Laced by the Rivers Authie, Bras de Brosne, Canche, Créquoise, Planquette, Ternoise and Lys – hence the Seven Valleys – this is pure unadulterated countryside. Major towns are few and far between, with the accommodation remote and more often of the *gîtes* and B&B variety. This means motoring, which for Brits at least is pure bliss – a number of whom have been encouraged to settle here from Kent, with the bonus of being back across the Channel in a just a few hours.

HESDIN Small it may be, but the town centre has plenty of reminders that Hesdin replaced a nearby village of the same name. The original village was destroyed in 1554 on the orders of the Emperor Charles V (Charles Quint), furious at the bloody excursions from France's Artois strongholds. Like Thérouanne (see page 133) the soil was rendered sterile with salt. Hesdin remained a bastion of Spanish power, facing the French stronghold at Montreuil until taken by King Louis XIII in 1639. For what was once a Spanish stronghold, this is now a quiet, almost unassuming, riverside market town where the Canche and Ternoise Valleys meet. The natural hub for the Seven Valleys on its eastern edge, Hesdin is distinguished by hump-backed bridges and a surprisingly large main square.

Tourist information

⚡ **Tourisme7Vallees** Hôtel de Ville, pl d'Armes; ☎ 03 21 86 19 19; e contact@tourisme-7vallees.com; www.tourisme7vallees.com; ⏰ mid-Sep–Mar

09.30–12.30 & 14.00–17.00 Tue–Sat, Apr–mid-Sep
09.30–12.30 & 14.00–18.00 daily

Where to stay and eat

🏠 **Hotel la Chope** (4 rooms) 48 rue d'Arras; ☎ 03 21 90 16 66; e info@la-chope.com; www.la-chope.com. Many congregate for lunch at this cosy, friendly hostelry with comfortable bedrooms, including a family suite. It will appeal to short break visitors wanting to put their Franglais to the test! The hotel is run by Katie & Eric Rush, English-born but Francophile by nature. They first saw La Chope in 1993 &, having already bought a weekend retreat in 1989, felt it was time for a fulltime move to France. Named the Hotel Belle Vue in the 1970s, the building probably dates back to the 17th century & has undergone a complete restoration since being bought by the Rushes in 2004. $$$

Shopping Hesdin has a smattering of small shops of the more family-run or specialist kind. Thursday sees the square thronged with market-goers, among them, no doubt, some of the small community of afore-mentioned retired Brits who have made the town their home.

What to see and do You can't miss the grandly Flemish 16th–17th-century **town hall**, whose balcony bears the Spanish Coats of Arms and Shields of Hesdin and Artois while the pediment bears the French arms. Behind is the **belfry**

6

MUSEUM MARKS THE SPOT

The original village of Hesdin, now Vieil Hesdin, 5km away, saw the opening in 2009 of **Le Site Historique de Vieil Hesdin** (*rue d'Hesdin*; ☎ 06 76 71 54 14; www.levieilhesdin.org; ⏰ 14.30–17.30 first Sat of each month; adult/child under 18 €4/2 for museum, last Sat of each month €6/3 museum & guided walk at 15.00 (2hrs; 5km)). Created by the local historical association, the site includes a museum containing antiques and artefacts tracing the town's history from Gallic-Roman to World War II.

(⊕ *mid–Sep–Mar 09.30–12.30 & 14.00–17.00 Mon–Fri, 09.30–12.30 Sat, Apr–mid Sep 09.30–12.30 & 14.00–18.00 Mon–Fri, 09.30–12.30 Sat; free entry*).

The **Musée Municipal** (*same details as for tourist office; see page 151*), located in what were once prison cells, gives a peep into the past, with paintings of Louis XIII's siege and general knick-knacks from pewter ware to pottery.

Nip into the **L'Église Notre-Dame** (*rue de la Paroisse*). Built between 1565 and 1585, it sports an impressive tile-hung tower and an ornate Renaissance-style stone porch surmounted by the Spanish Hapsburg arms. Remarkably it has withstood the French siege, the Revolution and two world wars.

HESDIN AND ST-POL REGIONS

It is easily forgotten that this land of pastoral peace, pierced only by a tractor trundling past your holiday *gîte*, was for centuries the crucible of European wars. Hesdin proves the point; so, too, do other half-forgotten villages where architectural whirls and swirls bear evidence of English, French and Spanish occupation.

Nowadays, however, the only roving army is the relatively small number of people – mainly motorists – who tour this region of babbling brooks, mellow valleys and all those other clichés which add to an image of bucolic bliss.

⌂ Where to stay

⌂ **Maison de Plumes** (4 dbl rooms) 73 rue d'Aire, Heuchin, 20mins from either Hesdin or St-Pol-de Ternoise; ☏ 03 21 41 47 85; www.maisondeplumes.com. Once the home of a 17th-century countess, this former *château*, meticulously restored by a British couple, remains a family home – but with a strong country house feel to it. This is just what Richard & Vanessa Rhoades-Brown were looking for when they stumbled upon the Seven Valleys property in what they confirm is a region remarkably unspoilt & where local fare is produced with pride. Since opening as a B&B in 2008, they have had rave reviews not least for the distinctive themed rooms, designed by Vanessa & based on 4 birds: ostrich, flamingo, parakeet & peacock. The Art Deco lounge has likewise won applause. Locally sourced seasonal produce for their menus has also helped. Eggs from their own corn-fed hens add that extra taste to b/fast. With pre-dinner aperitifs & a decidedly French-style €35 (children €16) dinner, this is an ideal stopover for a night or a w/end break. Le Touquet & Arras are less than an hour away, Montreuil is even closer. A €8 picnic lunch with 1 glass of wine can be arranged. Or you can simply sit in the garden, listen to the birds or jump in the hot tub. $$$$

⌂ **La Cour de Rémi** (7 rooms) 1 rue Baillet, Bermicourt, almost equidistant between Hesdin & St-Pol; ☏ 03 21 03 33 33; e sebastien@ lacourderemi.com; www.lacourderemi.com. The hotel's brick-&-timber bedrooms are a knock-out: seemingly big enough to hold a party in, they come equipped with comfortable furnishings & a top-notch coffee-making machine, They are also quiet, with views of the courtyard. 2 new rooms created from a farmhouse-style conversion (La Maison de Flore) were added in 2010. This stands in the grounds alongside a treehouse bedroom perched 4m from the ground. The kids will love it. $$$$

⌂ **Chambres d'Hôtes du Mont Blanc** (5 rooms) 313 rue du Mont Blanc, Beaurainville, 12km from Hesdin; ☏ 03 21 81 04 26; e jeannie@chambres-montblanc.fr; www.chambreshotesdumontblanc.fr. Set in woodlands, this cosy B&B with its home-from-home comforts sets the benchmark for the 100 or so B&Bs in the Seven Valleys. This is reflected in the rooms: 2 are crisply decorated in pastel shades with tiled floors & light-coloured furniture; 2 others have original roof timbers. The 2-room Poppy Cottage has the added incentive of a lounge/kitchen & a ground & 1st floor. $$$

🏠 **La Hotoire** (4 rooms) 2 pl de la Mairie, Guisy, 4km from Hesdin; ☏ 03 21 81 00 31; ℮ a.la.hotoire@wanadoo.fr; www.lahotoire.com. With its converted farmhouse setting, this family friendly B&B with 2 pet donkeys & a large garden comes highly recommended. 3 of the 4 bedrooms come equipped with a kitchenette. A 3-course €24 menu is available. $$

Rural accommodation

🏠 **Le Baladin** (19 rooms) 62 rue Principale, Torcy; ☏ 03 21 90 62 51; ℮ contact@lebaladin.fr; www.lebaladin.fr. The adjoining rustic-style *gîte* costs €20pp for 1 night to €2,000 for 18. $$$

🏠 **Les Charmilles** (3 rooms) 40 rue de Château, Torcy, Crequoise Valley, reached via Beaurainville & Hesmond; ☏ 03 21 90 61 85; ℮ francoisregisdelanoue@tiscali.fr. Sheltering in the shadow of the owners' 19th-century *château*, the old gardener's house with its own orangery is now a *gîte* for 8. Look one way & there's a field with cows. Look across the lane where even a passing car makes you jump & you spot the vane on the top of the château. Bored German troops, stationed there in World War II, used it for target practice. Yes, it's that quiet. As a base it's ideal, with tiny Torcy neatly positioned for trips to Montreuil, Hesdin & Azincourt. If it rains in the evening, there's always the indoor barbecue, & Le Baladin is a short car drive away. Alternatively stoke up the wood-burning fire & read a good book. With a relaxed farmhouse feel & furnishings to match, this is family territory of the hide-&-seek variety. Take up the offer to visit the *château* for an historical tour, including the garden with its herd of deer. $$$

✘ Where to eat

✘ **La Cour de Rémi** (7 rooms) 1 rue Baillet, Bermicourt, almost equidistant between Hesdin & St-Pol; ☏ 03 21 03 33 33; ℮ sebastien@lacourtderemi.com; www.lacourderemi.com; 🕐 12.00–14.00 & 18.00–22.00 Tue–Sat, 12.00–14.00 Sun, closed Mon. Don't be daunted by the imposing setting of this elegant restaurant set in the grounds of a *château*. Built in 1826 this was used as a hunting lodge until 1950 when it became home to the current owner's great-grandfather. That's

A FRENCH LOVE AFFAIR

One person who has grown to love the Nord-Pas de Calais region is Paris-born Chantal de la Noue who, with her husband François-Régis, lives at the Château Torcy (see *Where to Stay* opposite).

In a tribute written for this guide she puts a French slant on her escape, 'far away from the ever-growing towns to discover a land of nature, gardens, bocage and an amazing coastline'.

Pas de Calais is my own little hidden gem, a stone's throw from Paris, between the sea and the town of Lille. It has stolen my heart. Far from the existing clichés on the Nord and its flatland, I'm recharging my batteries in a very rural, gently undulating and superbly preserved setting.

I have quickly realised that discovering this area with its glorious past made of victories, defeats, pains and joys, has helped me understand the people and the stakes of today.

Pas de Calais is an amazing alchemy of charm, unexpected landscapes with a rich and varied architecture of castles, industrial heritage and historical sites as well as its natural beauty.

I wish you a warm welcome to Pas de Calais, and please, do as I've done as a French woman, go off to explore it.

not all. A bronze model of a British Mark I tank stands in the grounds, a reminder that the British Army's Tank Corps was headquartered here during World War I. It replaces the original one, which was melted down by the occupying German forces in World War II. All of this complements the cuisine, served in gracious surroundings dominated by a giant wooden table made from a mango tree. Thumbs up here to Sebastien de la Borde for producing such a fine lunch & dinner menu at €29. This is no-nonsense home cooking stylishly cooked & served. Top marks for the likes of grandmother's fowl fricasse & slow cooked lamb's shanks. (See also *Where to stay* page 152.) $$$
✕ **Le Baladin** 62 rue Principale, Torcy; ☎ 03 21 90 62 51; e contact@lebaladin.fr; www.lebaladin.fr; ⏱ year round 18.00–22.00 Fri–Sun & public holidays, extended to daily Jul–Aug, 12.00–14.00 Sun & public holidays. We are not the first in singing the praises of this delightfully quirky *estaminet* (bar-cum-restaurant) lying delightfully close to the River Créquoise & the hamlet of Torcy. Singing is the operative word…this cosy, hostelry plays host to regular Sat-night concerts, featuring some of the best in jazz, blues, folk & rock. Sit down & enjoy, while tucking into a hearty selection of dishes of 1–3 courses. Then see how many knick-knacks you can count in the wooden nooks & crannies. The more obvious include an upside-down school desk, a collection of hats & a puppet on a swing. It all adds up to a great family night out. (See also *Where to stay* page 153.) $$$
✕ **Le Val d'Authie** 60 la Place, Saulchoy, close to Picardy border 20km from Hesdin; ☎ 03 21 90 30 20; ⏱ 12.00–14.00 & 19.00–21.00 daily, closed Tue & Thu Jul–Aug. Basic but friendly spot to drop in for a coffee & a welcome country-cooked lunchtime snack. Stretch your legs with a stroll round the surrounding poppy fields. $$

Country crafts and cottage industries Complementing the pastoral scene is the commercial tenacity of a positive nest of entrepreneurs whose place in the guide is earned through their extraordinary efforts to bring personal flair to this most individual of areas.

Take Valerie Magniez, a quietly spoken mother of three with a flourishing cheese- and bread-making outlet at the 1ha **La Halte d'Autrefois** (*28 route d'Embry Hesmond 17km from Hesdin;* ☎ *03 21 81 97 14;* e *contact @halte-autrefois.com; www.halte-autrefois.com;* ⏱ *14.00–18.00 daily for cheese, Tue & Fri–Sat for homemade oven-baked bread ordered in advance*). The shop is some 300m from Hesmond village; from Montreuil take D349 towards Hesdin, turn left in Beaurainville following Loison-sur-Crequoise on the D130.

Following her strict principles of self-sufficiency, she bakes her bread using local flour three times a week in a wood-burning oven and produces the cheese from her small herd of goats which she hand milks daily. Take your pick from *terril*, moulded in an old ash coal plant, to a garlic or peppery variety. Even the bread comes molded, as a *faluche*, for toasting, or as a *parrulie*, or 'small stick'. Superb fruit tarts are also for sale.

HE'S THE BEE'S KNEES

Whether you're a bee lover or not, you'll find **The Bee Museum** (*Musée de l'Abeille d'Opale; 923 rue Nationale, Bouin-Plumoison, 3km west of* ☎ *03 21 81 46 24;* e *thery.apl@wandoo.fr;* ⏱ *14.00–18.00 mid-Apr–Oct; admission free*) buzzing with interest. The nectar-laden gardens indicate which flowers the bees hone in on, while indoors the small museum shows a range of historic equipment used by owner Robert Therry for extracting honey and for making of his award-winning mead, biscuits, candles and vinegar. A French-language video shows him talking about his five million bees. The shop (⏱ *14.00–19.00 Tue–Fri, all day Sat & 15.00–18.00 Sun, closed Jan*) stocks a range of honey-based souvenirs. A Bee Festival is held the second weekend in September and a Mead Festival the third Sunday of March.

Should you tire of the Seven Valleys you could always walk to the Côte d'Opale – with a donkey! It will take you five to six days, but just think what you will see on the way. Walks are limited to 12–18km daily, not for your sake, but for that of the donkey who carries you luggage, limited to 40kg. Overnight stops are in tents, teepees or lodges.
For further details contact **A Petits Pas** (*16 route de Canlers, Ruisseauville nr Fruges;* `03 21 41 70 07;` e *equipe@apetitspas.net; www.apetitspas.net*).

The centre-piece of this site which was once an abandoned *estaminet*, rebuilt over 12 years, is the eco-friendly chalet. This lies near a water mill constructed of local wood, and is suited to individual or family use. NB: there is no electricity, but plenty of candles and wood for the stove. Rates are available on request.

Between them Valerie, born on the French island of Rayon, off Mauritius, and husband Christophe, a carpenter, have attracted visitors from Paris, Boulogne and Belgium keen to experience *The Good Life* qualities with which the Seven Valleys abounds.

Also in the vicinity of Hesmond, in the tiny village of **Offin** a mere 2km southeast on the D130, you'll find François Delepierre's organic farm **Aux Légumes d'Atan** (*5 Grande rue;* `03 21 81 36 27;` e *francois.delepierre@orange.fr;* ⏱ *14.00–19.30 Mon, Wed & Thu, 17.00–19.30 Tue, 09.00–19.30 Fri–Sat, 10.00–12.00 & 15.00–18.00 Sun*). Specialising in old varieties, this is the place for self-caterers to pick their own vegetables. Look out for forgotten types of artichokes and parsnips, as well as 80 varieties of tomatoes, including the black Crimean. Seasonal fruit, from June strawberries to pears, cherries and plums, are available from his intriguingly small shop. Take time to stroll round the organic grounds. Better still stay overnight at his B&B (*small, fairly spartan but cosy with cheerily decorated 'flower' & 'fruit' rooms accommodating up to 3 & 2 people respectively; extra bed available;* $$).

Less than ten minutes on the D130 at **Loison-sur Créquoise** is **La Maison de la Perle** (*Pearl House, 50 rue Principale;* `03 21 81 30 85;` e *contact@perledegroseille.com; www.perledegroseille.com;* ⏱ *Oct–Apr 10.00–12.00 & 14.00–18.00, closed Sat–Sun, May, Jun & Sep 10.00–12.00 & 14.00–18.00, closed Sun am, Jul–Aug 10.00–19.00 daily*), where the 'currant wine' of Nord-Pas de Calais was created in 1985. Though simple fruit wines have long since been made by Artois farmers, it was left to producer Hubert Delobel, a professor of economics, to refine traditional recipes to create his own distinctive redcurrant wine. Now the sparkling *perlés de groseille*, based on what his grandma made in the Créquoise Valley, is a big-hitter. It sells some 75,000 bottles regionally and nationally, along with similar products made from gooseberry, raspberry and cherry. These and other regional food products involving the use of currants are on sale at the shop.

Delobel's gardens are open to the public with free tasting of the 90 or so varieties of soft fruit in July and August. Five looped trails from 1.5 to 15 miles leaving from the centre provide a unique chance to explore this richly wooded region. A crêperie provides a tasty choice of €8.50 or €12 menus.

Skating the Picardy border is **Beussent**, 8km north of Montreuil on the D117. You may have seen the name on the specialist chocolate shops in Dunkirk, Calais, Le Touquet, St-Omer and Montreuil among others. Now follow your nose to the **Chocolaterie de Beussent** (*66 route de Desvres;* `03 21 86 17 62;` e *info@choco-france.com; www.choco-france.com;* ⏱ *15.30, 16.30 & 17.15 for 45min free tour; shop:* ⏱ *09.00–12.45 & 14.00–19.00 Mon–Sat*).

Don't be fooled by the fact that this maker of high-quality chocolates has become the Course Valley's top cottage industry. The easy-to-miss factory entrance

Montreuil-sur-Mer and the Seven Valleys   SEVEN VALLEYS   6

(look out for the sign as you enter the village) takes you into a wonderful Willy Wonka world where oodles of dripping chocolate is magically massaged into mouth-watering shapes and flavours. There is a magnificent chocolate replica of St-Omer Cathedral.

The business was created in 1985 by family confectioners Maité and Bruno De Rick. They were joined by brother Alain De Rick in 1994. Expect to meet Alain or Bruno during the tour, which gives an overview of the history and production of chocolate, including a tasting. There is also a factory at Lachelle in the Oise region of France.

With 60 dairy cows, the Henguelle family has long held the key to fine cheese-making. At **Auberge de la Ferme Sire de Créquy** (*route de Créquy, 2km from Fruges;* ℡ *03 21 90 60 24;* e *siredecrequy@wanadoo.fr; www.siredecrequy.com;* ⊕ *09.00–18.00; adult/child €2.50/1. Admission is free of charge if you eat at the restaurant* ⊕ *12.00–14.00 Sun & daily Jul–Aug; reservation is advised*) three types of cheese are made, including a cousin to the famous Maroilles. They also make yoghurt and refine Tomme, the Seven Valleys local beer. A visit to the cellar and the chance to see cheese-making ends with a tasting session. They are open for lunch June–August, but book in advance.

ST-POL-SUR-TERNOISE Don't dismiss this somewhat straggling, lorry-ridden town that sits rather stuck out on a limb between Hesdin, 24km away, and Arras, 36km away. Though targeted in both world wars, the town has sufficient historical interest to warrant a stop for a coffee and a walk round the ramparts. It is also girdled by some great rural scenery.

Tourist information

🄸 **St-Pol Tourist Office** Hôtel de Ville; ℡ 03 21 47 08 08; e ot-saintpol@wanadoo.fr; ⊕ 09.00–12.00 & 13.45–17.00 Mon–Tue & Thu–Fri, 09.00–12.00 Sat

🄸 **Ternois Tourisme** 1 pl de Verdun; ℡ 03 21 03 46 16; e contact@ternois-tourisme.com; www.ternois-tourisme.com

✖ Where to eat

✖ **La Saint Poloise** 3 rue de la Calandre; ℡ 03 21 41 91 00; e stpoloise@wandaoo.fr; www.lastpoloise.com; ⊕ 11.00–22.00 Tue–Sun. Once a brewery, hence the rustic redbrick charm, this typical market-town restaurant is centrally located &, always a good sign, popular with the locals. An easy-to-understand menu ranges from a lunchtime €6.50 *planche* (a meat or cheese platter) to some great Flemish dishes. Set 2–3 course menus cost from €11.50–19.50, with a 2-course children's version at €3.50. $$$

What to see and do The best bet is to stroll round the ramparts, climbing steeply to where the ruins of a 15th-century castle are a reminder that the town was once the stronghold of the powerful counts of St-Pol. It was virtually destroyed when in 1537 Spain's Charles V (Charles Quint), on learning that the French forces under Francois I had failed to repair the ramparts, let rip on the city.

Some 4,500 people died including the elderly, children and monks. The city remained Spanish until the Treaty of Pyrenees ceded it to France's Louis XIV in 1659. What was left of the castle was razed to the ground in World War II. Nowadays the wooded ramparts play a more peaceful part in the July medieval jollities, with night-time – or should that be knight-time? – shows and concerts.

Drop in at the **Municipal Museum** (*Musée Bruno Danvin, rue Oscar Ricque;* ℡ *03 21 47 00 10;* e *c.camus@ville-saintpolssurternoise.fr;* ⊕ *11.00–12.30 Mon, 15.00–18.00 Wed & Sat, 11.00–12.30 & 15.00–18.00 Sun; admission free*). The history of the museum is probably of as much interest as the disparate collection put together by local doctor David Danvin. It began when the Black Nuns, so-called because of the colour of their dress, arrived in St-Omer in 1430, caring for the sick and tending

Of the 30-plus gardens in Nord-Pas de Calais (see pages 49–50), a large proportion lie within the Seven Valleys region (go to *www.parcsetjardins-npdc.com* for a full list). These are open to the public, providing a colourful family day out whether you're a gardener or not. Some are huge, others simply superbly maintained private gardens.

Sculptures et Jardin (*6 rue du mont, Bergueneuse, 20km from Hesdin on the D24 towards Anvin;* \ *03 21 04 38 64;* e *jacques.droulez@wanadoo.fr; www.sculpturesetjardin.com;* ① *Apr–Sep daily by appointment, Jun–Jul 10.00–19.00 Sat–Sun; adult/child under 12 €5/free*) is created around a thatched cottage typical of the area. This small but beautifully landscaped garden is the ideal setting for the wrought-iron sculptures of Jacques Droulez. Now retired, this talented art-teacher-cum-sculptor, photographer and graphic designer has ploughed all his skills into combining the art of metalwork with that of gardening. A lifelike bird, its wings ready for take-off, dominates the lawn. Giant insects lurk in the flowerbeds, rich in flowers, amid the shrubs or in the wooded area opening on to the Ternoise hills. The village is also worth a visit.

You need look no further than the names of the 24 themed sections in the 2.5ha of **Les Jardins d'Evea** (*252 route de Montreuil, Maresquel Ecquemicourt, take D349 from Hesdin, direction Montreuil via Beaurainville, for village centre;* \ *03 21 81 38 88;* e *alain.dautreppe@wanadoo.fr; www.lesjardinssdevea.fr;* ① *Apr–Oct 14.00–18.00 Wed–Sun; adult/child €5.40/2.80*) to realise that this is large-scale gardening, with the family in mind. Understandably so: Alain Dautreppe's family – his wife Sylvie and their children – all help with the bringing to life of Alain's childhood dream to create a world where water runs freely amid the floral pockets, from The Wall of Roses and the Island of Rhodos to the Robinson Crusoe and the little French gardens. Pace yourself to fully explore a virtual maze of around 8,500 shrubs and flowers. There is a nursery with plants for sale, and also a *gîte*.

Recommended even by rival gardens, the private **Le Jardin des Lianes** (*8 rue des Capucins, Chériennes, from Hesdin take D928 in the Abbeville direction & turn left after 3–4km;* e *guy.lebl@orange.fr;* ① *14.00–19.00 Mon–Tue & Thu–Fri, 10.00–19.00 Sat–Sun & public holidays May–Sep; adult/child under 12 €5/free*) is cultivated by enthusiastic amateurs and features over 400 scented roses, including English varieties. Trees and shrubs, chosen for their fragrance, foliage or autumn colours, include 180 varieties of hydrangea.

The 4ha **Les Jardins de Séricourt** (*2 rue du Bois, Séricourt, from St-Pol take D916 in the Frévent direction, in Nuncq take D82;* \ *03 21 03 64 42;* e *ygdeg@jardindesericourt.com; www.jardindesericourt.com;* ① *year round 09.00–12.00 & 14.00–18.00 Tue–Sat, & May–Sep Sun–Mon; adult/child under 12 €8.5/free*) is an undoubted showpiece for its sheer diversity. But much more than that, it is a mystical place, full of hidden messages and symbolism, that has won designer Yves Goose de Gorre multiple awards and the classification Remarkable Garden. Take a guided tour to fully understand, for example, the intricacies of The Path of Nostalgia with its weeping willows and neatly shaped box. In contrast, the fiery Warrior Garden is inspired by the Chinese terracotta army, and represented by a really quite frightening array of golden yew. And you don't need to be too esoteric to appreciate the Warrior Masks, a brilliant piece of topiary inspired by masks from Easter Island and similar locations. Then there are the craters, the procession, the grass labyrinth… The list seems endless – and more is planned.

to the elderly. Their chapel, in which the museum is now partially installed, belonged to their convent. This was burnt down by a careless baker in 1635; the conquering French later replaced it with a church.

With the Black Nuns chased out by the French Revolution, their chapel became, in turn, a hayloft, a granary and even a 19th-century tobacco warehouse. In the 19th century the ground floor became a shed for fire engines, a dance room, a judo room and finally a cinema.

The upper part eventually became the museum in 1967. An archaeology section, added in the 1990s, contains a well-preserved 7th-century skeleton, much to the delight of the local schoolchildren that make up the bulk of the visitors. There is now talk of focussing more on recent history and perhaps even running workshops – an indication there's more to St-Pol than you might suspect.

Out-of-town sights include the **Dungeon of Bours** (*Donjon de Bours, pl du Donjon;* ✎ *03 21 04 76 76; www.crahg.free.fr;* ⊕ *mid-Mar–mid-Nov 14.00–18.00 Sat–Sun & public holidays for 1hr 15min tours; admission free*). Purchased for a symbolic franc in 1962, this once-decaying six-turreted example of a medieval castle keep has since 1982 served as the town hall for the 520 or so villagers of Bours.

Packed with history, and with a turret's eye view of the superbly wooded landscape, it remains a defiant symbol of the 12th-century castle itself. Once protected by a moat and sturdy walls, it was burnt down by French troops in 1543. Close by is the 11th-century church of St-Austreberthe.

7

Arras and the Great War Battlefields

Arras is a city in overdrive. Not only is it the capital of the ancient province of Artois but, by building on its reputation as a city of culture and entertainment, it is attracting a new breed of short-break visitors keen to experience La Belle France in what is one of the most attractive cities close to Calais. It is also the hub for visiting the nearby World War I battlefields. Béthune and Lens, likewise, don't just reflect the horror of the Great War, but are shining examples of how once-great coal-mining centres have been transformed into thriving 21st-century towns. The fact that the new wing of the Louvre in Paris will be built on a former colliery site in Lens says it all.

ARRAS

Arras can conjure up more contradictions than a Harry Potter plot – take those glorious gabled buildings in the cobbled twin squares. They are replicas of the original 17th- and 18th-century timbered buildings which, thanks to a French restoration law passed in 1919, were faithfully rebuilt in brick and stone in the same style after being laid to waste in World War I.

Below ground lie the town hall cellars – part of the hidden world of the 10th-, 15th- and 16th-century limestone quarries on which the whole town is famously built. Not bad for a place which bounced back from World War I devastation to become one of the best-loved towns in northern France, attracting vast crowds to the squares with their café culture and specialist shops. Arras's Christmas fair, too, is now rated one of the best north of Paris.

This, and an almost stubborn belief in its cultural and economic role from Caesar to Arras-born Robespierre, has seen the town emerge not just as capital of the Pas de Calais Artois region, but as an elegant tourist centre with a fresh batch of hotels being built to meet demand, not least from the British.

Major exhibitions at the Fine Arts Museum and a varied programme of contemporary music and art events at the renovated Italianate theatre have likewise upped the ante in the cultural stakes. So, too, has the town's easy-going nature, helped by students from the 12,000-strong university.

HISTORY Originally known by the Gaulish name of Nemetocenna – from the Celtic Nemeton, meaning 'sacred place' – Arras became recognised for its colourful and luxurious draperies under the late Roman Empire. By then a fortress town called Atrebatum, it became capital of Atrébates – one of the last regions to resist Julius Caesar.

Destroyed by barbarians in AD407, it was rebuilt at the beginning of the 6th century by St-Vaast, whose monastic community developed into the immensely wealthy Benedictine Abbey of St-Vaast; it then developed in the 9th century as a grain market around which the modern town grew. It later fell into the hands of

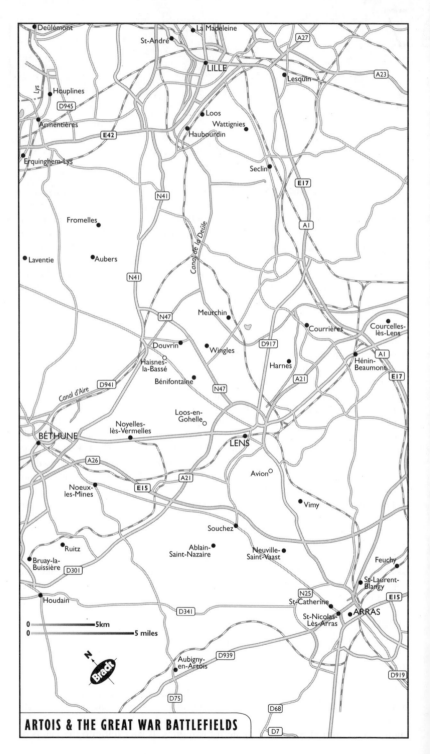

Deûlémont

La Madeleine

St-André

A27

LILLE

Lesquin

A23

Lys

Houplines

D945

Loos

Wattignies

Armentières

E42

Haubourdin

Seclin

Erquinghem-Lys

E17

N41

Fromelles

Canal de la Deûle

Laventie

Aubers

N41

Meurchin

N47

Courrières

Courcelles-lès-Lens

Douvrin

Wingles

D917

Haisnes-la-Bassé

Harnes

Hénin-Beaumont

A1

E17

Canal d'Aire

D941

Bénifontaine

N47

A21

Loos-en-Gohelle

Noyelles-lès-Vermelles

BÉTHUNE

LENS

A26

Avion

E15

A21

Noeux-les-Mines

Vimy

Souchez

Ruitz

Ablain-Saint-Nazaire

Neuville-Saint-Vaast

Feuchy

Bruay-la-Buissière

D301

St-Laurent-Blangy

Houdain

N25

St-Catherine

E15

D341

St-Nicolas-Lès-Arras

ARRAS

D919

0   5km

0   5 miles

N

Bradt

Aubigny-en-Artois

D939

D75

D68

D7

ARTOIS & THE GREAT WAR BATTLEFIELDS

the counts of Flanders before becoming a diocese in 1092 and finally part of the royal domain around 1180.

The name Arras did not appear until the 12th century, according to etymologists. Some say the name is supposedly related to the Celtic 'Ar', indicating water – a reference to the location of the city at the confluence of the Rivers Scarpe and Crinchon. Others suggest the name was created from a contraction of Atrébates to Ars, Aras, and finally Arras. Take your pick.

It was not until the 14th century that the town's previously mentioned talent for draperies really took off. Arras gained an international reputation and considerable wealth from the cloth and wool industry. Its tapestries were particularly sought after, with the word 'arras' (in Italian, *arrazzi*) adopted to refer to tapestries in general; Polonius made the fatal mistake of hiding behind one in Shakespeare's *Hamlet*. A rare example remains in the Fine Arts Museum (Musée des Beaux-Arts; see page 169). The patronage of wealthy cloth merchants also ensured that the town became an important cultural centre, with the poet Jean Bodel and the troubadour Adam de la Halle among those making their homes here.

Inevitably the town fell foul of the endless squabbles which bedevilled the Artois region generally during the Middle Ages. Following the death of the ambitious but over-stretched Charles the Bold, Duke of Burgundy, Arras became a fortified town boasting a large agricultural marketplace. This gave France, under Louis XI, the chance to seize a town which, still loyal to its old rival Burgundy, immediately threw out the French. Louis retaliated by razing the town's walls and replacing the townsfolk with French loyalists. He even changed the name, albeit temporarily, to Franchise.

In 1492 Arras was plundered again, on this occasion by the Spanish, by which time the textile industry had been surpassed by agriculture. In 1640, France, then ruled by Louis XIII, regained an interest in the city, with the Spanish departing in 1659 as agreed under the Treaty of the Pyrenees. In 1667 Vauban, the military engineer who masterminded so many fortifications both within Artois and throughout France (see page 12), was commissioned to build a fortress in his trademark star-shaped design. The citadel at Arras remains one of his finest achievements and gained World Heritage Site status on the 300th anniversary of his death in 2008.

ROBESPIERRE: HERO OR VILLAIN

Robespierre – or Maximilien Marie Isidore de Robespierre to give him his full name – has been cast historically as a Hollywood-style villain of the French Revolution. In fact, Robespierre, who studied law, took up the cause of the poor and was initally regarded as one of the best writers and most popular young men of his native Arras.

However his growing autocracy as head of the Revolution's Reign of Terror made him increasingly unpopular, and a conspiracy was launched to overthrow him. In 1794 he and 21 of his closest supporters were guillotined in Paris.

It was left to the lesser-known revolutionary Joseph Lebon, nicknamed The Butcher of Arras, to inflict his brutality on what, ironically, was also his birthplace. Aged only 28 when he replaced Robespierre, who by then was seconded to Paris, Lebon boasted in a report dated 26 November 1793 that, 'No twenty-four hour period passes in which I do not bring before the revolutionary criminal court in Arras two or three head of game for the guillotine.' It did not stop there and though Arras suffered most, other centres, such as Cambrai (page 181), also suffered through Lebon's role as administrator for the then *département* of Pas de Calais.

7

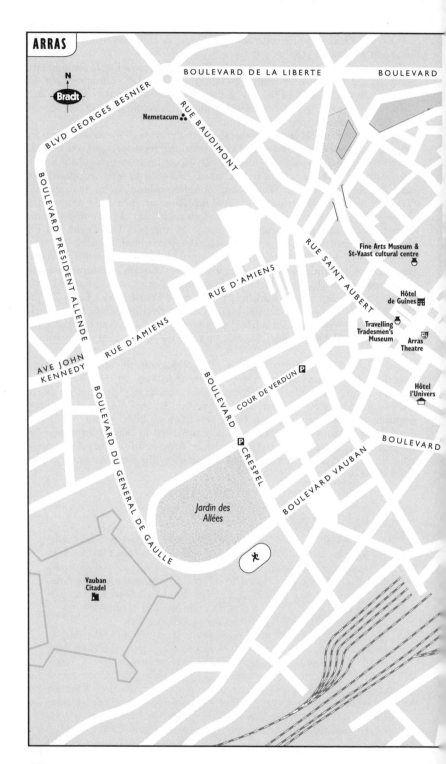

ARRAS

N

Bradt

BOULEVARD DE LA LIBERTE   BOULEVARD

BLVD GEORGES BESNIER

RUE BAUDIMONT

Nemetacum

BOULEVARD PRESIDENT ALLENDE

RUE SAINT AUBERT

Fine Arts Museum &
St-Vaast cultural centre

RUE D'AMIENS

Hôtel
de Guînes

Travelling
Tradesmen's
Museum

Arras
Theatre

RUE D'AMIENS

AVE JOHN
KENNEDY

BOULEVARD

COUR DE VERDUN

Hôtel
l'Univers

BOULEVARD DU GENERAL DE GAULLE

CRESPEL

BOULEVARD VAUBAN

BOULEVARD

Jardin des
Allées

Vauban
Citadel

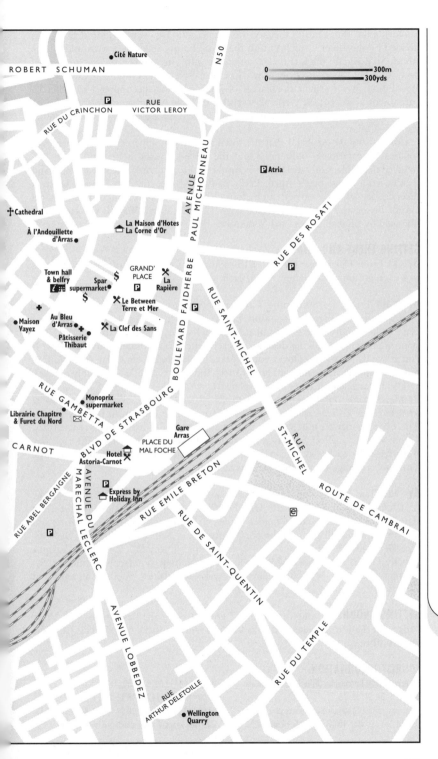

Cité Nature

ROBERT SCHUMAN

N50

0 ━━━━━━━━━━━━━ 300m
0 ━━━━━━━━━━━━━ 300yds

🅿
RUE DU CRINCHON

RUE
VICTOR LEROY

🅿 Atria

AVENUE PAUL MICHONNEAU

✝ Cathedral

À l'Andouillette
d'Arras ●

La Maison d'Hotes
La Corne d'Or

RUE DES ROSATI

🅿

Town hall
& belfry
Spar
supermarket ●

GRAND'
PLACE

🅿

$

$

$

✗ La
Rapière

✗ Le Between
Terre et Mer

🅿

BOULEVARD FAIDHERBE

RUE SAINT-MICHEL

✚
● Maison
Vayez

Au Bleu
d'Arras ●
Pâtisserie
Thibaut

● ✚
●

✗ La Clef des Sans

RUE GAMBETTA

Monoprix
supermarket

BLVD DE STRASBOURG

Librairie Chapitre
& Furet du Nord
✉

CARNOT

Gare
Arras

PLACE DU
MAL FOCHE

Hotel
Astoria-Carnot

RUE ST-MICHEL

RUE ABEL BERGAIGNE

AVENUE DU
MARECHAL LECLERC

🅿

Express by
Holiday Inn

RUE EMILE BRETON

ROUTE DE CAMBRAI

e

🅿

RUE DE SAINT-QUENTIN

AVENUE LOBBEDEZ

RUE DU TEMPLE

RUE
ARTHUR DELETOILLE

● Wellington
Quarry

During the 18th century the city, though peaceful for over a hundred years, was divided by the River Crinchon into the more bourgeois district surrounding the Abbey St-Vaast and the fortified town on the hill. The two became one municipal body in 1749. Soon after, in May 1758, Robespierre, key figure in the French Revolution, was born in the Parish of La Madeleine, becoming a member of parliament (*député*) at the General Assembly in 1789. A year later Arras was chosen as the capital of the Artois *département* after violent quarrels with its rivals, among them St-Omer.

But it is for World War I that the town is best remembered: the familiar twin squares were virtually obliterated and the gabled houses, belfry and town hall reduced to rubble. Only three houses round the great squares remained intact. And it was from here, on 9 April 1917, that the Battle of Arras began when a diversionary offensive carried out by four Canadian divisions launched a successful assault on nearby Vimy Ridge (see page 175). In World War II, the town was liberated by English forces on 1 September 1944.

GETTING THERE AND AWAY

By car From Calais take the A26/E15 motorway for the 112km journey; it takes just over an hour. Toll charge: €7.20 each way.

By train From the 80-minute Eurostar service to Gare Lille Europe, change platforms for the regular 30-minute fast TGV service to Arras. Alternatively use Gare Lille Flandres for the regular trains, which can take up to an hour. The stations are within walking distance of each other via an underground passage. If you arrive by ferry from Dover you can take a local train from Calais-Ville station, but you will have to change at Hazebrouck. Travelling via Lille is probably quicker.

The railway station **Gare Arras** (*pl du Maréchal Foch;* ⊕ *04.45–21.45 Mon–Thu, 04.45–22.45 Fri, 05.15–22.00 Sat, 08.15–23.50 Sun & public holidays; book online at www.sncf.co.uk & www.raileurope.co.uk*) is a ten-minute walk from the city centre. There are regular train departures to Douai: 26 each day from Monday to Friday, 13 on Saturday, 12 on Sunday and public holidays; to Valeciennes: 22 each day from Monday to Friday, 11 on Saturday and 9 on Sunday and public holidays. Timetables change frequently: see www.ter-sncf-com.

By bus The bus station (*contact Artis next to the station;* ☏ *03 21 51 40 30;* ⊕ *07.30–12.30 & 13.30–18.30 Mon–Fri, 08.00–12.00 Sat*) is close by the train station. Bus line 51 operates a regular service to Cambrai, also to the city centre and the surrounding villages of Achicourt, Agny, Anzin-Saint-Aubin, Athies, Bailleul-Sire-Bertoult, Beaumezt-les-Loges, Beaurains, Dainville, Fampoux, Farbus, Feuchy, Gavrelle, Mercatel, Monchy-le-Preux, Neuville-Vitasse, St-Catherine, St-Laurent-Blangy, St-Nicolas, Thélus, Tilloy-les-Mofflaines, Wailly, Wancourt and Willerval.

GETTING AROUND Though train Line 7 goes to Vimy, the best way to visit Vimy Ridge and the wartime sites is to take a taxi or join an official tour. Details from the tourist office.

TOURIST INFORMATION

🖪 **Arras Tourist Information Office** Town hall, pl des Héros; ☏ 03 21 51 26 95; e arras.tourisme@wanadoo.fr; www.ot-arras.fr; ⊕ 14 Sep–31 Mar 10.00–12.00 & 14.00–18.00 Mon, 09.00–12.00 & 14.00–18.00 Tue–Sat, 10.00–12.30 & 14.30–18.30 Sun, 1 Apr–13 Sep 09.00–18.30 Mon–Sat, 10.00–13.00 & 14.30–18.30 Sun. Free maps & accommodation information.

CITY PASSES AND GUIDED TOURS

Reduced city passes Bronze includes the belfry, historama and a guided tour of the boves for adult/child €7.60/4.60; silver is the same as bronze plus a guided tour of Wellington Quarry (see pages 170–1) for €11.40/5.60; gold includes everything under the silver pass plus the Fine Art Museum and Cité Nature for €19/10.

Audio-taped guided tours Rent headphones in English, French and Dutch for an independent one-hour, 1,900m-long history tour geared to descriptions at a dozen pavement stud stops (adult/child €6.30/3.40).

Guided tours A tour of the squares and St-Vaast costs adult/child €6.30/3.40, leaving at no set times; the town hall, belfry and boves plus a beer at 18.30 is €7/3.40; arcades, cellars gables and columns with a drink in a tavern also costs €7/3.40. All guided tours are bookable at the tourist information office throughout July–August.

WHERE TO STAY

⌂ **Hôtel de l'Univers** (38 rooms) 3 & 5 pl de la Croix Rouge; ☎ 03 21 71 34 01; e univers.hotel@najeti.com; www.hotel-univers-arras.com. A former Jesuit monastery dating back to the 16th century, it was converted first into a hospital & latterly used as a college. Such historic credentials have earned the Best Western hotel high ranking for old-world French-style charm, an aspect reflected in the smallish but comfortable rooms. Though quietly tucked away in a cobbled courtyard setting, with limited parking space, it is less than a 10-min walk from the town centre squares. A €26 3-course menu featuring regional dishes is offered at the hotel's Le Clusius restaurant; other eateries are close by. B/fast €14. Off-season breaks available. Business facilities. $$$$

⌂ **La Maison d'Hôtes La Corne d'Or** (5 rooms) 1 pl Guy Mollet just off Grand'Place; ☎ 03 21 58 85 94; e franck@lamaisondhotes.com; www.lamaisondhotes.com. This is a B&B with a difference – so much so it almost rates an entry in the sightseeing section. The heavy wooden door of the somewhat gaunt façade opens onto a jaw-dropping restoration of what was once the guest wing of a wealthy 18th-century merchant's house. On the first 3 floors are 5 highly individual bedrooms, including 1 in a storybook attic full of intriguing knick-knacks, nooks & crannies. On the ground floor crumbling steps lead to a vaulted brick cellar 3

levels down. This may well have once led to a nearby church, long since destroyed.

Owners Franck & Isabelle Smal had long had their eye on the property once owned by a family friend; their enthusiasm for the place is reflected in their hospitality – & a truly great b/fast at €7.50 served amid the antique collections in the lounge-cum-dining room. Free coffee, tea & fruit juices. Parking is available in the street. $$$

⌂ **Express by Holiday Inn** (32 dbl, 51 twin, 12 family, 3 disabled rooms) 3 rue du Docteur Brassart; ☎ 03 21 60 88 88; www.hiexpress-arras.com. A cut above similar standard business-cum-leisure hotels, it provides a convenient base, facing the railway station with its cluster of restaurants & bars. The main squares are a shortish walk away. Reasonable b/fast included in the price. Daily parking in underground public car park (98 spaces) with lift to reception. 24h €10 fee payable to hotel. $$$

⌂ **Hotel Astoria-Carnot** (29 rooms) 10–12 pl Foch; ☎ 03 21 71 08 14; e contact@hotelcarnot.com; www.hotelcarnot.com. With its own restaurant, this station-facing hotel offers a handy stopover room rate combining accommodation & dinner in the restaurant or brasserie. Buffet b/fast €7 06.00–10.00 & continental-style 10.00–11.30. The pastel-toned rooms are equipped with a shower or bath; facilities include free wireless internet connection. $$$

WHERE TO EAT AND DRINK

✗ **Restaurant Carnot** (see Hotel Astoria-Carnot above) ⏰ 11.45–15.00 & 19.00–22.45 daily. A cosy brasserie-cum-restaurant catering for an eclectic bunch of diners from families to backpackers. Good food, including a worthwhile 3-course regional menu for €23; the brasserie offers a main course plus

dessert with wine & coffee at €14.50. You may need to book as it can get very busy & a little cramped at peak times. There is a pleasant outside terrace. $$$

✗ **La Rapière** 44–46 Grand'Place; ☎ 03 21 55 09 92; www.larapiere.fr; ⏰ 12.00–13.45 &

19.00–22.00, closed Sun evening. This is Arras in a nutshell: not only do you have a vaulted 17th-century cellar dining area with a glassed-off section of an old quarry still showing, but a comprehensive regional menu at €19.50 featuring both the town's famous *andouillette* (see below) & a flan made from the ubiquitous Maroilles cheese (see page 216). Cheaper menus €13–18. It is worth a visit for the novelty value alone. $$$

✗ **Le Between Terre et Mer** 12 rue de la Taillerie; ✆ 03 21 73 57 79; www.betweenterreetmer.fr; ⏰ 12.00–14.30 (except Sat & Mon) & 19.00–22.30 (except Sun). A cheerful place with good cross-section of diners tucking into imaginative Earth & Sea dishes, hence the name. Try the sea bream, though steak in a *foie gras* crumble is pretty good too. The contemporary Zen type décor reflects 'creativity &

tradition'. Main dish & dessert €22, entrée & main dish €23.50, 3 courses €30.50; also 18 oysters plus dessert €26. Healthy portions & good value. Great for a family outing (there is a €12.60 children's menu) or with a group of friends. $$$

✗ **La Clef des Sens** 6062 pl des Héros; ✆ 03 21 51 00 50; www.laclefdessens.com; ⏰ 12.00–14.30 & 19.00–22.00. With its comfortable wooden panelled alcoves, its appeal lies in providing reassuring old-world charm overlaid with matching menus & helpful staff. The bistro menu (€26) offers a substantial introduction to the local fare including *potjevlesch* (homemade white meat pâté of veal, chicken or rabbit, in aspic); for an across-the-board alternative try the €32 house menu. Just the place for a relaxing evening out, though it does get busy. Great place for people-watching from the terrace. $$$

SHOPPING

Specialist shops Vaulted and hence covered arcades in both squares provide a shady spot for a beer or a meal on a sunny day or, in the in case of place des Héros,

---

SAUSAGE STARTED A MEATY CLAIM

The town's *andouillete* is no ordinary offal-based sausage – it's an Arras *andouillete*. And if the local Brotherhood of the Andouillete, formed in 1997, has its way, this will become an official label for this porky product produced only in the town of Arras since the Middle Ages. The Brotherhood has a strong case: way back in 1407 a letter signed by John, Duke of Burgundy, Count of Flanders and Artois, guaranteed the same sausage 'thanksgiving, franchises and liberties' in order to preserve its identity from those without the know-how or knack of making the genuine article.

The *andouillete* is not to everyone's taste. It basically consists of carefully prepared pork chitterlings cooked in milk. 'Chitterling' is the word for the small intestines of a pig in Old (or Middle) English, the language spoken roughly between 1066 and 1470. Arras *andouillete* was certainly favoured by Jacques Chirac when, as prime minister, his Minister of Agriculture drew it to his attention. Later, as president, he is said to have sent his driver out to buy his favourite sausage.

If you want to know more ask **Huges Becquart**, owner of À l'Andouillete d'Arras (*3 rue du Marché au filé;* ✆ *03 21 22 69 96; www.andouillette-arras-com;* ⏰ *08.30– 12.45 & 14.30–19.30 Tue–Fri, 08.00–13.00 & 14.30–19.00 Sat*). Arras *andouillete*, he will patiently explain, is now made mainly from a special part of pork chitterlings (not, as so many loosely say, of tripe), which is carefully cleaned and cooked in milk. The secret lies in preparing the ingredients by hand, then timing the boiling process to get rid of any fat. This leaves a smooth, yet not too strong, constituency. The sausage skin, likewise, must be made from beef caul, the fatty layer surrounding the intestines of cattle. He pooh-poohs *andouillette* produced commercially or elsewhere as being not quite the same.

The *andouillette* is traditionally served grilled and sliced as an aperitif or main dish. It can also be braised. Not only a winter warmer, it also enlivens many a summer barbecue. Try it for yourself – the annual Andouillette Festival, held in early September in the place des Héros, is as good a place to start as any.

a wet day chance to stroll past the clutch of specialist shops. Most are closed all day Sunday and Monday mornings; some close for lunch daily. Normal weekday opening hours are 09.00/10.00–19.00.

Look out particularly for the Coeurs d'Arras at **Pâtisserie Thibaut** (*50 pl des Héros;* ℡ *03 21 71 53 20;* ⊕ *08.00–19.30 Tue–Sun*). These are small heart-shaped pieces of spicy gingerbread which earned a registered trademark in 1821. They are still made by pâtissier Sébastian Thibaut from a smooth honey-tasting recipe stemming back to at least the 17th century. Try, too, the chocolate rats, a speciality of chocolate-maker Yannick Delestrez, commemorating the rat that appeared on the town's seal in the 14th century and which led to a local play on the words 'Arras' and 'a rat', pronounced, naturally, in a French accent.

A leaflet at the shop points out that a rat has appeared in various guises as a mark of chivalry; also that every time Arras was besieged an enigmatic verse reappeared which stated: 'When the French take Arras the mice will eat the cats, The French took Arras the mice did not eat the cats.' Make of it what you will... at least the chocolates, full of crunchy praline, are delicious.

At **Au Bleu d'Arras** (*32 pl des Héros;* ℡ *03 21 71 17 88; www.aubleudarras.fr;* ⊕ *10.00–12.30 & 14.00–19.00, closed Mon*) owner Maurice Ségard can be seen hand-painting a stack of porcelain plates to celebrate everything from a wedding to a sporting achievement, or even to celebrate the 40th anniversary of Albert Roux's famous London restaurant, Le Gavroche. It is not so much the porcelain but the use of cobalt blue that plays a primary role in the simple but highly effective designs on a range of china objects. These go back to 1774 when four sisters opened an Arras factory, using patterns from Tournai and Chantilly, although the factory closed in 1790 after less than 20 years in business. Maurice and two others who took over the current premises some 30 years ago are now unique in using the distinctive blue.

Other finds along the arcades include a handmade soap shop, a beer emporium and **Antiquités Nathalie Pourriez** (*40 pl des Héros;* ℡ *03 21 51 63 85;* ⊕ *10.00–12.00 & 15.00–19.00 Wed & Sat, 15.00–19.00 Sun–Tue & Thu–Fri*) as well as a local branch of **La Finarde** (*37 pl des Héros;* ℡ *03 21 07 82 86;* ⊕ *09.30–12.30 & 14.30–19.15*), named after a street in Hulluch where the original cheese shop still remains. Close by on place des Héros, off rue Delansorne, is **Maison Vayez** (*13 rue des Recolléts;* ℡ *03 21 51 51 95; www.maison-vayez.com;* ⊕ *08.30–13.00 & 14.00–19.00 Tue–Sat*). You can't miss the aroma of freshly-roasted coffee wafting from what the ever-helpful joint owners Luc-Olivier and Stéphane Vabois Joyez stress is not a shop but an importer of coffee beans, freshly-roasted to suit customers' tastes. Even the most ardent non-coffee drinker will be tempted by the huge array of coffee available, especially from Central America and Africa. Failing that, they also sell 60 varieties of tea, from the traditional English varieties to green tea from China and the distinctive caffeine-free red tea from South Africa. A unique chance to grab a cuppa – and they stock high quality chocolates as well.

Bookshops
Librairie Chapitre 21 rue Gambetta; ℡ 03 21 23 87 20; ⊕ 09.30–19.00 Mon–Sat

Furet du Nord 19 rue Gambetta; ℡ 03 21 15 25 00; ⊕ 14.00–19.00 Mon, 09.30–19.00 Tue–Sat

OTHER PRACTICALITIES
Internet café Cyber café citoyen; 2 rue du Commandant Dumetz (behind the station); ℡ 03 21 23 33 80; ⊕ 09.00–20.30 Mon–Fri, 10.30–19.00 Sat

Post Office 13 rue Gambetta; ⊕ 09.00–18.30 Mon–Fri, 09.00–12.30 & 14.00–17.00 Sat
Public toilet Town hall, pl des Héros

Banks

$ **Crédit Agricole (CA)** 9 Grand'Place;
🕐 09.00–12.30 & 13.45–17.30 Tue, 09.00–12.30 & 13.45–18.30 Wed–Fri, 09.00–12.30 Sat; closed Mon

$ **Caisse d'Epargne** 23 pl des Héros;
🕐 09.00–12.00 & 13.00–18.00 Mon–Wed & Fri, 09.00–12.00 & 14.30–18.00 Thu, 09.00–12.00 Sat; closed Mon. ATM accepts Visa & MasterCard.

Supermarkets

Monoprix 30 rue Gambetta; 📞 03 21 71 52 11; 🕐 08.30–20.00 Mon–Sat

Spar 19 rue de la Taillerie; 🕐 08.30–13.00 & 15.30–20.00 Mon–Sat, 09.00–13.00 & 17.30–20.00 Sun; closed Mon

Pharmacies

➕ **Pharmacie Sement** 46 pl des Héros; 📞 03 21 71 58 85; 🕐 09.00–12.30 & 13.00–19.00 Tue–Sat

➕ **Pharmacie du Beffroi** 7 rue Désiré Delansorne; 📞 03 21 51 06 42; 🕐 08.30–19.30 Mon–Sat, 08.30–19.00 Sat

WHAT TO SEE AND DO Arras is uniquely different, whichever way you look at it. What lies below ground in this troglodyte town can be matched by the sights above – some of which simply cannot be ignored.

A big-screen slide show sets the scene with 2,000 years of Arras history at the gloriously gothic-style **town hall** (🕐 *during tourist information office hours – see page 164; adult/child €2.70/1.80*). This is followed by the best view in town from the top of the ornate 75m belfry, one of many belfries in the region granted World Heritage Site status by UNESCO, and spectacularly illuminated nightly. But beware: the top is reached by a combination of lifts and stairs, the latter unsuitable for those wary of steepish steps. If doubtful, enjoy a guided tour of the town hall instead (*adult/child €2.30/1.50, summer season only*). Look out for the town's giants – Colas (papa), Jacqueline (mama) and baby Dédé.

Below ground the town hall *boves* (three tiers of cellars once used as warehouses by traders from the squares) help unlock the hidden world of the 10th-, 15th- and 16th-century limestone quarries on which the whole town is famously built. They were also used as the British Army HQ and as a military hospital during the Great War and as shelters during World War II.

Each year, roughly between 21 March and 21 June, they are transformed into delightful garden themes; these have included the extraordinary Jardin du Théâtre, a crafty wink at the reopening that year of the town's theatre, and, in 2009, the zany world of plastic artist Luc Brévart. During those months, special garden tours temporarily replace the regular 40-minute tours (*both tours adult/child €4.90/2.80*). It is jokingly suggested that the market squares are hosed down after Saturday trading and that by Sunday sufficient water has permeated the chalk to drip on the head of any visitor who has not been paying attention.

The closeness of the Arras attractions means you are generally within a short walking distance from the main squares; this is certainly so with St-Vaast Abbey and the cathedral. The latter is reputedly the most important 18th-century religious building in France while the gigantic size of the current abbey complex provides a clue to the economic and spiritual role played by the original 7th-century version, around which Arras was founded.

Sculptures of saints from the Pantheon, and Art-Deco style surprises from the tapestry town of Aubusson in the Central-Massif, feature in the **cathedral** (*entrance through the apse on rue Albert 1-de-Belgique; 🕐 15 May–15 Oct 10.30–12.30 & 14.00–18.00 Mon–Sat, 14.00–18.00 Sun; 16 Oct–14 May 14.30–17.30 Mon–Sat only. Guided tours Jul & Aug*).

But playing the trump card, and occupying a large area of the abbey, is the **Fine**

Arts Museum (*Le Musée des Beaux-Arts, 22 rue Paul-Doumer, entrance via the abbey courtyard;* ☎ *03 21 71 26 43;* e *musee.arras@ville-arrs.fr; www.musenor.com;* ⊕ *09.30–12.00 & 14.00–17.30, closed Tue & public holidays; adult/child €4/2*). Home to an extensive range of objects of artistic and cultural interest, it forms part of the huge St-Vaast project which, within the next decade, will bring together all the cultural elements of Arras in a single location. Covering 22,000m², this will be the largest centre of its kind north of Paris. It will also place Arras culturally in the same league as Lens, Valencienne and Béthune (see *Chapter 8*).

Current exhibitions include the work of 17th-century French and Dutch artists, including Vignon, Lebrun and Rubens, and the widest collection in France of 17th-century paintings. It also houses medieval sculptures, 18th-century Arras porcelain, landscapes from the Arras school of paintings, including paintings by Corot, plus a unique Arras tapestry (*arrazzi*, for which the town was renowned in the 15th century.

Head next for the nearby arts quarter which in 2007 saw the re-opening of **Arras Theatre** (*7 pl du Théâtre;* ☎ *03 21 71 66 16; www.theatredarras.com;* ⊕ *13.30–19.00 Tue–Sat; guided tours Jul–Aug*). Built in the 17th century on a former fish market in a Louis XVI style, it was inaugurated on the eve of the French Revolution in 1785. Though the somewhat sober façade was built in a neo-Classical style, the auditorium follows the Italianate architecture famed at the time for its beauty and acoustics. Following extensive renovation in 2003, the theatre is equipped with two fully refurbished rooms: one satisfies those dedicated to the Italian theatre, the other followers of contemporary arts.

Lying between the theatre and the museum is the eye-catching **Hôtel de Guînes** (*rue des Jongfleurs; contact tourist office on* ☎ *03 21 51 26 95 for opening hours & special events*), dedicated to encouraging the work of those involved in the arts generally. This falls in line with the original idea of the wealthy to build 'houses of pleasure' nicknamed 'mad houses'. Now, three centuries on, this delightful 'little palace' in yellow ochre in the aptly named Road of Jugglers, with its wrought-iron gates and cobbled courtyard, is a centre for performing arts as originally envisaged by the family of the Counts of Guînes.

Less colourful but historically important, on the remoter western edge of town, is the **Vauban Citadel** (*bd du Général-de-Gaulle; contact tourist office on* ☎ *03 21 51 26 95 to request guided tours in English Jul–Aug*). Masterminded by Vauban, military architect to Louis XIV, the citadel was created in his classic star-shaped design between 1667 and 1672. However, upheavals in France's frontiers meant this superb defence system, listed in 2008 as a UNESCO World Heritage Site, was never tested. Located outside the fortress walls is the Firing Squad Wall which pays homage to the 218 French Resistance members executed during World War II in the citadel trenches.

Also worthy of historic note is the site of **Nemetacum** (*entrance 77 rue Baudimont;* ⊕ *Jul–Aug 14.30–17.00 Tue–Sun; €3.40/children free for guided tours in French*). Part of the old Roman town, this shows everyday life in the capital of what was then Atrebates.

Robespierre, a key figure in the French Revolution and the town's most famous son, lived in what is now the **Travelling Tradesmen's Museum** (*9 rue Maximilien de Robespierre;* ⊕ *afternoons daily except Mon, also closed Wed & Fri 1 Oct–30 Apr*). A permanent exhibition retraces the history of travelling tradesmen.

In utter contrast is **Cité Nature** (*25 bd Schuman;* ☎ *03 21 21 59 59;* e *mail@citenature.com; www.citenature.com;* ⊕ *09.00–17.00 Tue–Sat, 14.00–18.00 Sat–Sun, closed public holidays; adult/child €5/3*). Converted from a former miner's lamp factory, it is now a cultural and scientific centre dedicated to food, agriculture, nature and health; there is also a discovery area for children.

It says much for a museum that it can convey the slaughter of the Great War by the simple act of scattering a few tin helmets by a stairway marked 'Number Ten Exit'. Though now blocked, it was through this exit and similar tunnels that some 25,000 soldiers emerged, blinking in the early-morning sleet, to fight an unsuspecting enemy in the spring offensive of 1917. These tunnels proved to be a pathway to a hell far worse than the appalling conditions the men endured below – many were to perish in the subsequent Battle of Arras (see page 164), one of the shortest but most brutal of World War I.

Wellington Quarry (*La Carrière Wellington, rue Deletoillé;* ✆ *03 21 51 26 95;* e *arras.tourisme@wanadoo.fr; www.carriere-wellington.com;* ⊕ *10.00–12.30 & 13.30– 18.00 daily; closed for 3 weeks following Christmas; adult/child €6.50/2.80*) is no ordinary museum. It is housed in one of the original medieval subterranean chalk quarries linked up in World War I by 500 New Zealand tunnellers, predominantly Maori coal and gold miners, aided by Bantams – Yorkshire miners who didn't meet the Army's minimum height requirement of five feet three inches. It was this unique network of two inter-connected labyrinths totalling 25km and accommodating over 24,000 British and Commonwealth soldiers – the equivalent of the population of Arras just before the outbreak of war – that played a strategic role in the Battle of Arras. But amid the postwar chaos, this incredible feat was forgotten. It was not until 1990 that they were rediscovered, when Alain Jacques, in charge of Arras's archaeology department, decided to investigate the *boves* (caves) in which a few still-living locals sheltered in World War II.

'It was so exciting to find history undisturbed,' he said. 'The first time we opened the tunnel we found an operating theatre, boots, helmets, dog-tags and even bullets that had been removed from wounded soldiers.'

Along with Arras's enthusiatic director of tourism, Jean-Marie Prestaux, he worked out that just one quarry – Wellington, one of a number named after the Kiwi tunnellers and home to the Suffolk Regiment – lay under a former council-owned campsite. This meant

The squares The twin squares are literally Arras's biggest assets. Laid out in the 1300s, the 155 gabled houses and galleried shops of the Grand'Place and the place des Héros (also called the Petite Place) encourage you to linger in the comfort of a pavement café.

Though home to the town hall (see page 168) the **place des Héros** is, strangely enough, the smaller of the two squares: it's more the size of a typical market square and, indeed, it's here that you can catch the colour and flavour of the weekly market each Wednesday.

The **Grand'Place**, on the other hand, is one of the largest squares in France. Like others in what was the old Southern Netherlands, the Grand'Place got is name for simply being the main town square. Look out for the red-brick gables of Les Trois Luppars, at its north end. A World War I survivor, this building is the oldest house in Arras and was last rebuilt in 1467.

The Grand'Place's biggest attraction is the annual Christmas market, spotlighting local specialities and other festive goodies, which runs from late November to Christmas Eve. There is also a giant skating rink. In early July it hosts the Main Square Festival attracting such pop luminaries as Radiohead, Coldplay, Kaiser Chiefs, Duffy and Lily Allen. It also shares the weekly Saturday market with the place des Héros and place de la Vacquerie.

Each property around the central squares has its own cellar, all part of the vast network of *boves*. Look out, too, for the bells, helmets, sheaves of wheat and cauldrons sculpted on the buildings – a reminder that at one time they were not numbered but known only by their trade.

that reconstruction work could make it accessible to the public; the remaining tunnels in both public and private hands had either collapsed or were unsafe. In some cases houses had been built over them. Now this €4 million visitor attraction offers a 75-minute not-to-be-missed portrayal of the underground privations leading up to the fateful 9 April 1917 spring offensive. 'Everyone knows the Somme and Verdun,' says Jean-Marie. 'Now people from all over the world will learn of Arras. Even most French people know nothing of all this.'

After a short introduction, visitors, accompanied by a bi-lingual expert and equipped with audio-guides, take a glass-walled lift 20m down to a compelling Great War world where drawings, fading photos and graffiti bring a terrible touch of authenticity. At each of some 20 pauses a short film and audio track touches on part of the life underground. Everywhere lie heaps of cans, old stone jars and, next to a 9m chalk pillar, two large rusting buckets discreetly placed beneath wooden holes. Above them the word 'latrine' is written. Elsewhere black traces of wax remain melted on a pillar which served as an Easter Sunday altar for the men of the Suffolk Regiment in their underground home. A powerful presentation involving the sounds of guns and the general noise and shouting of the battle raging above helps convey the true horror of the situation.

Canteens, chapels, power stations, a light railway and even a fully functioning hospital were all established in this chilly, damp world. The southern part of the network became known as New Zealand, where Wellington Quarry sat alongside others also named after well-known New Zealand cities; the northern section likewise linked Glasgow, Edinburgh, Crewe and London while a side-tunnel led to a trio of quarries called Jersey, Guernsey and Alderney.

Tunnels had to be wide enough for soldiers to march past stretcher bearers coming the opposite way. They were also a place of droll humour, of mickey-taking, which is cleverly conveyed through lighting and sound effects. More poignant are the letters home. Writing to his wife and baby son by candlelight, Private Harry Holland scribbled: 'Kiss our Harry for me. When I see him again, it will take me all my time to catch him.' But Private Holland never returned.

Other notable squares include **place de l'Ancien Rivage**, with traditional 18th-century houses, **place de la Prefecture** with a classical church in the middle, **place du Pont de la Cité** noted for the baroque fountain, **place du Wetz d'Amain**, and the circular **place Victor Hugo** with an obelisk in the centre.

BÉTHUNE AND LENS

This was once King Coal Country: the region was uncompromisingly described as such by Émile Zola in his novel *Germinal*, now revered as a classic. These days family groups enjoy weekend strolls on grass-covered slag heaps awash with fresh green shrubs and rare wild flowers. Walking, cycling and mountain bike trails criss-cross a region where pit-heads stood until the closures of the 1980s. Talk today is not of grime and poverty, but leisure parks and adventure trails, with sporting activities from canoeing and cycling to even skiing on one giant slag heap.

The region's industrial heritage is still celebrated, however, with the miners' union headquarters in Lens hailed as an historical monument, and now the cool breeze of high-tech industry blows where once the black gold of coal-mining held sway.

The area also felt the full fury of World War I, during which whole towns were virtually destroyed.

BÉTHUNE For a bewildering display of architectural styles, the cobbled town square takes some beating. The fact that the Flemish gable and Art Deco style façades you see today were lovingly rebuilt after the Great War is equally as remarkable. The town is an unsung hero deserving greater recognition, not just for its architecture but also its coal-mining heritage.

Tourist information

🛈 **Béthune-Bray Tourist Office** 3 rue Aristide Briand; ☎ 03 21 52 50 00; e accueil@tourisme-bethune-bruay.fr; www.tourisme-bethune-bruay.fr; ⊕ Oct–Apr 09.30–12.30 & 14.00–17.30 Mon–Sat except Tue am, May–Sep 09.30–12.30 & 14.00–18.00 Mon–Sat, closed Tue am except in Jul & Aug. A handy bilingual French–English tourist map is available. An audio-guide provides a 90-min step-by-step walk divided into 9 stops: adult/child & over 60s €5/3.50.

🏠 Where to stay, eat and drink

🏠 **La Suite** (7 rooms) 15 pl de la République; ☎ 03 21 01 78 88; e restaurant-lasuite@orange.fr; www.restaurant-lasuite.com. If old-world charm is your scene, then this family-run hotel conveniently close to the Grand'Place will do you nicely. The rooms are big, but cosy, hung with the draperies beloved of France & with soft furnishings to match. Thumbs up to a proper hotel b/fast which is included in the room rate. There is no need to go out for dinner – the 4-room restaurant in a huge setting of chandeliers & panelled walls has a relaxed atmosphere. The chef/owner can be counted on to come up with 1–3 set courses (€17–35), & meat & fish dishes suited to all tastes, & cooked to order; lunch €17. Closed Sat lunchtime, Sun evening & Mon ($$$). $$$

✗ **Au Depart** 1 pl François Mitterand; ☎ 03 21 01 18 20; www.jf-buche.fr; ⊕ 19.15–21.45 Tue, 12.00–13.45 & 19.15– 21.45 Wed–Sat, closed Sun–Mon. Opened by a talented young chef, Jean François Buche, the restaurant ranks among the critically praised eateries in the town. $$$$$

✗ **Kouign Amann** 32 pl Jules Senis; ☎ 03 21 56 04 91; ⊕ 09.00–12.00 Mon–Sat. Representative of snacking outlets, the crêperie (pancake bar) offers a €9–11 menu or à la carte courses from €4.50–10. A children's menu is €6.50. $$

Shopping Chocoholics could do no better than to head for **Chocolaterie Laloux** (*41 rue du Pot d'Etain; e contact@chocolaterielaloux.com; www.chocolaterielaloux.com; ⊕ 10.00–12.30 & 14.00–19.00 Tue–Sat*). Mady, Diane and Cassandre Laloux are not just chocolate-loving sisters – they make their own. Watch them at work while hand-picking your favourite pralines made from pure cocoa butter, before sitting down for a coffee, tea…or even a hot chocolate.

For cheeses and a wide range of other delicatessen delights try **La Prairie** (*20 rue Albert; ☎ 03 21 68 04 85; ⊕ 09.00–12.30 & 15.00–19.30 Mon, Wed & Thu–Sat, 15.00–19.30 Tue, closed Sun*). Local specialities include Béthune macaroons, Artois snails, white and smoked garlic, and La Saint Glinglin beer.

The main town centre **market** is held 08.00–13.00 on Monday; additional markets are held in other locations in and around the town.

What to see and do Béthune, brimming with British troops and close to the Great War front, bore the full brunt of enemy bombardment with 90% of the town destroyed in 1918. The Grand'Place patchwork of Flemish gable and Art Deco style façades you see today was built during 1920–27. Lined up like superb pastel-shaded dollhouses, they provide the backdrop to the still-standing 14th-century

RAISE YOUR GLASS TO A JOLLY GIANT!

Contributing to the jolly town of Béthune is Gambrinus, a pot-bellied giant sporting a broad grin. Dressed in ermine and wearing a crown, this 4m-plus carnival giant, weighing in at 180kg, never goes out without his mug containing 20 litres of beer – and he goes out roughly six times a day during the festival in March.

At a first glance it is merely a furniture shop. But Modern at 42 Grand'Place holds a secret. In the cellar is a mini museum, kitted out with a poignant collection of black-and-white photos of the ravaged town in World War I. This is not simply a unique private collection, including a medieval pottery and a bread oven, but a timely reminder that, from 1300 to 1500, the town's cellars were used as a shelter from constant wars raging around this much-coveted city.

belfry (☉ *Feb, Easter & Nov holidays 15.00 Wed & Sat, May–Jun 15.30 & 16.30 Sat–Sun & public holidays, Jul–Aug 15.30 Mon–Fri, 15.30 & 16.30 Sat–Sun & public holidays, 15.30 Christmas market; adult/child under 12 €3/2/free*). It's worth climbing the 144 steps for the bird's-eye view across the city to the Artois plain and the Monts des Flandres (see *Chapter 5*). Its carillon of 36 bells regularly rings out chirpy little tunes.

Also adding to the Grand'Place tapestry is the 1920s-rebuilt **town hall**, whose façades reflect the Military Cross and the Legion of Honour awarded to the town in 1919 for the resistance shown in World War I. The inside is remarkable for its Art-Deco style. This and the almost cathedral-sized **St-Vaast Church**, again rebuilt in the 1920s, are seen at their stunning best when floodlit, especially when the Christmas market brings a rosy glow to the Grand'Place.

Cultural links Confirming Béthune's cultural credentials is **Lab-Labanque** (*44 pl Cleménceau;* ☏ *03 21 63 04 70;* ℮ *contact@lab-labanque.fr; www.lab-labanque.fr;* ☉ *14.00–19.00 daily; admission free*). Opened in October 2007, in the rather grand early-20th-century Bank of France, this is now the visual arts centre for students. Involving the use of such diverse media as photography, video, sculpture and painting, it is not everyone's cup of tea. But if you love the contemporary style of, say, London's Tate Modern, you'll have fun interpreting the role of money in society. This is portrayed against the genuine background of the bank manager's office, with the great wrought-iron safe and the rows of wooden drawers with their hidden wealth. Walls and floor are used for exhibits and objects designed to interpret the link between art and the city. Euro coins nailed to the reception room floor (yes, everyone tries to pick them up) give a clue as to what to expect in terms of the abstract.

La Comédie de Bethune, in boulevard Victor Hugo, on the site of the once-derelict Cinéma du Palace, is now the contemporary setting for the National Drama Centre for Nord-Pas de Calais.

LENS While inevitably linked with the World War I battlefields, Lens, like Bethune, has seen hitherto industrial wastelands give way to leisure areas.

The dozens of slag heaps that once dotted the Lens plain are likewise being colonised by flora and fauna that flourishes from the heat that they still create.

Tourist information

🇫 **Office de Tourisme et du Patrimoine de Lens-Liéven** 23 rue de la Paix; ☏ 03 21 67 66 66; ℮ info@tourisme-lenslieven.fr; www.tourisme-lenslieven.fr; ☉ Oct–Apr 09.30–12.00 & 13.30–18.00 Mon–Sat, May–Sep 09.30–12.00 & 13.30–18.30 Mon–Sat. Get a free *Allo Visit* & use it to download a 7-stop audio guide; alternatively download it free from the tourist office website & listen on an MP3 player available for rental at €5. There is also a monthly guided 2½hr coach tour covering the mining heritage & a 1hr 30min walking tour (both adult/child under 12 €6/free).

Arras and the Great War Battlefields **BÉTHUNE AND LENS**

7

The affinity between the arts and industry, dating back even beyond coal mining to the creative crafts of the Middle Ages, is nowhere stronger than at Lens – chosen as the site of a new wing of the Louvre, Paris. This is quite a coup, with keen competition coming from Amiens, Arras, Boulogne, Calais and Valenciennes. The clincher was exceptional transport links, provided by the A21 and A26 motorways, the TGV railway station and Lille-Lesquin airport. Lens also has seven million inhabitants within a 100km radius, the majority of them young, all adding grist to the aim of reaching a new audience, many of whom are the grandchildren of miners.

The winning proposal will see what was once Colliery No 9, the old Theodore Barrois Colliery, replaced by a Japanese-designed building with glass roofs and polished aluminium walls. Visitors will not follow a structured floor plan, but will be urged to wander at will. Louvre exhibits, formerly closed to the public, will be on display.

The €142-million museum in rue Bernados, due to open in 2012, is symbolically placed between slag heaps numbered 11/19, familiar to a generation of World War I forces (see below), and the famous Bollaert football stadium. A guided tour is part of a preview provided by **The House of the Louvre-Lens Project** (*Maison du Projet Louvre-Lens, rue Bernados; www.louvrelens.fr; ⊕ 11.00–18.00 Wed–Sun; free admission*).

What to see and do The main sights relate to the 150-year history of coal mining. Pride of place goes the **Union House** (*Maison Syndicate, 32 rue Casimar Beugnet;* ☏ *03 21 67 48 93; ⊕ 10.00–12.00 & 14.00–17.00; admission free*) which remains a major symbol of the Pas de Calais miners' struggle for a better life. It now houses temporary exhibitions of mining interest.

Contrasting neatly is a real industrial giant, Les Grands Bureaux as they were known locally, which was the administrative headquarters of the Lens Mining Company. The building, basically an industrial castle, is surrounded by 3ha of French landscaped garden, now home to Artois University faculty of science. Visitors can tour the **Faculty Jean Perrin Gardens** (*rue Elie Reumaux; ⊕ 10.00–17.00 in winter & 10.00–18.00 in summer; admission free*).

Do take time to look at the **railway station**. Built in 1926, it is shaped like a steam locomotive and was the first Art Deco building in the coal-mining area. The mosaics reflect this accordingly.

Other attractions include the 60ha Parc de la Glissoire at Avion off the N17 close to the main memorial. You can even climb Terril du 11/19, *terril* meaning 'slag heap', 11/19 being the number of the pit. At around 190m it is the highest in Europe. It is located at Loos-en-Gohelle, site of the World War I battle of Loos (see page 176).

THE WORLD WAR I BATTLEFIELDS

Imagine drawing an imaginary circle between Arras and Lens and you will have covered many of the major sites in this cockpit of war; others, like Loos, lie between Lens and Béthune. The savagery of the World War I battles seems intensified when one considers how small this area is – and the devastation appears all the worse as one admires this now peaceful region of green hills and lovingly restored towns.

Make full use of the tours available from the respective tourist offices at Arras, Béthune and Lens; some are organised, others are self-guided. Additionally, many specialist tour operators include the region in their intineraries (see page 20).

MAJOR SITES

Canadian National Vimy Memorial We defy anyone not to be deeply affected by the Canadian National Vimy Memorial (*follow signs from Vimy off the N17, reached via junction 7 on the E15/A26, the monument & other sites are well signposted; ⊕ year round; free admission*). The white, twin-columned monolith seemingly soaring to the clouds stands alone in open country slightly north of the 240-acre Canadian Memorial Park, of which it forms a part. The park is located at the top of Hill 145, fiercely fought for during the Battle of Arras. Even now, red zone areas are fenced off as they might contain unexploded munitions – though the sheep graze happily enough.

The sandstone structure commemorates the Battle of Vimy Ridge, where 4,000 Canadian soldiers died. It also records the 66,000 Canadians killed overall in the Great War and the 11,285 with no known graves. It took 11 years and C$1.5 million to build, and rests on a bed of 11,000 tons of concrete, reinforced with hundreds of tons of steel. The work of Toronto sculptor and designer Walter Seymour Allward, it was unveiled on 26 July 1936 by Edward VIII, who, while Prince of Wales, had served on the staff of the Canadian Corps in France. A recent restoration, including general cleaning and the re-carving of the names of those that died, was completed in 2007.

The towering columns each stand 45m high. One bears a maple leaf, and the other a fleur-de-lis; these symbolise the sacrifices of both Canada and France. The columns and the sculptured figures (created by Canadian artists) together contain almost 6,000 tons of limestone brought from an abandoned Roman quarry on the Adriatic Sea (in present-day Croatia). The largest piece, carved from a 30-ton block, shows a cloaked figure – the figure of a grieving woman representing Canada in mourning. The memorial ultimately provided Canada's previously divided provinces with a true sense of national unity.

Canadian Memorial Park trenches and craters This sense of unity is strikingly confirmed in the area containing the main part of the parkland. This was granted by the French to Canada in 1922 on the territory of the commune of Givenchy-en-Gohelle.

Here amid 11,285 Canadian trees and shrubs – the number of those 'missing' in war – families stroll over grass-covered shell holes and mine craters. Other visitors play games or jog along gravel paths which run alongside one huge crater that at first glance could easily be mistaken for a golf-course bunker. But look closer, and you see sand-bagged trenches clearly indicating the closeness of the German and Allied front lines.

This is just one of 14 craters created when hidden Allied mines were exploded on Easter Monday, 9 April 1917, as the four Canadian Divisions, aided by the 5th British Division and a considerable number of artillery units, launched their attack in driving snow. By mid-afternoon they had achieved most of their objectives; it took another day to take Hill 145, and on 12 April a plateau called the Pimple.

There is also a monument to the Moroccan Division; several plaques commemorate the volunteers from different countries who fought in this particular division of the French Foreign Legion.

Comprehensive displays in English are featured at the **visitor centre** (☏ *03 21 50 68 68; www.vac-acc.gc.ca; ⊕ late Jan–Feb 09.00–17.00 daily, Mar–24 Oct 10.00–18.00, 25 Oct–13 Dec 09.00–17.00; closed public holidays*) which is manned by Canadian students who act as guides. Free guided tours are available Tuesday to Sunday during opening hours. These explain the boring of 10km of tunnels to protect Allied troops and supplies. There are no catering facilities at the visitor centre, but picnic tables are provided.

Fromelles In 1916, Fromelles (*about 2.5km to the east of the Australian Memorial Park on the D22 via the N41 from Lille*) lay behind German lines and was the site of regional fighting by Australian forces. A special signposted car route around the Fromelles–Aubers area still shows it dotted with cemeteries and memorials. Remnants of German concrete bunkers can be spotted on roadsides, in the middle of fields or even used as part of private homes.

It's most notorious, however, for the horrific **Battle of Fromelles**. This was originally planned as a minor – and what later proved futile – British attack to prevent the Germans moving troops from their quiet sectors to the Battle of the Somme. Fought on 19–20 July 1916 in open fields just northwest of the village – 16km west of Lille – it resulted in some 5,500 Australian and more than 1,500 British killed, wounded or missing in less than 24 hours. Many were teenagers. Adolf Hitler, then a 27-year-old corporal, is rumoured to have been among the German ranks.

The bodies of around 400, mainly Australian, soldiers were hurriedly buried in pits by the German army just hours after the battle. They remained unidentified for over 90 years until 2008 when two Australian amateur historians discovered the site. Its importance was confirmed by University of Glasgow archaeologists and a three-week dig found conclusive evidence that substantial numbers of Australian and some British soldiers had been buried in five of the eight pits identified.

In 2009 DNA testing on buckles, buttons, press-studs and fragments of fabric from the 1908 pattern webbing equipment enabled archaeologists to identify 250 of the bodies. Of these, 205 were Australians, and 96 of those were able to be identified by name. Three others were identified as British, although their full identities had still not been discovered at the time of writing; the identities of a further 42 remain totally unknown. Further investigations will continue until 2014.

During the winter of 2009/10 the remains of 249 of the soldiers were transferred from the old VC Corner Australian Cemetery at Pheasants Wood, 2km northwest of the village on the road to Sailly, to a new cemetery on the other side of St-Jean-Baptist Church for ceremonial burial at individual plots. This is the first cemetery in 50 years to be built by the Commonwealth War Graves Commission. For further details see www.cwgc.org/fromelles.

On 19 July 2010 Prince Charles joined scores of relatives to mark the dedication of the new cemetery and also the burial, with full military honours, of the 250th soldier. The coffin of this last, and unidentified, soldier was taken to the new cemetery by a military wagon drawn by horses from the King's Troop, Royal Artillery.

Among the relatives attending the ceremony was Alastair Matheson, 48, of London, who was told the sad story of his 'great-uncle Christy' as a young boy. 'It's over 90 years ago since this happened, yet it still creates a kind of turbulence in the family after all this time,' said Mr Matheson.

A good collection of original Australian artefacts of the battle as well as many other items relating to German and British forces that fought hereabouts between 1914 and 1918 can be found at Fromelles's **War Museum** (*Musée de la Guerre, in the Mairie (town hall), 7 rue de Verdun;* ✆ *03 20 50 20 43;* ⊕ *09.00–12.00 & 14.00–19.00 on 2nd Sun of each month & 1 day during Nov, closed Aug except by appointment; €3.50/3 adult/child*). The museum is run by the Association pour le Souvenir de la Bataille de Fromelles (ASBF) whose website, www.asbf14-18.org, has an excellent English-language section. The association is also trying to excavate and preserve significant World War I sites, such as underground bunkers and defensive positions, in the area.

Battle of Loos Lying to the north, 5km northwest of the former mining town of Lens, is the village of Loos-en-Gohelle (*off A26 at junction 6 or junction 6.1 – follow* *the signs via the D943*) around which the brutal Battle of Loos (roughly pronounced, perhaps somewhat aptly, as 'Loss') was fought. It was here that General Douglas Haig, short of artillery shells and needing to soften up the enemy for the emerging trench warfare, ordered gas to be used for the first time by British forces. However, many British soldiers, unable to see through the fogged-up eye-pieces of inefficient masks, removed them, leading to some being choked by their own chlorine gas as it blew back across the lines.

The combined Anglo-French offensive, which became known as the Third Battle of Artois, began early on 25 September 1915; the objective was to take precious German advantage posts. These included Hill 70, now northwest of junction 10 on the A21, and the Double Crassier, two long, flat-topped slag heaps, the basis of today's twin *terrils* (slag heaps) which dominate the flat mining area for miles.

An initial attempt to dislodge the Germans in May 1915 had led to a catastrophic loss among the French forces. Four months later, thanks mainly to their superiority in number, the British forces – predominantly Scottish – were able to break through the weaker German trenches and at least capture Loos. But supply and communications problems, combined with the late arrival of reserves, prevented them from holding Hill 70.

TV'S MY BOY JACK DIED HERE

The son of Rudyard Kipling – John (Jack) Kipling played by *Harry Potter* star Daniel Radcliffe in the much-acclaimed British TV drama *My Boy Jack* – died aged 18 on 27 September 1915 during the battle of Loos. But whether a grave in St Mary's Advanced Dressing Station Cemetery, a post-war battlefield clearance cemetery (see page 178) correctly bears his name is still under discussion.

The argument arises due to the rank markings worn by the deceased officer: they were a 2nd lieutenant's markings, yet Jack Kipling – whose famous father used his connections to convince the Irish Guards to commission his shortsighted son – was promoted to full lieutenant, but admittedly not gazetted, on his arrival in France.

There's also confusion regarding the location of the body. Jack Kipling was last seen about a mile and three-quarters southeast of where the cemetery now lies, yet the body listed as his was found about two miles to the southwest. There's even some question as to whether the uniform of the deceased officer, originally described simply as 'A lieutenant of the Irish Guards' was actually that of the Irish Guards.

What is certain is that a distraught and guilt-ridden Rudyard Kipling and his wife spent years searching for their son's body which was never recovered after the advance of the Guards Division during the Battle of Loos. Their mission proved fruitless. It was not until June 1992 that the Commonwealth War Graves Commission finally decided that the 'lieutenant' buried had to be Kipling, because they could account for all the others who had fallen during the battle.

Even so, his name still appears on Panel 9 at the Loos Memorial as 'missing'. This is possibly because the inscriptions are updated in batches rather than on a case-by-case basis. His name is no longer listed as being on Panel 9 on the commission's online database, however.

Above all, though, Jack's story, as told in *My Boy Jack* (written by David Haig who played Rudyard Kipling in the TV production), illustrates the dangers of unbridled patriotism. To grow up the seriously shortsighted child of a celebrated author was bad enough. To have to embody the beliefs of the man could be devastating; in Jack's case, his father's passion for king and country led to a preventable tragedy.

A further complication was the failure of artillery to cut vital German wires before attacking. British losses were devastating: in the first day alone some 8,500 soldiers were killed while advancing over open fields in full range of German machine guns and artillery. When the battle resumed the following day, the Germans were ready to repulse all attempts to continue the advance. By 28 September fighting fizzled out with the British, having suffered 50,000 casualties, retreating to their starting positions. The Germans likewise lost some 25,000 men. The nature of the fighting also meant that most of the dead were unrecoverable from the battlefield until after the war three years later. By then their bodies were unidentifiable, and many cemeteries around Loos contain a high percentage of 'unknown' graves.

In mid-July 1917 Canadian soldiers, following the liberation of Hill 154 at Vimy, captured the last part of Loos from the Germans. On 15 August they took the elusive Hill 70, having spent 15 days hidden in tunnels pending an attack which was constantly postponed. Some 9,000 were killed or missing; the youngest was just 15 years old.

Some historians regard the Battle of Loos as the British version of Verdun, the Great War battle in which 163,000 French soldiers died. The human side of the battle, in particular, is provided by the **Museum Alexandre Villedieu** (*Musée Alexandre Villedieu; 14/18 pl de la République in Loos-en-Gohelle;* ℡ *03 21 70 59 75/03 21 28 99 82;* e *a.villedieu@wanadoo.fr for advanced booking;* ⊕ *09.00–11.00 & by appointment 14.00–17.00 daily; €3 guided tour of museum only, €6 each for group of 5 minimum, €5 each for groups of more than 10 for guided tour of museum & 'double crassier', the slag heaps known as 11/19, guided walk*) which displays everyday objects from the battlefield. Exhibits include a Waterman fountain pen that still worked after 80 years buried in the earth. The museum is named after its owner, 28-year-old Alexandre Villedieu – a French soldier from a wealthy family in Lyon. Lively anecdotes in French, by Alfred Duparcq, president of the association behind the project, include the story of how a piece of wood used by a soldier to defend himself came from the altar of the church in Loos. Allow around 90 minutes for a fascinating glimpse at souvenirs, grouped by nationality, of soldiers' possessions. These range from bottles and mugs to grenades and guns, some of which were used to launch gas canisters.

St Mary's Advanced Dressing Station Cemetery

The village of Haisnes-la-Bassée (*follow the Commonwealth War Graves Commission sign on the D947 Lens to La Bassée road, the cemetery lies off this on the D39 Hulloch to Vermelles road;* ℡ *03 21 25 43 43;* ⊕ *all year round; free*), at which this cemetery is located, was reached, or nearly reached, by the 9th (Scottish) and 7th Divisions on the first day of the Battle of Loos. Other parts of the commune saw desperate fighting at Hohenzollern Redoubt from 13–15 October. This was a subsidiary action during which Temporary Captain Charles Geoffrey Vickers of the Robin Hood Rifles – the popular name for the 1st Nottinghamshire (Robin Hood) Volunteer Rifle Corps – was awarded the Victoria Cross. No further advance was made in this sector until October 1918.

The battlefield clearance cemetery, which lies in farmland, was created after the Armistice; the great majority of the graves are of those killed in action between September and October 1915. Of the nearly 2,000 Great War casualties commemorated, over two-thirds are unidentified. This explains the extremely high percentage of 'Known Unto God' graves, the words being those of Rudyard Kipling whose own son, John (Jack), was killed at Loos (see page 177). Few of the headstones bear names, although some that do have more than one name, indicating multiple burials. There are also memorials to those 'believed to be buried in this cemetery'. A French cemetery, on the opposite side of the road, contained 800 graves but they were removed in 1922.

OTHER SITES The cemetery of **Notre-Dame de Lorette** (*Ablain-Saint-Nazaire, signposted off the D937 between Arras & Bethune;* ⊕ *08.00–18.30; free admission*) is France's largest military cemetery containing 20,000 gravestones. It also has eight communal graves in which 20,000 unknown soldiers are buried. The 52m Lantern Tower, symbolising the flame of remembrance, sweeps rays of light across the surrounding plains from twilight to late at night.

From the plateau of Notre-Dame de Lorette, 165m above sea level, there is a remarkable view of the eastern part of the Gohelle Plain dominated by the twin slag heaps, 11/19, and the Artois hills in the west.

Also nearby is the **Musée vivant 14/18** (*Colline de Notre-Dame de Lorette, behind the cemetery;* ⊕ *09.00–08.00; adult/child €5/3 plus €1 for recreated battlefield*) which traces the daily experiences of Great War soldiers. The museum, which has a collection of more than 300 items, also has reconstructed underground shelters. Organised bilingual activities are offered in English and French. A recreated battlefield covering more than 1,000m of trenches is another reminder of the harshness of the Great War.

Cimetière Allemand de la Maison Blanche (*Neuville-Saint-Vaast; 8km off D973/D55 to Béthune*) was created by the French military from 1919 to 1923; it is the largest German war cemetery in France. A relief map at the entrance represents the battlefield on which the cemetery was built. A total of 44,830 soldiers are buried in mass graves under black crosses. Like all such German cemeteries, it resembles a peaceful forest of firs symbolising the paradise of warriors where trees keep vigil.

Mémoire d'Artois (*100 rue Pasteur, Souchez; 12km on the D937 from Arras;* ℡ *03 21 44 07 04;* e *contact@memoire-artois.fr*) was created as a public institution of intercommunity co-operation in 2001; it retraces the effects World War I had on the people of the Artois through a series of activities. These include literary walks and mountain-bike outings. Musical readings of letters written by soldiers are often given greater impetus by artists who add their own perspective on the area and its history.

✗ WHERE TO EAT AND DRINK

✗ **Al' Fosse 7** 94 bd Henri Martel, Avion; ℡ 03 21 43 06 98; ⊕ 12.00–14.30 Tue–Thu, 12.00–14.30 & 19.00–22.00 Fri & Sun, 19.00–22.00 Sat. Black is the colour, coal is the name… this superb recreation of a pithead, hence the name, is a credit to local lad Jonathan Fardoux for the sheer audacity in design alone. Close your eyes, blink, & then look again. The ceiling of cut pine pit props, the blackened brick walls & the miners' clothes hanging as though ready for use all bring an authentic ring to a family-run restaurant proud to be associated with a once-powerful coal-mining region. Settle down to a choice of menus, which any self-respecting miner would have judged the finest in local fare. Doff your hat to the old black & white photos of local miners as you leave. Their legacy lingers on in this little known part of Lens. Vimy, however, is a mere 4km off the N17, Lens around the same & Arras 14km. $$$

✗ **A'l Potée d'Léandre** 107 rue Pasteur, Souchez; ℡ 03 21 45 16 40; e contact@alpotee.eu; www.alpotee.eu; ⊕ 12.00–14.00 & 18.00–22.00. Go, as we did, at Sun lunchtime. The place was brimming with families, from tiny tots to grannies & grandpas, enjoying the best of what *estaminets* (pubs-cum-cafés-cum-restaurants) offer & this was not in summer, but on a foul mid-Feb day. The fug was tremendous, the Flemish food was its robust best & a rousing performance by an accordionist rounded off a perfect escape from the wintry weather. Set menus €11.50 for 2 courses – €25 for a Sun special. Ask Pascal the owner to show you his 1st edition copy of Émile Zola's *Germinal*. He's proud to reflect the mining culture & cuisine so aptly captured in the French author's famous book. $$$

8

Cultural Cities of Le Nord

For centuries the region has been a crucible for creativity. Even the decline of the flourishing medieval drapery trade ushered in new skills as china, crystal and linen took over as the new money-spinners. Today Desvres china and fine lace from Caudry and Calais are still reknowned worldwide. And while Arras (see page 157), once famed for its tapestry, is also seen as a cultural giant, it is the big cities of Le Nord that portray the powerful part played by industrial wealth in the creation of centres of learning, museums and the funding of the arts generally. The arts museum at Valenciennes, birthplace of the 18th-century artist Jean-Antoine Watteau, is rated alongside the Louvre in Paris. Likewise, The Matisse Museum in Le Cateau-Cambrésis gives pride of place to the works of Henri Matisse, a locally born artist whose early paintings reflect the working-class life at the end of the 19th century. But then he did spend his childhood and youth from 1870 to 1890 in a region dominated by the textile trade, where pride was taken in providing the most beautiful fabrics and furnishings in France.

LE CAMBRÉSIS

Combining the whole of the Cambrai region, and marketed as such (see *www.touriseme-cambresis.fr*), Le Cambrésis offers an intriguing glimpse into how a former coal-mining region has dusted itself down to reveal the rich cultural seam which originally brought it fame and fortune.

CAMBRAI Cambrai holds three trump cards up its tourist sleeves: it is compact, crammed with architectural history of the genteel cobbled-streets-and-gables kind, and can count on a steady stream of visitors looking for an easily digestible approach to Le Cambrésis. It is also remembered, perhaps somewhat vaguely, as the World War I town in which British tanks were deployed for the first time. It is the birthplace, too, of Louis Blériot, who in 1909 was the first pilot to fly across the Channel (see page 192). Probably less well-known is that the local lace from Caudry is lauded by top fashion designers, and that the *bêtise de Cambrai,* a refreshing minty-flavoured sweet, is once more in vogue.

Add the fact that Cambrai was the first town in the Nord to be granted the prestigious title of Ville d'Art et d'Histoire by the Ministry of Culture in 1992 and you get the measure of the place. The birth of the artist Henri Matisse close by, in Le Cateau-Cambrésis (see page 192), likewise adds credence to a centre built on a rich cultural, and at times, deeply religious, past. Cambrai may not pack the huge tourist punch of some towns, but two days in and around the town is time well spent.

History Cambrai has good reason to thank its turbulent past as it has created a city whose religious and cultural reputation has always sat easily with its commercial

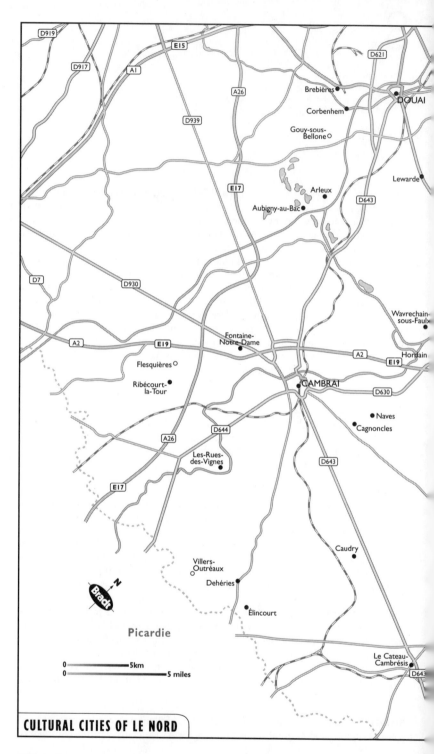

D919
D917
A1
E15
D621
A26
D939
Brebières
Corbenhem
DOUAI
Gouy-sous-
Bellone
Lewarde
E17
Arleux
D643
Aubigny-au-Bac
D7
D930
Wavrechain-
sous-Faulx
A2
E19
Fontaine-
Notre-Dame
A2
E19
Flesquières
Hordain
Ribécourt-
la-Tour
CAMBRAI
D630
Naves
Cagnoncles
D644
A26
Les-Rues-
des-Vignes
D643
E17
Caudry
Villers-
Outréaux
Dehéries
Élincourt
N
Bradt
Picardie
Le Cateau-
Cambrésis
0   5km
0   5 miles
D643

CULTURAL CITIES OF LE NORD

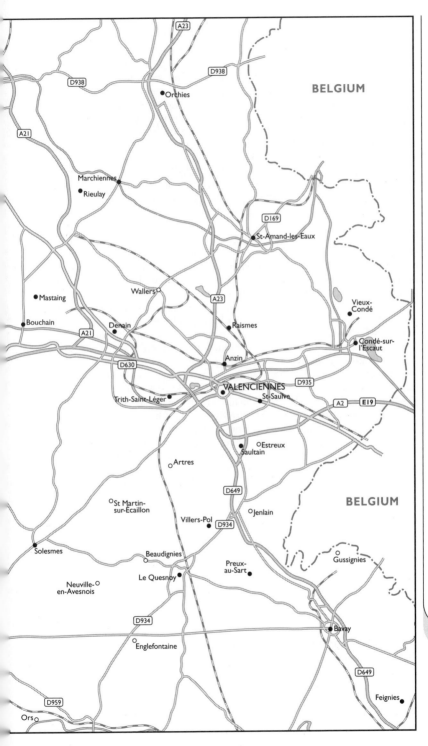

BELGIUM

A23

D938

D938

●Orchies

A21

Marchiennes●

● Rieulay

D169

St-Amand-les-Eaux ●

Wallers○

A23

●Mastaing

Vieux-
Condé ●

Bouchain ●

A21

Denain ●

● Raismes

Condé-sur-
l'Escaut ●

D630

Anzin ●

VALENCIENNES

D935

Trith-Saint-Léger ●

St-Saulve ●

A2   E19

○Estreux

●Saultain

○Artres

D649

○St Martin-
sur-Écaillon

BELGIUM

○Jenlain

Villers-Pol
●   D934

Solesmes ●

Beaudignies
○

○
Gussignies

Neuville-○
en-Avesnois

Le Quesnoy ●

Preux-
au-Sart ●

D934

○
Englefontaine

● Bavay

D649

D959

Feignies ●

Ors ○

growth – from a famous medieval centre for weaving to a major city in Le Nord's industrial heartland.

First the 6th-century Saint Gaugericus, or Bishop Gery, shrewdly transferred the bishopric from Arras creating not just a religious, but also a civil, powerbase to what was an important Frankish town.

Throughout the political and military upheavals which followed the Norman invasion, Cambrai clung on to its virtual independence – including being granted a Citizens' Charter in 1227. This was reinforced between 1150 and 1250 when a cathedral – 'the wonder of the low countries' – was built. The town also rebuilt its fortifications to protect itself not only from France and England during their 100 Years War from 1337–1453, but from other dangerous neighbours, such as the Earls of Flanders and the Dukes of Burgundy. In 1543 the Habsburg Emperor Charles V (King Charles I of Spain, known as Charles Quint) conquered Cambrai, adding the town to his already vast wealth. However, in 1677, Louis XIV, having botched an earlier attempt to take Cambrai from the Spanish, decided to safeguard what he called 'the tranquillity of his borders' for ever. Thanks, inevitably, to Vauban, his military mastermind (see page 12), his troops successfully laid siege to the town. Cambrai fell into French hands on 19 April that year. The following year the city officially became French under the Treaty of Nijmegen.

Cambrai suffered badly during the French Revolution when most religious buildings, including 17 churches, were destroyed. As for the cathedral, it was sold to a coal merchant who used it as a stone quarry. Only the main tower was left standing, and this eventually collapsed during a storm in 1809. The town also suffered, like Arras, from the excesses of Joseph Le Bon who sent 162 citizens to the guillotine.

In World War I the heavily defended Hindenburg Line ran through the town centre; in World War II Cambrai was hit by air strikes against the railway, destroying 803 buildings and damaging 3,329 others.

Getting there and away

By car From Calais take the A26/E15 motorway for the 146km journey taking 95 minutes. Toll charge: €7.20 each way. From Dunkirk take the A25/23/22; the 194km journey takes two hours 20 minutes. Toll charge: €2.50 each way.

By train From the Eurostar service to Gare Lille Europe (see page 25), change platforms for the regular 30-minute fast TGV service to Douai; at Douai, change for the local (TER) train for Cambrai – again, the journey takes 30 minutes. Alternatively use Gare Lille Flandres for the regular direct trains which can take up to an hour. The two stations are within walking distance of each other via an underground passage. The railway station **Gare Cambrai** (*pl de la Gare; ⊕ 07.30–18.00; book online at www.sncf.co.uk & www.raileurope.co.uk; see also www.ter-sncf.com*) is a five-minute walk from the city centre. There are 20 trains daily to Douai, 10 to Valenciennes and 13 to Arras via Douai.

By bus The bus station is near the train station (☎ *03 27 83 67 59; www.reseau-arcenciel.fr/cambresis/reseau/grilles-horaires*). Line 501 joins Caudry and Le Cateau Cambrésis area. There are three number 51 buses to Arras daily.

Tourist information

🖳 **Office de tourisme de Cambrai** 48 rue de Noyon; ☎ 03 27 78 36 15; e contact@tourisme-cambrai.fr; www.tourisme-cambrai.fr; ⊕ 10.00–12.30 & 14.00–18.00 Mon–Sat, 14.30–17.30 Sun. Details of guided tours, with or without guides, from tourist office.

Where to stay

🏠 **Château de la Motte Fénelon** (40 rooms) square de Château; ☎ 03 27 85 25 84; e contact@cambrai-chateau-motte-feleon.com; www.cambrai-chateau-motte-fenelon.com. Even though it's tucked away somewhat bizarrely in the midst of a rather scruffy suburban area, you can scarcely miss this swanky 1850 building swanning in 8ha of parkland. The work of Hittorff, one of the greatest Parisian architects, the chateau boasts 2 Louis XV & Louis XVI state rooms & a magnificent staircase adorned with more portraits than you can shake a stick at. Plump for one of the 22 *château* bedrooms which are correspondingly classy; others located elsewhere in the wooded parkland have received mixed reviews. Lovely setting for a relaxing break, with bargain HB offers availaible. You really need a car as the hotel is some 2km from the town centre, & there are no nearby bars or restaurants. Free parking, b/fast €10.

You don't need to eat out. The hotel has its own restaurant in the vaulted castle caves. **Les Douves** (⊕ *12.00–14.00 & 19.30–22.00 daily*) offers choices from a 2-course business lunch with free coffee (Mon–Fri, €18), to a 3-course lunch & dinner menu (Mon–Sat, lunch only Sun, €26), & a 6-course lunch & dinner gourmet menu (Mon–Sat, lunch only Sun, €55). Wines can be expensive. $$$$

🏠 **Hotel Béatus** (32 rooms) 718 ave de Paris; ☎ 33 27 81 45 70; e hotel.beatus@wanadoo.fr; www.hotelbeatus.fr. Though only a short distance from the city centre, this hotel's relaxing country-style ambience & shaded flowerbeds have won praise from short-breakers winding down from a day in town. The rooms, quietly comfortable with garden views, are well equipped; b/fast (€9.50) & a good-value dinner menu (€15–50), featuring local dishes, are served in a rather splendid timbered setting. Your genial host Philippe Gorcynski's rescue of Dorothy, a rusting World War I British tank, is legendary (see page 195). A model & other memorabilia are prominent in the foyer. English is widely spoken. Good parking, & ample business & tourist facilities. $$$

🏠 **Le Mouton Blanc** (23 rooms) 33 rue Alsace Lorraine; ☎ 03 27 81 30 16; e hotel-de-mouton-blanc@wanadoo.fr; www.mouton-blanc.com. Only 200m from the station, this well-established Flemish-style hotel has been family run for some 20 years. B/fast €9. Its restaurant is likewise known for good regional fare in a charmingly rustic setting (⊕ 12.00–14.00 & 19.30–21.30, closed Mon & Sun evening; menus €23.50–48.50). $$$

🏠 **Le Clos St Jacques** (5 rooms) 9 rue St Jacques; ☎ 03 27 74 37 61; e leclosstjacques@wandoo.fr; www.leclosstjacques.com. Surprises come thick & fast with this enchanting B&B. The site, whose current façade & interiors date back to 1980, not only has a history of offering hospitality to 12th-century pilgrims *en route* to the tomb of Cambrai's much-loved St Gery, but provides a perfect exercise in how to recreate the same philosophy in a 21st-century context. Even in winter the Campaign, 1 of 5 individually themed rooms, provides a loft-level womb in which to doze amid a criss-cross of beams & an intriguing collection of knick-knacks. Honeymooners may opt for the House of Angels or the contemporary style of Escape. All rooms, adaptable to suit families, speaks volumes for the flair of Roger Quéro & his wife, Babeth – the creative brains behind the décor – owners of this brilliant city-centre bolthole. B/fast at €9.50 is worthy of the price. $$$

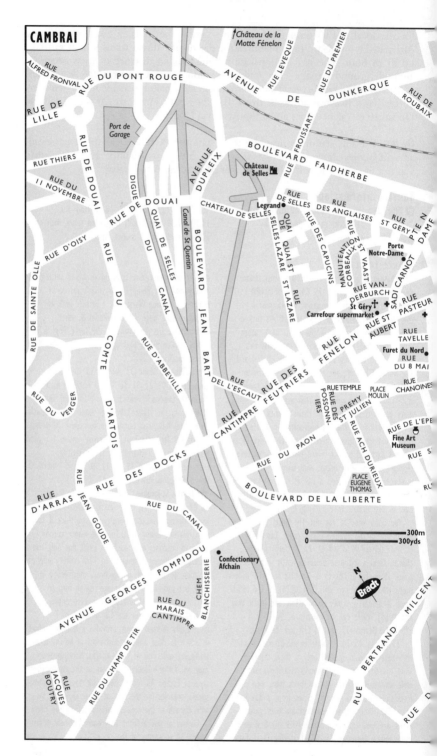

CAMBRAI

Château de la Motte Fénelon

RUE ALFRED FRONVAL
RUE DU PONT ROUGE
AVENUE DE DUNKERQUE
RUE LEVEQUE
RUE DU PREMIER
RUE DE ROUBAIX
RUE DE LILLE
Port de Garage
RUE THIERS
RUE DE DOUAI
RUE DU 11 NOVEMBRE
DIGUE
RUE DE DOUAI
AVENUE DUPLEIX
BOULEVARD FROISSART
BOULEVARD FAIDHERBE
Château de Selles
Legrand
RUE DE SELLES
RUE DES ANGLAISES
RUE ST GERY
RUE ST VAAST
RUE DE DAME
QUAI DE SELLES
CHATEAU DE SELLES
QUAI DE SELLES ST LAZARE
RUE DES CAPUCINS
MANUTENTION CORBEAUX
Porte Notre-Dame
RUE SADI CARNOT
RUE D'OISY
RUE DE SAINTE OLLE
RUE DU COMTE D'ARTOIS
QUAI DU CANAL
Canal de St Quentin
BOULEVARD JEAN BART
QUAI ST LAZARE
RUE ST LAZARE
RUE VAN-DERBURCH
St Géry
RUE ST AUBERT
RUE PASTEUR
Carrefour supermarket
RUE TAVELLE
RUE D'ABBEVILLE
RUE FENELON
Furet du Nord
RUE DU 8 MAI
RUE DU VERGER
RUE DEL L'ESCAUT
RUE DES FEUTRIERS
RUE DES POSSONN-IERS
RUE TEMPLE
PLACE ST JULIEN
PLACE MOULIN
RUE CHANOINES
RUE CANTIMPRE
RUE DES POSSONN-IERS
RUE PREMY
RUE DE L'EPE
Fine Art Museum
RUE S
RUE DES DOCKS
RUE DU PAON
RUE ACH DURIEUX
RUE D'ARRAS
JEAN GOUDE
RUE DU CANAL
PLACE EUGENE THOMAS
BOULEVARD DE LA LIBERTE
RU
0 300m
0 300yds
AVENUE GEORGES POMPIDOU
Confectionary Afchain
CHEM BLANCHISSERIE
RUE DU MARAIS CANTIMPRE
N
Bradt
RUE DU CHAMP DE TIR
RUE BERTRAND MILCENT
RUE JACQUES BOUTRY
RUE D

186

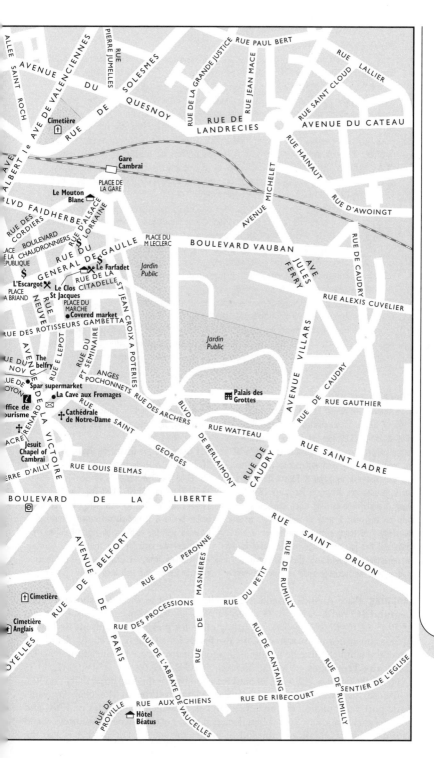

Have you heard the story of how an apprentice's mistake made a mint for his family's firm? If not, you soon will. Cambrai is proud of its *bêtise* (roughly translated as 'a bit of a mess up') – a minty sweet swathed with stripes of tongue-tickling flavours.

It all began, so the story goes, when young Emil Afchain, a scatter-brained apprentice in his parents' *confiserie*, was scolded by his mum for not following the family recipe. His sweets, she shouted, were *bêtises*. But his stupid errors proved so popular that the family business, founded in 1830, prospered to become part of local folklore. Though latterly hit by low sales, **les bêtises de Cambrai**'s (*Confectionery Afchain, ZI de Cantimpré, rue de Champ de Tir – reached via ave Georges Pompidou;* ✆ *03 27 81 25 49;* e *betises-de-cambrai@wanadoo.fr; www.betises-de-cambrai.fr;* ⏰ *08.00–12.00 Mon–Thu. 1hr tours, minimum 20 people – check first for availability*) production has been given a promotional boost by new owners from Dunkirk, creating quite a craze for the humbug-shaped sweets. And it is not just the original minty flavours that have taken off, but the lemon, orange and raspberry ones as well.

Join a factory tour to watch stripes of softening caramel being applied to the basic mint-flavoured swirls in an intriguing setting of ancient copper boilers and sugar-paste machines. For the record, 400 tons of the award-winning sticky stuff is produced annually at the modern plant which in 1985 replaced the original site in the Grand'Place. The recipe itself remains faithful to the original with a bespectacled Granny Afchain still a comforting trademark figure on a huge array of products, well worth buying from the factory shop for the tins alone. Many of the antique containers are now collectors' items and these, along with medals, diplomas, and old hardware clothing that belonged to Emile the apprentice, are on display at the museum.

✖ Where to eat and drink

✖ **Le Farfadet** (The Sprite) 13 rue de la Citadelle; ✆ 03 27 82 81 53; www.farfadet.fr; ⏰ 12.00–14.00 & 19.00–23.00 Tue–Sat. Expect a welcome from a puppet – yes, you read that correctly – at this most jolly & all-round entertaining eaterie, run, with the same flair, by Roger & Babeth Quéro of Le Clos St Jacques (see *Where to Stay*, page 185). The young & enthusiastic catering team, which includes their son, engenders a sense of well-being – as does an elderly genuflecting gent who greets you with a handshake! He's just one of the puppets made in the restaurant's own workshop. The food's pretty good as well, the speciality being stone-grilled meat dishes of beef or pork to salmon & giant prawns. Prices vary, depending on size, but allow from €15 to €21. $$$$

✖ **L'Escargot** 10 rue Général de Gaulle; ✆ 03 27 81 24 54; e restaurantlescargot@wanadoo,fr; ⏰ 12.00–14.00 & 19.00–22.00 Mon–Tue, 19.00–22.00 Thu, 12.00–14.00 Thu–Sun & 19.00–22.00 Sat–Sun. An easy-going place, of the timber beams & stained-glassed variety, patronised by locals with the emphasis on regional dishes. Try their namesake speciality – a crusty snails croustade with Cambrai Tome, the local cheese (€16). It can get crowded but the staff keep smiling. $$$

Shopping Place Aristide Briand is generally regarded as the main shopping area. **Legrand** (*19 rue de Selles;* ✆ *03 27 78 53 58; www.legrand-macarons.com;* ⏰ *08.00–12.30 & 14.30–19.00 Tue–Sat*) is a handy place for picking up pattiserie-style gifts such as chocolates and macaroons. It's also handy for an afternoon cuppa. And don't forget the famous Tome de Cambrai, a smooth farm cheese produced locally – **La Cave aux Fromages** (*9 rue St Nicholas;* ✆ *03 27 37 09 74;* ⏰ *08.00–12.30 & 15.00–19.00 Tue–Sat, 09.15–12.30 Sun*) is a good bet for this and other dairy goodies.

Try, too, the **covered market** in place du Marché off rue du Merechal. An avant-garde post-war building of concrete and glass, in which the façades of 17th- and 18th-century houses are superbly reflected, it now hosts the weekly Wednesday and Saturday markets. Look out for end-of-line factory deals. The market is also the start, on Sundays, of a remarkable tour of *les carrières souterraines*, the ancient stone quarries dug out from the chalk mainly in the Middle Ages and whose use fizzled out in the 16th and 17th centuries. Some city centre ones, however, continued to be used for storage, as well as providing valuable shelter in two world wars (*tour starts 16.00 Sun from the market hall elevator; €3.50; not recommended for children under 6*).

Bookshop
Furet du Nord Mail St Martin; ☏ 03 27 81 33 77;
🕐 09.30–19.00 Mon–Fri, 09.00–19.00 Sat

Other practicalities
Internet Extrem, 33 bd de la Liberte;
🕐 14.00–20.00 Mon, 10.00–19.00 Tue–Fri,
09.00–14.00 Sat; closed Sun

Post Office 1 pl du Saint Sépulcre; 🕐 09.00–18.30 Mon–Fri, 09.00–15.30 Sat
Public toilet City hall in rue d'Alger

Banks
$ Société Générale 9 rue du Général de Gaulle;
🕐 08.30–12.15 & 13.45–17.45 Tue–Fri,
08.30–12.30 Sat
$ Crédit Mutuel 24 rue du Général de Gaulle;

🕐 08.30–12.00 & 13.30–17.15 Tue–Fri,
09.00–12.00 Sat
$ Crédit du Nord 14 rue d'Alsace-Lorraine; 🕐 08.30–12.15 & 13.30–17.40 Tue–Fri, 08.30–12.15 Sat

Supermarkets
Carrefour 3 rue de Saint Aubert; 🕐 07.00–22.00 Mon–Sat, 08.00–13.00 Sun

Spar ave de la Victoire; 🕐 14.30–19.30 Mon, 09.00–13.00 & 14.30–19.30 Tue–Sat

LACE WORK STILL LOOMS LARGE

Caudry lace is much sought after by the rich and famous. The gown Hilary Clinton wore for husband Bill's presidential inauguration in 1993 was made here; so, too, was the tulle mantilla worn by Jackie Kennedy during her Vatican visit back in 1962. Dresses worn by Nicole Kidman and Madonna have also been made in the unprepossessing factory lying on the commercial outskirts of Cambrai.

Though business reportedly has been hit by Asian competitors, the company's role as a premiere lace-maker seems secure. While Calais (see page 69), they argue, can count on quantity, Caudry can boast of being a top-quality supplier to the prestigious world of haute couture. Both centres, however, owe their prosperity to the know-how passed down by the Leaver looms smuggled in by Nottingham lace-makers in the 19th century (see page 69). The first was installed in Caudry in 1826; by 1913 there were some 650 looms employing several thousand workers. The town's population likewise expanded from 1,926 in 1804 to 13,360 in 1911.

Today the looms rumble on at the **Lace Museum** (*Musée des Dentelles at Broderies, pl des Mantilles;* ☏ *03 27 76 29 77;* ✉ *musee-dentelle-caudry.fr.tc; www.museedentelle-caudry.fr;* 🕐 *09.00–12.00 & 14.00–18.30 Mon–Fri, 14.30–18.00 w/ends & public holidays; adult/child aged 6–16 €3/1.50, under 3 free*). Located on the site of an 1898 tulle and lace shop, the museum offers a 15-minute ground-floor video show on the history and technique of Caudry's lace industry and visits to the workshop. Upstairs, a temporary exhibition renewed every four months provides a behind-the-scenes look at high fashion with finished lace, tulle and embroidery products.

Distinct from the museum is the **House of Embroidery** (*Maison de la Broderie, 20 rue Victor Hugo, Villers Outreaux – 18km from Cambrai via the D76/96;* ☏ *03 27 70 88 54; www.veritable-macrame.com;* 🕐 *10.00–12.00 & 14.00–17.00 Mon–Fri, closed Aug & public holidays*) which explains the evolution of industrial embroidery.

Pharmacies

✚ **Pharmacie du Centre** 34 Place Aristide Briand; ⏲ 14.00–19.30 Mon, 09.00–12.30 & 14.00–19.30 Tue–Sat

✚ **Phamarcie Saint Géry** 19 pl du 9 Octobre; ⏲ 09.00–12.30 & 14.00–19.00 Mon–Sat

What to see and do Though short on major crowd-pulling attractions, the city centre, painstakingly reconstructed following the ravages of World War I, offers a dazzling display of architectural styles reflecting Cambrai's chequered history.

The so-called Spanish House (Maison Espagnole) is an eye-catching reminder of the days when Cambrai was under Spanish rule. It dates back to 1595 and is now the gabled home of the tourist office (see page 185) in rue de Noyon. The wooden sculptures that once decorated the exterior are seen inside. Once most such buildings in Cambrai were made of wood; it wasn't until Louis XIV declared wooden buildings to be too Spanish that the familiar French and Flemish styles were adopted.

Reinforced with literature from the tourist office, head for the **Fine Arts Museum** (*Musée des Beaux-Arts, 15 rue de l'Epée*; ☏ *03 27 82 27 90;* e *musee.cambrai@wanadoo.fr; www.musenor.com/et/cambrai;* ⏲ *10.00–12.00 & 14.00–18.00 Wed–Sun except public holidays; advanced booking for groups Mon–Tue; adult/under 25 €3.10/free*). The audio-visual show in the heritage section helps set the overall scene, while a relief map of the town is a handy introduction to the town's cobbled streets and squares.

Housed since 1890 in a 16th-century mansion, the museum is rich in Nord artefacts from prehistoric times to the present day. The important collection of fine arts concentrates on portraiture and landscapes of the 19th century, with works by Ingres, Chassériau, Claudel, Rodin, Boudin, Le Sidaner and Bourdelle.

The **Cathédrale de Notre-Dame** (*pl Jean-Paul II;* ⏲ *08.00–20.00 daily; free*), built on the site of an older abbey church, is one of four major sights reflecting the episcopal importance of Cambrai. Built between 1696 and 1702, in the classical religious style called for by Louis XIV, it contains the tomb of François Fénelon, the much-loved bishop of Cambrai from 1695 to 1715. The church and the guesthouse, home to the post office since 1911, formerly belonged to the Saint-Sépulcre abbey, founded in the 11th century. Among works of art on display are the 1745 trompe-l'oeil paintings by the artist Martin Geeraerts from Antwerp, and the Notre-Dame-de-Grâce (Our-Lady-of-Grace) icon brought from Rome and installed in Cambrai Cathedral in 1452. The icon also features in the annual Notre-Dame-de-Grâce procession on 15 August, part of a week-long carnival with fairground, fireworks, concerts and competitions.

The same celebrations mark the return of the town's **belfry** bell, snatched by the retreating Germans in 1918 and recovered after the armistice was signed. The belfry (*Le beffroi, rue du Beffroi*) – the original of which is said to date back to the 11th century – was built in Gothic style between 1447 and 1474. Despite a long history of damage, including being struck by lightning, partial demolition and eventual reconstruction, it survived the French Revolution to become classified as an historical monument in 1965. In 2005 it was registered, like 23 others in Nord-Pas de Calais and the Somme region (see page 13), as a World Heritage Site. The four sculptures adorning the top of the 62m building represent figures in the history of Cambrai.

The part played by local hero Bishop Géry in creating Cambrai as both a 6th-century religious and civil powerbase is recognised through **St-Géry Church** (*Église Saint-Géry, Grande rue Vanderburch;* ⏲ *08.00–20.00 daily*). Founded in the 6th century, and rebuilt between 1697 and 1745, it illustrates two traditional types of architecture: Dutch Baroque and French Classicism. During the Revolution, the

Look out for Martin and Martine. The legendary figures either appear as giants in the town's August festival frolickings or as the colourful characters who noisily strike each hour in the bell tower of Cambrai's town hall – a resplendent building in the Grand'Place rebuilt in its original grand Classical-style at the end of World War I.

The story goes that around 1370 Martin, a Cambrai blacksmith of Moorish descent, along with his wife Martine, led a revolt against the wicked lord of Thun-Lévêque. Though armed only with his heavy iron hammer, Martin managed to drive his opponent's solid steel helmet down over his eyes. Dazed and blinded, the lord of Thun quickly surrendered – leaving Martin's legendary hammer blow to symbolise freedom and the triumph of law over brute force.

A second, more questionable, version of the story dates back to the 16th century when the Moors accompanied Charles V to quell a revolt in Bruges. One of them, Hakem, settled in Cambrai only to fall in love with a young Christian girl named Martine. The Cambrésiens were outraged and the lovers were locked in the clock tower where, under the threat of a whipping, they were ordered to ring the hours with a heavy hammer. An old priest, moved by their misfortune, intervened and Hakem, converted to Christianity and baptised under the name Martin, married Martine. During World War I Martin and Martine, originally made from wood but later adapted to metal for their ringing role, were torn from the town hall, but they were returned in April 1919. Refurbished in 1922, they were classified as historical monuments in 1926.

church was saved from destruction and used instead to store the clergy's seized goods. The church now houses numerous works of art, including *The Entombment* by Rubens (1616).

Built between 1678 and 1694, the **Jesuit Chapel of Cambrai** (*La Chapelle des Jésuites, pl du Saint-Sépulcre*) is ranked among the finest Baroque-style buildings in the north of France. Completed in 1694, it features ten sumptuous columns of blue stone and some great sculptures. With the arrival of the Jesuits in 1592 to prevent the spreading of Protestantism, the chapel was rebuilt according to the rules of the Counter-Reformation. The abundance of Northern Baroque Art sculpted decorations was completed with a series of works by painter Arnoult de Vuez, illustrating scenes from the life of Christ.

Though Cambrai's fortifications have been for the most part demolished to make way for suburban avenues, the remains of Vauban's 17th-century **citadel** are to be found in gardens in the southeast of the town. The **Château de Selles** in Quai de Selles provides a good specimen of the military architecture of the 13th century while **Porte Notre-Dame**, a stone-and-brick structure of the early 17th century, and **La Porte de Paris**, a former castle gate saved by a single vote majority by the city council in 1893, are foremost among a variety of gates.

Lesser-known sights Small fry perhaps, and easily overlooked, is **rue des Anglaises** (look out for the road signs), home to an English Benedictine convent set up by nuns fleeing religious persecution in 1623. This and the surrounding streets are stuffed full of often-forgotten history. There are architectural surprises too, such as the Art Deco buildings in **rue des liniers** and the alliance of both Art Deco and Flemish styles in **place de la République**. The nearby animal and crop cartouches at the **Crédit Agricole** can also be quite eye-catching, as can the magnificent red-brick railway station which, built in 1907 in neo-classical style, knocks spots off others in the region.

On 25 July 1909 Cambrai-born Louis Blériot flew his crudely constructed monoplane across the English Channel – winning the *Daily Mail's* £1,000 prize for the first pilot to cross by air. The centenary of this remarkable achievement was duly commemorated on both sides of the Channel in 2009. There was even a re-enactment of the famous flight by French pilot Edmond Salis whose replica plane took off from Blériot-Plage near Calais (see page 88), arriving 40 minutes later in Dover. Blériot took 38 minutes.

While his flight in a plane constructed of little but steel and wooden tubes with wings covered in rubberised cloth earned worldwide admiration, it is often forgotten that Blériot was born in Cambrai, some 128km from the coast. The town duly celebrated throughout 2009 with special events and memorabilia. A dinner was attended by his grandson, aged 93. There was even talk about creating a permanent Blériot museum.

Blériot was born into a wealthy industrial family on 1 July 1872, at the Hôtel Chateau de Simencourt (see page 88). After studying at Notre-Dame-de-Grâce in Cambrai he studied in Paris, and by 1897 had founded his own firm; two years on, he tested a flapping sailed plane, which reminded him off a flying bird. By 1901, obsessed with aviation, he invested all his firm's money, as well as well as most of his wife Alicia's dowry, in creating a working aeroplane.

Though most of the money was spent on models and unsuccessful testings, he did manage to take off for the first time in 1909, flying five metres, albeit six years after the first powered flight by the Wright Brothers. Undeterred, he continued to risk life and limb testing his own prototypes, and in March 1909 founded the first French aeronautical firm in Courbevoie in the suburbs of Paris. But with no money, he desperately needed to win one of the big cash prizes granted to aviators beating a record. That same year he created his masterpiece, the Blériot XI – a mere eight metres long and weighing 220 kgs – and went on to win the the *Daily Mail* £1,000 challenge.

The exploit gained him immense recognition. In 1910 he and his father watched while a monument to him was unveiled in Cambrai. During World War I his firm supplied planes to both the French and British forces. After the war, he diversified into motorcycles, cars and boats. But he was first and foremost an aeronautics genius, and in the 1930s devised the B110 which won the world record for a non-stop flight in 1932. In 1936 the Blériot factories were nationalised, much to the displeasure of their owner. He died the same year of a heart attack in Paris, aged 64.

LE CATEAU-CAMBRÉSIS
Forget for a moment the traffic trundling through the town centre. Le Cateau-Cambrésis is every bit an architectural gem as big sister Cambrai. It's just a smaller version, whose considerable chocolate-box charm includes the Matisse Museum (see page 194).

History In 1001 an edict from Otto III, Emperor of Germany, authorised the Bishop of Cambrai to fortify St-Marie Castle. From this stemmed the town known as due Chastel (old French for 'castle'), later to become Le Cateau-Cambrésis.

Despite being besieged and devastated many times, its often narrow streets and architecture reflect a rich cultural and artistic heritage, mainly dating from the 17th century. By the 19th century it was also a major textile centre. During World War I the city was again seriously damaged but, as with Cambrai, was rebuilt along identical lines in the 1920s.

Getting there and away Le Cateau-Cambrésis lies 22km from Cambrai via the RN43; it is also served by train from Lille Flandres, though this involves at least one change. Take the Line 501 bus for Cambrai.

Tourist information

🛈 **Tourist office of Le Cateau-Cambrésis** 9 pl du Commandant Edward Richez; 📞 03 27 84 10 94; www.tourisme-lecateau.fr; ⏱ 09.00–12.30 & 14.00–17.15 Mon–Thu, 09.00–12.30 & 14.00–18.00 Fri–Sat, 14.30–17.00 Sun, 10.00–12.30 & 14.30–17.00 1st Sun of month; closed Tue & public holidays

---

BRITISH WARTIME POET HONOURED

Wilfred Owen is a very British wartime poet, yet he is to be honoured on French soil: the forester's house in which he lived, and close to where he was killed in World War I, will be the centre-piece of a new museum due to open on 4 November 2011, the 93rd anniversary of his death.

The project is the culmination of the curiosity shown since 1991 by the small farming community of Ors (7km from Cateau-Cambresis off the D643) in the annual pilgrimage of British people looking for Owen's grave.

They quickly discovered that the mysterious British officer started as a private in the Manchester Regiment in his early 20s, was gassed during the Battle of the Somme and later in the war spent 28 hours in a hole with the dismembered body of a brother officer. His nerves understandably snapped and doctors declared him unfit to command. In June 1917 he returned to Britain for a long spell in hospital on the outskirts of Edinburgh. It was here that he met the celebrated anti-war poet Siegfried Sassoon and formed a relationship that produced such works of genius as *Anthem for Doomed Youth*, *Disabled*, and *Exposure*.

So intrigued was Jacky Duminy, the Mayor of Ors, by Owen's prowess as a poet, that he set out to secure funds to commission Turner Prize nominee Simon Patterson to turn the property into a shrine to this man who lived a wartime existence deep in nearby woods. Now with funding of €1.3million, the modest house in which Owen lived will have the walls rendered white and incorporated into a white sculpted building to stand out like a bleached bone against the dark forest. The dank, dark cellar which we visited early in 2009 will be untouched. It was here Owen scribbled by candlelight his last letter on 31 October 1918; he was writing to his mother reassuring her 'there is no danger down here'. The text will now run alongside a ramp leading to the cellar.

It was on 4 November 1918 that Owen marched a mile south to take part in the assault on the Sambre-Oise Canal, a battle so vicious that two Victoria Crosses were won and 169 lives lost. These included the life of then second lieutenant Wilfred Owen. He was 25 years old, had published four poems and had written a hundred other unpublished texts, half of which had been produced between 1916 and 1918.

On 5 November, the *London Gazette* announced Owen's posthumous promotion to lieutenant from that of second lieutenant – the rank he had held since 4 June 1916 – to be backdated from 4 December 1917. Three days later, on 8 November, he was awarded the Military Cross for capturing a German machine-gun on the Beaurevoir-Fonsomme line where he held his position for 24 hours before being relieved. That same day, he was buried with his comrades in the small square reserved for British military graves in the village of Ors's communal cemetery; his grave lies third from the left on the back row. Ironically, his mother did not get the official news of his death until 11 November 1918, the very day the victory bells rang.

Where to stay and eat

Hotel Restaurant des Digues (9 rooms) 13–15 rue Charles Seydoux; 03 27 84 12 07; e hoteldesdigues@hotamil.fr; www.hoteldesdigues.eu. Anywhere which brings a warm glow on a cold, wet Feb evening deserves a round of applause. A former *estaminet*, converted into a post office & brought back as a welcome watering hole after Word War II, its theme rooms bring a strong touch of old-world charm without losing out on showers, whirlpools & free Wi-Fi. As with other smaller hotels in Le Nord, the best is where you least expect it – in this case on the main stretch close to the tourist office & the main attractions. Equally as cosy & only a courtyard away is **Des Digues** restaurant (12.00–14.00 & 19.00–21.00, closed Sat; $$$) which draws the locals for a wholesome menu based on regional products. Do look at the acrylic paintings by the owner, of which he's rightly proud. $$$

What to see and do The **Matisse Museum** (*Palais Fénelon;* 03 27 84 64 50; e museematisse@cg59.fr; www.cg59.fr; 10.00–18.00 Wed–Mon, closed Tue & public holidays; adult/child & concessions €7/3) replaced the old town hall museum, founded in 1952 by the locally born artist himself. Relocated in 1982 to the tree-lined grounds and flowerbeds of this former 18th-century palace, a hugely enlarged version reopened in the fully renovated palace in 2002. The museum houses France's third-largest collection of Matisse's drawings, paintings and sculptures. It also features the geometric works of the abstract artist Auguste Herbin. More recently the Tériade donation (Tériade was a friend of Matisse) gave 31 items to the museum, including work by Piccaso and Chagall.

The museum offers no-reservation guided visits (15.00 Sat & 10.30 Sun), as well as workshops for all ages. A 'following in Matisse's footsteps' tour takes in the artist's birthplace, the local school and Matisse's stained glass window, *The Bees*.

Also demanding attention is the Baroque-style façade and onion-shaped bell of **St-Martin Church**, a former Benedictine abbey built in 1634 and much admired for the richness of its sculptures and the proportions of the nave. Elsewhere the stepped gables, a reminder of the Spanish influence, blend almost bizarrely with the Renaissance architecture of the **town hall**.

This is beer country – and less than 1km away from the town centre is the lovingly restored red-brick brewery of the **Abbey of Le Cateau** (*Brasserie Historique de l'Abbaye du Cateau; 16 rue du Marché aux Chevaux;* 03 27 07 19 19; www.brasserieducateau.com; 10.00–15.00 Tue, 10.00–18.00 Wed–Thu, 10.00–23.00 Fri–Sat, 10.00–19.00 Sun; admission €2). Partly renovated during the popular beer-drinking days of the 19th century, it is now enjoying a renewed reputation for real ale. The enthusiasm shown by Julie Butez in managing the plant for her beer-

---

CALL IN FOR A CACOULE

Now here's a sweet story. Once upon a time a 19th-century fairground confectioner invented a caramel surprise called La Cacoule. A favourite of Matisse, it was made with sugar, honey and glucose. The secret recipe was handed down through the family until the early 1970s when, sadly, it looked as if interest in La Cacoule had died. But rescue was at hand in the shape of two pastry cooks, Crapet and Bervoet, who quickly licked the boiled sweet back into shape. Years went by until Bervoet, who was about to retire from the shop (*Patisserie Hosdez, 7 rue Charles Seydoux;* 03 27 84 24 02; 08.00–12.15 & 14.00–19.00 Wed–Fri, 08.00–19.00 Sat–Sun; €4.50 for 100g bag) whispered the recipe to his apprentice Philippe Hosdez. In 1987, Philipe bought the outstanding stock on the strict understanding that La Cacoule should not be made outside of Le Cateau. When it comes to the crunch, it seems, there's nothing like adding a bit of local flavour!

Historian and hotelier Philippe Gorcynski is a man in love with a tank called Dorothy – so much so that his persistence in rescuing the rusting World War I warrior from the battlefield mud around the village of Flesquières (11km from Cambrai off the E19/A2) in 1998 remains the stuff of local legend. And if Philipe eventually has his way, she – for tanks, depending on their design, do have a gender – will leave her temporary home to become centre-piece of a museum dedicated to the ferocious Battle of Cambrai in which the tank took part.

Dorothy, officially tank Number D41, was one of some 400 employed by the British for the first time in 1917, appearing out of the November mist to cause confusion, and considerable damage, among the defending German forces.

A vicious counter-attack inevitably followed. Tragically Dorothy took at a direct hit from five German shells killing four of her eight-man crew. They were buried locally in the Flesquières Hill British Cemetery. Dorothy, meanwhile, remained lost in the aftermath of a war most people wanted to forget. That was until until Philipe, frustrated for many years by rumours of a buried tank, began his mission both to find, and save, the rusting hulk. One villager, Madame Bouleux, reported that as a teenager she had seen prisoners being ordered by the Germans to push a tank into an enormous hole; beyond this, he had little to go on. Initial investigations with metal detectors proved fruitless – though Philippe's instinct kept drawing him back to the area indicated by Madame Bouleux.

His instincts – and her memory – were right. Six years later, after research visits to England's National Archives, the Tank Museum in Bovington, and the Imperial War Museum in London, his dream of finding the precise location was fulfilled. Studies of original and contemporary aerial photographs, together with infra-red photos and powerful metal detection tests, showed there was indeed a large metal object buried in a local field.

After one hour of digging on 5 November 1998, the roof hatch was revealed. By 20 November, the 81st anniversary of the Battle of Cambrai, the tank was fully exposed. A special ceremony attracting worldwide interest was held and a wreath laid in memory of the soldiers from the Tank Corps killed in the Battle of Cambrai.

brewing family business is as lively as their Vivat. A malt variety beer, it is described as a 'clear golden coloured ale with a large pure white foamy head', and as 'having an aroma of perfect peach with delicate floral notes.' Try it for yourself at the bar. The cosy, heavily timbered restaurant bedecked with hanging hops serves a blackboard-style menu of regional dishes, all begging for an accompanying pint. Look out for the *Cambrai andouillette*. It's said to be unique in France as it has the distinction of being prepared from veal rather than pork. As at Arras (see page 166), the defenders of the sausage have a brotherhood – in Cambrai their dress is red, yellow and black.

DOUAI

There's nothing like a river, or a canal, to liven up a place. Douai boasts both, and its pleasing blend of 18th-century gabled buildings and contemporary low-level red-brick residences are seen at their best on a riverside stroll. They each bring a muted charm to a city which erupts noisily just once a year during its three-day festival of giants in July. While other towns hold similar events (see page 45), Douai does its better, providing one literally huge reason to linger a little longer in this surprisingly sparky post-industrial centre.

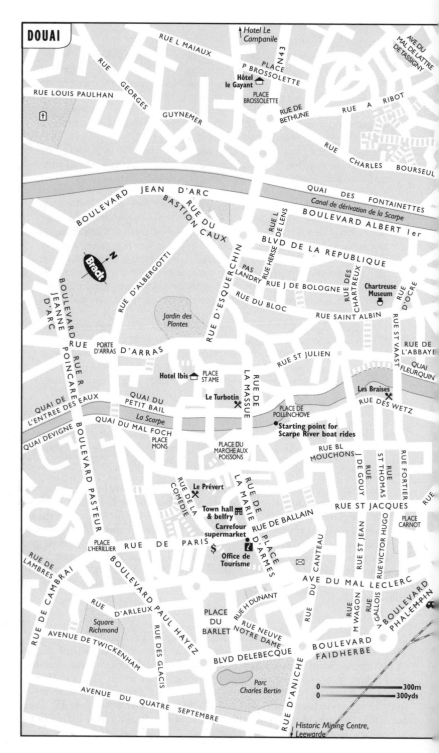

DOUAI

RUE L MAIAUX

Hotel Le Campanile

AVE DU MAL DE LATTRE DE TASSIGNY

PLACE P BROSSOLETTE

RUE GEORGES GUYNEMER

Hôtel le Gayant

RUE LOUIS PAULHAN

PLACE BROSSOLETTE

RUE DE BETHUNE

RUE A RIBOT

RUE CHARLES BOURSEUL

BOULEVARD JEAN D'ARC

QUAI DES FONTAINETTES

Canal de dérivation de la Scarpe

BOULEVARD ALBERT 1er

RUE DU BASTION CAUX

RUE L DE LENS

RUE HERSE

BLVD DE LA REPUBLIQUE

RUE D'ALBERGOTTI

PAS LANDRY

RUE J DE BOLOGNE

RUE DES CHARTREUX

Chartreuse Museum

RUE D'OCRE

Jardin des Plantes

RUE D'ESQUERCHIN

RUE DU BLOC

RUE SAINT ALBIN

RUE ST VAAST

RUE DE L'ABBAYE

BOULEVARD JEANNE D'ARC

PORTE D'ARRAS

RUE D'ARRAS

RUE ST JULIEN

QUAI FLEURQUIN

RUE R POINCARE

Hotel Ibis

PLACE ST AME

RUE DE LA MASSUE

Les Braises

QUAI DE L'ENTREE DES EAUX

QUAI DU PETIT BAIL

Le Turbotin

RUE DES WETZ

La Scarpe

QUAI DU MAL FOCH

PLACE DE POLLINCHOVE

QUAI DEVIGNE

BOULEVARD PASTEUR

PLACE MONS

Starting point for Scarpe River boat rides

PLACE DU MARCHE AUX POISSONS

RUE BL MOUCHONS

RUE DE GOUY

RUE ST THOMAS

RUE FORTIER

Le Prévert

RUE DE LA COMEDIE

RUE DE LA MARIE

RUE DE BALLAIN

RUE ST JACQUES

Town hall & belfry

Carrefour supermarket

PLACE CARNOT

Office de Tourisme

RUE DE PARIS

RUE CANTEAU

RUE ST JEAN

RUE VICTOR HUGO

PLACE L'HERILLIER

PLACE D'ARMES

AVE DU MAL LECLERC

RUE DE LAMBRES

RUE DE CAMBRAI

BOULEVARD PAUL HAYEZ

RUE D'ARLEUX

RUE H DUNANT

RUE DU

RUE M WAGON

V GALLOIS

BOULEVARD PHALEMPIN

Square Richmond

AVENUE DE TWICKENHAM

RUE DES GLACIS

PLACE DU BARLET

RUE NEUVE NOTRE DAME

BOULEVARD FAIDHERBE

BLVD DELEBECQUE

RUE D'ANICHE

Parc Charles Bertin

0 ——— 300m
0 ——— 300yds

AVENUE DU QUATRE SEPTEMBRE

Historic Mining Centre, Leewarde

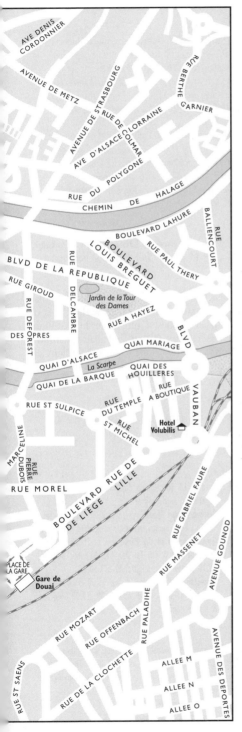

HISTORY

Douai seems to have begun as a settlement on the site of Duacum, a 4th-century Roman fortress. The Flemish counts later developed a flourishing 12th-century cloth trade along the River Scarpe, ideally placed for commerce and on which Douai lies at the highest navigable point. Known initially as Douay ('Doway' in English) the town fell first into the hands of the Counts of Burgundy in 1384, and hence the Spanish Netherlands, until finally being taken by the troops of Louis XIV. In 1713, following successive sieges during which it was virtually destroyed, the town was fully integrated into France.

Religion has played a prominent role in Douai's past. From the 1560s until the fomentation of the French Revolution, it was the centre of education for English Catholics on the run from religious persecution. It was, however, another revolution, the industrial one, that dramatically changed the face of Douai: with the boom in coal-mining, it became the capital of the Bassin des Houillières (coal basin) of Nord-Pas de Calais. But in December 1990 the coal boards for northern France and Pas de Calais shut down the last shaft, closing the book on three centuries of mining history in the region. Douai, already badly damaged in two world wars, defiantly drew up a huge regeneration programme designed to face a bright new future still in keeping with its cultural roots.

GETTING THERE AND AWAY

By car From Calais, take the A26 motorway then the A21 in direction of Douai; the 131km journey takes one hour and 20 minutes.

By train From the Eurostar service to Lille Europe (see page 25) go to the regional station Lille Flandres (the stations are within walking distance of each other via an underground passage) to take a direct train to Douai; the journey from Lille to

Douai's English College was founded in 1568 by William Allen, formerly of Queen's College, Oxford, and Canon of York. It was used as a bolt-hole for Catholics escaping religious persecution in England, and for training priests whose aim was to encourage Protestant England back into the Catholic fold. It was connected with Douai University which, founded under the Spanish Netherlands, was also prominent until the French Revolution as a centre for the education of English Catholics escaping persecution in England.

It was here that the English Catholics first translated the Latin version of the Old Testament into English, a task that was completed by 1609. This, combined with the New Testament, which had been translated and published at Rheims 27 years earlier, became the so-called Douay (the town's old name) Bible. The much-later Haydock Douay-Rhiems version of the Bible was used by John F Kennedy during his inauguration as the first Catholic President of the United States.

Douai takes about 25 minutes. The railway station **Gare de Douai** (*place de la Gare;* ⊕ *06.15–20.00 Mon–Fri, 07.15–20.00 Sat, 08.15–20.30 Sun & public holidays*) is a five-minute walk from the city centre.

By bus All 15 of Douai's bus routes stop at the train station and operate a regular service to the city centre. They also serve the surrounding towns and villages of Aniche, Auby, Auberchicourt, Bruille lez Marchiennes, Cuincy, Dechy, Ecaillon, Emerchicourt, Erchin, Esquerchin, Flers en Escrebieux, Guesnain, Lallaing, Lambres Lez Douai, Lauwin Planque, Lewarde, Loffre, Masny, Monchecourt, Montigny en Ostrevent, Pecquencourt, Raimbeaucourt, Roost Warendin, Roucourt, Sin le Noble and Waziers. For further information: ☎ 03 27 95 77 77; www.transportsdudouaisis.fr.

TOURIST INFORMATION

🔲 **Office de Tourisme** 70 pl d'Armes; ☎ 03 27 88 26 79; e tourisme@ville-douai.fr; www.ville-douai.fr; ⊕ Oct–Mar 10.00–12.30 & 14.00–18.30 Mon–Sat,

Apr–Sep 10.00–13.00 & 14.00–18.30 Mon–Sat, 15.00–18.00 Sun & public holidays

CITY PASSES AND GUIDED TOURS

Audio-taped guided tours Rent headphones in English, French, German & Dutch for 5 differing aspects including city centre, River Scarpe, Flemish & French periods, & city in the 19th–20th centuries. Adult/under 18 €4/3, no rental to unaccompanied children.
Guided tours Belfry & Town Hall Sep–Jun 11.00, 15.00, 16.00 & 17.00 daily (except Mon morning), Jul–Aug 10.00, 11.00, 14.00, 15.00, 16.00, 17.00 & 18.00; adult/child €3.50/2; carillon concert 11.00 Sat except school holidays. Fun visit for children

aged 6–12 on selected days during Jul–Aug; €5: register at tourist office.
Discovery Tours Douai generally: 15.30 Sun Apr–Sep & 1st Sun each month Oct–Mar, adult/child €6.50/4.50; Great Chamber of the Parliament of Flanders: 18.30 or 15.30 2nd & 4th Tue Apr–Sep & public holidays, 15.30 Sat Jul–Aug, adult/child €3.50/2.
Riverside stroll May, Jun & Sep 15.00–19.00 Sat, Sun & public holidays, Jul & Aug 14.00–19.00 Thu–Sun & public holidays, adult/child €4.50/3.

🏠 WHERE TO STAY

🏠 **Hôtel Le Gayant** (43 rooms inc 1 family room, 8 with bath) 20 pl Pierre Brossolette; ☎ 03 27 88 29 97; e contact@hotel-le-gayant.fr; www.hotel-le-gayant.com. Tucked away on the edge of the city centre, it fulfils its purpose as a modern, functional & comfortable overnight stop, close to a park &

providing a quietish escape from the jollities of the July giants festival. HB available but with bar times limited & very little else close by, it's probably best to dine in town & stick to B&B. W/end rates available. Free Wi-Fi access, large flat-screen TV in dining area. Secure parking. $$$

🏠 **La Ferme de la Sensée** (5 rooms) 5 rue de l'Eglise, Gouy sous Bellone; 📞 03 21 50 21 68; e contact@fermedelasensee.com; www.fermedelasensee.free.fr. This is more a family home than a B&B. Nothing is more welcome, especially on a wet winter's day, than a hot home-cooked meal before dragging your weary legs up the creaking stairs for a hot bath & a soft comfortable bed. The fact that owners Fanny Martin & Gerard Nicolas join you for table talk makes the atmosphere that much more convivial. You can learn about regional fare from Gerard who is also the chef, & a good one at that. Add the converted 18th-century farmhouse, Fanny's stable yard of horses & some stunning countryside, & you can't really go wrong with this ideal out-of-town hideaway (8km from Douai, 24km from Cambrai). B/fast is included. Evening meal is available on reservation from €25. $$$

🏠 **Hotel Volubilis** (59 rooms) bd Vauban; 📞 03 27 88 00 11; www.hotel-volubilis.fr. An independent

hotel located in green & quiet surroundings between the railway station & the Gayant Expo exhibit centre. It has its own restaurant serving regional set menus (€20–40). Parking is free. $$$

🏠 **Hotel Ibis** (42 rooms) pl Saint Amé; 📞 03 27 87 27 27; e h0956@accor.com; www.accorhotels.com. Located 200m from the Belfry, this converted 18th-century building is typical of the group's economy priced hotels ie: the rooms are comfortable & round-the-clock snacks & drinks are of an international nature. But it is well placed for local eateries & sightseeing. Street parking is available; book early if attending major events such as the giants festival. $$

🏠 **Hotel Le Campanile** (50 rooms) rue Maximilien Robespierre, Cuincy; 📞 03 27 96 97 00; www.campanile.fr. Though located in a suburb of Cuincy, the hotel is a handy stopover for the town centre 5km away. It has its own terrace, caters for the disabled & offers a healthy b/fast. Parking is free. $$

✖ WHERE TO EAT AND DRINK

✖ **Le Prévert** 28 rue de la Comedie; 📞 03 27 98 59 51; 🕐 12.00–14.00 & 19.00–22.00 Mon & Thu, 12.00–14.00 Tue–Wed, 12.00–14.00 & 19.00–23.00 Fri, 19.00–23.00 Sat. Snug is the best way to describe this almost student-style restaurant with blackboard menus. Whether dining in a warming February fug or as a welcome stop on a fair-weather walk round town, it's a nice place to rest your legs, admire the colourful artists' prints & listen to the general chatter in a venue that

becomes crowded with locals, especially around lunchtime – its popularity speaks volumes. $$$

✖ **Les Braises** 165 rue des Wetz; 📞 03 27 97 43 04; 🕐 12.00–14.00 Mon–Thu, 12.00–14.00 & 19.00–22.00 Fri, 19.00–22.00 Sat. One of those small family-run finds in a quiet corner of town. Varied regional dishes are of the lighter, rather than the robust, kind. A homely atmosphere is helped by courteous service. Find a table by the window & wind down in a traditional tearoom-type setting. $$$

OTHER PRACTICALITIES

Bank Crédit Agricole, 179 rue de Paris; 📞 0 810 000 512; 🕐 08.45–12.45 & 13.45–17.45 Tue–Fri, 08.45–12.15 Sat
Supermarket Carrefour Market, Gallérie du Dauphin, pl d'Armes; 🕐 08.30–20.00 Mon–Sat
Internet Tourist Information Centre, pl d'Armes; 🕐 10.00–13.00 & 14.00–18.30 Mon–Sat, 15.00–18.00 Sun

Pharmacy de la Place d'Armes pl d'Armes; 📞 03 27 88 96 05; 🕐 09.00–12.30 & 13.30–19.00 Mon–Sat
Post Office 81 pl Charles de Gaulle à Douai; 📞 03 27 93 55 00; 🕐 08.00–18.30 Mon–Fri, 08.00–12.30 Sat
Public Toilet Tourist Information Centre, pl d'Armes; 🕐 10.00–13.00 & 14.00–18.30 Mon–Sat, 15.00–18.00 Sun

WHAT TO SEE AND DO The great joy about Douai is the huge choice of self-guided or guided tours both on land and on water (see *Tourist information* opposite), with choice largely dictated by personal preferences or by seasonal weather. All include, to some extent, six not-to-miss sites or attractions that are mostly within manageable walking distance from the tourist office in place d'Armes. Most can be seen in a day, with a two-day summer break soon filled.

The most noteworthy attraction must be the 61m **belfry** (*le beffroi, rue de la Mairie*; 🕐 *10 Aug–30 Jun 11.00, 15.00, 16.00, 17.00 daily, 1 Jul–10 Aug 11.00, 14.00, 15.00, 16.00, 17.00, 18.00 daily*). Even if you don't immediately spot the 600-year-old

In 1945, Douai was the coal-mining capital for the Nord-Pas de Calais region. Nowadays it reflects a different era, that of a town at ease with the high-tech era, shown at its best through the electronic wizardry displayed at the **Historic Mining Centre** (*Centre Historique Minier, Lewarde – 8km from Douai off the D645; ☎ 03 27 95 82 82;* e *contact@chm-lewarde.com; www.chm-lewarde.com;* ☐ *Mar–Oct, 09.00–17.30 daily, Nov–Dec & Feb 13.00–17.00 Mon–Sat, 10.00–17.00 Sun, school & public holidays, closed Jan; adult/child €11.50/5.90, audio-guided tour available in English; free car-parking & covered picnic area*). Established in 1982, this is now France's foremost mining museum. The centre is based upon what was once the Delloye pithead; from 1930 to 1971 around 1,000 miners were employed here producing on average 1,000 tons of coal a day.

The museum's size is impressive at some 7,000m²: allow a good half day to get round it. Take the 480m 'descent' to visit the tunnels – your stomach lurches at the speed, only for you to discover later that clever simulation means you are back where you began! But at least you have enjoyed being guided by an ex-miner along a shaft reconstructed from authentic materials. The children will love it, while many an adult will recall scenes and objects from the more recent past among the 15,000 items on display. One section shows still-familiar mining machinery. Elswhere, photographs depict elements of mining life: one display features the social life of women, while another brings to life the tiny 19th-century pithead cafés and bars where miners drank, discussed pigeons and formed brass bands.

The use of pit ponies and the stables where they were kept is also covered. Most memorable is the hanging-room where row upon row of miners' overalls dangle like many brightly coloured bats, each belonging to one of the 800 men who not so long ago toiled in what now is a 21st-century shrine to Douai's powerful industrial past.

The restaurant alone is a good wet weather retreat, though booking is recommended at peak periods. Named Le Briquet, after the miners' break time snack, it offers a reasonably priced family-style menu of regional dishes including *flamiche au Maroilles* (made from the famous cheese), chicory pie, and the ubiquitous Flemish *carbonade* beef braised in beer and just right for a nippy day. Cassonade sugar and beer tarts and northern waffles with chicory coffee ice cream are also representative of hearty northern fare, very much part of the mining life the museum dramatically, and sometimes craftily, captures.

building – its outrageously ornate tower seems to pop into view wherever you are – the 62-bell carillon will certainly strike an appealing note every quarter of an hour. Visit on Saturday and you can enjoy a carillon concert while shopping at the weekly market; better still take a guided tour and the carillon master or one of his pupils will play the organ-style keyboard for you. He may even let you or your children tinkle the ivories yourself. The visit ends with a breathtaking top-floor view of the town and an admiring glance at the biggest bell of the carillon, which weighs in at 5,550kg.

The 196 steps to the *chambre des cloches* (room of the bells) might not appeal to some, but, even from below, the bells provide a ringing endorsement of this surprisingly attractive city. One devotee was Victor Hugo who, while visiting Douai in 1837, wrote enthusiastically of 'a gothic tower, topped by a slate roof composed of numerous small conical stacked windows …'

Close by the **town hall** in rue de la Mairie (*mairie* is French for 'town hall') – and best enjoyed in the joint English-speaking guided visit with the belfry – includes the 19th-century White Room used for weddings and the Gothic Room, with a superb chimney, where council meetings are held. In St-Michel's Chapel,

IT'S A GIANT-SIZED FAMILY SUCCESS

It may seem a tall order, but each July the Gayant family delivers a huge three-day knees-up for the thousands who throng the streets and squares of Douai. They are giants after all. Made from wickerwork, Monsieur Gayant measures in at 8.50m – around 28 feet sounds so much more impressive – and weighs 370kg. His wife Marie is a mere 6.25m, around 20 feet, and weighs 250kg. Their children, Jacquot, Fillon and little Binbin, each rise to a mere 2.40m, or around seven feet. They tower above the crowds that noisily celebrate these doughty dignitaries, whose origins date back to 1479 when a festival honoured the part played by the town patron St Maurand in the escape of the Count of Flanders from a French armed gang.

Following a further defeat of the French in 1530, Flanders's Spanish rulers suggested the town's basket-makers construct a celebratory wickerwork giant called Gayant, the Picardy word for the French *géant*. A year later the fruiterers' guild made him a wife, Marie Cagenon. The rest, as they say is history, though it proved far from plain sailing. When Douai finally became part of France in 1667, the Bishop of Arras ordered a new festival – this time to celebrate a *French* victory. The Gayants, initially banned as being too profane, were later revived in 1780, then banned again during the French Revolution as portraying aristocrats. Undeterred they reappeared in 1801, and again in 1821 dressed in the costumes they still wear today.

Though the original mum and dad have been replaced, the whole family, dressed in its finery – which is worked on year-round – has, like its fellow giants in Cassel, been classified as a UNESCO heritage treasure. Deservedly so. From the time families gather for chips and *potjevlesch* (a dish of cold meats) served from stalls in tree-lined streets on the Saturday to the colour and cacophony of sound during Sunday's big parade, the atmosphere is one of aggro-free fun. The anticipation is enormous as the town hall courtyard crowds await the first glimpse of the giants, housed for the rest of the year in high-ceilinged quarters.

Watch out for the six pairs of trainers worn by their hefty bearers, hidden from sight, as Monsieur Gayant and his wife shuffle across the cobbles – providing a curtain-raiser for a string of events, including the release of pigeons and the throwing of sweets.

There is even a dance by the giants, swirling and swaying as the bands play, the belfry carillons ring out and children cluster round a decorated cart drawn by a rare breed of heavy horse from Le Nord. This contains a Wheel of Fortune, featuring such diverse characters as a lawyer and a policeman to a thief and, to quote one onlooker, 'a lady who gives pleasure to men'.

Take a peep beneath the giants' finery: the separate six-man teams who each lift Mr and Mrs Gayant belong to the 53-strong 'family' of bearers who begin as money collectors before becoming a *chef de lunette* (the one who guides the way through a small peephole of wire mesh) or a *chef de protocole*. The position of Gayant-bearer is handed down from father to son or son-in-law, with recruitment starting at 18. Even the one-man bearers for each of the four Gayant children – who were not 'born' until the 17th and 18th centuries – deserve their well-earned lunchtime rest, as does the Sot des Canonniers (a fool on a hobby-horse) who cavorts in front of visitors. Regularly included amongst the visitors is a group from the London borough of Harrow with which Douai is twinned.

The high-jinks restart early Sunday afternoon so grab a convenient café seat well in advance for a ringside view of a succession of floats. Though varying in theme from year to year, they provide a perfect blend of the classical and frankly surreal, including a selection of smaller giants (you may even get the chance to lift one) plus street artists and performers.

Cultural Cities of Le Nord DOUAI

8

built in 1475, there's a wooden panel etched with the names of Douai soldiers and civilian victims killed in wars since 1870.

Some buildings are seen at their most sumptuous on the **Scarpe River boat rides** (⊕ *May, Jun & Sep 15.00 & 19.00 Sat, Sun & public holidays, Jul & Aug 14.00 & 19.00 Fri–Sun & public holidays; adult/child €4.50/3*). These start from the Parliament of Flanders (proceedings were transferred here from Tournai in neighbouring Belgium in 1714), whose building is now the Court of Assizes for Le Nord. Developed on the site of a former refuge for 13th-century Benedictine monks from Marchiennes Abbey (see page 198), the Parliament's 65m façade has eight arches covering a dock designed to feed an upstairs grain loft. The boat trip includes a peep into the old Parliament cells where visitors can spot a trussed-up model of Eugene Vidocq, an 18th-century Arras-born criminal whose remarkable jail-breaking skills led to his being signed up as Chief of Police. Who says crime doesn't pay?

If the day turns damp leave the riverside for the shortish walk to the **Chartreuse Museum** (*Musée de la Chartreuse, 130 rue des Chartreux;* ☏ *03 27 71 38 80;* e *musee@villedouai.fr; www.musenor.com/gm/douai;* ⊕ *10.00–12.00 & 14.00–18.00 daily except Tue & public holidays; adult/child €4/2, audio-guide in English €1.50*). Established since 1958 in the former Carthusian monastery, the museum, lying between the river and the canal, houses 17th- and 18th-century Flemish and Dutch paintings, as well as works by the Italian and French schools from the 17th to 19th centuries. The restoration of the chapel now leaves the nave to shed light, literally, on a fine set of sculptures from the 19th century. Look out for the scale model of Douai as it was in 1709 – it helps you find your bearings even now.

Mix and match the riverside with the lanes and alleys for a long, fine-day walk. These not only neatly thread their way through the town but take in some of the sights already mentioned. **La ruelle des Archers** (Archers' Alley) off place d'Armes close to the tourist office, for instance, leads neatly into **la ruelle des Arbalétriers** (Crossbowmen's Alley) and the garden where the Brotherhood of Archers practised their crossbow techniques. At this point you can double back slightly via rue St Nicholas and rue Theophile Bra into **la ruelle de la Vierge Marie** (Alley of the Virgin Mary). This was once known as the lane of *pradel* (meaning 'small meadow'); the current name probably relates to a sign or a small chapel. Otherwise continue on to the river and cross the main bridge for a further maze of around a dozen tiny streets leading back to place d'Armes. This includes **la ruelle de la Blanchisserie** (Laundry Alley) which recalls the laundry that existed in the 17th century, and **la ruelle de l'Etoile** (Star Alley).

The alley entrance passes under a building reconstructed in original style after World War I when the whole of the north side of place d'Armes was destroyed. The south side of the square, likewise suffered bombing in World War II and was rebuilt as apartment buildings in the architectural style of the 18th century. The only site dating to the Middle Ages is that of the Dolphin Hotel (Hôtel du Dauphin), built in 1755 by the city of Douai, within which the tourist office is housed.

VALENCIENNES

Valenciennes is not true tourist territory in the accepted sense, more a bruiser of a town fighting back after a wartime battering and economic decline. Virtually rebuilt following the Nazi bombing in May 1940, it suffered a double whammy with the closure of its coalpits in the 1980s. Valenciennes responded by launching a 20-year regeneration plan, and is now boldly punching its way back into the 21st century.

What it lacks in historical charm is compensated for by a buzzy café culture where concrete-and-glass shopping malls and offices coexist with an arts museum matched only by the Louvre in Paris. The town's ambitious cultural policy has also

Valenciennes (*Valencjn* in Latin) is used to calamities. In AD881 it was invaded by the Vikings and in 1008 the plague brought famine to the town. But, so the story goes, on 7 September of that year the Virgin appeared to wind a red thread round the town and this kept out the devil. She later reappeared with a warning to the townsfolk: they must repeat the process annually around 8 September or the plague and starvation will return. And so they do, by walking the 14km road round the town in what is called the tour of the Holy Cordon.

created a theatre with national stage status, a multi-media library, a fine arts school and a music academy.

So is it worth a visit? Yes, if you enjoy big-city bustle where late-night ethnic and regional restaurants are two a penny, and silent eco-friendly trams are a powerful symbol of the town's dream of a more sustainable future. There are also 800 shops and one huge shopping centre on the main square. (Check your car's satnav is up-to-date or you could land up facing one of its walls.) This is a town in a hurry, where landmarks change overnight.

GETTING THERE AND AWAY

By car From Calais, take the A25 (Dunkirk–Lille) motorway then the A23 (Valenciennes–St-Amand–Bruxelles), and take exit 21 for Valenciennes city centre. The 162km journey should take one hour and 38 minutes.

By public transport The railway station (*Gare de Valenciennes, pl de la Gare;* ⊕ *06.00–19.45 Mon–Thu & Sat, 06.00–20.10 Fri, 07.45–20.40 Sun & public holidays*) is a five-minute walk from the city centre.

All ten bus routes (plus the tramway to Université du Mont Houy and Denain, Espace Villars) stop at the railway station. Buses also serve all the surrounding towns and villages from the station.

For further information: ✆ 03 27 14 52 52 or visit www.transvilles.fr.

TOURIST INFORMATION

🇪 **Office de Tourisme** Spanish Hse, 1 rue Askièvre; ✆ 03 27 28 89 10; e otdduvalenciennois@ wanadoo.fr; www.tourismevalenciennois.fr; ⊕ 14.00–18.00 Mon, 09.30–12.00 & 14.00–18.00 Tue–Sat, Sun & school summer holidays; also offices at The Belfry, 26 pl Pierre Delcourt; ⊕ 09.30–12.00 & 14.00–18.00 Tue–Sat, Sun & school summer

holidays; town hall ⊕ 09.30–12.00 & 14.00–18.00 Wed, 09.30–12.00 Sat, Sun & summer holidays. Offers city tours: historical guide to the city €1.50; self-guided audio-tour €7 or guided tour €10; tours with lecture/guide by arrangement. Seasonal discount offers are available. The office also rents bikes: adult/child: €10/5 full day & €7/3 half day.

WHERE TO STAY AND EAT

🏠 **Auberge au Bon Fermier** (16 rooms) 64 rue de Famars; ✆ 03 27 46 68 25; e beinethierry@ hotmail.com; www.bonfermier.com. Hold your horses here! The stagecoach spirit of this delightful inn is as great now as it must have been in the 16th century. Sit in the cobbled courtyard for a substantial 3-course regional meal of wild terrine with onion jam, farm-reared guinea fowl with cream, white beer & truffle with a homemade *tarte tatin* for dessert (€35.50). Don't worry if it rains – the

timber & red-brick walls of the restaurant provide a perfect setting for a special night out. Just avoid knocking over the full suit of gleaming armour on the way out! 10 out of 10 for showing that historic Valenciennes is still alive & kicking (**$$$**) Better still, stay overnight or on a w/end offer. The rooms, too, have that touch of historical magic. **$$$$**

🏠 **Grand Hotel** (95 rooms) 8 pl de la Gare; ✆ 03 27 46 32 01; e grandhotel.val@wanadoo.fr; www.grandhotel-de-valenciennes.fr. Comfortable,

Try *La Lucullus de Valenciennes*. Named after Lucullus Lucullus, a Roman general fond of his food, the delicacy made from smoked ox-tongue with *fois gras* in a flaky pastry was created to meet the demand for a luxury family meal. Nowadays the specialty can be tasted on a tour of **Les Foies Gras de Saulzoir** (*rue de Viel Escaut;* ☎ 03 27 49 49 10; e *lesfoiesgrasdesaulzoir@club-internet.fr; wwsw.clublucullus.fr;* ⊕ *08.00–12.00 & 14.00–18.00 Mon–Fri, 08.00–12.00 Sat;* €5), where the genial Regis Baroncini is at hand to help you pick a pâté or two.

traditionally furnished rooms, 10 of them en suite, have earned the hotel, facing the TGV railway station, a reliable reputation for an overnight stop. A substantial b/fast is €15. Parking costs €7 per night. The hotel's restaurant **Les 4 Saisons** offers a €39 Sun menu, €48 with wine, or a €30 3-course meal Mon–Sat; the brasserie with Alsace-style specialties has a 2-course menu at €14.90 ($$$). $$$$

🏠 **Hotel Notre Dame** (35 rooms) 1 pl de l'Abbé;

☎ 03 27 42 30 00; e hotel.notredame@ wanadoo.fr; www.hotel-valenciennes-notredame.com. Combining the charm of a former convent with the high-tech TV & business whims of today, this quirky, close-to-the-centre hotel with a private garden is a short-break winner. Look out for the room with the 19th-century stained-glass windows. Family-style rooms are another bonus. B/fast is €8, free for children under 6. $$$

✗ Where to eat cheaply

✗ **Le Kervegan** 7 pl des Wantiers; ☎ 03 27 45 98 47; ⊕ 11.45–14.00 & 19.00–22.00. Stop here for filling lunchtime Breton-style crêpes. $$

✗ **Au Chat qui lit** 16 sq Crasseau; ☎ 03 27 77 45; www.auchatquilit.fr; ⊕ 11.45–14.00 & 19.00–22.30, closed Sun, Mon evening & Wed. Dine out on crêpes, salads or soups. $$

SHOPPING Hone in on the **rue de Paris** area for homemade chocolates while the rue de la Paix and rue de Quesnoy are geared to regional goodies. The **rue du Famars**, in the still-quaint old part of town, is home to antique shops: **Galerie Philippe Kozak** (*90 rue de Famars;* ☎ *03 27 47 11 48;* e *galeriekozak@cegetal.net*) is worth a quick call. And when you're done, drop in for a coffee at the **Café Bar** (*23 rue de Famars*). Its tea salon is terrific.

Bookshops

Office de Tourisme Sells books about Valenciennes in its 3 outlets: Valenciennes, Condé-sur-Escaut & Sebourg.
FNAC Centre commercial, pl d'Armes; ☎ 08 25 02 00 20; ⊕ 10.00–19.30 Mon–Sat
L'Etiquette 6 rue Tholozé; ☎ 03 27 47 34 38;

⊕ 14.00–19.00 Mon, 09.00–12.15 & 19.00 Tue–Fri, 09.00–12.15 & 14.30–18.30 Sat; closed Jul–Aug
Le Furet du Nord 21 rue de Quesnoy; ☎ 03 27 20 13 90; ⊕ 09.30–19.00 Mon–Sat

OTHER PRACTICALITIES
Banks

$ **Le Crédit Lyonnais** 7 rue du Quesnoy; ☎ 08 20 82 30 25; ⊕ 09.00–12.30 & 14.00–18.00 Tue–Thu

$ **Crédit mutual** 2 rue de la poste; ☎ 08 20 35 22 07; ⊕ 08:30–12.15 & 13.30–17.00 Tue–Thu, 08.30–12.00 Sat

Supermarkets

Supermarché Match pl d'Armes; ☎ 03 27 29 04 04; ⊕ 08.30–20.00 Mon–Sat

Carrefour Market bld Harpignies; ☎ 03 27 20 37 77; ⊕ 08.30–20.00 Mon–Sat, 09.00–12:30 Sun

Internet cafés

e **Cyberbase à la bibliothèque (library) de Valenciennes** 2 rue Ferrand; ☎ 03 27 22 57 00; ⏰ 14.00–18.00 Tue & Thu, 10.00–12.00 & 14.00–18.30 Wed & Sat, 10.00–20.00 Fri. Booking is compulsory.

e **Cyber direct** 11 rue Ferrand; ☎ 03 27 43 06 56; ⏰ 10.00–19.00 Mon–Fri

Pharmacies

✚ **Pharmacie du Beffroi** 7 pl d'Armes; ☎ 03 27 46 23 08; ⏰ 08.30–19.30 Mon–Sat

✚ **Pharmacie de la Fontaine** 10 rue de Paris; ☎ 03 27 46 20 75; ⏰ 09.00–19.00 Mon–Sat

Post Office

✉ 2 place du Marché aux herbes; ☎ 08 99 70 14 31; ⏰ 09.00–18.30 & 09.00–12.30 Sat

Public toilets

Town Hall pl d'Armes; ☎ 03 27 22 59 00; ⏰ 08.00–12.30 & 13.30–17.30 Mon–Fri, 08.00–12.30 Sat

Office de Tourisme du Valenciennois Spanish House – see page 203 for opening hours

WHAT TO SEE AND DO It was not for nothing that Valenciennes was voted the Regional Capital of Culture in 2007; some call the city 'The Athens of the North' because of its interest in the arts and the number of artists born there. The painter Antoine Watteau (1684–1721) and the sculptor Jean-Baptiste (1827–75) were just two. Each have their work reflected in the **Musée des Beaux-Arts** (*bld Watteau;* ☎ *03 27 22 57 20;* e *mba@city-valenciennes.fr; www.valenciennes.fr;* ⏰ *10.00–18.00 daily except Tue; adult/child* €*3.90/1.95*). Renovated throughout, this impressive Palace of Fine Arts, comparable to the Louvre and covering an area of 4,400m², is home to an outstanding collection of 16th- and 17th-century Flemish paintings. Rubens's *Descent from the Cross* is here, admirably backed up by the works of Van Dyck, Jordaens Bosch and Bruegel.

However, it's the works of Watteau, their magic mixed with melancholy, that are the real crowd-pullers. The verdant trees, the courting couples and the sumptuous silks in some way reflect the sensuousness, as well as the extravagance, of the Court of Louis XIV at Versailles. Carpeux, too, gets a specific space for his paintings and sculptures. This opens with a special rotunda where the works of Lemaire, Hiolle, Crauk, Chapu and Degas form a delightful sculpture garden.

The archaeological crypt is given over to the history of the Hainaut region from Celtic times to the Middle Ages. This has been enriched by Gallo-Roman relics found in the bed of a monastery between 1999 and 2003.

But while the museum has more old masters than you can shake a palette at – attracting culture vultures and the merely curious alike – the town's artistic attractions don't end there. Valenciennes's creative spirit began in the 17th century with the wood and fabric trade. It was also known for its lace. Then, with the advent of the coal mines and other heavy industry, again came the need for workers skilled in the art of drawing, perspective, geometry and maths. Carpeux's own father was a skilled bricklayer who urged his son to become a stone-cutter. Others

8

YOUNG ARTISTS BRINGS NEW SKILLS

Typical of contemporary young artists are Geoffrey Guiot, a digital artist and 3D creator who studied in the city before setting up his own company that produces virtual reality for advertising and also for industry. The concept, he says, brings yet another dimension to the dynamism of Valenciennes.

were to follow suit in a region where industry and art maintain strong links. Sculptor Lucien Brasseur (1878–1960) made his living in Paris thanks to the support of the owner of a local steel works. Two of his works are in the museum.

Today, the town takes art to the people as much as its museum brings people to its art. Sculptures are everywhere; the town centre featured around 20 by 2009. Most striking of all is the glistening 44m-high stainless-steel needle that stands alongside the gabled charm of the main square. With its pavement cafés bursting with students and lunch-break businessmen, this is the sort of scene that makes this town tick.

Other Valenciennes sites worth a look-in include the church **belfry of St-Gery**, the 18th-century **Jesuit library and chapel** and the 1960s-built **Carmelite Chapel at St-Saulve** 2km northeast of town.

ST-AMAND-LES-EAUX

This mild-mannered town, though conveniently close to the big-city benefits of Metropolitan Lille and 15km from Valenciennes, is cloaked by green, courtesy of surrounding woodland and the Scarpe-Escaut Regional Nature Park. It's a great place for a day visit.

HISTORY The spa town derives its name from an evangelist monk, St Amandus, who built the original Elnone Abbey on marshy land where the Scarpe and Elnon rivers meet. This was to become one of the most respected abbeys in the north of France, before a much-rebuilt version was eventually destroyed during the French Revolution (see page 208). The waters, recognised since Roman times for their healing powers, were one of the first hot springs to be harnessed by Vauban, the great military engineer of the 17th century. This was carried out on the orders of Louis XIV to preserve their curative powers. In the 18th century, the town, then called St Amandus, was famed as a prosperous centre for pottery.

GETTING THERE AND AWAY
By car From Calais take the A16/E40 for the 154km journey taking one hour 40 minutes.

By train From the Eurostar service to Gare Lille Europe (see page 25), transfer to Gare Lille Flandres (the stations are within walking distance via an underground

---

DRIFTING ALONG WITH A SINGING TENT

Watch out for the floating pink tent drifting down river if you take the tourist train along the Valley of the Scarpe at festival time. It's not really a tent, but a skirt for the blonde singer sitting on stilts nearly 4m above the water. You can't fault her voice, which befits the all-singing, all-dancing group of actors that stroll on and off the train throughout the 45-minute trip. You'll meet her again on the way back, this time playing an accordion. It's surreal, and full of French fun with the actors joining in. Don't expect to understand a single word, though. They're talking – or singing – Ch'ti-mi (see page 12), the patois of this once-industrial region, which is as foreign to many French visitors as it is to those from overseas. Don't blame the guide if the stilt lady is missing. This is ad-libbing at its purist, and could be different but just as zany another time.

Scarpe Valley Tourist Train Train Touristique de la Valleé de la Scarpe; see tourist office for details; ⊕ May–Sep from 14.30 then hourly Sun; adult/child aged 5–12 €3/1.50 steam train & €2/1 for diesel.

No one can deny that the Lewarde Museum (see page 200) portrays the mining industry in a remarkable manner. But whereas it relies on modern high-tech interpretations, the **Arenberg Mines** (*Site Minier d'Arenberg, rue de Croy, Wallers;* ✆ *03 27 24 02 67;* ⏰ *09.00–11.00 Tue & Thu; adult/child €4/3*) is low key and benefits from being so. Though the mine closed in 1989, you feel as if the miners who show you around have just finished a shift. But then it did become one of the most famous film sets in France when, during 1992–93, Émile Zola's *Germinal*, starring movie legend Gérard Depardieu, was shot here. Location shots hang proudly alongside mining paraphernalia; one miner is even pictured with the actor.

The smell of coal still seems to hang heavy here. The clanking of the metal steps, as you hang on tight to the railings round the pithead, resonates with the grittiness around you. There is one hands-on exhibit, a heavy coal-filled truck that you are invited to push – don't put your back out, it's far from easy.

passage) and take the TER train to St Amand-les-Eaux. If you arrive by ferry from Dover take the TGV train from Calais-Ville Station; you will have to change at Lille.

St Amand-les-Eaux railway station is a ten-minute walk from the city centre or ten minutes by AMD bus.

TOURIST INFORMATION
🛈 **La Porte du Hainaut Office de Tourisme** 89 Grand'Place; ✆ 03 27 48 39 65; www.tourisme-portedhainaut.fr; ⏰ 10.00–12.00 & 14.00–17.00 Mon, 10.00–12.00 & 14.00–18.00 Tue–Sat, 10.00–12.30 Sun

WHERE TO STAY
🏠 **Hotel de Pasino** (60 rooms) bypass 79; ✆ 03 27 48 19 00; www.pasino-saintamand.com. Try your luck at blackjack, take in a show or dine in one of the ethnic restaurants. The Pasino is open 10.00–04.00, but the air-conditioned rooms are quiet & well equipped in contemporary styles. $$$$

🏠 **Le Spartiate** 1 rue des Choret, Bruille St Amand; ✆ 006 24 03 04 42; www.le-spartiate.abcsalles.com. This hotel-cum-meeting-&-seminar-venue relies on cutting-edge technology as much as wood-burning stoves to fire its role as a 21st-century eco-friendly establishment. It is unashamedly open plan, with giant windows looking out over the Forest of St Amand-les-Eaux. Located 6km from the town itself, its 4 all-wood *gîtes* each sleeping 4 are geared to families. There is a large terrace, swimming pool & plenty of parking spaces. The Leroys, who developed the concept, can arrange tours from following in the footsteps of wild boars to discovering & cooking with plants. They also arrange cookery courses. $$$$

WHERE TO EAT AND DRINK
✖ **La Grignotière** 6 rue Jean Jaurès, Raismes – 9km from St Amand-les-Eaux via D169/169A; ✆ 03 27 36 91 99; ⏰ 12.00–14.00 Tue, Thu & Sun, 12.00–14.00 & 19.00–22.00 Fri & Sat; ✉ lagrignotiere@free.fr; www.lagrignotiere.fr. Favourable reviews have been given to this gastronomic restaurant. Average cost pp €50+. $$$$$

✖ **Restaurant au Chaudron De Celine** 29 rue Henri Lasts, Bellaing – 12km from St Amand-les-Eaux via D169a/A23; ✆ 03 27 40 41 59; ⏰ 12.00–14.00 Tue–Thu & Sun, 12.00–14.00 & 19.00–22.00 Fri & Sat. Country-kitchen-style menus are the forte of this restaurant; it is, after all, the heart of a working farm. Set menus €25–60. $$$$

WHAT TO SEE AND DO Dominating the main square is the 17th-century **Abbey Tower** (⏰ *10.30 & 15.00 Wed & Sat for 90-min tour; adult/child €5/2.50, under 12 free*), impressive for its Baroque-style architecture. A huge piece of sculpture carved in white stone from the Avesnes-le-Sec quarries, it's currently undergoing a massive €45 million restoration, which is due for completion in 2012. The work has helped

St Amand-les-Eaux is a town of festivals. Time it right and you can take part in the end of June/early July Water Festival. This is the time to make whoopee either in, or around, the inland harbour basin serving the canalised River Scarpe.

Alternatively take a spin down the river on the good ship *Eureka* (*2 Chemin du Halage, Valenciennes;* \ *03 27 25 34 57;* e *contact@eureka-tfg.com; www.eureka-tfg.com;* ⊕ *from €50 for cruise inclusive of choice from traditional menus*). Captain and English-speaking owner David Guermonprez is a genial host, whose 'Allo, à l'eau' line on his brochure shows time spent in Sheffield, England, including watching the all-time favourite British comedy. Exploratory cruises feature stops at Cambrai (see page 181).

Eureka also calls at the **Choulette Brewery** (*La Choulette, 16 rue des écoles, Hordain;* \ *03 27 35 72 44; www.lachoulette.com;* ⊕ *08.30–12.00 & 14.00–18.00 Mon–Fri; advance booking required for 30-min tour; adult/child €10/5*). One survivor of the 300 or so breweries once established in the Valenciennes area, the name derives from the ancient game of *choulette*.

Back in town the **Sources Brewery** (*Brasserie des Sources, 2 ave du college;* \ *03 27 48 777 71; www.brasseriedesaintamand.fr;* ⊕*09.00–12.00; adult/child €5/2*) features speciality beers such as Germinal, based on the Émile Zola novel of the same name, and Raoul, brewed to celebrate a local dialect singer, Raoul de Godewaersvelde.

The surrounding area includes **The Forest Centre** (*Le Maison de la Fôret, Etoile de la Princess, Raismes;* \ *03 27 36 72 72; www.pnr-scarpe-escaut.fr;* ⊕ *Apr–Nov 14.30–18.30 Sun, 13.00–18.00 Wed, in school holidays 14.00–18.00 Sun–Fri, closed Sat; adult/child €2/1*). Call in here or at the tourist office for advice on walking, horseriding and mountain bike trails in the surrounding 4,600ha forest.

peel away the architectural history of this splendidly ornate symbol of town power.

The tower and the priory are the sole survivors of a tremendous Benedictine abbey. Founded in AD633, the abbey was rebuilt between 1626 and 1640 on such a scale that two passing monks claimed: 'The outside looks more like a palace than a monastery.' Old prints show the jaw-dropping enormity of the abbey estate before it was destroyed in 1791 during the French Revolution. Look carefully at some of the town houses and you'll see they have been part-built from the abbey's ruins, which in effect became one large builders' yard.

If tours of the works are not possible then the **Abbey Tower Museum** (⊕ *14.00–17.00 Mon & Wed–Fri, 10.00–12.30 & 15.00–18.00 Sat–Sun & public holidays; admission €2*) has a fine collection of glazed earthenware from the 18th century when the town's thriving economy was built on its pottery. Chinese porcelain was the forte of the huge Fauquez factory.

If you miss both, you'll certainly notice the carillon of 48 bells. These ring daily between 12.00 and 12.30, and additionally in summer from 17.00 to 18.00 on Saturdays and 18.00 to 19.00 on Sundays.

If all else fails relax at the **Thermes** (*1303 route de la Fontaine Bouillon;* \ *03 27 48 25 00; www.chainethermale.fr;* ⊕ *Mar–Nov 09.00–12.00 & 14.00–18.00; €49 for a day package, €120 for w/end or €480 6-day B&B & fitness course*). Recognised since Roman times, the hot springs were first harnessed by Vauban (see page 12). Today they centre on the edge of a forest; the complex offers bubbling baths, hydro massage and a handful of other respiratory and rheumatology treatments.

If all this lying around makes you thirsty you can always buy a bottle of the local liquid. The **Mineral Water Company of Saint-Amand-les-Eaux** (*www.saint-amand.com*) has its origins in four local sources, providing an annual production of 350 million bottles.

9

Rural Avesnois

This is the green face of Le Nord. It was not always so; this is a region with an industrial history, where 18th- and 19th-century water mills powered spinning wheels, and bellows breathed life into specialist glass and ironworks. By the end of the 19th century, the Avesnois workshops had closed and heavy-duty factories, fuelled by the burgeoning coalfields around Lille and Lens, were churning out cheaper mass-market goods.

It's all changed now. The factories are long gone and today this is a place for individual exploration by car, bicycle, boat, on horseback or even from the air. Hotels, *gîtes* and B&Bs help define the diversity by their individuality and settings.

The region links in nicely with a visit to Le Cateau-Cambrésis, 20km, or a 30-minute drive, away from the Avesnois border. It is a similar distance from Valenciennes, which is why this chapter includes a number of highly individual rural B&Bs and hotels that lie conveniently between the city and the Avesnois. This perfect combination of town and country does not end here: motorways and other major roads serving the region's major cities quickly funnel traffic close to the green toe of Nord-Pas de Calais. Getting here, then, is easy, while the Avesnois itself stays relatively traffic-free.

VALENCIENNES TO LE QUESNOY

Lying on the surprisingly rural outskirts of Valenciennes (see pages 202) are a scattering of villages. These offer accommodation ideally suited to those seeking a base from which to tour the Avenois or combine it with visits to such tourist cities as Cambrai, Douai and even Lille. They are equally as attractive for those who prefer the on-the-doorstep advantages of Le Quesnoy or Valenciennes for eating out or shopping. Hiking and horseriding are among activities featured locally.

 WHERE TO STAY

⌂ **Hotel La Gentilhommière** (10 rooms) 2 rue de l'Eglise, Artres; ↘ 03 27 28 18 80; e la.gentilhommiere@wanadoo.fr; www.hotel-lagentilhommiere.com. This former 18th-century farmhouse, with extensive rose beds, offers a country house retreat located between Valenciennes & Le Quesnoy. The rooms have that nicely draped luxury look along with all the hi-tech trimmings. $$$$

⌂ **La Rose Latiére** (2 rooms) 59213 St-Martin-Sur-Ecaillon; ↘ 03 27 29 97 85; e contact@laroselatiere.fr; www.laroselatiere.fr. There's a storybook quality to this lovingly restored 18th-century farmhouse, with its bags of red-brick arches,

delightfully terraced gardens & pots of flowers on the windowsills. Cows, chickens & a tree-lined pond add to the sense of pastoral peace. So, too, does the valley setting. Bedrooms & the dining room reflect the soft rustic approach. Tours of the farm, bike rental (€6) & the closeness of Le Quesnoy, 15mins, Valenciennes, 20mins, & Cambrai, 30mins, make it a suitable town & country setting for families. $$$

⌂ **Domaine de la Frênaie** (4 rooms) 27 rue de la Liberté, Estreux; ↘ 03 27 42 91 19; www.lafrenaie.fr or www.gites-de-france-nord.fr. Perhaps it's the overall charm of the place, or simply the cosiness of the cottages with their

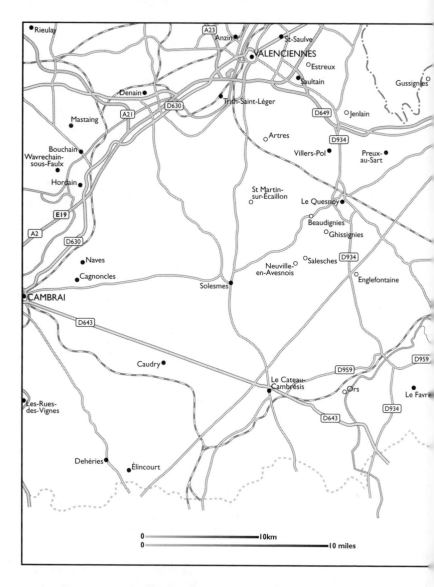

easy-on-the-eye creamy brown décor, but this B&B wins hands down for its homeliness. B/fast, served in the fiery colours of the dining-rooms, is a daily bonus. A large wooded park, complete with waterfall, a tennis court & seasonally heated swimming pool complete the picture. Valenciennes is 10km away; Le Quesnoy 13 km. HB is also available. $$$

LE QUESNOY

Take time to explore Nord-Pas de Calais's most extensive walled town. Le Quesnoy's perfectly preserved fortifications of coarse stone, flint and lime mortar covered with bricks quickly win you over. A stroll, or a two- to three-hour guided tour, helps slot the history into place. It has particular significance for New

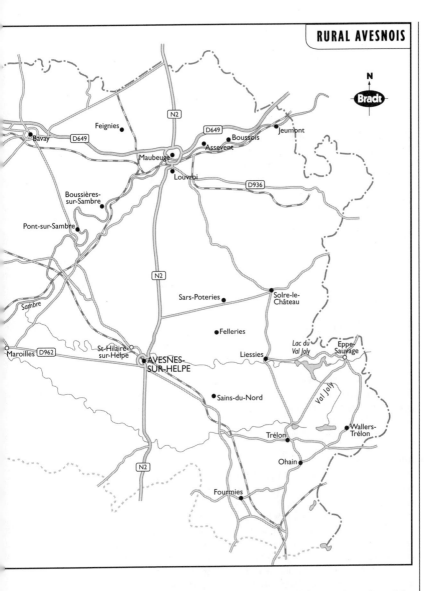

N

Bradt

Zealanders: it was here in 1918 that a plucky band of Kiwi soldiers took on the might of the Germans in a raid of considerable derring-do – and won (see page 213).

HISTORY Le Quesnoy (pronounce it 'kenwaw' and you'll get by) is thought to have derived from the Latin *quercitum*, meaning an area covered with oak. Forests gave way to agricultural land and, in the 12th century, the Earls of Hainaut chose to build their castle here. From then on it became more heavily fortified, growing considerably in stature. In the 15th century it was captured by Louis XI during the land squabbles between the Valois and Burgundians, and became a stronghold of Chares Quint (Charles V) in 1536, only to fall to the French under Louis XIV in 1654. Captured and recaptured during the late 17th century European wars, the town later became victim of the upheavals caused by the French Revolution.

The 19th-century arrival of the railways on the Valenciennes line brought new prosperity, but by World War I it was once more in the thick of things, and occupied by the Germans after a harsh battle near Mormal Forest. Its liberation by New Zealand forces remains the stuff of legend (see opposite). It was reoccupied by the Germans in World War II. Interestingly, it was a popular weekend retreat between the two wars.

GETTING THERE AND AWAY

By car From Calais take the A16 in the Dunkirk direction then the A25/E42 towards Lille before joining the A23 to Valenciennes and the junction for Le Quesnoy. There are no toll charges. Alternatively take the A26/E15 towards Reims to join the A21 to Lens then the A2 to Valeciennes for the junction to Le Quesnoy. There is a €7.20 toll both ways on the A26.

By train Although there is a way of getting there from Calais involving changes, it is rather convoluted and takes nearly four hours. It is far wiser, therefore, to take the Eurostar service to Gare Lille Europe and from there go to the regional Gare Lille Flandres (within walking distance via an underground passage) for a direct train via Valenciennes to Le Quesnoy using line 16 or 17. The journey takes two hours 12 minutes.

GETTING AROUND There is no bus network within the Avesnois region except for the Arc en Ciel school buses which operate during the week. You can buy ten tickets for €8 on board or at the railway station.

TOURIST INFORMATION

🛈 **Office de Tourisme du Quesnoy** I rue Maréchal Joffre; ☏ 03 27 20 54 70; e otsi.le.quesnoy@ wanadoo.fr; www.tourisme.fr/office-de-tourisme/le-quesnoy; ⏲ Oct–Apr 09.00–12.00 & 14.00–17.00 Mon–Fri, Jun–Sep 09.00–12.00 & 14.00–18.00 Tue–Fri, 09.00–12.00 & 15.00–18.00 Sun & public holidays

WHERE TO STAY

🏠 **Auberge du Bracmar** (4 rooms) 284 rue du Bracmar Amfroipret; ☏ 03 27 66 38 82; www.gites-de-france-nord.fr. Take a friendly farming family, 4 rustic-style cottages & a converted barn for b/fast & dinner & you have this highly rural, but remote, B&B property in a nutshell. The children will love exploring the farmhouse trappings, from the stables where the donkey once worked to the site of the dairy. Le Quesnoy is 9km away, Valenciennes 20km. Farmhouse dinner (€22) is available on request. Suitable for the disabled. $$$

🏠 **Petit Comte/La Petite Couronne** (2 rooms) 3 rue de la Couronne; ☏ 03 27 41 36 36; e Mariannik.ledinwantellet@9online.fr or lamaisondupetitcomte@gmail.com. Quietly tucked away from the town centre, this comprises a small B&B with a dbl bed & *gîte* with 2 rooms, I with a dbl bed, the other with twin beds. It provides an attractive stopover for exploring the surrounding countryside. $$

✘ WHERE TO EAT

✘ **La Brumaudière** 3 route de Le Quesnoy, Locquignol; ☏ 03 27 44 53 39; www.la-brumaudiere.com; ⏲ 12.00–22.00, closed on Mon. Located in the centre of Locquignol, 8km from Le Quesnoy via the D934/33, the restaurant is in the former 19th-century home of a shepherdess. It offers beamed ceilings, a large fireplace & a healthy slice of local fare. The €15 menu includes Flemish leek & Maroilles, the famous cheese made in Maroilles (see page 216), home-made *potjevlesch* (3 white meats in aspic) & a cream waffle. $$$

Le Quesnoy is also home to the **New Zealand Memorial**, possibly one of the most underrated of World War I in terms of importance. There is no huge monument, only a modest plaque that reminds us just how much the town owes its liberation from the Germans to a plucky band of Kiwis.

Refusing to use artillery, due to potential casualties among the 1,500-strong population, the New Zealand Division based a few miles away launched instead an astonishing surprise attack a week before the Armistice in November 1918. On 4 November at 05.30, using heavy mortar fire and smoke from burning oil drums as cover, a few soldiers from the 4th Battalion 3rd Rifle Brigade planned to scale the ramparts by propping up a ladder. This proved too short for the first location so they used a narrow stone wall which crossed the moat instead.

At the same time Captain Napier, a mortar expert, bombed the top of the walls and by 16.00 that day astonished German soldiers faced an onslaught of rampart-scaling soldiers. After strong resistance, during which the New Zealand Division suffered 400 casualties – of which 93 were killed in action – the 1,500 Germans surrendered.

Sixty-five of those that died are buried in Le Quesnoy. Not one of the 55,000 French residents lost their life. Though the population is now less than 5,000, its gratitude to its Kiwi liberators is as strong as ever.

WHAT TO SEE AND DO While the star-shaped defences and floodable moats surrounding the town recall the brilliant 17th-century military engineering of Vauban (see page 12), the formidable bastions and projecting towers of **Le Quesnoy Castle** date back to the rule of the 16th-century Spanish Emperor Charles V (Charles Quint). The castle grounds present a variety of gardening trends, while the ramparts provide stunning views and sufficient ducking and diving in dank dungeon-like ruins to interest the children. But do take care: there are some nerve-racking drops.

The **town centre** has its own architectural charm. The *Terroir 'en Poche* (part of a superb €3 pocket guide series, some in French only, and available from tourist offices or bookshops) will guide you round the more intriguing parts. These include rue Thiers which since 2004 has borne the name of Adrian Macey, the New Zealand ambassador to France, in recognition of the bravery of the Kiwis in World War I. Number 15, Maison Quercitaine de Nouvelle-Zélande, the town's exhibition hall, regularly hosts renowned artists.

One antipodean link you can't fail to notice is **Teko Teko**, the town's Maori giant with his tongue sticking out. Given to the town in 1972 by the New Zealand Rifle Brigade, he wins pride of place next to Pierre Bimberlot, the town's tradtional wicker giant near the town hall. The partnership with the New Zealand town of Cambridge is also marked at **Le Quesnoy railway station** – located on the other side of the arrival platform is a station sign translated into Maori.

End off a visit to the town with a stroll round the lush, lake filled parkland outside the city gates; alternatively head for a picnic lunch in the nearby 9,000ha **Mormal Forest** whose rich agricultural potential was a major factor in the town's economic development. The forest's name stems from a battle that took place around 700BC called Mors Malorum (Death of the Bad). Oaks were planted for the men and beeches for the women, who lost their lives in this ferocious battle.

Rural Avesnois LE QUESNOY

9

The spiderweb of villages surrounding Le Quesnoy include **Beaudignies**, reached via the D942, where a farm was used as a supply base for the New Zealand forces, **Salesches**, known for St-Quinibert Church whose porch was once a defence tower, and **Neuville en Avesnois**, famed for its 14th-century fortified church.

ENGLEFONTAINE At **Englefontaine** (7km from Le Quesnoy, via the D934) turn off for the village itself and walk to St-George's fountain. Legend has it that the horse of the English saint discovered the source by stamping on the ground.

Where to stay

7 Rue des Tuileries Englefontaine; 03 27 28 35 19; www.gites-de-france.com & key in Englefontaine for the property details. Don't be deceived by the roadside location. This red-brick *gîte* has 3 large bedrooms; once the gardener's house, it adjoins the owners' 19th-century vine-covered property, & it feels as though it's deep in the country, not 500m from the town centre. Horses clatter in the old stables where Corinne Simon, joint owner with her husband, also has her own pottery workshop. Relax with a drink in the acacia & lime shaded courtyard, or chat with the family. You may even be greeted with a large bunch of flowers by the Simons' young daughter. Full range of facilities include TV, microwave & internet access. $$$

BAVAY Around 15km from Englefontaine, and a similar distance from Le Quesnoy, Bavay is the largest Gallo-Roman archaeological site north of the Loire.

Tourist information

Bavay Office of Tourism rue Saint-Maur; 03 27 39 81 65; e ot-bavaisis@wanadoo.fr; www.bavay.com; 08.30–12.30 & 13.30–17.30 Mon–Fri, closed w/ends

Where to stay

Chateau den Haut (5 rooms) 20 route Nationale, Jenlain; 03 27 4971 80; e chateaudenhaut@free.fr; www.chateaudenhaut.free.fr. One of the *foillies* built by nobility, this elegant, mostly late-18th-century manor offers large, tastefully furnished theme rooms with many personal touches in the way of antiques. It is located in wooded grounds some 15km from Bavay & 13km from Le Quesnoy. $$$

A STORY WORTH CHEWING OVER

Following the Battle of Waterloo in 1815, local farmers tending a wounded veteran of Napoleon's fleeing army noticed he still had most of his teeth. Questioned closely, he pulled out a packet of caramels. These were made, he claimed, by wives desperate to woo soldiers away from the habit of chewing teeth-rotting tobacco. This was used to try to rid themselves of the taste of rotting lead swallowed while ripping open gun powder bags.

A form of Chiques de Bavay, as the sweets became known, was taken up much later by Favier-Fortin to produce a similar peppermint-flavoured sweet. In 1922 it was registered as the Chiggers Bavay.

Even so, if it had not been for Christian Kamet, who after a long lapse resumed production in 1993, the famous sweet could have been chewed for the last time. Now the caramels, under the trademark 'chewing Bavay' have acquired a regional reputation. You can see and taste for yourself at Kamet's shop **La Romaine** (*30 pl Charles-de-Gaulle;* 03 27 63 10 06; e leschiques@france.com; 10.00–19.00 daily; 50-min tours by arrangment €2).

The sleepy village square at Gussignies, 7km from Bavay via the D24, is scarcely the sort of place to find a spa centre. But if you want to tie in B&B with the benefits of essential oils, a jacuzzi, steam bath and sauna then the **La Grange au Corps** (7–9 la Place; ☎ 03 27 66 99 59; e info@diffusion-exclusive.com; www.info@diffusion-exclusive.com) offers an alternative approach to healthy holidaying.

If you simply want a slice of serenity in this pastoral setting opt for **Koan Lodge** and its Asian-inspired décor with multi-coloured bedrooms. Alongside the calming influence of the floral screens and futons is a terrace overlooking a Japanese garden. Another lodge, **L'ilot Kazakhe**, reflects Kazakhstan-born Arina Platteau's deep love for his country. Having removed their sandals or shoes, guests are treated to his childhood memories both through the furnishings and personal items on display. The kitchen, very close in nature to that of his grandparents, is given over to casseroles, vegetables, pasta, poultry and meat ingredients cooked slowly to bring out the flavour of Kazakh cooking.

Both lodges offer one to four night formulas, based on outdoor activities from walking to golf, as well as aqua and other treatments. Though geared towards a more specialist healthy-living market, its very existence speaks volumes for the scope of holiday options in this rural region ($$$ to $$$$ depending on length of stay and use of facilities).

What to see and do Don't be too surprised if you're greeted in Bavay by a fierce battle being conducted in full warrior dress. The combatants will be a bunch of schoolchildren enthusiastically engaging in a noisy set-to between the Gauls and Romans in the courtyard of the **Archaeological Museum** (*Musee d'Archeologie, 2 rue des Gommeries;* ☎ *03 27 63 13 95;* e *museebavay@cg59.fr; www.musenor.com;* ☉ *Apr–Sep 09.00–18.00, closed Tue, Oct–Mar 09.00–12.00 & 14.00–17.30 Mon–Fri, 10.30–12.30 & 14.00–18.00 Sat–Sun; adult/child €4.5/3 & €2 for 1½hr guided tour. English speaker on advance request*). Now owned by Le Nord *département*, as opposed to the French state, the archaeological site on which the museum stands is currently undergoing a massive €2 million restoration. Centre-piece will be the renovation and landscaping of the forum which, covering nearly 2.5ha, is the largest of its kind north of Rome. Its basilica is considered one of the three largest in the Roman Empire, ranking alongside Carthage and Ostia.

Ironically it was only when Bavay was bombed in World War II that attention was drawn to what for centuries had been recognised as a pretty well preserved site, but nothing much else. The extensive excavations that followed revealed its true worth. A wander around the forum, including the underground portico, gives a startling sense of the monumental size of the buildings.

The museum itself contains collections of bronze, pottery and glassware that contributed to life in what was then Bagatum; at the time of Caesar Augustus, this was an important centre in Roman Belgium. Traces of ruts, formed by carts using the still-recognisable network of Roman military roads, can be seen in the forum.

GUSSIGNIES A 7km drive from Bavay along the D24 is **Gussignies** and the red-bricked micro-brewery **Au Baron** (*pl du Fond des Rocs;* ☎ *03 27 66 88 61;* e *aubaron&nord.net.fr;* ☉ *08.00–12.00 & 14.00–16.30 Mon–Thu, 08.00–12.00 Fri*). Relax on the riverside terrace, sip a local St-Medard beer from the brewery (€6.50), or stop for lunch at the tavern (☉ *mid-Jun–mid-Sep 11.00 daily, off-season Fri–Sun;* $$), which does a great *planche* – a sort of ploughman's lunch of assorted specialities – for €10.50.

MAROILLES If you have not heard the name of the famous cheese within a few hours of arrival in cross-Channel France we will be a little surprised. This powerful symbol of Nord-Pas de Calais crops up everywhere. The joke goes it is even eaten at breakfast, and, heaven help us, dipped in coffee! (The author confesses that he has actually eaten it in one form or another at every meal.) 'Evil to him who, without Maroilles, claims to hold fair table,' is the motto of the Brotherhood of Maroilles created in 1983. Maroilles has three cousins: The Dolphin, so-called because of its shape, the conical La Boulette Avesnes and the Le Vieux-Lille (Old Lille), also called Maroilles gray.

This is no factory-produced cheese (see below); it is lovingly nurtured in the quiet rural village where the only real noise comes from the watermill, and the main activity is fishing amid the surrounding lakes and meadows.

What to see and do You could call it Maroilles's magical garden. Created in 1994 from Avesnois pastureland by Sylvie Fontaine is **Le Jardin de Sylvie Fontaine** *(12 pl Verte; ⟍ 03 27 77 17 54; www.lejardindesylviefontaine.fr; ⊕ pre-booked guided 1½hr tour 10.00 Sat–Sun from Mar to autumn, with dates dependent on weather; adult/child aged 3–12 €7.50/4; tea & coffee by reservation €2.50).* The 1ha organic plot produces a dazzling display of summertime blooms and a parkland brimming with many rare trees and shrubs.

Take time to chat to this delightful lady. A doctor for 15 years, she turned her passion for plants and floral art into an educational centre for children as well as becoming known as a landscape gardener and writer. You can't miss her: she will be wearing wellie boots and a floppy cotton hat and will be accompanied by her dog and a flock of multi-coloured chickens.

A second Maroilles garden is **Le Courtil Saint Roch** *(35 Grande-Rue; ⟍ 03 27 77 13 54; e dominique.hiubert18@wandaoo.fr; www.parcsetjardins-npdc.fr; ⊕ mid-Apr– mid-Oct 10.00–12.00 & 14.00–19.00; adult/child under 12 €5/free; guided tours available).*

THE TRUE SMELL OF SUCCESS

OK, so it pongs. But, unlike its softer Gallic counterparts, Maroilles, *the* cheese of Nord-Pas de Calais, has great texture, with a rich brown-red rind reinforcing a distinctive tangy taste. The perfecting of the cheese goes back 800 years to when the Abbey of Maroilles collected cheese instead of dues from local peasants.

Now only a handful of actual farms produce the subtle square cheeses, including **Ferme du Pont des Loups** *(Farm of the Bridge of the Wolves, 2 rue du Pont des Loups; ⟍ 03 27 57 84 09; e fermedupontdesloups@orange.fr; ⊕ 09.30–12.00 & 14.00–18.00 daily; €3 tours by arrangement).* This is run by the Gravez family, a third generation of farmers at Saint Aubin, close to Maroilles, and produces 60 tons of cheese annually. Thanks to its herd of 150 black-and-white Holsteiner cows, a ready supply of rich milk goes into making Maroilles – one of only 22 cheeses that can carry the official French quality control slogan *appellation d'origine contrôlée.*

It's not just the lush pastureland that helps provide the wow factor, it's the special Gravez cattle feed resembling a fruit cake mixture. Not for nothing has the Maroilles aroma been described as suggesting fermenting fruit and the flavour of smoky bacon.

The taste, however, comes not from the cheese but from the rind which, washed daily in a saline solution, takes around three months to mature from yellow to the familiar browny red. It is then sold in the farm shop or to the likes of Philippe Olivier's famous cheese store in Boulogne. A unique smell of success in every sense.

The garden, set in the grounds of a 19th-century family home, recaptures the spirit of free garden planting. Trees, roses, shrubs and perennials prevail. Sit down and admire the scenery.

AROUND MAROILLES The tiny village of **Saint Hilaire sur Helpe**, 11km west of Maroilles off the D962, provides an ideal overnight stop or even a base for the Avesnois region generally.

Where to stay

La Grange de Saint Hilaire (5 rooms) 8 route d'Aulnoye, St-Hilaire-sur-Helpe; 03 27 57 07 15; e luc.vancompemolle@wanadoo.fr; www.grange.saint. hilaire.free.fr. You'd be hard pushed not to find this remarkable one-off treasure hidden away in the depths of the country. Just look for the blue porchway to this splendid Scandinavian-style chalet, an unassuming entrance to a wondrous world of timbered stairways & shelves choc-a-bloc with knick-knacks of all kinds. These include ornaments, garlands of dried flowers, jars of spices & old tin cans. It's a jolly place, full of warmth & charm & big, comfortable beds. B/fast is a big-time booster for an active day out on a rental bike, horseriding or exploring the area in a horse-drawn open carriage. It has now opened a tearoom serving homemade pastries. $$$

AVESNOIS'S SOUTHERN TOE From Saint Hilaire sur Helpe return to the D962 and to **Avesnes-sur-Helpe**. The Grand'Place is worth a look for its old houses with high slated roofs and the 60m belfry porch of **St-Nicolas**, built in 1534, is a local landmark.

To the increasingly wooded south lie four museums featured by **Écomusée de l'Avesnois** (*pl Maria Blondeau, Fourmies;* 03 27 60 66 11; e *contact@ecomusee-avesnois.fr; www.ecomusee-avesnois.fr*). This is basically the name for an umbrella organisation which in the 1970s set out to save textile machines built between 1880 and 1930 from destruction.

The first museum, **Maison du Bocage** (⊕ *Apr–Oct 14.00–18.00 Mon–Fri, 14.30–18.30 Sat–Sun & public holidays; adult/child €5/3.50, free for children under 8*), is located in a late 19th-century farm at Sains-du-Nord, 8km from Avesnes-sur-Helpe via the D951. It is devoted mainly to agriculture and, inevitably, the secrets of making Maroilles cheese. It includes a blacksmith's shop. There is also an orchard, with a tasting of fruit juices, and beer.

The second museum, 11km away via the D951/D42, is at **Fourmies**, tucked away in the deeply rural southern toe of the Avesnois. The **Museum of Textile and Workaday Life** (*Museé du Textile et de la Vie Sociale;* 03 27 60 66 11 *for guided tour in English;* ⊕ *early Feb–mid-Dec 09.00–12.00 & 14.00–18.00 Mon–Sat, 14.30–18.30 Sat–Sun & public holidays; adult/child €5.5.50/3, free under 8*) is housed in an old spinnery which was in use from 1874 to 1978. The museum traces the manufacture of yarn making; a visit ends with a trip along a typical 19th-century cobbled street with a bakery, school, pub and a haberdashery.

Wend your way 9km from Fourmies via the D20/963 through the forested countryside to **Trélon**, where interest centres round the **Studio Glass Museum** (*Museé du Verre;* 03 27 59 71 02; ⊕ *Apr–Oct 09.00–12.00 & 14.00–18.00 Mon–Fri, 14.30–18.30 Sat–Sun & public holidays; adult/child €5.50/3, free for children under 8*). Watching the glassblowers at work is what makes this museum worthwhile. If you're keen and your French is up to scratch, there is an introductory course to the art.

But this is not the end of the story. The museum forms part of an old 19th-century glassworks that took 15 years to convert to **The Green Bowl** (*Centre Bol Vert, rue Clavon;* 03 27 60 84 84; e *contact@bolvert.com; www.bolvert.com*). Here, you can eat or play at what is basically a top-notch heritage centre celebrating its comeback from industrial decline. With a swimming pool, archery and horseriding easily to hand, the 3ha woodland setting is a boon for those with a family. The 40-seater **La Poterie** serves a good regional lunch ($$$). It's possible to sleep there too, in apartments and *gîtes* (see page 36). The original blue stones, ceilings, brick arches, beams and pulleys complete an air of authenticity.

Where to stay

Hotel des Verriers (10 rooms) 28 rue Clavon Collignon, Trélon; ☎ 03 27 60 84 84; e contact@bolvert.com; www.bolvert.com. The 'Hotel of Glass' in English, this was once the owner's home — and it looks like it. The floral lounge greets you with Art Nouveau wooden panelling & painted ceramics, while sculptures adorn the fireplace in the Salon Cariatides. A €4 b/fast is served in the traditional kitchen. A pleasant blend of old & new, the hotel, fully accessible to those with reduced mobility, makes a handy base for the south of the region. $$$

Les Jolis Prés (3 sgl rooms & 2 suites) 7 rue de l'Alouette, Ohain, 3km from Trélon; ☎ 03 27 59 02

42; www.lesjolispres.com. Deeply devoted to the environment, without being too earnest, this is a B&B where walks take on a sense of exploration & family fun. One activity takes visitors on a 6km walk that includes Ohain village, the orchards, woods & forest; they then listen to tales at the Abbey Liessies & the watermill setting for the Musée des Bois Jolis at Felleries (see page 219). Another takes a look at local flora & fauna. Meals are jolly affairs around a communal table, suited to hungry kids & with a great French flavour. The barn-converted bedrooms include 1 adapted for the disabled. Special €150 inclusive w/end & other deals are available. $$–$$$.

VALJOLY

ValJoly is not a town. It is not even a region, but a mega resort a few kilometres away from the Belgian border. The entrance is on the D133 via Eppe-Sauvage.

The setting is undeniably stunning. Lying on the shores of a 189ha lake which, in turn, nestles in 411ha of wooded landscape, this is rural Avesnois at its most bounteous. If you like an embracing family resort, this is the place for you. If not, cherry-pick from the vast year-round facilities, which now include restaurants, a pedestrian shopping mall, an indoor–outdoor water activities park, and an acrobatic circuit through the trees.

Horseriding, with great lakeside hacking, sailing, canoeing, cycling and hiking can be added to birdwatching and fishing as activities. Aquatica is a 300m² water park with a series of pools and also masssaging showers, a sauna and a jacuzzi; swimming and gym classes are available. A team from Maison des Enfants take care of toddlers from one to five years old.

Additionally, a number of creative and and environmental courses are held — the use of wild flowers in cooking was in progress when we visited.

TOURIST INFORMATION

Station Touristique du ValJoly Maison de Valjoly, Eppe Sauvage; e valjolyresa@valjoly.com; www.valjoly.com; ⏰ Jan–Mar & Nov–Dec 09.00–12.00 & 14.00–18.00 Mon–Thu, 09.00–12.00 & 14.00–19.00 Fri–Sun, Jul–Aug 09.00–19.00

Mon–Thu, 09.00–20.00 Fri–Sun, Apr–Jun & Sept–Oct 09.00–12.00 & 14.00–18.00 Mon–Thu, 09.00–12.00 & 14.00–19.00 Fri, 09.00–20.00 Sat–Sun & public holidays. A PassJoly costs €1.50–17.80 depending on season & facilities used.

 WHERE TO STAY AND EAT There are 180 **woodland cottages** that sleep two to eight people; the longer the stay the greater the access to facilities ($$$). Check on **self-catering supplements** such as €6 breakfast delivery. There is also a 30-chalet village with access to campsite facilities and group lodgings ($$).

If you don't want to stay in the ValJoly complex itself head for the village of **Eppe-Sauvage** via the D83. It is conveniently close the lake of ValJoly. Like similar sleepy villages, it may seem a haven of peace — as indeed it is — but a total of some 100 local events, from concerts and festivals to farmers' markets and nature walks, take place in the region during the summer months: see www.estivales-sudavenois.fr.

🏠 **Chateau Maillard** (I room & suite: can be used as 2 rooms) 59132 Eppe-Sauvage close to ValJoly; ☎ 03 27 61 84 04; www.chateaumaillard.com. This nicely timbered restoration of an 18th-century home has rightly been praised as a guesthouse of character. It's big & jolly, rather like the tail-wagging dog that greets you on arrival. The beam & brick bedrooms are modern traditional, & the bathrooms are well equipped. The lake of ValJoly is close by. Look out for w/end deals. $$$

🏠 **Château de la Motte** (9 rooms) rue de la Motte, Liessies; ☎ 03 27 61 81 94; e contact@chateaudelamotte.fr; www.chateaudelamotte.fr. The 18th-century monks knew what they were doing when they built the outbuilding bordering forests &

ponds, which was to become Château de la Motte. Now family-run for 70 years, it offers stylish rooms overlooking the grounds with Wi-Fi, TV etc. The lake at ValJoly is 3km away, the glass museum at Sars-Poteries 11km. B/fast is €9. The restaurant's menus offer a wide choice of dishes; the €40 is a good middling bet for a pleasant evening out in a classy setting ($$$). $$$

🏠 **La Forge de l'Abbaye** (4 rooms) 13 rue de la Forge, Liessies; ☎ 03 27 60 74 27; www.laforgedelabbaye.com. Offering a smaller, but still comfortable, alternative to the *château*, this B&B is again a reliable base for the main south Avesnois attractions. $$

AROUND VALJOLY

From ValJoly head west via the D133d/D133, then continue 17km along the D963 and D104 to **Felleries** and the museum **Des Bois Jolis** (*18 rue de la Place;* ☎ *03 27 59 03 46; www.musenor.com;* ⊕ *14.00–18.00 Mon–Fri, 14.00–18.30 Sat–Sun & public holidays; adult/child aged 8–17 €3.50/2.50, free for children under 8*). The museum, located in a watermill said to go back to 1466, provides a chance to watch flour being produced from a unique Nord-Pas de Calais two-wheel milling system. The galleries contain an intriguing collection of household objects related to rural life, including traditional games. Working tools and photos from 1880–1900 are also on display.

Some 5km northeast of Felleries is **Sars-Poteries** whose **Glass Museum** (*Musee-atelier du Verre de Sars-Poteries, 1 rue de Général de Gaulle;* ☎ *03 27 61 61 64; e museeduverre@cg59.fr; www.cg59.fr;* ⊕ *10.00–12.30 & 13.30–18.00, closed Tue & public holidays; adult/child €3/1.50*) is well worth a stop. Established in 1967 as a centre showing botched (in the true sense of the word) items, it quickly became home to exhibits from the industrial era and the work of international artists in glassware design. It is now one of the largest of its kind in France, shedding fresh light on its subject in an airy setting. Since 2008 it has worked in conjunction with the glass museum in Trélon (see page 217). A joint €7.50 ticket is available.

To complete what is basically a circular tour around southern Avesnois, drive southwest via the D80/D962 for the D104/D 93 for Ohain and Trélon and hence back towards Avesnes-Sur-Helpe.

GREATER LILLE

0 ⊨━━━━⊨ 5km
0 ⊨━━━━━⊨ 5 miles

N

Bradt

Halluin

Comines

D617

Deûlémont

Tourcoing

Quesnoy-
sur-Deûle

Bondues

A22

Wattrelos

Houplines

Wambrechies

Roubaix

D945

Croix

St-André

Wasquehal

La Madeleine

E42

LILLE

Haubourdin

Loos

Villeneuve d'Ascq

N41

Lesquin

A27

E42

Wattignies

Canal de la Deûle

A23

10

Métropolitan Lille

Laurence Phillips, author of Lille: the Bradt City Guide, *offers an expert's view on Lille, a city he has grown to love over two decades.*

LILLE

It was a Sunday evening. Summer had already surrendered to the anticlimactic half season prologue to autumn and Lille lay between excuses. A rare weekend with no festival, no season, no theatre. And it was raining.

I had only just completed the third edition of my Bradt guide to the city and was contemplating the heresy that Lille held no more teasing for me, when I looked up and stared across the uncharacteristically empty squares.

Yellow syrupy pools of lights that slipped from glistening gable to bright washed cobbles lured me across the place Général de Gaulle towards the inexcusably beautiful Vieille Bourse. The sounds of music filtered through, echoing cracked shellac tones of a long forgotten crooner at 78rpm and from the Renaissance arched doorways escaped the unmistakable Latin sound of the tango.

Long shadows sliced the glow from the cloisters and I prowled around the building, looking for an open door. From the place du Théâtre I stepped up and through the entrance to Bourse, Lille's timeless Rialto for bibliophiles and chess players.

Before me was movement, the seductive synchronicity of backs arching, toes pointing forward then sliding up close, calves pressed, waists pulled, shoulders shrugged, and eyes locked in concentrated complicity.

A great bearded bear of a working man in heavy plaid woodsman's shirt lumbered rhythmically and steadily through each stride and turn of the dance, while his whisper-waisted partner, hair a pre-Raphaelite tumble of curls, neatly picked her way around his strides, turning his bulk into gallantry.

For me, this is the spirit of Lille. In a city defined by youth this was in fact and deed, a genteel coup of measured effusion, sagesse and experience over unrefined jeunesse and exuberance. It was that self-same spirit that greeted me on my first visit two decades earlier when strangers welcomed me to *estaminets* and bars and a museum curator shared scandalous gossip about artists and heroes past.

But Lille is not just about heroes – it is defined by its people. Whether they be hordes of merrymakers at the grand festivals, carnivals and parades under the midsummer sunshine, a hundred thousand students bent on changing the world, or the marriage of stilettoed society and barefoot Bohemia in the measured maelstrom delicately turning and tripping through the Vieille Bourse in the modest Sunday evening ball with one last dance under the stars of a freshly rinsed clean indigo sky before bedtime.

And so, I headed back to the métro having learnt the happy lesson never to take the city for granted.

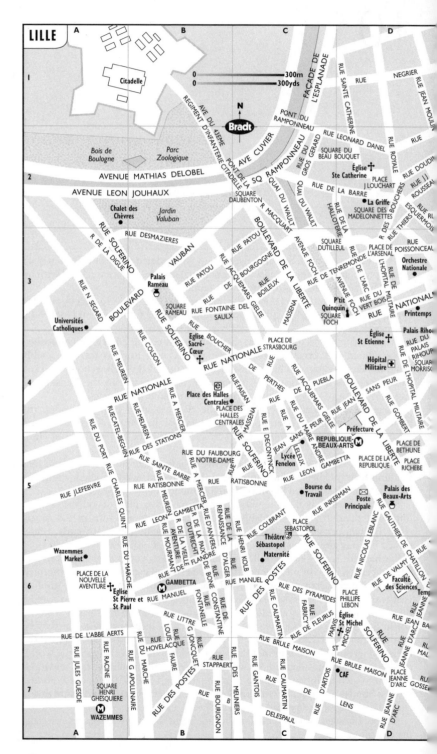

LILLE

A

Citadelle

0 ————————— 300m
0 ————————— 300yds

Bradt

N

B

Bois de Boulogne

Parc Zoologique

RÉGIMENT D'INFANTERIE CITADELLE

AVE DU 4ÈME

PONT DE LA SQ RAMPONNEAU

AVE CUVIER

PONT DU RAMPONNEAU

FAÇADE DE L'ESPLANADE

RUE SAINTE CATHERINE

RUE

NEGRIER

RUE JEAN MOULIN

C

D

RUE LEONARD DANEL

SQUARE DU BEAU BOUQUET

RUE DU GROS GERARD

RUE ROYALE

RUE DOUDIN

Église Ste Catherine

PLACE J LOUCHART

RUE II ROUSSEAU

AVENUE MATHIAS DELOBEL

AVENUE LEON JOUHAUX

SQUARE DAUBENTON

QUAI DU WAULT

QUAI DU WAULT

RUE DE LA BARRE

RUE DE LA HALLOTERIE

• La Griffe

SQUARE DES MADELONNETTES

RUE DES BOUCHERS

RUE THIERS

ESQUERMOIS

Chalet des Chèvres •

Jardin Valuban

RUE DESMAZIERES

R MACQUART

SQUARE DUTILLEUL

RUE DE

PLACE DE L'ARSENAL

RUE POISSONCEAL

R DE SOLFERINO

RUE DE LA DIGUE

VAUBAN

RUE PATOU

RUE JACQUEMARS

BOULEVARD DE BOURGOGNE

BOULEVARD DE LA LIBERTÉ

AVENUE FOCH

RUE DE TENREMONDE

RUE DE L'ARC

RUE DE L'HOPITAL MILITAIRE

Orchestre Nationale •

Palais Rameau •

SQUARE RAMEAU

RUE PATOU

RUE BOILEUX

RUE FONTAINE DEL SAULX

AVENUE FOCH

RUE DU VERT BOIS

RUE NATIONAL

P'tit Quinquin

SQUARE FOCH

RUE N SÉGARD

BOULEVARD

RUE SOLFERINO

MASSENA

Printemps •

Universités Catholiques •

RUE COLSON

Eglise Sacré-Cœur ✝

Eglise Boucher

PLACE DE STRASBOURG

Église St Etienne ✝

Palais Rihou

RUE DU PALAIS RIHOUR

RUE MEUREIN

RUE NATIONALE

DE

PERTHES

RUE JACQUEMARS GIÉLÉE

DE PUEBLA

Hôpital Militaire

RUE DE L'HOPITAL

SQUARE MORRISO

RUE NATIONALE

RUE FAISAN

Place des Halles Centrales •

PLACE DES HALLES CENTRALES

RUE E DECONYNCK

MASSENA

RUE A

RUE DU MAIRE ANDRÉ

JEAN SANS PEUR

SANS PEUR

BOULEVARD DE LA LIBERTE

RUE JEAN JAURES

Préfecture •

RUE GOMBERT

PLACE DE BETHUNE

RUECATEL-BEGHIN

RUE MEUREIN

RUE A MERCIER

RUE DES STATIONS

RUE SAINTE BARBE

RUE DU FAUBOURG NOTRE-DAME

RUE SOLFERINO

JEAN SANS MAIRE

RÉPUBLIQUE-BEAUX-ARTS Ⓜ

Lycée Fenelon

LELEUX

RUE LEON GAMBETTA

PLACE DE LA REPUBLIQUE

PLACE RICHEBE

RUE DU PORT

RUE JLEFEBVRE

RUE RATISBONNE

A MERCIER

RUE

RATISBONNE

Bourse du Travail •

RUE INKERMAN

✉ Poste Principale

Palais des Beaux-Arts •

RUE CHARLES QUINT

RUE LEON GAMBETTA

RUE MEUREIN

RUE DE LA RENAISSANCE

RUE DE LA PAIX D'UTRECH

RUE D'ANVERS

RUE HENRI KOLB

RUE COLBRANT

PLACE SEBASTOPOL

Théâtre Sébastopol 🎭

RUE NICOLAS LEBLANC

RUE GAUTHIER DE CHATILLON

Wazemmes Market •

PLACE DE LA NOUVELLE AVENTURE

Église St Pierre et St Paul ✝

Ⓜ GAMBETTA

RUE MANUEL

RUE DU MARCHE

RUE MOURMANT

AVENTURE

RUE DE LA VIEILLE

RUE DE FLANDRE

RUE DE BONE

RUE D'ALGER

Maternité

RUE MANUEL POSTES

RUE DES PYRAMIDES

RUE DES POSTES

RUE CALMARTIN

RUE FABRICY

PLACE PHILLIPE LEBON

Faculté des Sciences •

RUE DE VALMY

Temp

RUE DE L'ABBE AERTS

RUE DU MARCHE

RUE LITTRE

RUE DE FONTANELLE

RUE DE CONSTANTINE

RUE DE FLEURUS

Église St Michel ✝

PARVIS ST MICHEL

RUE JEAN BA

RUE JEANNE D'ARC

RL MAL

RUE JULES GUESDE

RUE RACINE

RUE G APOLLINAIRE

RUE DU MARCHE

RUE LOUIS FAURE

RUE G JONQUET

RUE HOVELACQUE

RUE STAPPAERT

RUE DES MEUNIERS

RUE GANTOIS

RUE CALMARTIN

RUE BRULE MAISON

RUE BRULE MAISON

• CAF

D'ARTOIS

PLACE JEANNE D'ARC

RUE SOLFERINO

RUE JEANNE D'ARC

RL GOSSE

SQUARE HENRI GHESQUIERE

Ⓜ WAZEMMES

RUE DES POSTES

RUE BOURIGNON

RUE

DE

DELESPAUL

LENS

A

B

C

D

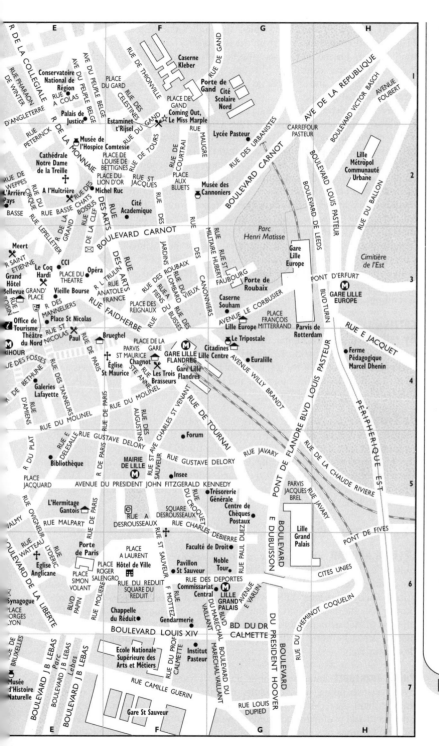

HISTORY It was in this same spirit that Lille, the historic trading post twixt Flanders and France, evolved from the island (*l'isle*) to a royal city. The city allowed the patroness Jeanne de Constantinople to launch a tradition of benevolence and hospitality which continued through the diverse regimes of the houses of Burgundy, Spain and France, as the city's ownership shuttled between the powerhouses of Europe.

After the Hapsburg incarnation, Louis XIV, the Sun King, brought Lille into his kingdom, established a garrison (the Citadelle) under the rule of legendary architect Vauban and literary hero d'Artagnan, and built a royal quarter to house generations of prosperous upper and middle classes.

Lille continued to make its mark on French life, producing heroes to suit each era: Mayor André withstood the Austrian siege of 1792; in 1888, before the winds of discontent and change blew across the continent, Pierre Degeyter wrote the revolutionary anthem the *Internationale* (even though the city itself adopted a lullaby *Le Petit Quinquin* as its own theme song); Charles de Gaulle led Free France through World War II and long-time mayor and one-time prime minister Pierre Mauroy took the city out of industrial decline and reinvented it to become a Eurostar staging post and eventually European Capital of Culture in 2004.

In the far and recent past, Lille has been both capital city of Flanders and of Culture. But then, now and always, Lille is surely the unchallenged capital of serendipity.

GETTING THERE

By rail As the regional capital, there is no shortage of railway links to the city's two main stations, Lille Flandres [223 F4] (for predominantly local services) and Lille Europe [223 G3] (TGV routes, intercity and international). The stations are 500m apart, and both are on the bus, tram and métro routes. For getting to Lille from the UK by Eurostar see page 25.

By ferry The cross-Channel ferries and Eurotunnel (see pages 22–4) are 60–90 minutes away by car. From Calais or Dunkirk take the A16 then the A25 motorway (signposted for Lille). From Zeebrugge take the N31 (via Bruges), which leads to the A17 motorway, and then the A14 (which becomes the A22 as it crosses the French border). Remember that Belgian motorway signs may list Lille by its Flemish name, Rijsel. At Marcq-en-Baroeul, leave the motorway and follow the N356 into Lille.

By air For getting to Lille by air see pages 24–5.

GETTING AROUND Lille is pretty much manageable on foot (with the odd trip by métro); each key area is around 15 minutes' maximum walk from the centre. From the main place de Gaulle (known colloquially as Grand'Place) walk through the 'Alcide' arch to Vieux Lille with its cobbled streets, traditional bistros and boutiques; alternatively cross the square to find the pedestrianised shopping quarter of department stores, cinemas and brasseries. The main artery of this district is rue Bethune, leading to place de la République, and home to the Palais des Beaux Arts.

Public transport Integrated public transport features the unmanned VAL **métro**, two ever-expanding lines crossing central Lille and serving the suburbs and métropolitan area. Métro lines in France do not have names, instead they are numbered and platforms indicated by the terminus. Thus Line One will be marked either 4 Cantons or CHRB Calmette, and Line Two CH Dron or St-Philibert.

Twin **tramways** run out to Roubaix and Tourcoing, passing the pretty Parc Barbieux, which, on sunny days, provide a pleasant alternative to the underground. Métro and tram services run from 05.15 to midnight (from 06.20 at weekends).

Buses generally run from around 05.30 until 20.30. The Citadine bus route is a circuit taking in the principal boulevards and both railway stations in a continuous loop sweeping around the city. It operates from around 05.30 to 21.30. Tickets are available singly or in *carnets* of ten from machines in métro stations or from bus drivers. You may use one ticket for a single journey taking in any or all of the transport options: métro, tram or bus. Day passes are also available.

Taxis and **bike hire** are available by the principal bus station outside Gare Flandres[223 F4].

TOURIST INFORMATION

☑ **Lille tourist office** [223 E3] Palais Rihour, pl Rihour, 59002; ☎ 03 59 57 94 00; e info@lilletourism.com; www.lilletourism.com; ⏱ 09.30–18.30 Mon–Sat, 10.00–12.00, 14.00–17.00 Sun & public holidays. Nearest métro: Rihour; from the Eurostar take Métro 2 to Gare Lille Flandres, then line 1 to Rihour. Minibus guided city tour departs hourly from the tourist office. Additional information desks at Lille Europe station & Lille Lesquin Airport are open during peak season.

WHERE TO STAY

🏠 **L'Hermitage Gantois** [223 E5] 224 rue de Paris, 59800; ☎ 03 20 85 30 30; e contact@hotelhermitagegantois.com; www.hotelhermitagegantois.com. Nearest métro: Mairie de Lille; from the Eurostar take Métro 2 to Mairie de Lille. Walk westwards along av du Président Kennedy then turn left on to rue de Paris.

Don't just see the sights — stay in one of them. Lille's only 4-star-luxe hotel is one of the best-kept secrets in the city. Just a bit further along the rue de Paris than most visitors would think of walking, the hotel, a listed building since 1923, was formerly the Hospice Gantois, a hospital & old people's home. Its courtyard remains a peaceful haven & escape from the bustle of everyday life.

The original hospice was founded in 1462 as a rest home for retired prostitutes, & continued to provide care for the poor (albeit for those of less scandalous lifestyles) until the end of the 20th century. This cluster of religious & secular buildings has been united by architect Hubert Maes into an exciting celebration of one of the few survivors of the long demolished St-Saveur quarter. The imaginative revival of the street façades gives not a clue to the thrilling marriage within: contemporary design ties the knot with a respect for history, with beamed ceilings, panelled walls & smart tiled floors. The former dormitories & wards make way for 67 bedrooms & suites, clustered around 4 courtyards. Rooms at €204–425, boast good-sized bathrooms. Even if you can't afford the room rates & the full €18 breakfast, the central atrium bar is at least open to everyone. Flop in a comfy sofa & gaze heavenward through glass at the architectural harmonies or relax in the sauna.

Among the eclectic treasures housed within the hotel are sundry vintage medical instruments (including a 1926 X-ray machine) & the body of the hospice's founder, buried in the chapel. There are Tue-morning tours of the building; alternatively take sneaky peeks when you take the coffee & croissant bar breakfast at €9 or similarly priced afternoon tea. $$$$$

🏠 **Grand Hôtel Bellevue** [223 E3] 5 rue Jean Roisin; ☎ 03 20 57 45 64; e grand.hotel.bellevue@wanadoo.fr; www.grandhotelbellevue.com. Nearest métro: Rihour; from the Eurostar take Métro 2 to Gare Lille Flandres then line 1 to Rihour. The hotel has double-glazed rooms on the Grand'Place itself, while still giving a *belle* goodnight view of a city at play. But it's no mere onlooker. Ever since the evening that the young Mozart played in one of the building's original salons (the 9-year-old prodigy stayed here for 4 weeks with his father Leopold when he was taken ill *en route* from England to the Netherlands), the address has been dabbling in the arts. A function room occasionally doubles as a theatre & b/fast is served in the Vivaldi room, whatever the season. The reception area adds a hint of a flourish to the décor, & the Windsor piano bar is *the* place for w/end cocktails. The marbled en-suite facilities add a certain indulgence to prices that are comfortably lower 3-star (€120–185). Complimentary daily newspaper & Wi-Fi. $$$$$

🏠 **Brueghel** [223 E4] 3–5 parvis St-Maurice; ☎ 03 20 06 06 69; e hotel.brueghel@nordnet.fr;

www.hotel-brueghel.com. Nearest métro: Gare Lille Flandres; from the Eurostar take ave le Corbusier to Gare Flandres, left into rue de Priez & walk round the church. The least known & most charming of the central hotels, this little gem is very much a word-of-mouth favourite. Tucked away in a quiet pedestrianised street between the old Gare Flandres & the shops of rue de Paris, the hotel faces the recently scrubbed & shining church of St-Maurice. This hosts some excellent classical concerts & organ recitals every summer Sun afternoon.

Overflowing window boxes announce the hospitality guaranteed within. Inside the cosy reception area an authentic 1920s cage lift takes guests Noah-fashion, 2-by-2, to the bedrooms. Each year another floor is carefully restored. With impeccable taste, the rooms have been styled to combine minimalism with elegance & comfort. Natural coir carpets, wrought-iron mirrors, picture frames from salvaged wood, & classic bathrooms are used — all proof that a budget hotel need not lack artistic inspiration. If you are planning to spend any considerable time in your room, do pack some slippers. Coir is lovely on the eye but less so on the soles of the feet (you can usually pick up a pair of slippers for under €4 at Tati around the corner). Only the very smallest rooms miss the sophisticated touch, but with rates at €67–120, comfort & a warm welcome it is genuine value for money. You may want to forego the lift just once to look at the excellent collection of paintings, prints & posters on each landing. $$$$
🏠 **Chagnot** [223 F4] 24 pl de la Gare; ☎ 03 20 74 11 87; 📧 contact@chagnot.com; www.chagnot.com. Nearest métro: Gare Lille Flandres; from the Eurostar take ave le Corbusier to Gare Flandres & pl de la Gare. Lying at the side of the

Gare Flandres & above the fabulous Trois Brasseurs, this hotel offers surprisingly comfortable & quiet (if bland & compact) rooms; service, too, is helpful. The slowest lift in Christendom serves an astonishing 75 bedrooms. But be warned, as with so many of the hotels around the stations, the elevator does not go all the way down to the ground floor, so there's still one flight of stairs to negotiate. Reception & rooms are stocked with local entertainment guides for visitors & the location provides for a quick getaway if you have an early train in the morning. Unexpectedly, for the price, the hotel can offer ethernet cables for the laptop. With rates from around €60 not including the uninspiring b/fast, opt for a quick coffee at the Ralleye bar next door, then amble into town for hot chocolate & fresh bread by the Grand'Place. $$$
🏠 **Lille Europe** [223 G3] ave le Corbusier, 59777; ☎ 03 28 36 76 76; 📧 infos@hotel-lille-europe.com; www.hotel-lille-europe.com. Nearest métro: Lille Europe; from the Eurostar take ave le Corbusier to Euralille. An anonymous modern hotel in a suitably anonymous modern building, the *hôtel de la gare de nos jours* has charming, helpful staff, lots of identikit rooms & a buffet b/fast in a fully glazed 1st-floor salon. The hotel is part of the Euralille tower-block shopping & business complex. The plus point for overnighters & travellers with heavy luggage & plans to strip bare the shelves of the en-suite shopping mall is its location, close to the TGV Eurostar station. But with the Grand'Place & old town just 5mins away, this is unlikely to be a first choice for visitors seeking the charm of old Flanders. Rooms €74–90. After a period experimenting with pay-as-you-go internet options, the hotel now offers broadband to all guests at the 1st-floor business centre, with views over the city. $$$

Self-catering option
🏠 **Citadines Lille Centre** [223 G4] 83 ave Willy Brandt; ☎ 03 28 36 75 00; 📧 lillecentre@citadines.com; www.citadines.com. Nearest métro: Gare Lille Flandres; from the Eurostar take ave le Corbusier to Euralille. Left into ave Willy Brandt. Located in the Euralille building, this central self-catering option offers extremely competitively priced modern studios & larger apartments with well-equipped kitchenettes & extra facilities, from €8 buffet b/fasts to an in-house laundrette — wash, dry, & detergent for €10. Studios

are from around €98–145 per night, reductions for weekly bookings. A slightly higher rate is charged for those requiring the full hotel package, with daily maid service. Otherwise pay the basic price & use the dishwasher, vacuum cleaner & ironing board provided. Security is pretty good, with the front doors locked & guests given private entry codes whenever the main desk is unmanned. Very helpful staff at reception, & basement parking among the bonuses. Internet connection in rooms, Wi-Fi in reception area. $$$$

✖ WHERE TO EAT AND DRINK
✖ **A l'Huîtrière** [223 E2] 3 rue des Chats Bossus, 59000; ☎ 03 20 55 43 41; www.huitriere.fr; 🕐 closed Sun evening. From the Eurostar take bus 3,

6 or 9 from Gare Flandres to Lion d'Or. If I were a rich man, I'd spend the rest of my life introducing my friends to l'Huîtrière, if only to bask in the glow of

unalloyed pleasure that this jewel-box of a fish shop presses upon even the sternest of gastronomes. Once in the narrow vestibule twixt the domains of the fishmonger & the *maître cuisinier*, a warm welcome from the fabulously efficient & courteous staff instantly sets the standard for the evening. In the restaurant itself all is calm, all is bright. Light wood panels are adorned by lovely wool tapestry. Table appointments are charming, with the white & navy Limoges service atop crisp white linen. A sense of quality pervades with exquisite & discreet service that is attentive without a hint of intimidation. The cuisine too never fails to stimulate or enchant. An entrée of wild Scottish salmon *mi-cru mi-cuit* is lovingly prepared, briefly roasted, pan-fried & seared in spices on the outside, yet succulent & raw within & laced with a fine horseradish dressing. The *trois petites royales* reveal themselves as truffled-up seductions of leek, cabbage & *petit pois*, simply superb.

Though this is a fish restaurant, honourable mention must go to the *escalope de foie gras de canard* in a *pot-au-feu de nouveaux legumes*. The main course varies with the catch & the season & according to the taste of the diner. A *sorbet à la fleur de bière* is the northern answer to a *trou normand* & clears the appetite for game or *volaille*. Desserts are impeccable — do try the *mi-gratin, mi-soufflé* of wild woodland strawberries — & the pastries, chocolates & *petits fours* are simply heavenly. Budget a good €100 per head, or €138 for a seasonally truffled or lobstered 7-course gastronomic menu. A very reasonable 3-course business lunch is served at €45. The Huîtrière has recently opened its new oyster bar for more modest lunching. $$$$$

✕ **Estaminet t'Rijsel** [223 F1] 25 rue de Gand; ℡ 03 20 15 01 59; ⊕ closed Sun, Mon & much of Aug. From the Eurostar take bus 3, 6 or 9 from Gare Lille Flandres to Lion d'Or. Cross pl Louise de Bettignies to rue de Gand. Rijsel is the Flemish name for Lille, so no surprise to find a warm corner of old Flanders in the heart of a modern city. Jean-Luc Lacante, founder of the *estaminet* t'Kasteel-Hof in Cassel (see page 136), a long-time favourite with those who explore the countryside of Le Nord, brought his trademark combination of wit, style & homeliness to town at the turn of the millennium. Expect all the regional specialities here, from *potjevlesch* to sugar flans, on menus printed in old school-exercise books. Budget comfortably around €20 for dinner, & lunch for around €13. The success of real northern hospitality & home-style cooking in this fashionable quarter has led to a brace of sister *estaminets*. So try Chez La Vieille, the

one across the way at number 60 & the newest estaminet, Le Vieux de la Vielle, off rue de la Monnaie. $$$

✕ **Les Trois Brasseurs** [223 F4] 22 pl de la Gare; ℡ 03 20 06 46 25. Nearest métro station: Gare Lille Flandres; from the Eurostar follow ave le Corbusier to Gare Lille Flandres & pl de la Gare. Flanders is famed for its beers, so do try at least 1 of the region's distinctive flavours. Many local *artisanales* beers are made in the traditional method, & some larger breweries offer guided tours & tastings for the public. As for me, I stay in central Lille & pay a regular visit to Les Trois Brasseurs opposite the old Lille Flandres station. A director of Pelforth — the commercial brewery behind the Pelican lagers favoured by Calais-trippers — created this genuine brasserie. Monsieur Bonduel decided to get back to brewing basics, & it was the welcome I found here that first drew me to Lille. I will never cease to be thankful. The clientele ranges from solo business types at the bar to groups of friends, locals & visitors. The bar staff are rarely less than convivial, the waiters never less than harassed. In this always-packed bar-restaurant the only beers served are those brewed in copper vats on the premises.

For €4.50 buy a *pallette* — a tasting tray of four small glasses of the various home brews, the *blonde*, *brune*, *ambrée* & *Blanche de Lille*, the refreshing bitter-sweet thirst quencher ideally served with a slice of lemon. This tasting tray is the best way to get to know the beers of Lille. March & Christmas see special seasonal beers added to the range. The menu is excellent northern home cooking: rabbit stews, roasts & the cholesterol-packed *Welsh*, a bowl of melted cheese, ham & beer with a slice of bread & chips. If you are feeling really adventurous, try the beer tart or beer sorbet! Set-menu deals are the best value at around €11, as are the house *flammekeuche*, & the daily special, such as marrow-bone or a *carbonnade*, is always reasonably priced. A range of promotional combinations can be found on the blackboards or in the newspaper-style menus. Otherwise budget at €20 & you won't go far wrong. The restaurant next door serves the same food in a more traditional bistro setting, but I like to dine amongst the dark wood & bright copper of this convivial & very special brewery. $$$

✕ **Paul** [223 E4] 8–12 rue de Paris; ℡ 03 20 78 20 78. Nearest métro station: Rihour; from the Eurostar take bus 12 from Gare Lille Flandres to Théâtre. Or walk ave le Corbusier & right into rue Faidherbe, then left to the Vieille Bourse. Forget the hotel: come to Paul instead for the best b/fast in town. Not the biggest, nor the most varied, but certainly the best. This corner-site bakery opposite the Vieille Bourse is the place for fresh croissants, just-baked bread & creamy, piping-hot chocolate first thing in the morning. The b/fast tray served on solid wooden tables against the blue-&-white tiled walls & heavy tapestries of the bread & cake shop is the perfect way to start the day. Find inspiration in the words of wisdom painted on the old wooden beams, or concentrate on the scrumptious homemade jams & crunchy, crusty baguettes. I have good news for long-time fans: each edition of my Lille guide has announced the closure or reopening of the upstairs restaurant & at the time of writing, the curving wooden staircase once again led to the famously bright & airy 1st-floor restaurant dining room. Paul has now spawned scores of satellite bakeries & *viennoiserie* counters across Lille, throughout Paris, France & beyond. But this old corner shop between the Opéra & the main square remains something special. $$$

✗ **Le Coq Hardi** [223 E3] 44 pl Général de Gaulle; ☎ 03 20 55 21 08. Nearest métro station: Rihour; from the Eurostar take bus 12 from Gare Lille Flandres to de Gaulle. Or walk ave le Corbusier & right into rue Faidherbe then left to Grand'Place. Though this small restaurant has been an institution on the central square of Lille for donkeys' years, it's the tables spreading out across the pavement that are even better known. In fact it was only when the winter weather grumbled ominously that I ventured to check out the interior of the restaurant itself. Small but perfectly busy, with service on 2 floors, the Coq Hardi is unashamedly rustic. Untreated wooden ceilings & sacks of baguettes inside the front door

greet a constant flow of customers keen on value-for-money lunching. Huge portions are the order of the day, whether *andouillette de Cambrai* with *frites* or a *tartare des deux saumons*, served ready-mixed or with the additional ingredients on the side. Allow around €7–12. In the sunshine take a big bowl of *moules* or a huge summer salad & lunch outdoors for well under €15, indulging in good old-fashioned people-watching at this key corner between the old town & the main square. $$

✗ **Meert** [223 E3] 27 rue Esquermoise; ☎ 03 20 57 07 44. Nearest métro: Rihour; from the Eurostar take bus 12 from Gare Lille Flandres to de Gaulle. Charles de Gaulle himself would never have dreamt of saying 'Non' to the celebrated *gaufrette* – or filled waffle – that has graced many a palace & presidential biscuit barrel since this shop started trading in the 1760s. This unassuming house speciality of the chocolate-box quaint *pâtisserie* is a tiny miracle: a light, feathery crispy wafer packed with a sugared explosion of flavour. The town's most famous son continued his regular order for the *gaufrettes* all his life, & ate them, so he wrote, 'with great pleasure'. The Belgian royal family gave their warrant to Monsieur Meert in 1849. The pretty cake shop, decorated in 1839 with mirrors, balconies & *Arabian Nights* exotica, is a feast for the eyes. The tea room behind the shop provides savoury lunchtime snacks & sumptuous afternoon teas. A selection of cakes & a pot of tea should set you back around €6–12. Lemon meringue tarts are creamy delights; the *safari* a surprisingly heavy dose of fluffiness for hard-core chocolate addicts only. A new dining room behind the shop & wrapped around a courtyard is a recent addition to the restaurant scene $$

SHOPPING Secondhand clothes and shoes from the continent's leading fashion houses can be found at **La Griffe** [222 D2] (*27 rue de la Barre;* ☎ *03 20 57 47 20;* ⏰ *14.30–19.00 Mon, 13.00–19.00 Tue & Thu–Sat, closed Wed*); everything is in good condition and costs about a third of the original retail price. Another good place to shop for clothes is **Michel Ruc** [223 E2] (*23–25 rue des Chats Bossus;* ☎ *03 20 15 96 16;* ⏰ *14.00–19.00 Mon, 10.30–19.00 Tue–Sat*). The shopfront may be centuries old but the window features the latest looks from Milan and Paris: Gaultier for the girls, Boss for the boys and Armani for everyone.

For edible treats, **L'Arriére Pays** [223 E2] (*47 rue Basse;* ☎ *03 20 13 80 07*) sells incredible and wonderful preserves, oils and pâtés in little bottles and jars as well as doubling as a *restaurant salon de thé*. And don't forget to pick up some of **Meert**'s famous waffles (see above).

Wazemmes Market [222 A6] (*pl de la Nouvelle Aventure;* ⏰ *Sun morn; covered produce market* ⏰ *from 06.00 until late aft Tue–Sun*) is a feast for the senses. Mounds of gloriously plump fresh chicory, rosered radishes and tear-blushed artichokes from the market gardens of Artois and Flanders sit next to everything from puppets and playthings to smart coats and swimwear. In the red-brick market hall itself you will find fresh North Sea fish on the slab and crates of seafood; cheeses from the region and beyond; exotic sausages and pristine plucked poultry. Through the hall is the flower market where carnations and lilies mix with spring blooms or Christmas wreaths. On street corners, enormous rotisseries drip the juices from turning chickens on to trays of roast potatoes and vegetables, the scent of a traditional Sunday lunch competing with the more exotic aromas from the enormous drums of couscous and paella. Follow your nose and keep your hand on your wallet. Wazemmes on a Sunday morning is an unforgettable experience for bargain hunters and browsers alike.

The long-awaited validation of Lille as a key destination for the fashion conscious came with the opening of **Galeries Lafayette** [223 E4] (*31 rue de Béthune;* \ *03 20 14 76 50;* ⏲ *10.00–22.00 Mon–Thu, 10.00–21.00 Fri–Sat*) in 2007. It boats all you'd expect from the A-listers' emporium, plus a branch of the Zein spa. There is also a branch of **Printemps** [222 D3] (*41–45 rue Nationale;* \ *03 20 63 62 00;* ⏲ *09.30–19.30 Tue–Thu & Sat, 09.30–20.00 Fri*), the famous Parisian department store.

Between the two railway stations, **Euralille** [223 G4] (*Av le Corbusier;* \ *03 20 14 52 20 (Euralille), 03 28 38 50 50 (Aeronef)*) is one of France's biggest shopping centres with 140 shops spread over two storeys. Hardcore consumers will squeak with excitement at the massive Carrefour hypermarket and specialist shops such as the temple to new-age consumerism, Nature et Découvertes, and the arts and crafts wonderland of Loisirs et Créations.

Bookshop
Le Furet du Nord [223 E3] Grand'Place (see page 230); \ 03 20 78 43 43; ⏲ 09.30–19.30 Mon–Sat

OTHER PRACTICALITIES
Bank Most major French banks can be found along rue Nationale. Generally they are open ⏲ 10.00–17.00 Mon–Fri (some close 12.00–14.00), some also open 10.00–13.00 Sat.
Supermarket Carrefour see Euralille in *Shopping* above

Internet cafés *Espace Web: Cyber-Laverie* [223 F5] 14 rue Desrousseaux; ⏲ 08.00–19.00 Mon–Sat, 11.00–19.00 Sun; *Atlanteam* [222 B4] 93 rue Solférino; ⏲ 10.30–00.00 Mon–Sat, 11.00–19.00 Sun
Post Office [223 E3] bld Carnot; ⏲ 08.00–18.30 Mon–Fri, 08.00–12.00 Sat

WHAT TO SEE AND DO Lille offers many sightseeing opportunities; here are some of the highlights.

Palais des Beaux Arts [222 D5] (*Fine Arts Museum, pl de la République, 59000;* \ *03 20 06 78 00; www.pba-lille.fr;* ⏲ *14.00–18.00 Mon, 10.00–18.00 Fri, 10.00–19.00 Wed–Thu & Sat–Sun; closed Tue, public holidays; adult €5 (discounts for under 25s), but free admission on the 1st Sun of the month. Free access to atrium. Nearest métro station: République-Beaux Arts; from the Eurostar take Métro 2 to Gare Lille Flandres, changing to line 1 to République- Beaux Arts*) France's second museum after the Louvre houses Goyas, Rubens, Picassos, Lautrecs and Monets. So who said that crime doesn't pay? The breathtaking art collection was brought to Lille on the orders of Napoleon, who stripped the walls of palaces and private galleries throughout his European empire, from Italy to the Low Countries. On the first floor, room after room offers French, Flemish and European masterpieces from the 17th to the 19th centuries. Highlights include Rubens's *Descente de la Croix*, an entire room devoted to Jordaens, and a succession of high-ceilinged galleries housing the works of Van Dyck, Corot and Delacroix as well as Watteau, the collection's first curator. Best of all is the celebrated pair of Goyas, *Les Jeunes* and *Les Vieilles*, the former a timeless portrayal of a teenage

10

crush, as relevant to the SMS generation as to its own time, and the latter a cruelly satirical dissection of old age: crones at one with their malevolence. With so many riches, it is easy to overlook the modest corridor devoted to the Impressionists. Make time for Monet, Van Gogh, Renoir and Sisley, not to mention a Lautrec and models of Rodin's *The Six Burghers of Calais* (see page 68).

The ground-floor sculpture gallery includes the best of 19th-century classical statuary, some imperial, some disturbing. The collection leads to the rear courtyard – a good halfway refreshment point for your visit – and the modern architect's remarkable prism comprising the glass-fronted administration block and a sheet of water that turns the grey skies of the north into pure natural light to illuminate the basement galleries.

The basement rooms should not be missed. The Renaissance room includes Donatello's bas-relief *Festin d'Herod*, and many sketches by Raphaël. It also houses 19 of Vauban's detailed models of Louis XIV's fortified towns of the north – among them Lille and Calais – frozen in time and space between sheets of glass in an otherwise blacked-out exhibition of the landscape of 18th-century France and Flanders.

Musée de l'Hospice Comtesse

[223 E2] (*32 rue de la Monnaie;* ℡ *03 28 36 84 00;* ⊕ *14.00–18.00 Mon, 10.00–12.30 & 14.00–18.00 Wed–Sun, closed holidays; adult €3. Joint tickets also available with Palais des Beaux Arts. From the Eurostar take bus 3, 6 or 9 from Gare Lille Flandres to Lion d'Or*) Tucked away behind the shops and archways of the oldest street in town, the former 13th-century hospital captures the life and talents of another Lille in another time. Once both a hospital and a convent, the site has been restored as a museum of local arts and crafts. Outside is a medicinal herb garden. Inside is an eclectic collection of carved furniture and rare musical instruments, domestic tableaux and wooden panels adorned with paintings of local children. The art collection includes paintings by Flemish and northern French masters, among them Louis and François Watteau, as well as tapestries by Lille's famous weaver Guillaume Werniers. The kitchen is typically tiled with the traditional blue-and-white tiles of the Low Countries, and vestiges of the original murals can be seen in the 17th-century convent chapel. The chapel, the 15th-century ward and other buildings around the central courtyard are favourite locations for informal concerts and intimate musical recitals. Guided tours are available at no extra charge most afternoons.

Place du Général de Gaulle (Grand'Place)

[223 E3] (*Nearest métro station: Rihour; from the Eurostar take bus 12 from Gare Lille Flandres to de Gaulle. Or walk ave le Corbusier & right into rue Faidherbe then left to Grand'Place*) Named after Lille's most famous son, but known to everyone simply as the Grand'Place, the main square is the very heartbeat of the city. Almost pedestrianised, although a serpentine trail of traffic slithers safely along two sides, this is a veritable forum where shoppers break their day, friends plot an evening and revellers celebrate the night.

The essential rendezvous is the central fountain around the column of the Déesse, the goddess and symbol of the spirit of the city. The statue commemorates the bravery of the townsfolk who withstood the siege of Lille by 35,000 Austrian soldiers in 1792. Her crown represents Lille's ramparts, her right hand ever ready to fire another cannon, her left pointing to a plaque inscribed with the brave words of Mayor André's rebuttal of Austria's demands.

Under her watchful gaze, students hold their protest rallies, bands play on Gay Pride Weekend and the city's tame giants parade during the Fêtes de Lille. Grand'Place has a habit of dressing for every occasion – most famously as a Christmas grotto in December and January, when, surrounded by Cinderella candelabra, a huge Ferris wheel swings sensation seekers into the skies to take in the panorama of gables and belfries from a swaying cradle high above the cobblestones.

Around the square are gilded images of the sun, symbol of King Louis XIV, whose royal bodyguard lived in the Grande Garde, a splendid galleried building that today houses the Théâtre du Nord. Alongside the theatre is the striking frontage of the home of *La Voix du Nord*, once a wartime Resistance news-sheet and now the regional daily newspaper. Dominating the square, its tiered roof is topped out by three golden Graces, symbolising the regional provinces of Artois, Flanders and Hainaut.

Continental Europe's biggest bookshop, the Furet du Nord, boasts half a million volumes in stock, and is spread over eight storeys on different levels served by a complicated arrangement of lifts, staircases and walkways. Across the square, linking Grand'Place with place du Théâtre, is the stunning Vieille Bourse. Step inside the contemplative cloister to find a charming weekday market selling antiquarian books under the gaze of busts of local pioneers of science and literature. A sanctuary from summer sun and winter winds alike, people come here to sit and read or play chess from mid-morning until early evening.

Notre Dame de la Treille [223 E2] (*pl Gilleson;* ☎ *03 20 55 28 72;* ⏰ *10.00–12.00 & 14.00–18.30 Mon–Wed & Fri–Sat, 10.00–18.30 Thu. On Sun respect service times. Remains open 1hr later May–Sep; free. From the Eurostar take bus 3, 6 or 9 from Gare Lille Flandres to Lion d'Or. Take rue de la Monnaie then 1st left to pl Gilleson.*) Notre Dame de la Treille straddles several time zones with its fine Gothic chapel and apse dating from the mid-19th-century and its grand façade finally unveiled in 1999. From outside, architect P L Carlier's designs are very much of the age of the out-of-town shopping mall: B&Q perpendicular. But inside, it is quite a different story: imposing yet welcoming, a delicate blend of light and shade. The new rose window by Kijno produces a remarkable effect within, and the remarkable doors created by Holocaust survivor sculptor George Jeanclos, representing a barbed-wire vine of human suffering and dignity, are quite magnificent.

The cathedral stands on the Îlot Comtesse, site of the former *château* of the counts of Flanders, and the surrounding streets follow the line of the old fortifications, with traces of a moat still visible. A Museum of Religious Art in the crypt opens on Saturday afternoons from 16.00–17.00, housing 200 works of art and historic objects, including the original statue of Notre Dame de la Treille, dating from 1270.

OUTSIDE THE CITY LIMITS

Pretty gardens of the Parc Barbieux and Disney-quaint houses line the roads on the half-hour tram route to the major satellite towns of Tourcoing and Roubaix. These days the métro cuts journey times in half, blurring the boundaries between the city of Lille and the other towns that make up Lille Métropole.

ROUBAIX One good reason to visit Roubaix (apart from the twin outlet malls and fashion shopping at half the regular high-street prices) is **La Piscine – Musée d'Art et d'Industrie** (*Art & Industry Museum; 23 rue de l'Espérance;* ☎ *03 20 69 23 60;* ⏰ *11.00–18.00 Tue–Thu, 11.00–20.00 Fri, 13.00–18.00 Sat–Sun; adult €4.50. Nearest métro station: Gare Jean Lebas; from the Eurostar take Métro 2 to Gare Jean Lebas. Walk down ave Jean Lebas & turn right to rue des Champs & left onto rue de l'Espérance*).

It took five years to convert the former municipal swimming pool into this stunning museum where a dramatic Art Deco stained-glass window radiates stylised sunbeams over this most ambitious of projects. Restored and reinvented as

10

a combination art gallery and sensual archive of textiles, the building itself takes the breath away.

Once you've gasped at the architecture, browse the art: Bonnard, Dufy and Gallé are among the big-name draws. Most dating from the end of the 19th and the first half of the 20th century, the artworks provide a forensic examination of the lives and people of Roubaix.

The museum grew from a collection of fabrics from the textile factories to include works of art accumulated and acquired by the industrialist families of the town. Some of these works show remarkable glimpses into the lives of local working men and women.

Social politics merge with artistic merit in a gallery devoted to the emancipation of women through art: a wry evocation of the *Mona Lisa* shows a modern woman of learning; Camille Claudel's evocative bust of a child was a challenge to Rodin, her mentor and former lover, to acknowledge the paternity of her own daughter.

As you wander through the galleries, the occasional sound of splashing and shrieking within the unmistakable acoustic of swimming baths leads you to the heart of the museum, the pool itself. It's a witty sound effect that is even more effective *in situ*. A sheet of water still runs almost the length of the Olympic baths, fed by the fountain head of Neptune at the end of the dazzling mosaic basin. This continues to reflect brilliant-coloured glass sunrise and sunset windows at each end of the building. Catch your breath then walk along the boardwalks lined with 19th- and 20th-century sculpture. These, like the Cogghe and Weerts paintings in earlier galleries, reflect the social history of the town. Some are worthy religious icons, others starkly socialist interpretations of the dignity of the working man. A massive Moorish arch in Sèvres porcelain dominates the room, and along each side of the pool are ranged tiers of original shower and changing cubicles. Glazed to protect their exhibits, these are now treasure houses, including a remarkable range of ceramics by Picasso.

On upper levels the textile collection brings gowns and underwear, accessories and shoes of bygone ages. The *tissuthèque* is an archive of thousands of years of material patterns, from ancient Egypt to the present day. And, around the museum, filing-cabinet drawers of fabrics allow visitors to plunge their hands into a sensory wonderland of the soft and silky, matted and furred.

Take time to reflect on the day with a cool drink in the restaurant or on its terrace, run by Meert of Lille (see page 228), flicking through an art book from the excellent museum shop.

TOURCOING

Musée des Beaux Arts *(2 rue Paul Doumer, 59200 Tourcoing;* ✆ *03 20 28 91 60;* e *museebeauxarts@ville-tourcoing.fr;* ⏱ *13.30–18.00 Wed–Mon; free. Nearest métro station: Tourcoing Centre; from the Eurostar take a tram or métro to Tourcoing Centre. Rue Leclerc to rue Paul Doumer)* Eclectic, imaginative and never less than stimulating, Tourcoing's art collection spans the artistic spectrum from Brueghelesque Flemish works to the Cubists. The archives are regularly ransacked by the curator to keep exhibitions fresh and nicely incongruous. This way you find a Rembrandt next to some local artist's portrait of a much-loved grandmother or discover a Picasso between a couple of mundane still lives.

VILLENEUVE D'ASCQ

Musée d'Art Moderne *(1 allée du Musée, Villeneuve d'Ascq;* ✆ *03 20 19 68 68;* http://mam.cudl-lille.fr; ⏱ *10.00–18.00 Wed–Mon, closed 1 Jan, 1 May, 25 Dec. From the Eurostar take Métro 2 to Gare Lille Flandres then line 1 to Pont de Bois, then bus 41 to Parc Urbain-Musée, & follow the footpath into the park)* Reopened in 2010, this unexpected cultural park in Villeneuve d'Ascq, Lille's university campus suburb, is packed with national treasures. A comprehensive tour through the most influential painters of each of the key artistic movements of the past 100 years includes a half-dozen Picassos, Bracque's *Maison et Arbres*, works by Rouault, Miró and Masson, and some renowned canvases by Modigliani, including his *Nu Assis à la Chemise*. Fauvist and Cubist rooms are most popular, but post-war artists are equally well represented through more recent acquisitions. Outside, walk through the park to find installation sculptures, including Picasso's *Femme aux Bras Ecartés* and Alexander Calder's *Southern Cross*.

WAMBRECHIES There is no tourist office, but the town hall (*Mairie, 5 pl Général de Gaulle;* ☏ *03 28 38 84 00*) stocks visitor information. A vintage tram (☏ *03 28 42 44 58; www.amitram.asso.fr*) from 1906 runs from 14.30–19.00 every 15 minutes along the canal bank between Wambrechies and Marquette on Sundays and public holidays between April and September. Passengers may join the tram at Vent de Bise at Wambrechies or rue de la Deûle at Marquette. Pay €4 for a return fare and sit on authentic wooden benches, as refurbished in 1926.

Well worth a visit is **Distillerie Claeyssens** (*1 rue de la Distillerie;* ☏ *03 20 14 91 91; www.wambrechies.com;* ⊕ *tours 09.30–12.30, 13.30–17.30, closed holidays; adult €6, reservation essential. From the Eurostar take bus 9 from Gare Lille Flandres to Wambrechies Château or bus 3 from Gare Lille Flandres to Wambrechies Mairie. From rue 11 Nov 1918 take rue Leclerc to rue de la Distillerie*). There is nothing high-tech about this 200-year-old distillery making *genièvre* gin. Original wooden equipment still sifts seeds and mill flour and heats, cools and distils the spirit, just as it did in Napoleonic times, when the waterways of the Deûle brought grain from Belgium after an edict banned the use of French crops. The hour-long tour is an anecdote-filled meander through a past that can hold its own in the present.

In total contrast is the **Doll and Antique Toy Museum** (*Musée de la Poupée et du Jouet Ancien Château de Robersart;* ☏ *03 20 39 69 28; www.musee-du-jouet-ancien.com;* ⊕ *14.00–18.00 Sun, Wed & school holidays, closed 25 Dec & 1 Jan; adult €4. From the Eurostar take bus 9 from Gare Lille Flandres to Wambrechies Château*). Victorian dolls and inter-war kitsch form part of this charming museum of childhood in the family *château* of Juliette, the last countess of Robersart. Amid mini couture dolls and more traditional china babies are regular toys and train sets from generations past.

10

Appendix I

LANGUAGE

The majority of English speakers will probably still retain a few memories of school-day words and phrases of French. And with the same alphabet and some three-fifths of everyday English said to have arrived via France, we somehow get by – even though French is far more associated with its romantic counterparts, Spanish and Italian. So, in the spirit of the Entente-Cordiale, swallow hard – literally – and swot up on a few of the more familiar aspects of the official language of some 30 countries worldwide.

Most words at least sound familiar. But watch out for the different sounds for 'u' and the rolling, almost growling, noise from the back of the throat needed to tackle the letter 'r'. Listen, too, for the stress and rhythm of words – for example '*café*', which is close to the English sound but with the 'ay' shorter and sharper.

Most importantly of all, however, have fun. Practise makes perfect even if your French is all too often of the Franglais variety. Remember also that local dialects differ a lot, especially in Nord-Pas de Calais.

PRONUNCIATION French pronunciation of the letters of the alphabet is given below. Their pronunciation within words is similar to the English, unless specified otherwise.

A, a	'ah', 'ai', 'air' or 'ay'	with tonal variations
B, b	'bay'	
C, c	'say'	with '**ch**' – as in *Ch'tis* or *chapeau* – pronounced like 'sh' in English
D, d	'day'	
E, e	'e', 'ee', 'eu'	with tonal variations
F, f	'ef'	
G, g	'zhay'	sometimes softened as with the 'g' in 'aubergine'
H, h	'ash'	
I, i	'ee'	
J, j	'djee'	
K, k	'kah'	
L, l	'ell'	
M, m	'em'	
N, n	'en'	pronounced with tongue against upper teeth
O, o	'oh'	with slight variations called open and closed o
P, p	'pay'	more clipped than in English
Q, q	'koo'	while it must be followed by u as in English, it sounds much more like French 'k' see above
R, r	'air'	along with u this is the most difficult sound; think of saying the r in rumble while clearing your throat in a rasping fashion

S, s	'es'	
T, t	'tay'	
U, u	'ew', 'oo', 'er'	this is the most difficult of vowels, with tonal variations: corresponding French examples are *tu, chou* and *deux*
V, v	'vay'	
W, w	'dobluvay'	rather like French 'v' above, with 'wagon' pronounced roughly as 'vagon'
X, x	'eex'	
Y, y	'ee'	
Z, z	'zed'	

ESSENTIALS
Basics

Good morning/afternoon	*bonjour* (bon-zhoor)
Good evening/night	*bonsoir* (bon-swahr)
Hello	*salut* (sah-loo)
Goodbye	*au revoir* (oh rer-vwahr)
My name is …	*Je m'appelle…* (zher ma-pel)
What is your name?	*Comment vous appelez-vous?* (kom-mohn voo-za-peh-lay voo?)
I am…	*Je suis …* (zher swee …)
English	*Anglais(e)* (ong-lay)
American	*Américain(e)* (am-er-i-ken)
Australian	*Australien(ne)* (os-tray-lien)
a New Zealander	*Néo–zélandais(e)* (nay-o zay-lon-day)
How are you?	*Comment ça va?/Ça va?* (komon sa va?/sa va?) or *Comment allez-vous?* (komon talay voo?) which is more formal, such as when addressing a stranger
Fine, thanks and you?	*Bien merci, et vous?* (bee-ehn mair-see ay voo?)
Pleased to meet you	*Enchanté(e)* (ohn-shon-tay)
Thank you	*Merci* (mare-see)
That's OK	*De rien* (dah ree-ehn) or *c'est bien* (say byun)
Cheers!	*Santé!* (son-tay!)
Pardon me/sorry	*Pardon* (pahr-dohn) or *excusez-moi* (ek-skew-zay-mwa)
yes	*oui* (wee)
no	*non* (nohn)
I don't understand	*Je ne comprends pas* (jhuhn kom-prohn pah)
Please speak slowly	*Parlez lentement, s'il vous plaît* (par-lay lehn-ta-mohn seel voo play)
Do you understand?	*Comprenez-vous?* (kom-prer-nay-voo?)

Questions

Where?	*Où?* (oo?)
When?	*Quand?* (kohn?)
Why?	*Pourquoi?* (poorkwa?)
What is it?	*Qu'est-ce que/qui?* (kes kuh seh?)
Who?	*Qui?* (kee?)
Which?	*Quel/quelle?* (kel?)
How?	*Comment?* (komont?)
How much/many?	*Combien?* (kom byan?)
Is/are there?	*Y a–t–il?* (ya til?)

Numbers

0	*zéro* (zayroh)	16	*seize* (sez)
1	*un* (un)	17	*dix-sept* (deez-set)
2	*deux* (duh)	18	*dix-huit* (deez-weet)
3	*trois* (trwah)	19	*dix-neuf* (deez-nerf)
4	*quatre* (katr)	20	*vingt* (van)
5	*cinq* (sank)	21	*vingt et un* (vant ay un)
6	*six* (sees)	30	*trente* (tront)
7	*sept* (set)	40	*quarante* (karont)
8	*huit* (weet)	50	*cinquante* (sankont)
9	*neuf* (nerf)	60	*soixante* (swasont)
10	*dix* (dees)	70	*soixante-dix* (swasont dees)
11	*onze* (onz)	80	*quatre-vingts* (katr van)
12	*douze* (dooz)	81	*quatre-vingt-un* (katr van un)
13	*treize* (trez)	90	*quatre-vingt-dix* (katr van dees)
14	*quatorze* (katorz)	100	*cent* (son)
15	*quinze* (kanz)	1,000	*mille* (meel)

Time

What time is it?	*Qu'elle heure est-il?* (kel uhr ay-teel?)
afternoon	*l'après–midi* (lah-pray-mee-dee)
evening	*le soir* (le swar)
morning	*le matin* (leh ma-tahn)
night	*la nuit* (lah new-wee)
now	*maintenant* (mun-ter-non)
today	*aujourd'hui* (oh-zhoor-dwee)
tomorrow	*demain* (deh-mahn)
yesterday	*hier* (ee-yehr)

Days

Monday	*lundi* (lahn-dee)
Tuesday	*mardi* (mahr-dee)
Wednesday	*mercredi* (mare-kruh-dee)
Thursday	*jeudi* (zer-dee)
Friday	*vendredi* (vahn-drer-dee)
Saturday	*samedi* (sahm-e-dee)
Sunday	*dimanche* (dee-mahnsh)

Months

January	*janvier* (zhan-vee-ay)
February	*février* (fey-vree-ay)
March	*mars* (marz)
April	*avril* (ah-vril)
May	*mai* (may)
June	*juin* (zhwun)
July	*juillet* (zhwee-yay)
August	*août* (ooht)
September	*septembre* (sep-tahm-bhr)
October	*octobre* (ok-to-brer)
November	*novembre* (nov-em-brer)
December	*decembre* (day-som-brer)

Getting around
Transport

I would like...	*Je voudrais...* (zher voo-dray)
a one-way ticket	*un billet simple* (uhn bee-yai sahm-ple)
a return ticket	*un billet d'aller et retour* (uhn bee-yai dah-lay eh reh-toor)
first-class ticket	*un billet en première* (uhn bee-yai ehn pre-meer)
second-class ticket	*un billet en deuxième* (uhn bee-yai ehn do-zeem)
How much is a ticket to...?	*Combien coûte un billet pour...?* (cohm-bee-ehn koot uhn bee-yai poor...?)
What time does the train leave?	*À quelle heure part le train?* (ah kell uhr par leh trahn?)
What time does the train arrive?	*À quelle heure arrive le train?* (ah kell uhr ahrive leh trahn?)
Is this the train for...?	*Est-ce bien le train pour...?* (ehs-ce bee-ehn leh trahn poor...?)
Where is the platform for...?	*Où est le quai pour...?* (oo eh leh kai poor...?)
The train has been cancelled	*Le train a été annulé* (le trahn ah etay a-new-lay)
The train is delayed	*Le train est retardé* (leh trahn eh re-tar-day)
station platform	*le quai* (leh kay)
timetable	*les horaires* (leh-zoh-rare)
railway station	*la gare* (la gahr)
airport	*l'aéroport* (la-ehro-por)
port	*le port* (leh-por)
bus	*l'autobus* (lohto-boos)
train	*le train* (leh trahn)
plane	*l'avion* (lave-ion)
ferry	*le ferry* (leh fayree)
car	*la voiture* (la vwatoor)
4 × 4	*un quatre-quatre* (ung katr-katr)
motorcycle	*la moto* (lah moto)
bicycle	*la vélo* (lah vay-lo)
arrival	*l'arrivée* (lare-vay)
departure	*le départ* (leh daypar)
here	*ici* (ee-see)
there	*là* (lah)

Driving

Which road do I take for... please?	*La route pour aller à... s'il vous plait?* (la root pur alay a... sel voo pleh?)
Is this the turning for...?	*Est-ce que c'est là que je tourne pour...?* (es-keh say la kuh zhuh torn pour...?)
Where is a petrol station?	*Où est-ce qu'il y a une station-service?* (oo es-keel ya ewn sta-syon servees?)
Fill up the tank please	*Le plein, s'il vous plaît* (ler plun seel vvoo play)
diesel	*le diesel* (dyay-zel)
unleaded petrol	*sans plomb* (son plom)
The car has broken down	*La voiture est tombée en panne* (la vwa-ter tom–bay on pan)

Road signs

give way	*cédez le priorité/passage* (say-day la pree-oreetay)

danger	*danger!* (don-jay!) or perhaps *danger de mort!* (don-jay de moor!)
detour	*deviation* (de-viation)
one-way	*sens unique* (sons ew-neek)
toll	*péage* (pay-azh)
no entry	*sens interdit* (sons un-ter-dee)
Beware, roadworks	*Attention travaux* (attension travo)

Directions

Where is…?	*Où est...?* (ooh eh…?)
Go straight ahead	*Allez tout droit* (alay too draw)
It's right/left	*C'est à droite/à gauche* (say a drawt/a gosh)
Turn right/left at the traffic lights	*Tournez à droite/à gauche aux feux* (toor–nay a drawt/a gosh o fer)
Turn right/left at the roundabout	*Tournez à droite au rond-point* (toor-nay adrawt/a gosh o rom-pwun)

Food

bread	*le pain* (leh pahn)
croissant	*le croissant* (leh kuwah-sahn)
chocolate croissant	*le pain au chocolat* (leh pahn oh show-koh-lah)
sweet bread	*la brioche* (lah bree-ohsh)
butter	*le beurre* (leh burr)
cheese	*le fromage* (leh fro-mahjz)
blue cheese	*le fromage bleu* (leh fro-mahjz blew)
salt	*le sel* (leh sell)
pepper	*le poivre* (leh pwavr)
oil	*l'huile* (l'weel)
olive oil	*l'huile d'olive* (l'weel doleev)
sugar	*le sucre* (leh sookr)

Fruit

apple	*la pomme* (lah puhm)
banana	*la banane* (lah bah-nan)
grape	*le raisin* (leh ray-zehn)
melon	*le melon* (leh meh-lohn)
orange	*l'orange* (l'or-an-jhe)
pear	*la poivre* (lah pwar)
raspberry	*la framboise* (lah frahm-bwahz)
strawberry	*la fraise* (lah frehz)

Vegetables

broccoli	*le brocoli* (leh broh-koh-lee)
carrot	*la carotte* (lah cah-rot)
onion	*l'oignon* (loh-nyohn)
cabbage	*le chou* (leh shoo)
Brussels sprouts	*les choux de Bruxelles* (lay shoo de brux-elles)
cauliflower	*le chou-fleur* (leh shoo-flur)
celeriac	*le céleri-rave* (leh say-leri lav)
celery	*le céleri* (leh say-leri)
chicory	*la chicorée* (lah shikoree) for coffee
	l'endive (l'ondeev) for salad, also known locally as 'witloof' (vitloof)

garlic	*l'ail* (l'eye)
potatoes	*les pommes de terre* (lay puhm deh tehr)
leeks	*les poireaux* (lay pwaro)

Fish

mussels	*les moules* (lay mool)
mussels in white wine with herbs and shallots	*moules marinières* (mool mah-ree-nee-air)
oysters	*les huîtres* (lay wee-truh)
sea bass	*le loup de mer/le bar* (leh lew deh mehr/bahr)
shellfish	*les crustacés* (lay kroos-ta-say)
shrimps	*les crevettes* (lay kruh-vet)
smoked salmon	*le saumon fumé* (leh sow-mohn foo-may)
sole	*la sole* (lah sohl)
trout	*la truite* (lah tru-eet)
tuna	*le thon* (leh tohn)

See also page 39.

Meat

beef	*le bœuf* (leh buhf)
chicken	*le poulet* (leh poo-lay)
pork	*le porc* (leh pohr)
lamb	*l'agneau* (l'eh-ah-nyo)
sausages	*les saucisses* (lay so-sees)
ham	*le jambon* (leh jahm-bohn)

Drinks

beer (dark/light/tap)	*la bière (brune/blonde/a la pression)* (lah bee-yehr (brewn/blohnd/ah lah pres-see-ohn))
coffee(with cream/with milk/black/decaffeinated)	*le café (crème/au lait/noir/décaféine)* (leh ka-fay (krem/oh lay/nwahr/day-kah-fay-nay))
fruit juice	*le jus de fruit* (leh zhoo duh frwee)
orange juice, fresh	*le jus d'orange pressé* (leh juj doh-rahnzj pray-say)
milk	*le lait* (leh lay)
tea (with lemon)	*le thé (au citron)* (leh tay (oh see–trohn))
water (tap/sparkling mineral/still mineral)	*l'eau (du robinet/minéral gazeuse/minéral plate)* (low (dew row-bee-nay/mee-nay-rahl gah-zuhz/mee-nay-rahl plaht)
wine (red/rosé/sparkling/white)	*le vin (rouge/rosé/mousseux/blanc)* (leh vihn (rooj/row-zay/moo-soh/blohn))

Shopping

How much is it please?	*Combien est-il, s'il vous plait?*
I'm just looking	*Je regarde seulement* (zhuh ruhgard suhlmon)
It is too expensive	*C'est trop cher* (say tro shair)
Can I try it on?	*Est-ce que je peux l'essayer?* (es-kuk zhuh puy lessay yay?)
Can I pay by credit card?	*Est-ce qu'il est possible de payer ave une carte de crédit?* (es keel eh poseebl du pay-ay evek oon kart duh kryadee?)

Help!	*Au secours!* (o-skoor!)
I need a doctor (who speaks English)	*J'ai besoin d'un médecin (qui parle anglais)* (zhay ber-zwun dun maydi-sun (kee parl onglay))
I had an accident	*J'ai eu un accident* (zhay ew un ak-asee-don)
I am lost	*Je suis perdu(e)* (zhay swee pair-dew)
police	*la police* (lah po-lees)
ambulance	*l'ambulance* (l'om-bew-lons)
thief	*le voleur/ la voleuse* (leh vo-ler/lah vol-lerz)
hospital	*l'hôpital* (l'o-pee-tal)
I am ill	*Je suis malade* (zhay swee ma-lad)

more (than)	*plus (que)* (ploos (kuh))
less (than)	*moins (que)* (mwah (kuh))
smaller (than)	*plus petit (que)* (ploo puhtee (kuh))
bigger (than)	*plus grand (que)* (plos gron (kuh))

Communications

I am looking for…	*Je cherche…* (zher shairsh…)
bank	*la banque* (lah bonk)
post office	*la poste* (la poste)
church	*l'église* (l'aygleez)
tourist office	*l'office de tourisme* (loffice de tour-eez-muh)

Health

I have…	*J'ai…* (zhay…)
diarrhoea	*la diarrhée* (la dya-ray)
I feel nauseous	*J'ai des nausées* (zhay day no-zay)
doctor	*le médicin* (leh mahdî-sun)
prescription	*l'ordonnance* (l'or-do-nons)
pharmacy	*la pharmacie* (lah far-ma-see)
paracetamol	*le paracétamol* (leh para-set-amol)
antibiotics	*les antibiotiques* (lay on-tee-by-oteek)
antiseptic	*l'antiseptique* (l'on-tee-sep-teek)
tampons	*les tampon* (lay tom-pon)
condom	*le préservatif* (leh pray-zair-vateef)
sunblock	*l'écran solaire totale* (l'ay-cron so-lair total)
I am …	*Je suis* (zhay swee)
asthmatic	*asthmatique* (as-mer-teek)
epileptic	*épileptique* (ay-pee-lepteek)
diabetic	*diabétique* (dya-bet-teek)
I'm allergic to …	*Je suis allergique à …* (zhay swee alair-zheek a…)
penicillin	*la pénicilline* (lah pay-nee-see-leen)
nuts	*les noix* (lay nwa)
bees	*les abeilles* (lez-a-bay)

Travel with children

Is there …?	*Y a-t-il…?* (ee a-teel?)

GALLIC SHRUG Watch out for the famous – some might say infamous – Gallic shrug. It involves raising your eyebrows, holding up your hands with the palms facing upwards and sticking out your lower lip. It means anything from 'it's not my fault' or 'I don't know' to 'I doubt if anything can be done' or 'I don't really agree.'

KISSING French friends and acquaintances exchange kisses on alternating cheeks upon meeting and separating. Two people introduced by a mutual friend may also *faire la bise*, particularly children and young adults. There are variations, so just wait and see what happens.

THE POUT This is a classic French facial gesture which expresses discontent, disdain, disgust – and any other negative emotion starting with 'dis'.

HANDSHAKE This is quick and light, with no pumping up and down or iron grips. If hands are full, dirty, or wet, you may be offered an elbow or a finger for the other person to grasp.

a baby changing room	*un endroit pour changer le bébé* (un-drwa poor shon-zhay ler bay-bay)
children's menu	*un menu pour enfant* (un mer-new poor on-fon)
Do you have...?	*Avez-vous...?* (a-vayvoo...?)
nappies	*les couches* (lay koosh)
potty	*un pot de bébé*
babysitter (who speaks English)	*une baby-sitter (qui parle anglais?)* (ewn bay-bay-seeter (kee par long-glay)
highchair	*une chaise haute* (ewn shayzot)
Are children allowed?	*Les enfants sont permis?* (lay zonfon son pait-mee?)

Other

my	*mon/ma* (mon/ma)
mine	*mien/mienne* (mee-ann/mee-enne)
our	*notre* (no-trer)
yours	*le/la votre*
and	*et* (ay)
some	*du/de la /des* (dew/der la/day)
but	*mais* (may)
this/that	*ce/cette* (suh/set) male/female
expensive/cheap	*cher/chère* (share/share) male/female
beautiful	*beau/belle* (bo/bel) male/female
ugly	*laide(e)* (lay/led)
old	*vieux/vielle* (vyer/vyay) male/female
new	*nouveau/nouvelle* (noo-vol/noo-vel) male/female
early	*tôt* (too)
late	*en retard* (on rer-tar)
hot	*chaud(e)* (shod)
cold	*froid (e)* (fraw)
difficult	*difficile* (dee-fee-seel)
easy	*facile* (fa-seel)

It's raining cats and dogs	*Il pleut comme vache qui pisse* (literal translation: 'it's raining like a weeing cow')
Don't exaggerate/go too far	*Faut pas pousser mémé (grand-mère) dans les orties* (literal translation: 'don't push granny (grandma) into the stinging nettles')
Having eyes bigger than your tummy or don't overestimate yourself	*Avoir les yeux plus gros que le ventre* (literal translation: 'to have one's eyes bigger than one's stomach')
Never! Not likely! (as in 'yes, when pigs fly')	*Quand les poules auront des dents!* (literal translation: 'when hens have teeth!')
A powerful wind, enough to blow off your hat, chimney pots etc	*Un vent à décorner les boeufs* (literal translation: 'strong enough wind to blow the horns off a bull')
To take French leave	*Filer à l'anglaise* (similar to 'to take French leave', and means the same thing)
French fries	*frites belges* (meaning 'Belgian fries' – it seems no-one wants to bear the burden of inventing them!)
To faint	*Tomber dans les pommes* (literal translation: 'to fall into the apples')
To get on someone's 'wick	*Courir sur le haricot* (literal translation: 'to run on someone's bean')
It's nothing to write home about/trifling	*Ca ne casse pas trois pattes à un canard* (literal translation: 'that does not break three legs of a duck')
No way!	*Pas question!* (as in 'no way, mate!' or 'over my dead body!')

boring	*ennuyeux/ennuyeuse* (on-nwee-yer/on-nwee-yerz)
interesting	*interéssante(e)* (un-tayray-son(t))

Appendix 2

FURTHER INFORMATION

BOOKS In addition to the titles listed here, there are many books written in French on the region; for more information enquire at one the many English-speaking bookshops referred to in Part Two.

Literature
Dumas, Alexandre *The Taking of Calais* Fredonia Book, 2002. Part of series of stories by the author of *The Three Musketeers*.

Griffiths, Arthur *The Passenger from Calais* BiblioBazaar, 2008. Detective story of a mysterious lady's flight through France pursued by detectives.

Hugo, Victor *Les Misérables* Vintage Classics, 2008. Hugo's albeit brief stay in Montreuil-sur-Mer inspired him to use the unique setting in his famous novel – later adapted into the awarding musical *Les Mis*, as it's affectionately known.

Merle, Robert *Weekend at Zuydcoote* Mass Market Paperback, 1972. The 1949 novel, which provides a harrowingly realistic portrayal of one of the darker episodes in World War II, was based on his own experiences during the evacuation of Dunkirk.

Wodehouse, P G *P G Wodehouse on Golf* Valuablebook, 2006. Le Touquet features in this now rare book, along with references to the course in his legendary Jeeves and Wooster books. The author also owned property in the chic resort.

Zola, Émile *Germinal* Penguin Classics, 1998. The struggle of a mining community facing collapse in the market for coal provides a vivid insight into late 19th-century life in northern France generally.

Travel and language
Bird, Angel *Northern France* Malnoue Publications, 2007

Duquénoy, Anne (Editor) *Nord Pas de Calais – Picardie (Turtleback)* Travel House Media Group, 2010. Written in French.

Fenn, Patricia *Calais, Boulogne and the North of France (restaurants & hotels)* Aspect Guides, 2002

Phillips, Laurence *Paris, Lille & Brussels* Bradt Travel Guides, 2010

Rider, Nick *Short breaks in Northern France* Cadogan Guides, 2005

Sadaune, Samuel *Nord-Pas-de-Calais Editions* Ouest-France, 2009. English version. A French author reflects on the 'indescribable pleasure' of a much-caricatured region.

Smith, Mike *Exploring Northern France* Landmark Publishing, 2008

Walking the Walls Jointly published by Kent County Council & Syndicate Mixte de la Côte d'Opale, 1999. Historic twin defences in Kent, Côte d'Opale and West Flanders

Watkins, Gaven R (editor) *Northern France and the Paris Region* Michelin, 2010

Louis Blériot

Charpentier, Henri *100 years: Louis Blériot* Atlantica Editions, 2009

Elliot, Brian A *Blériot – Herald of an Age* Tempus Publishing, 2000. English-language biography of Louis Blériot, the Cambrai born flier, with foreword by his grandson.

Maps

Calais and Boulogne Philip's Red Books Shoppers Map (Leisure & Tourist Maps)

Nord-Pas-de-Calais Berlitz Motoring Map (Berlitz Motoring Maps)

Nord-Pas de Calais, Picardy Michelin regional no 511

Pas de Calais, Somme Michelin local no 301

Food and drink

Reynaud, Stéphane *French Feasts: 299 Traditional Recipes for Family Meals & Gatherings* Stewart, Tabori, & Chang, 2009

Taylor, Arthur *Northern France Good Beer Guide (Paperback)* CAMRA Books, 1998

Willan, Anne *Country Cooking of France* Chronicle Books, 2007

World War I

Bridger, Geoff *The Battle of Neuve Chapelle, French Flanders* Pen & Sword Books, 2000. Part of the Battleground Europe series, it covers the often forgotten area between Armentiéres and Loos.

Cave, Nigel *Vimy Ridge: Arras (Battleground Europe)* Pen & Sword Books, 1995

Cherry, Niall *Most unfavourable ground* Helion & Company, 2008. This also relates to Loos.

Coombs, Rose E B *Before Endeavours Fade* After The Battle, 2006

Copp, Terry and Bechthold, Mike *Canadian Battlefields in Northern France: A Visitor's Guide* Laurier Centre for Military, Strategic and Disarmament Studies, 2010

Gavaghan, Michael *The British Unknown Warrior & other Great War titles* M&L Publications, 2003

MacDonald, Lyn *1915: The Death of Innocence* Johns Hopkins University Press, 2000. A widely acclaimed compendium of military history and poignant, often humorous, memories from the Great War.

Somewhere on the Western Front Published in 2003 by, and available from, the tourist office. An absorbing account of the Battle of Arras.

Warner, Philip *The Battle of Loos* Cassell, 2000

Culture

Catalogue Du Muse de Peinture & Sculpture de La Ville de Valenciennes: Et Du Muse Bnezech 2010

Spurling, Hilary *Matisse the Master: A Life of Henri Matisse 1909–1954: 1909–1954 v 2; the Unknown Matisse: Man of the North: 1869-1908: Man of the North: 1869-1908 v 1* Penguin, 2009

Various contributors *The World of Watteau 1684–1721* Time Incorporated, 1974

Sporting activities

Granveaud-Vallat, Claude and Routhier, Benjamin *Le Guide des Golfs de France* Motor Presse France, 2010

Golfs De France: Golf Courses (IGN Grey 910) Institut Géographique National

Holmes, Richard *War Walks from Agincourt to Normandy* BBC Books, 1997

Kent and Nord/Pas de Calais on Horseback British Horse Society (BHS). 2002. Describing 21 regional routes for horseriders, the book includes maps, route descriptions, and lists of accommodation, food outlets and stabling. Handy for walkers and cyclists too.

Simpson, Jerry H *Cycling France: The Best Bike Tours in All of Gaul* Bicycle Books, 1992

History
McPhail, Helen *The Long Silence* I B Tauris & Co, 2001. Life under German occupation in World War I.
Tingey, Frederick *North of France: Picardy & Artois* Spurbooks, 1979

Buying property
Davey, Charles *The Complete Guide to Buying Property in France: Buying, Renting, Letting, Selling* Kogan Page, 2004
Pybus, Victoria *Retiring to France* Crimson Publishing, 2009

Natural history
Botting, Douglas and Rigge, Simon (editors) *Wild France* Sheldrake Press, 2000
Melbeck Balades, David *Nature en Pas-de-Calais* Dakota Editions, 2009

WEBSITES
www.realfrancerealclose.fr Keep up-to-date with what's on in Nord-Pas de Calais with Nicole's newsletter.
www.uk.pas-de-calais.com All-singing, all-dancing introduction to Pas de Calais – contains everything you could want to know about this coast-hugging region.
www.tourisme-nord.fr The definitive site for Le Nord, with bags of information on the major centres and activities.
www.northernfrance-tourism.com All the lowdown on the region, from major events to gastronomy and shopping.
www.franceguide.com Website of ATOUT France, the national tourist board in London.
www.theotherside.co.uk A miscellany of what makes Nord-Pas de Calais tick, from traditional games to the lives of Matisse and Émile Zola.
www.about-france.com/regions/nord-pas-de-calais A deep look at the region with a good smattering of history.
www.informationfrance.com/nord_pas_de_calais A good source of information, with snappy guides to the towns and resorts along the Côte d'Opale, including hotel and restaurant recommendations.
www.holidayfrancedirect.co.uk A quick glance at some of the region's highlights.
www.holidayfrance.org.uk An overview of highlights, with some good click-on subjects to follow-up.
www.france.com/nord-pas–de–calais Potted history with guide to hotels etc.
www.day-tripper.net/events-in-nord-pas-de-calais Events throughout northern France, with links to French websites.
www.frenchduck.com General information on France.
www.whatsonwhen.com Look up the nightlife in brief.
www.pinkchoice.com Guide to the gay scene in Lille, along with eating out and where to stay.
www.francekeys.com Quick way to brush up on some French facts and figures, with an overview of Nord-Pas de Calais.
www.webinfrance.com/nord-pas-de-calais Useful round-up of the region.
www.allfranceinfo.com/nordpasdecalais A general overview of the region, but meatier in details than other websites and with some useful links.
www.french-at-a-touch.com Ideal for swotting up on the region's history, with an insight into the economy.

www.discoverfrance.net Brief historic facts with some useful links.

www.greeters62.com A new initiative derived from the New York Greeters website in which locals invite visitors to share their love of their town or city. Likely to extend to Le Nord.

www.nordmag.fr Some intriguing cultural facts from this consistently good regional magazine.

www.travellingbirder.com Reports on birdwatching in the region.

www.demeure-historique.org Association representing more than 3,000 private monuments throughout France.

www.nordpasdeclais.fr Administration site of the Regional Council.

www.europa.eu Search regional policy for Nord Pas de Calais, and future prospects.

Transport

www.norfolkline.com Norfolkline Dover–Dunkirk ferries.

www.poferries.com Dover–Calais ferries.

www.seafrance.com SeaFrance Dover–Calais ferries.

www.eurotunnel.com Eurotunnel car-shuttle service.

www.lyddair.com Flights to Le Touquet from Lydd airport, Kent.

www.raileurope.co.uk Information and booking with French Railways.

www.defra.gov.uk Information on travelling with pets.

www.Bison-fute.Equipment.Gov't.en Avoid the traffic jams: information on road traffic throughout France.

Food and drink

www.saveurs-npdc.com Gastronomic goodies throughout the region.

www.toutsurlenord.fr/fr/estaminets/produits.aspx A detailed look at the origins of *estaminets* (pubs-cum-cafés) and their history.

www.ferrybooker.com/nord/gastronomy.asp A look at local food and drink.

Accommodation

www.gitesdefrance-pas-de-calais *Gîtes* in Pas de Calais *département*.

www.gites-de-france-nord.com *Gîtes* in Le Nord *département*.

www.bienvenue-a-la-ferme.com Farms in Nord-Pas de Calais

Buying property

www.frenchconnections.co.uk A useful source if thinking of buying or letting accommodation.

www.french-property.com Round-up of a region which is becoming increasingly popular with the Brits.

Index

Page numbers in **bold** indicate major entries; those in *italic* indicate maps.